CHECHNYA

CHECHNYA

CALAMITY IN THE CAUCASUS

Carlotta Gall and Thomas de Waal

NEW YORK UNIVERSITY PRESS

New York and London

NEW YORK UNIVERSITY PRESS
New York and London

First published in Great Britain by Macmillan Publishers Ltd.

Library of Congress Cataloging-in-Publication Data
Gall, Carlotta.
Chechnya : calamity in the Caucasus / Carlotta Gall and Thomas de
Waal.
p. cm.
Includes bibliographical references and index.
ISBN 0-8147-2963-0 (alk. paper)
1. Chechnia (Russia)—History—Civil War, 1994–1996. I. De Waal,
Thomas. II. Title.
DK511.C37G35 1998
947.5'2—dc21   97-26694
                        CIP

10 9 8 7 6 5 4 3 2 1

Contents

Contents

List of Illustrations

Imam Shamil. Portrait by Thomas Horscheldt.

Murids crossing a river during the Caucasian Wars. A drawing by Prince Gagarin.

Ruslan Khasbulatov. (*Vladimir Filonov*)

Pavel Grachev, Russian Defence Minister. (*Yevgeny Stetsko*)

Jokhar Dudayev on the terrace of the House of Commons in October 1993. (*Tomas Jaski*)

Jokhar Dudayev at a rally in 1994. (*Thomas Dworzak*, Wostok Press)

Men performing the *zikr* in the village of Itum-Kale on the third day of mourning after Dudayev's death. (*Michael Yasskovich*)

The aftermath of the New Year's battle in Grozny. (*Heidi Bradner*)

Russian conscript prisoners in the bunker of the Presidential Palace. (*Heidi Bradner*)

Chechen fighters moving through the city. (*Heidi Bradner*)

Russian soldiers camped in the heart of Grozny. (*Heidi Bradner*)

Central Grozny, February 1995. (*Heidi Bradner*)

A mother searching for her missing son at the Orthodox cemetery in Grozny. (*Heidi Bradner*)

Introduction

The images of the war in Chechnya are some of the most harrowing of modern times. A modern European city bombed to ruins while its citizens cower in bunkers. Streets littered with dead bodies, uncollected for weeks. Mass graves. Mothers combing the hills for their missing sons.

It is all the more terrible for being a war that started so suddenly. The issue of Chechen President Jokhar Dudayev's self-declared independence had dragged out for three years and the decision to try to end it was made hastily by an inner circle in the Kremlin in a matter of days. What followed was a disaster for Chechnya and for Russia.

Much of the story is quite fantastic. A rogue regime survived within Russian territory for three years, trading oil with a government that was supposedly 'blockading' it. Kremlin politics turned on trivial incidents and personal rivalries in the making of decisions of the greatest global importance. Chechen fighters bought weapons off soldiers who were meant to be 'disarming' them. Internal documents intended for government use in Moscow ended up in the hands of Dudayev. And – most incredibly – a small Chechen guerrilla army that had been dismissed as 'bandit groups' brought the Russian army to its knees and forced it to withdraw.

This book aims to tell the story of the conflict and put it in its historical context. The Chechens have long suffered from world-wide ignorance about their history and who they are. Too often during the war they were simply sidelined in reports on Chechnya, reduced to a mere factor in the political survival or otherwise of

Boris Yeltsin, or the first wave in a supposed 'domino reaction' of bids for independence by other regions in post-Soviet Russia. In fact their story is in many ways unique: no one but the Chechens has ever properly tried to claim independence from Moscow.

There are many historical clues to why the Chechens have been so rebellious. Chechnya was the centre of one of the longest guerrilla campaigns in history in the nineteenth century. The Chechens' tight clan and religious structures made them especially resistant to assimilation by Russia. In 1944 they were the largest ethnic group on a compact territory to be deported en masse by Stalin. In the late Soviet era they were one of the poorest peoples in Russia. This history should have warned any Moscow strategist that, if forced to, many of them would be prepared to fight a savage war to defend themselves.

Chechnya's self-declared independence was also the most extraordinary side-effect of the collapse of the Soviet Union. The seizure of power in Chechnya by the former Soviet air force general and commander of a strategic bomber division, Jokhar Dudayev, came as the Soviet Union itself was crumbling. The eccentric, self-declared state he set up survived by exploiting the economic and political weaknesses of the post-Soviet carve-up and the corruption and confusion that reigned in Russia. It was a regime founded equally on nationalism and dirty money.

Dudayev himself has to take much of the blame for setting out on the rash project of defying Moscow and failing to come to a compromise. Dudayev's 'independent' Chechnya was a deeply unattractive regime. He provoked Russia and prepared Chechnya for a coming war and did little to prevent it. Together with Boris Yeltsin he was the co-author of the Chechen war. Ultimately, however, the bigger player must take more responsibility and the evidence is that Yeltsin personally and ruthlessly decided to order a military crackdown in Chechnya. Consistently over the last 200 years Moscow has eschewed subtlety in dealing with the Chechens and used brute force. Chechnya in 1991–4 was a tricky problem but the use of force was not the way to solve it: the decision to go to war over the rebel region was only the latest chapter in a long story of misunderstanding between the centre and the edges of empire.

The war that was unleashed was a triumph of brutality over reason. The level of destruction in Chechnya was phenomenal – proof of what heavy weapons and bombs can do to a small place if no regard is taken for civilian casualties. Russian actions on the ground, though less reported, were if anything even more terrible. All armies in all wars do terrible things and the Chechens also committed acts of savagery, as witnessed in the hostage-taking incidents in Budyonnovsk and Pervomaiskoye. But the chaotic, underfed, vicious Russian army did something quite apocalyptic in small Chechnya. It became a war against all Chechens, both those who wanted to stay in Russia and those who did not.

The Chechens in their turn possessed at best several hundred properly trained men at the start of the war. They not only decimated the Russian attackers trying to capture Grozny on New Year's Eve 1994, they delayed the capture of the city for three months. When the Russians seemed to be advancing deep into the mountains, they were able to launch a brutal and brilliant raid into the heart of Russian territory in June 1995 that forced Moscow to sit down at the negotiating table. A year later they had formed such an effective guerrilla army that they were able to perform the most amazing feat of all – to recapture Grozny from the Russian army and force on Moscow the terms of a victorious peace settlement.

It is impossible to tell the story of this senseless war without also trying to tell the story of the Kremlin politics that precipitated it. 'Politics' is in fact hardly the word for the poisonous mix of intrigue, corruption and improvisation that has characterized much Russian high-level decision-making over the last few years. With regard to the ethnic problems of a country where 20 per cent of the population is non-Russian, this was to prove disastrous.

In 1992 Boris Yeltsin's first post-Soviet government made an honourable attempt at formulating a proper nationalities policy, but the specialists did not survive the complex currents of Kremlin politics, and much more authoritarian figures came to the fore. Galina Starovoitova, an ethnographer and an early adviser to Yeltsin on nationalities policy, sees the roots of the Chechen conflict partly in the Soviet cast of mind of the Russian leadership, when confronted by a complex ethnic problem: 'They were brought up under the Soviet regime, they had an imperial cast of mind and thought that these peoples understand only the use of force. It was an important factor, of course. Plus the personal factor, a personal sense of offence at disloyal [regional] leaders.'

The idea of a 'small victorious war' to solve domestic problems dates back to 1904. The phrase was uttered by the then Russian Interior Minister Vyacheslav Plehve, who was talking to Alexei Kuropatkin, the commander of Russian forces in the Far East. Plehve said, 'We need a small victorious war to avert the revolution.' The war turned out to be the Russo-Japanese War of 1904, in which Russia suffered a catastrophic defeat, and as for 'averting the revolution', the 1905 Revolution followed directly on from Russia's defeat. So when Oleg Lobov, the Secretary of the Kremlin Security Council, uttered the same phrase in November 1994, declaring that Yeltsin needed a small victorious war to win re-election as President, he should have been more mindful of what he was saying.

Imperialist habits die hard and sometimes the attitudes of top Kremlin officials on Chechnya have been quite grotesque. Thus the hawkish head of the counter-intelligence service, Mikhail Barsukov, reportedly blurted out at a meeting of the government commission on Chechnya in June 1996: 'Stalin sorted the Chechens out in two weeks. What are we afraid of? Are we afraid of the West?' The bitter irony of this comment is that Barsukov was half right – the West mostly ignored Chechnya and treated it as an 'internal matter of Russia', which was one reason why the war was allowed to go on as long as it did.

The reporting in the book is the product of many months spent by both authors in the area between January 1994 and January 1997. During that time we have come to know the Chechens well and learned to like and respect them a great deal. Thomas de Waal, a reporter for *The Moscow Times* and then *The Times* of London, first visited Chechnya to write about the fiftieth anniversary of the 1944 deportations. He returned to follow the showdown between Dudayev and his opponents and was in Grozny as the first Russian jets flew over the city. Later, his wanderings led him to discussing the Caucasian Wars with Chechen commander Aslan Maskhadov in an improvised press conference in a beech wood; being almost deported from Kazakhstan by an officious bureaucrat; and staying the night in what used to be Dudayev's office and is now the Jokhar Dudayev suite in the Hotel Barclay in Tartu, Estonia. He has concentrated on the earlier part of the story, Chechen history and culture and both internal Chechen and Kremlin politics.

Carlotta Gall, who worked throughout for *The Moscow Times*, first flew down to Chechnya on the day of the Russian invasion, and stayed in Grozny until late December into the thick of the aerial bombardments. She covered the war intensively from that point, was one of the first journalists into Grozny when the Chechens recaptured the city twenty months later, and suffered both the intense heat of the mass hostage seizure at Budyonnovsk and the bitter cold of the second hostage crisis at Pervomaiskoye. She spent many weeks in the mountains with Chechen guerrillas, tipping into the River Argun in the middle of the night, running the gauntlet of Russian checkpoints, and twice interviewing Dudayev in his secret mountain hide-outs.

Our account of the Chechen war is also indirectly a portrait of modern Russia and of its hitherto failed attempt to make the transition to a democratic society. Russia is not a dictatorship like the Soviet Union. In many ways it is one of the freest societies in the world. We were, for example, able to fly down from Moscow and drive straight into Chechnya to report the war. The Russian media also provided some devastating insights into the awfulness of the war; but instead of dictatorship or democracy there is a kind of chaos in which those in power can do what they want and the individual has no legal recourse against his masters. The undernourished and untrained Russian teenage conscripts who perished in Grozny were as much the victims of the war in Chechnya as the Chechens. The apparently 'Russian' citizens – Chechens, Russians and others – who were bombed and murdered in Chechnya have received no compensation for what their government has done to them. The men who wreaked this destruction on them are still sitting in senior jobs. The most senior of all, Boris Yeltsin, has been re-elected President. Both the Chechens and the Russians deserved something better.

1

New Year's Eve

The people of Grozny were woken before dawn by a thundering bombardment crashing around them. It was New Year's Eve 1994 and they should have been preparing for what was traditionally their biggest holiday of the year. Instead, from 5 a.m. until mid-morning they cowered as attack aircraft roared overhead, diving low to hurl bombs at the city. In the high-rise apartment blocks on the east of Grozny, a few residents, already weary from nights spent in their cellars during weeks of bombing, climbed to the top floors to watch the planes. A one-storey house was already burning furiously, the rafters cracking in the intense heat. Some Russian pensioners, white with shock and brick dust, crawled out of their bombed building and sat wailing on the pavement, still in their nightclothes. Tank shells and mortars were now slamming into the city with steady consistency, growing closer and harder by the hour. Everyone in the Chechen capital knew this was more serious than anything that had come before.

For nearly three weeks Russian tanks had been massing on the ridges above Grozny as Moscow called on the Chechen separatist fighters to surrender and disarm. The embattled President of Chechnya, Jokhar Dudayev, locked in a dangerous game of brinkmanship with Russian President Boris Yeltsin, had moved his office into the bunker of his Presidential Palace but was refusing to back down on his bid for independence from Russia. Dudayev had declared his tiny mountainous republic independent when he came to power in 1991. Now Russian tanks had invaded Chechnya to force him out of office and some 6000 troops were moving in on his city.

Over 1000 men of Russia's 131st Maikop Brigade had spent the night in the fields just north of Grozny, poised to advance at dawn. Viktor Kim, a nineteen-year-old conscript in command of a unit of four driving a self-propelled anti-aircraft gun, received the order to move at 6.40 a.m. Their task was to take the airport, and they moved across the open fields to it with surprising ease. When they met no opposition they were told to head into the centre of town and occupy the railway station. Nikolai Ryabtsev was in the first battalion that pressed on to the centre, driving slowly in a column of thirty vehicles, tanks, armoured troop-carriers and self-propelled guns rumbling on their thick tank treads. A big, tall nineteen-year-old, Ryabtsev had started his military service six months before, one of tens of thousands of barely trained conscripts who made up the bulk of the Russian army. Now amongst the infantry, he was walking alongside the column, sometimes hopping back on to his armoured personnel carrier to ride a few blocks. They turned on to the wide avenue, Staropromyslovskoye Chaussee, that leads from the north-west into the city centre, packed with high-rise apartment blocks and other residential buildings. A few people were watching from their balconies, but the streets were deserted, with no traffic at all.[1]

By mid-morning the whole sky over Grozny was black. A noxious blanket of oily smoke poured from fierce fires burning on the west side of the city where bombs had hit the oil refineries' storage tanks. The smoke hung low over the city, a line of bright light only showing at the horizon. The Oil Institute in the centre of Grozny was on fire, the top floors blazing orange and red, billowing thick smoke across the central square, reducing visibility for the men guarding the Palace. Tank fire was now landing in the city centre, pounding the buildings at thirty-second intervals.

The massive Soviet-style concrete building of the Presidential Palace was the nerve centre of the Chechen resistance, its extensive, well-protected bunker serving as the headquarters of the defence of Grozny. Akhmed Zupkukhajiev, a commander of the Chechen Presidential Guard, a huge, bearded Chechen with a deceptively gentle manner, was on duty on New Year's Eve. A group of Russian parliamentary deputies arrived mid-morning to consult with the Chechen leadership in what was becoming an increasingly hopeless attempt to try to avert the destruction of the city.

Around lunch-time Akhmed was in the main entrance hall of the Palace when someone ran in saying tanks were coming down the street. The men with grenade-launchers ran to take up positions, and Akhmed, armed only with a Kalashnikov, leapt up the stairs to a look-out point on the first floor. Standing in a corner room overlooking the square and the side street, he watched a Chechen fighter fire an anti-tank grenade on an armoured troop-carrier. Four soldiers spilled out of the burning vehicle, and Akhmed and another fighter fired from the second floor, mowing down the Russian soldiers before they could take cover.

Tanks and armoured troop-carriers coming along behind tried to turn around, jerkily reversing over pavements to get away. One of the two Ukrainian volunteer fighters[2] who had joined the Chechens in the Presidential Palace showed Akhmed how to fire a Mukha, a shoulder-held anti-tank grenade launched straight from its tube. 'I fired and I did not know if I hit the tank or not, but when I ran over to look, it was already burning. All the remaining windows had blown out. I was in a state of shock. The sound was deafening,' he said.[3] Within ten minutes he had fired four missiles, intent on keeping the fire coming from the Palace, careless of his own safety. The powerful backlash of the weapon wrecked the corridor behind him. Below on the corner of Freedom Square five tanks were burning, the ammunition inside exploding in spectacular showers of sparks, the flames bright against the fading daylight. A tank was a 'moving coffin', as a Chechen commander had boasted a few days before: 'One hit is enough.'

Musost Khutiyev was a few blocks south, across the river on Subbotnikov Street, when word came in the early afternoon that Russian tanks were approaching. His group of sixteen men had eleven automatic rifles between them and only one rocket-propelled grenade, the only weapon that was any competition against a tank. All bearded, they were dressed in a motley uniform of Russian army surplus gear, jeans and sheepskin jackets, and wore black knitted hats. A few sported green headbands, the colour that symbolized both Chechen independence and Islam. They waited in a small cellar at a crossroads, listening to the rumble of the approaching armour. When someone with the grenade-launcher opened fire, disabling a tank, fighters erupted from their hiding-places all along the street to ambush the stragglers.

Across town on Pervomaiskaya Street, a long, broad avenue leading in from the airport, another fierce battle was raging where the 81st Motor Rifle Regiment came under ambush as it drove into town. Strung out for a mile along the avenue, the whole column came under fire from Chechen fighters positioned all the way down. Fighters were suddenly on the attack, running out in search of more tanks, plundering what did not burn for weapons and ammunition. By evening they gathered in the centre of the town, swarming around the market-place and moving towards the railway station.

The Maikop Brigade had occupied Grozny's railway station by early afternoon, parking its tanks and APCs in the square in front, facing the Presidential Palace, several hundred yards away down Orjonikidze Prospekt. They were unaware that they were a target for a very hostile and fierce Chechen resistance. Some members of the Presidential Guard even remember one Russian soldier poking his head out of the tank hatch to ask them where he could buy cigarettes. The Chechens answered him with a bullet to the head.

The Chechens took up positions in the depot buildings behind the railway station, the post office to the right and the five-storey building opposite. Over the radio they called on the Russians to surrender, warning them they were surrounded, but the Russians replied they had their orders and would not. Ryabtsev was standing under the arch of the railway building when a bullet nicked his uniform. It was early evening, still light, he remembered. It began slowly, with sniper fire and machine-guns rattling from nearby buildings. As the Russians answered with the big guns mounted on their armoured vehicles, the Chechens blasted them from the side with rocket-propelled grenades.

Within hours the square had turned into a horrific inferno of burning tanks and dead bodies. Ryabtsev was shot in the legs trying to haul a heavy machine-gun into the railway station building. He dragged himself behind the tanks and was pulled in through the window to a room that filled rapidly with wounded soldiers. Nikolai Zarovny, another young conscript, was inside his light tank firing the gun when an anti-tank grenade seared into the side, bursting like a fireball. His clothes on fire, his face and hands scorched, he yanked open the hatch at the back and leapt out, stumbling over the dead bodies of his comrades as he dashed blindly into the station building. Badly burnt, he joined the growing number of wounded in the impromptu field hospital. As the fighting raged through the night, Ryabtsev remembers drifting in and out of sleep, hearing loud explosions and someone saying another tank had been hit.

The commander of the Brigade, Colonel Ivan Savin, radioed all night for reinforcements but none came. Kim's unit only made it to the station at five in the morning but was in no position to help. His vehicle was hit in the street by the Presidential Palace around three in the afternoon. His team leapt free and made it into the light tank ahead. Fifteen of them then took cover in a building until the early hours of the morning when they managed to duck and weave their way to the station buildings. At midnight the men stopped for fifteen minutes while their commander offered them a swig of vodka. It was by now New Year's Day but they had little to celebrate.

In a bunker beneath the station Khavaj Khajbekarov, one of a small unit of Chechen railway police, was listening in terror. He had come to work that day as usual but as the bombardment grew heavier, he took cover underground with a group of colleagues. When the battle suddenly exploded above their heads, they thought they were the target. They radioed frantically to their Russian headquarters in Rostov but raised no response. Technically they were employees of the federal Russian railway police and they wanted to tell the Russians there was a mistake and they were not the enemy.

'Every fifteen minutes they hurled grenades against the building. They were trying to make us come out. We had automatic pistols but we didn't shoot. We were hoping they would talk to us, that they would even protect us,' Khajbekarov recounted as he fled the city two days later. In fact it was the Chechen fighters who were attacking the station, but even two days later, when Khajbekarov pushed away the rubble and crawled out to find the station destroyed and dozens of pieces of Russian armour burnt out in the square in front, he could still barely comprehend what was going on.

*

That evening the Chechen Information Minister, Movladi Udugov, managed to broadcast an appeal on Chechen television before the transmission was cut: 'Guard the borders. Take up your arms, move on Grozny. Today, once and for all, we should solve the problem of the Russian occupation,' he said. He was in the Presidential Palace along with the entire group of men who were to lead the rebel movement over the next two years. Vice-President Zelimkhan Yandarbiyev, donning his tall grey lambskin hat, gave interviews to journalists from his underground office, where his pet parrot was still with him.

The lean, grey-haired Chief of Staff, Aslan Maskhadov, commanded the fighting from a small room crammed with fighters bringing reports of the battle or Russian prisoners they had captured. Sitting in his Russian army field uniform, a thick grey fur collar on his jacket, he looked tense and tired, dark rings marking his eyes. He was a former colonel of the Russian army and had commanded an artillery division based in Lithuania before returning to Chechnya in 1992. Aged forty-three, he was to prove the mastermind of the Chechen military success and two years later would become Chechnya's post-war President.

His top commander, Shamil Basayev, a low-key twenty-nine-year-old who hung his head as he talked, came and went. He had a thick black beard and wore a grey and blue camouflage jacket of the Russian Interior Ministry, a green ribbon with Koranic inscription round his blue woollen hat. He carried a Kalashnikov assault rifle slung casually over his shoulder.

New Year's Eve was a big Russian holiday, a time when everyone throughout the country would be gathered round the table at home, drinking champagne toasts and watching television. All over Russia they would be watching Yeltsin's annual New Year's address: 'My New Year congratulations to all servicemen. When you carry out your duties, when you risk your lives even on New Year's Eve, remember that you are serving Russia and that you are defending Russia and the Russians,' he said ponderously.

Few in blacked-out Grozny were listening. An estimated 100,000 civilians were trapped in the city, sheltering in overcrowded bunkers, deafened by the explosions. The majority of them were Russian families who had not had the means or the foresight to leave. They had heard Yeltsin promise to end the bombing a few days before and yet the bombing had continued. Russian television even announced that evening that Grozny had fallen, but the former Soviet dissident and presidential human rights commissioner Sergei Kovalyov and the group of Russian parliamentarians denied it. Kovalyov, once a close ally of Yeltsin, like many of his liberal colleagues, became one of the most outspoken critics of the Chechen war and of the President himself. Now, from the basement of the Palace bunker, they denounced Yeltsin and appealed to all their fellow-countrymen to demand an end to the war.

'From the basement of the heavily shelled residence of Jokhar Dudayev, we who fought with you for democracy in Russia in 1991 to 1994, tell you that we are on different sides of the barricades today,' they said, reading an open letter to Yeltsin. 'We are not for Dudayev. We are against the war launched against the whole Chechen people . . . and unfortunately you are the commander-in-chief in this war. Today the problem is not about Chechnya but the democratic future of Russia.'

'Respected citizens of Russia, the situation is desperate for Grozny and desperate for Russia,' Kovalyov added. 'There stands before you a brutal choice.'

*

Patrick Chauvel, a French photographer, walked into Grozny at dawn on New Year's Day. He was the only independent journalist with the fighters in the centre of the city that day and he found the hunt for Russian tanks still going on.

The third battalion of the Maikop Brigade, some forty tanks and armoured vehicles, finally responded to calls for help and headed into Grozny mid-morning to try to break through to the station. Like the second battalion, they never made it and were blasted at close quarters as they trundled down the surrounding streets. Warned by those in the station to avoid the Presidential Palace and Orjonikidze Prospekt, they cut down side streets, only to run into more ambushes.

With no idea what to do, where to take cover or how to break out of the nightmare, soldiers were thrown into panic. Tank drivers backed frantically away to hide, crashing over pavements and through courtyards in a desperate attempt to get to safety. As the afternoon wore on and the light began to fade, tanks careered wildly down the streets, often lost, reversing in panic when they saw trouble, yanking their machine-guns round and firing in all directions. Some soldiers dived into nearby buildings, barricading themselves into the basements. 'They are hiding like chickens,' one fighter laughed scornfully.

'The Chechens would hit the first tank and the Russians in the tanks behind would run into nearby buildings to escape. There was a crazy game of hide-and-seek, with Russian soldiers hiding in apartments, bunkers and even toilets, and the Chechens hunting them with swords, knives and pistols,' Chauvel recalled. 'There were lots of tanks hiding in back yards and behind walls. The Chechens said they were waiting for night-time. They let lots of tanks in, then blocked the streets, they wanted to capture them.[4]

The Russian soldiers were so poorly trained that when the fighting erupted they were incapable of defending themselves. None of the eighteen- and nineteen-year-old conscript soldiers had any training for urban warfare and had no idea of the dangers. 'We only practised shooting lying flat in a field,' Zarovny said bitterly as two years later he watched documentary film of Chechen fighters firing from multi-storey buildings. They were also totally unprepared for the grenade attacks on their tanks. For all their heavy weaponry, their communications and back-up were abysmal, and isolated units blundered around without orders, even clashing with each other.

The Chechens, by comparison, were fearless and often merciless. Natural marksmen who learn to handle a gun as young boys, they picked off fleeing soldiers easily. Hundreds of volunteers ran in to grab weapons from the dead Russian soldiers, especially seeking the prized sniper rifles with night-sights, the more experienced hacking off the big machine-guns from the armoured vehicles.

Many Chechens carried daggers and even swords they had forged themselves or carried as a family heirloom; the *kinzhal*, the Caucasian dagger, being the most precious of possessions, intrinsic with a Chechen's manhood and honour. One commander, Batia, a big-bearded Chechen, led his group of fighters into battle brandishing a sword above his head. It was not for show, as countless dismembered and decapitated Russian corpses around the city bore witness.

Their most deadly weapon, though, was the Russian-made rocket-propelled grenade. Fired from the shoulder, it could pierce the vulnerable parts of tanks and armoured vehicles with extraordinary efficiency. Aimed from the top of Grozny's multi-storey buildings at the base of a tank turret, it would rip into the heavy armour, blasting off the gun in one go. Most of the Russian tanks and troop-carriers sent into Grozny were old and did not have full armoured protection against anti-tank weapons, proving easy prey for the Chechen fighters who would run in perilously close, aiming at the treads of the tanks or the fuel tank at the back part of the undercarriage. The ammunition inside the vehicle would do the rest, igniting and exploding with terrific force, giving the striker only seconds to leap aside.

Shelling picked up around 2 p.m. on New Year's Day and pounded on until dark. The Maikop Brigade was now under desperate pressure as the Chechens began hitting the station building where they were all sheltering. Colonel Savin called in artillery strikes to the immediate area around the station but it did little to ease his predicament. 'They are firing from all sides, where is the assistance? The whole battalion is wounded and lying in the station,' he radioed, his voice cracking under the strain. 'Think about how to get all the wounded out, we have no vehicles left, do you understand, work out how to get the wounded out. We are all dying, we need help, do you understand?' he said in one of his last radio messages, now passed around on cassette tape among the Brigade's survivors.

After dark he finally decided to evacuate the wounded to the only armoured vehicle still working. Two soldiers helped Ryabtsev hobble along the length of the station, two more were carried in blankets. A total of forty wounded men were loaded up, the badly wounded lying inside, the rest, Ryabtsev, Zarovny and Kim among them, somehow clinging on top. One of the only officers to survive, Mamed Kerim-Zade, sat at the front behind the driver. They left at speed, then suddenly stopped and turned back the way they had come, as the major in command reckoned they were heading the wrong way. 'We turned round and we were going back into the centre of town,' recalled Kim. 'We had nearly made it, too.' They were in fact less than half a mile from a Russian paratroop regiment who had set up base in a park. As they slowed to turn a corner, fighters caught them with several grenades. Soldiers spilled off in all directions as the APC crashed to a stop and gunfire broke out. Several tried to make a run for it, Zarovny, his wounded hands in bandages, guiding a friend who was blinded. They tried to climb a wall, only to come face to face with an armed Chechen. Kim dived into the drain. Kerim-Zade, badly wounded, could not move. Ryabtsev alone got away to an apartment building. He found some Chechen civilians who took him in but they alerted the nearest fighters, who came for him minutes later. Only thirteen of the forty wounded survived to be taken prisoner. Savin abandoned the railway station on the evening of 2 January, leaving on foot with the remaining officers and soldiers until they found several abandoned armoured vehicles. They headed out of town but they too were caught by the Chechens. The Colonel died on the street from shrapnel wounds beside his wrecked vehicle. The entire Maikop Brigade, over 1000 men, had been wiped out in just sixty hours.

*

Chechen fighters took Chauvel for a long and dangerous tour of the battleground on 2 January. Dodging snipers, they worked their way towards the airport up a wide avenue several miles long, littered with the wreckage of the Russian army. Chauvel counted 100 burnt-out pieces of armour that day and estimated he saw 800 dead Russian bodies – and he did not even make it as far as the railway station. 'It was a slaughter. Every 10 metres there were groups of four or five burnt-out vehicles. Along that street there are spaces of grass and trees in front of the houses. Two tanks would be lying hit in the middle of the road, and the others had panicked and turned in between houses. We even found dead Russians on the third floors of buildings.'

As he looked at wreck after wreck and bodies of soldiers strewn in pieces, Chauvel realized he was witnessing a humiliating disaster for the Russian army on a scale that no one could have imagined. 'There were twenty heavy tanks and troop-carriers, ten armoured personnel-carriers and troop trucks completely burnt, the bodies still inside. There was a mobile headquarters truck with communications. Everything was completely destroyed, the bodies burnt inside. They had hit the commander's vehicle, the Chechens were pleased with that. They kept saying "Command. Command."'

There were body parts everywhere, blown apart by explosions and blasted up on to the trees and trolley-bus wires above, where they still hung. Some bodies had been systematically butchered, a head sliced cleanly and placed apart on the pavement, undoubtedly the work of Chechen swordsmen. 'It was unbelievable. I had never seen anything like it,' Chauvel said.

Amongst the wreckage was a massive self-propelled gun, lying 10 yards away from the tank body that carried it. The gun, with its huge muzzle, can hurl its missiles over 10 miles, yet was lightly armoured and needed careful protection from anti-tank grenades. This terrifying piece of artillery had been broken like a toy, its huge gun tossed aside and the tank body 'popped open like a tin can', as Chauvel put it. Around it, scattered like bowling pins, were dozens of unexploded ammunition shells.

All the dead men were in tank fatigues. It was clear from the scene that no infantry had accompanied this column, something which every soldier knows is essential to protect a convoy from attack. Even Russia's Defence Minister, Pavel Grachev, who had taken over personal command of the operation, had said so when he laughed at the failure of an earlier attack on Grozny by Chechen forces opposed to Dudayev. 'Where were the infantry?' he asked. 'You must not send tanks in without infantry.' He called the use of tanks in a city 'wild ignorance' and said a single parachute regiment could have sorted out the affair in two hours. But he had sent tanks in and the Chechen fighters had blasted the columns easily at close range.

A story circulated that the decision to storm Grozny was taken during Grachev's birthday party, when top military and political chiefs were gathered in the Russian military base at Mozdok, just over Chechnya's border. Grachev, a strong Yeltsin loyalist, had invited two other Kremlin hawks, Oleg Soskovets and Mikhail Barsukov, to join him. Liberal Member of Parliament Sergei Yushenkov learned that during what he described as a 'drunken orgy', 'the order was given that whoever takes Dudayev's palace will get three stars'.[5]

There was every indication that in fact this was not a storm at all but a big show to push the Chechens to capitulate. Survivors of the Maikop Brigade said they had no idea they were driving towards such a big battle. Their orders were vague and unrealistic. Kim remembers they were ordered to go into the city 'without arms, and no shooting'. Later, when the fighting started, 'The order was to annihilate those who had weapons,' he said.

The Russian parliamentarian Anatoly Shabad, who spent New Year's Eve and New Year's Day in Grozny, believes that there was never actually a plan to storm the city. The bombing in the morning had little military purpose, but was more a frightening tactic, he argues. Then the tanks rolled in, as they had in Czechoslovakia to crush the Prague Spring in 1968, and again into Moscow in the attempted coup of 1991. 'When the tanks came into the centre of the town, it was clear that they were not storming anyone. It was a Prague-type operation. Or like that in Moscow in August 1991. They suggested they go and park in the town, and that way create political pressure so the government would not be able to survive any longer,' Shabad said.[6] 'It was a kind of military-cum-political act, a demonstration. They thought it would be different, they had not even formulated their ideas.' He had toured parts of the city on New Year's Day and the square in front of the railway station was like a cemetery, he said, the still-smouldering wrecks of vehicles jammed so close together it was hard to walk between them.

Grachev later appeared before the State Duma, Russia's Parliament, in a closed session and admitted he had never intended to storm the city as such. 'He became indignant and said there was no plan to storm Grozny. As he told the Duma, they were ordered to occupy specified positions in the town and they occupied them,' Shabad recalled. It was a catastrophically short-sighted order.

On another occasion Grachev blamed the high losses on lower-ranking officers. 'The operation to take the town was planned and was carried out with the least losses . . . And losses occurred, here I tell you in all honesty, through the absent-mindedness of commanders of the lower units, who sensed an easy victory and quite simply relaxed,' he said.

In Grozny, though, the picture was quite the reverse. Major-General Ivan Babichev, who commanded the assault from the west, could barely contain his frustration, blurting out his disgust for his bosses to a visiting delegation from the Organization for Security and Cooperation in Europe. 'The first thing he said was: "Our commanders in Moscow have let us down. They sent us in and then left us on our own." It was very interesting to hear a Russian general saying that,' Hungarian diplomat Istvan Gyarmati, who headed the delegation, recalled.[7]

*

No one knows the full count of the Russian dead. The official figures are far too low, partly because many of the soldiers were not wearing tags and their bodies, burnt to a cinder, were unidentifiable. Almost every soldier can name someone who died who does not appear on the official list. Survivors of the 131st Maikop Brigade said that over 1000 men died in Grozny. In Maikop, the capital of Adygeya, the North Caucasian town where the Brigade is based, one of the tanks destroyed on New Year's Eve stands on a plinth. Repainted but still bearing the hole from a grenade hit, it dominates a memorial to those who died. Lists of the fallen are carved on six black granite slabs. They bear just 110 names.[8]

The 81st Motor Rifle Regiment lost half its 1114 men, according to survivors. The 503rd and 45th Regiments also took a hammering, with casualties running into the hundreds. Their bodies lay for weeks beside their burnt-out tanks all over central Grozny, prey to stray dogs and cats that roamed the abandoned city. Several soldiers were burnt alive trying to climb out of the top of their tanks. Their blackened bodies and charred limbs, reaching out, were frozen in action, in some of the most gruesome images of the war.

The extent of the slaughter was never admitted at the time and only emerged gradually. Two days after the disaster an official statement from the Defence Ministry said that Russian forces in the city were 'regrouping', and admitted they had encountered intense resistance but consistently refused to issue casualty figures. It was up to the parliamentary deputies emerging from the bunker of the Palace to break the news. Kovalyov told how he stumbled around in horror at the railway station. 'A little wagon stood there, the sort builders use as temporary quarters. We went past it and underneath a little dog was eating something. Growling maliciously, it shot out at us. That is my most terrible impression from Grozny, because right beside it lay a dead body and I know what that dog was eating.'[9] From what they counted themselves the next day, the deputies estimated 1500 Russian troops had been killed on New Year's Eve. The figure may have been even higher; indeed, the word on the ground among Russian troops was 2000.[10]

Russian soldiers fighting in and around Grozny were also never told of the calamity but guessed as much. Denis Fedulov, a slightly built nineteen-year-old with a lock of dark hair falling over his eyes, was woken at 4 a.m. on New Year's Day and sent into the city in his big military-green Ural truck. The second battalion of his regiment, the 503rd Motor Rifle Regiment, about 500 men, had gone in the day before. 'We brought out 120 of them, dead and wounded, that first day,' he recalled.[11]

For days he did not stop ferrying wounded and dead soldiers out of the west part of the city and towing burnt and broken wrecks back to base. Grozny was still alive with gunfire as he ventured close to the railway station and market, listening to the horrifying battle raging the other side. 'The first night I hardly slept, I was so exhausted and cold,' he said.

Alexander Zavyolov, a twenty-year-old conscript in command of a battery of howitzers just north of Grozny, remembers how none of his team slept for five days as they were called on to fire salvo after salvo into the city. 'We were constantly firing, at night, afternoon, morning, all the time, throughout the day,' he said. 'Our units went in to take Grozny and were constantly demanding artillery support.'[12]

They suspected that their men of the 81st Motor Rifle Regiment were in big trouble. Dug in at the Rodina collective farm near the airport, they crouched in the gun emplacements, eating their cold rations between loads. 'Those first days during the storm of Grozny were the worst. No one knew exactly where to fire, where the enemy was, even who the enemy was.' It was only after a week that they learned of the fate of their comrades. Zavyolov remembered a single battle-scarred APC limping home to the base. Alone, out of the company of fifteen armoured vehicles and 225 men, they had survived and fought their way out. The shell-shocked men could barely speak, but slowly over the next days, away from their officers, the story came out. 'They told us how they were trapped for a whole week, they did not know where to go, they did not know even what to try to do, how or where to go,' Zavyolov said. 'They told us how our tanks burned. How they moved from one place to another, trying to break out but always pinned down. They broke out with real difficulty, they were completely surrounded.'

*

By now the scene in the Palace bunker had turned into one from hell. Some 100 Chechen fighters, over seventy Russian prisoners and a handful of doctors, nurses and civilians were living in the warren of dank, dark rooms of the Presidential Palace. There was no water, no heating and no light, and food was running out. The doctors and nurses worked around the clock, administering emergency aid with the barest supplies and equipment. One surgeon, his fur hat clamped on his head against the bone-aching cold, operated in a cramped room by the light of a single light-bulb, rigged up to a truck battery. There were no antibiotics or painkillers and men were screaming with pain. Nurses gave first aid by candlelight to the dozens of wounded fighters and civilians who lay alongside injured Russian soldiers, filling the corridors and small rooms.

The Russian prisoners lay together under grey army blankets in pitch-black rooms, listening to the tank fire of their own army advancing towards them. Most of them were conscripts. They were frightened not only of what the Chechens might do with them, but also of how their own military would treat them if they seized the Palace. Kim remembers thinking he would never get out alive. Vladimir Povetkin, whose unit had surrendered at the railway depot, now dreaded being recaptured and facing a court martial. Zarovny, his burnt face, head and hands wrapped in bandages, had to beg a friend to hold a cigarette to his mouth for him.

More nurses came in and out of the Palace, helping to evacuate the wounded over the River Sunzha to the south of the city. A few volunteers skidded in under sniper fire across the bridge, car tyres squealing as they hurtled into the Palace with supplies and ammunition and ferried out the wounded. One young driver, Shaman, had promised his mother he would not fight, but instead risked his life several times a day to race journalists into the Presidential Palace, flashing a broad smile full of gold teeth every time he emerged.

Civilians hiding in basements all over the centre of the city were also growing desperate. Pensioner Shura Rudina sat with Slava, her neighbour, watching over his invalid wife in the bunker of the Hotel Kavkaz, just yards from the Presidential Palace. They lived there for almost a month, begging bread from the fighters, bludgeoned by one of the heaviest bombardments any city has seen since the Second World War. Slava's wife finally died, and they pushed her body outside into the snow but did not dare to go outside to bury her for weeks.

*

The New Year's Eve battle seemed at first a great Chechen victory. A small band of Chechen fighters had humiliated a superpower, deflecting the assault of Europe's largest army and turning on its head the Cold War assumptions that made Russia's armed forces the most feared in the world. By one estimate Russian forces lost more tanks in Grozny than they did in the battle for Berlin in 1945.[13] The Chechens had seized countless weapons and ammunition and gained a breathing space as the Russian command slowly took in the scale of the catastrophe on their hands. Jubilant, the Chechen fighters roared around the city centre on captured tanks, flying the green Chechen flag. Basayev was one who did not brag. 'It was a senseless battle, without logic,' he said. 'They just threw their men in.' But as if he knew what was to come, he said the Chechens had shown they were deadly serious. 'It is not an empty threat that we will fight to the death.'

The Chechens had also suffered under the heavy bombardment. Their city was already half destroyed and many hundreds of people killed. The backlash, when Russia vented its wrath for its early failure, would bring down even more terrible death and destruction upon the hapless residents of the city. Their President, meanwhile, who had been predicting this war for three years, had fled town. The Presidential Guard evacuated Dudayev from the Palace in the early afternoon on New Year's Eve. Although it remained a well-kept secret, relatives in his personal guard drove him away as soon as the tanks appeared on the Palace Square. Yandarbiyev and Maskhadov stayed on in the Palace basement for over two weeks more, but Dudayev was never to return.

Nevertheless, Grozny had turned into one of the worst humiliations in Russian military history at the hands of a small force of lightly armed irregular fighters. It also proved a political defeat for Russia's leadership, who had not only failed to contain the crisis but had aggravated it, bringing the entire Chechen people out against them. An explanation for this extraordinary reversal lay in the Russian leadership's whole attitude to a people they had never really understood. They had ignored Chechnya's history of resistance to Russian rule and its ancient warrior traditions. And they had failed to calculate how a quick military campaign in Chechnya could turn into a quagmire for the whole of Russia.

2

The French of the Caucasus

The roots of the conflict dig deep. Long before they came to fight a guerrilla war with Russia at the end of the twentieth century, the Chechens were the most rebellious people in the Russian empire.

This is partly a fact of the landscape. Chechnya lies on the north side of the Caucasus, Europe's highest mountain range, and more than 1000 miles south of Moscow. It is not a large country, being smaller than Wales. The northern part is a grassy plain stretching down from the River Terek as it winds peacefully towards the Caspian Sea, but the heartland is in the south, a wild and rugged region in which serpentine rivers thread their way down through long gorges from the ridge of the Caucasus. The high hills are still coated with the thick beech forests, perfect terrain for guerrilla warfare in the last century, that used to cover the whole of Chechnya.

But the Chechens' rebellious spirit is also a matter of historical memory. Despite the Soviet Union's attempts to erase history, the thread of memory linking Chechens to their ancestors has not been cut. A Chechen should be able to recall the names of his forefathers back through six or seven generations, and former heroes from the wars of the last century still figure in the conversation of old men.

Chechnya is still dotted with shrines that are physical reminders of the Chechens' resistance to Russian rule. One autumn morning we went to one such spot folded into the hills just outside the ancient village of Vedeno in south-eastern Chechnya, a mausoleum looked after by three old men and lying on the high bank of a boulder-strewn river. In the early morning as we came up to the graveyard the mist was still rising from the long grass. Slowly its grey shreds lifted to open up a clear vista to the mountains and to the oak and beech woods blazing with reds and oranges at the turn of the seasons.

Said-Hasan Kaimov, the grandson of the man who built the shrine in the 1920s, is now its custodian. A small, wiry man with a mouth full of gold teeth, he is extremely proud of the plot he tends. Kaimov pushed his way down an untidy row of tall, pointed Chechen gravestones overgrown with brambles and stunted, gnarled apples trees. The graves, painted in vivid blues and greens, each topped by a jagged metal cap that let the rain run off, housed different generations of people who had fought Russia over the centuries, including the son and daughter of the great warrior Imam Shamil. At one edge of the graveyard three high poles soared up, with metal flags jutting out of them at angles, monuments to fighters killed in the recent war.

Kaimov led us to a low, broad mausoleum known as a *ziyarat*, resembling a pitched tent in stone, whose whitewashed walls were indented with inscriptions from the Koran. Inside the simple, concrete-coated tomb of the *imam* and warrior Uzun Haji was lit only by two small windows in the gloom, one looking to the sky and the other to Mecca. Uzun Haji was a Sufi religious leader from neighbouring Dagestan, a short man, almost a dwarf, who survived fifteen years in a Tsarist Siberian camp. A fierce Islamic militant, he declared, 'I weave a rope to hang engineers, students and all those who write from left to right.' In August 1919 the *imam* led a force of Chechens and helped the Bolsheviks defeat the White army of General Anton Denikin. He died in May 1920 before he had a chance to start fighting the Bolsheviks as well.

For years the old custodians received pilgrims streaming to Uzun Haji's mausoleum until the Soviet authorities tried to ban the pilgrims in the 1960s. They kept coming, just more surreptitiously: 'We posted guards so we knew if the KGB were coming,' said Kaimov. His grandfather, Kaim Haji, was a pupil of Uzun Haji, who built the mausoleum and later disappeared into Stalin's Gulag. The old man wearing the tall grey lambskin hat, called the *papakha*, a hunting rifle slung over his shoulder, revealed that he was the great-grandson of Shamil Haji, the Islamic scholar who founded the little hamlet on the river-bank. They plied us with apples and walnuts from the orchard and chatted in a friendly way in Russian. One of them even had a daughter living in Moscow, it emerged, but they were most proud of their famous ancestors buried in the graveyard who had fought the Russians.

The palpable sense of history at the graveyard outside Vedeno is common in Chechnya and a clue to the Chechens' outstanding confidence in their own identity. No one who has spent long among the Chechens can fail to warm to them, their pride in their country and their *joie de vivre*. They are highlanders with a hardy way of life and deep generosity to strangers and they are also southerners with a love of repartee and flamboyant gesture. 'Chechens are gay and witty. Russian officers nicknamed them the French of the Caucasus,' said the nineteenth-century French anthropologist Ernest Chantre.

The Chechens were farmers and horsemen who always lived close to the land. John Baddeley, the British historian and correspondent for the *Observer*, who travelled in the North Caucasus at the turn of the century, noticed their hospitality, thrift and neatness. The mountain villagers lived in mud-baked houses adorned with carpets and quilts: 'Each house commonly had its garden or orchard, and round the *aul* [village], in the forest clearing, stretched the cultivated fields, sown with maize, oats, barley, rye or millet, according to the locality – but as the villages were unfortified, care was taken to keep one side ever in contact with the forest, whither at the first threat of danger the women and children fled with all portable wealth.'[1] Not much has changed. There are cars in the courtyards and turquoise, green and blue cast-iron fences around the houses, but the care lavished on a Chechen village is a striking contrast to the decaying Russian countryside to the north.

Chechen society was formed around a complex system of *adats*, or codes of customary law, that took precedence over civil laws imposed from outside. The culture exalts two stereotypes: the old man respected for his wisdom and the young warrior showing off his flamboyance and bravery. Women generally kept in the background although they had more freedom than the veiled wives of Dagestan on the other side of the mountains. The Russian geographer Adolf Berzhe, writing in 1859, said the Chechen women 'wind long white scarves round their necks but do not wear veils and do not hide from men.'[2]

In the marriage ritual, the onus fell completely on the male. A young Chechen male could win his bride only after amassing a large bride-price and undergoing ritual tribulation. In the 1850s, the Russian writer A. P. Ippolitov watched as the groom sent a detachment of friends on a cart to the bride's house, where they were pelted with stones by children and then had their clothes ripped open by the pins and fingernails of the bride's girlfriends. When the bride was finally ritually bought and taken to the groom's house, he was not allowed to appear for three days. Often, Ippolitov says, the groom took the short cut and simply kidnapped the bride: '[I]t very often happens that the groom instead of taking the betrothed girl from the house of her relatives in the normal settled way steals her secretly with the knowledge of the relatives themselves. In former times two-thirds of weddings, both in Chechnya and in places here, were completed in this way: it was considered undignified and shameful for a man and decent person to take his wife in another way.'[3]

Ten months into the war, during the autumn of 1995, a wedding was held in the village of Alleroi of a young fighter and a sixteen-year-old girl who had worked as a nurse. The guest of honour was the chief Chechen commander Aslan Maskhadov. Maskhadov sat inside the house at the head of a long table, talking to the male members of the bride's family. Muslim law was in force and the table was lined with bottles of Pepsi and Fanta. The bride herself, in a white flounced dress to her feet, kept apart, a few steps outside the dining-room, chatting shyly to her friends. The groom was nowhere to be seen.

The main activity was outside in the square. The wedding was an event for the whole village. A 1000-watt bulb had been strung up over an empty patch of ground, creating a sea of intense light round which the men sat in one half of a huge circle and the women in the other. A man with a long cane went round the circle, seeking a man to dance. The dancer would then nod towards his chosen partner and the cane-tapper would select a woman from the other side of the ring. Then the couple entered the light and danced without touching. The man showed off, stamping his feet and thrusting his arms out like pistons, grinning to his friends. The girl, dressed in a shimmering aquamarine or pink Chechen long dress, glided serenely, eyes fixed on the ground with occasional shy looks at her partner. The dancing and the stamping went on all night and only a few people drifted away as once or twice the lights went out and someone had to fix the generator. The atmosphere of unity and togetherness, the unbroken ring, was extraordinarily intense, and the Russian soldiers camped on the edge of the village could have been a million miles away.

*

The origins of the Chechens and their close kin and neighbours the Ingush are obscure and ancient. Strongly built stone towers in the mountains show that in the Middle Ages they had mastered a high art of masonry and were living in fear of attack by their neighbours. The two peoples form a distinct ethnic group and have little in common with their neighbours to the east and west. The two other mountain peoples who fought the Russian armies as fiercely in the nineteenth century, the Circassians to the west and the Dagestanis to the east, were very different: both had an aristocracy and clear class divisions and Dagestan had a rich ethnic mix and a much older tradition of Islam.

The Chechens and Ingush call themselves *Vainakhs*. They speak languages that are mutually comprehensible but remain quite distinct and there are only modest levels of intermarriage between them. The Chechens call themselves *Nokhchi*. The name 'Chechen' comes from a village the Russians called 'Bolshoi Chechen', on the River Argun south of Grozny, now known as Chechen Aul and first mentioned in Russian chronicles in 1708. The centre of the Chechens' resistance, both in the nineteenth century and in 1995–6, was the region that the Russians called Great Chechnya, with its highland territory known as Ichkeria, starting south of the Argun and stretching up into the mountains.

The Ingush call themselves *Galgai*, whilst their Russian name derives from the village of Angusht. The Ingush also come from the mountains but resettled in the western plains in the eighteenth and nineteenth centuries, a process that made them much more vulnerable to Russian conquest. At times they have been together with the Chechens, at times apart. When Chechnya broke away from Russia in 1991, the Ingush voted to remain inside the Russian Federation. The Chechens' stereotype of the Ingush is as more middle-of-the-road and conformist than they are, whilst the Ingush regard their cousins as hot-headed romantics.

The Chechens have never had an aristocracy. In the pre-modern era they had only two categories of person – an *uzden*, a free man or commoner, and a *lai* or slave, usually a prisoner-of-war who worked on the land and had no social rights. Key decisions were taken collectively by the elders of each village in conference, a system that has been called 'mountain democracy'. According to Chantre:

> At the time of their independence, the Chechens formed several separate communities placed under the rule of a popular

assembly. Today they live as people unaware of class distinctions. They are very different from the Circassians whose gentry
occupies a very high place. This is the essential difference
between the aristocratic Circassian state and the wholly democratic constitution of Chechen and Dagestani tribes. It is this
that determined the specific character of their struggle . . .[4]

Instead of having a strong vertical hierarchy, Chechen society
breaks down into a web of tight cells and overlapping communities, so every Chechen belongs to a particular village, family and
religious brotherhood which have certain claims on him. The
most important attachment is to a certain *teip*. A *teip* is literally a
clan, but it is much more than that: according to the foremost
scholar of *teips*, Yan Chesnov, the *teip* has its origin in common
land ownership, and a newcomer to a region could join a *teip* by
acquiring land. *Teip* membership ties a Chechen to a large
extended family and to an ancestral piece of land.[5]

Teip members should provide support for the weak and work
for the unemployed. A more recent development is that they
should help each other to do deals in the black economy. There is
a strong parallel with Sicily's ties of honour and blood, which
gave birth to the Mafia and are much firmer than any obligations
to the state. The North Italian police inspector reflecting on the
lawless Sicilians in Leonardo Sciascia's novella *The Day of the
Owl* could be talking about the Chechens:

All this, thought the captain, is the result of the fact that the
only institution in the Sicilian conscience that really counts is
the family; counts, that is to say, more as a dramatic juridical
contract or bond than as a natural association based on
affection. The family is the Sicilian's state. The State, as it is for
us, is extraneous to them, merely a *de facto* based on force; an
entity imposing taxes, military service, war, police. Within the
family institution the Sicilian can cross the frontier of his own
natural tragic solitude and fit into a communal life where
relationships are governed by hair-splitting contractual ties. To

ask him to cross the frontier between family and State would be too much.[6]

There are more than 150 *teips* in Chechnya, of which around two dozen pride themselves on their purity and ancient descent. In one legend the ancestors of the pure *teips* used to have a huge bronze cauldron with their names inscribed on it in the mountain village of Nashkho, but members of the 'impure' outside *teips* seized the cauldron and melted it down on the fire so the purity of ancestry can never now be proved. The oldest *teips* have been stereotyped by other Chechens; thus, for example, the *tsentoro* are reputed to be tough and hard-working; the *chinkho* are so brazen that one of them once outwitted the Devil, another told God, 'Come down or I'll shoot'; the *kharacho*'s ancestors came from a cave, which is why they talk so loudly, whilst members of the largest *teip*, the *beno*, are the butt of jokes.

Beyond *teip* distinctions there is a bigger Chechen divide between people from the mountains and those from the plains. The mountain Chechens, protected by the natural defences of the landscape, have always been more independent, whilst the more placid Chechens in the north have lived and worked side by side with Russians and Cossacks for centuries. In 1989 the new Chechen leader, Doku Zavgayev, a plainsman from the Nadter-echny Region, openly patronized people from the plains, but two years later the mountain-born Jokhar Dudayev came to power and supported the claims of the mountain *teips*. The core of support for the war effort came from the mountain villages.

Russian law and customs remained alien in Chechnya until very recently. Rather than apply to the courts, Chechens, particularly in the mountains, used to settle their scores by violence. The codes of violence created a system of the blood feud and in Soviet times it was quite common for a Chechen to serve a long prison sentence for murder in a Russian jail, only to be murdered in a revenge killing on his release.

Amkhad Abayev, who died in 1990 at the age of 100, fought a vendetta that lasted seventy years. In the early years of the century his elder brother Akhma was driving cattle along the road between the villages of Gekhi and Roshni-Chu. A raucous wedding party swept along, the bride in a horse-drawn cart and the guests careering behind on horseback. One of the horsemen made a swipe and struck the *papakha* from Akhma's head – a great insult. Akhma turned in fury and hit his assailant a heavy blow across the back with his stick, whereupon the other man turned round his horse, drew his dagger and stabbed Akhma in the back. The village elders were called in to stop a blood feud breaking out and ruled that the two blows cancelled each other out. Akhma Abayev was murdered twenty years later in a different feud, but his brother nurtured a hatred for the original attacker, Akhmed Bazayev. In 1928 he found his enemy and slashed him across the back with a *kinzhal*. The feud was resumed and nurtured over the years with a host of small incidents. In the autumn of 1975 Amkhad and his son Alvi, who tells the story, were cutting hay outside Roshni-Chu and drinking tea. He suddenly saw that the man in the next orchard was his old enemy Bazayev. He called out to him three times before the other old man came over, then he said, 'I don't know how long we'll both live. We're both old men now. Let's make up.' The two old men embraced and the feud was over.

The threat of blood revenge is supposed to deter the first blow, and the fear that one feud can set off a chain-reaction of violence is one reason why Chechnya has avoided large-scale civil war. But that is not enough to suppress crime. Lawlessness, nurtured by the lack of a single central authority and tolerance of a culture of violence, thrives in the gaps between Chechnya's tight communities. Kidnapping – of Cossacks, Russian civilians, even Georgian princesses – was a constant menace in the nineteenth century. In the recent war the targets changed but the practice continued. Russian workers, priests, journalists and Western aid workers have all been abducted at various times and held for ransom. Banditry has always been rife in these parts. In 1901 John Baddeley heard the unfortunate story of an Englishman, a Mr Walton, who was robbed the year before. He 'was stopped at high noon midway between Grozny and the oil-fields by two horsemen, who robbed him of his money and other valuables and even of his boots'. One of the robbers was a Dagestani prince.[7]

Baddeley then adds a passage that is also still true, that once you are under the protection of your Chechen hosts you are completely safe.

> The net result was that to drive or ride – no one of course walked – in the lowlands of Chechnya was always to run a very serious risk of being robbed, and the nearer the town the greater the danger; whereas, once you had entered the mountain regions, if truly you knew the ways of the people, you were as safe as – even safer than – in the most civilized countries of Europe.[8]

Another outsider, an observant young Russian soldier, S. Belyayev, who spent ten months in captivity among the Chechens in 1843, also experienced the Chechens' strict codes of behaviour and strong sense of dignity that could lead to violence. Belyayev learned how to talk in Chechen and even fell in love with a Chechen girl. He won the trust of his captors and was treated as a member of the family, but saw how a fellow-captive sweated in shackles among less forgiving masters. Belyayev's description of being surrounded by a group of laughing, chattering, wise-cracking Chechens talking military tactics and asking questions nineteen to the dozen is a snapshot of time spent with Chechen men:

> They demanded my opinion: how it was best to attack them, from which side. They supposed it was more appropriate from the rear. They laughed at our attempt to go through the Ichkerian forest. Full of curiosity, they wanted to know how

we live, and when I told them about our famous towns they were all astonished and cried out 'Astafyur Allah! Astafyur Allah!' Their curiosity stretched very far. They love talking and they are masters at laughing at something they see is not right. They are able to value dignity in a man very highly, but in a moment of fury even the greatest man may die for no reason at all.[9]

Generally, however, the Russian invaders never bothered to investigate the complexity of the society they were conquering. They provoked the Chechens to violence and then concluded that they were mere savages. Even the relatively enlightened nineteenth-century geographer Berzhe, who wrote a thorough ethnographic study of the Chechens in which he gave credit to their elaborate codes of hospitality, decided they could only benefit from complete military conquest:

> The Chechens are, more than all the other mountain tribes, far from civilization and close to barbarism, the beastly ways of a half-wild people predominate in their lives, they have a highly developed propensity to plundering and murder and this rules out any chance of industry or other peaceful occupations amongst them.[10]

Some of the more free-thinking Russians who came down to the Caucasus to fight the long-running colonial war regarded the mountain peoples as at best gallant savages. For these children of the Romantic era, like the poets Pushkin and Lermontov, service in the Caucasus was equivalent to a Victorian English officer's time on the North-West Frontier; a place to escape the capital, live the simple life and encounter the primordial natives in all their wildness and simplicity. Lermontov's image in the first lines of his 'Cossack Lullaby' of the Chechen in his long felt cloak with his silver-encrusted *kinzhal*, ready to spring out from the trees, has unfortunately stuck in Russian folklore:

> The Terek streams over boulders,
> the murky waves splash;
> a wicked Chechen crawls on to the bank
> and sharpens his *kinzhal*;
> But your father is an old warrior
> forged in battle;
> sleep, my darling, be calm,
> sing lullaby.

The image lived on in the work of the French author Alexandre Dumas the Elder, who went in search of the romance of the Caucasus in 1858 and wrote up a racy account of his travels. Dumas describes an incident of man-to-man combat on the bank of the Terek. A Chechen *abrek* or gallant fighter appeared in the forest, shot one of the Cossacks' horses and challenged a Cossack to a duel. Dumas offered 20 rubles to anyone willing to take up the challenge. The first Cossack to take the writer's money was killed and slung over the Chechen's saddle. His Cossack comrade then fought the Chechen and killed him with a guileful trick. The Cossack blew a mouthful of pipe smoke out at the Chechen, who was deceived into thinking his enemy had fired his musket first. When the Chechen fired and missed, the Cossack was at liberty to finish the Chechen off. He cut off the head of the victim to keep as a trophy. The pure romanticism of the story leads one to suspect that Dumas may have made it up.

*

One more element – Islam – alienated the Chechens from the Russians. Islam did not become well established until the eighteenth century among the Chechens and even later among the Ingush. There are traces of some Christian monuments from the early medieval period in the mountains of western Chechnya and Ingushetia, but on the whole both people were animist until two or three centuries ago. The Islam that took hold, however, was very fervent. Most Chechens became members of one of two Sufi orders, the Naqshbandiya or the Qadiriya. Sufism is the mystical tradition in Islam. The *murid* or disciple must follow the *tariqat* or holy path under the guidance of a master. Being a member of a brotherhood obliges you to pay dues to the order and to visit holy shrines. Although early Sufism began as a non-worldly spiritual way, the North Caucasian teachers also began to preach *ghazavat* or holy war once the Russian threat increased.

The Naqshbandiya from Bukhara in Central Asia, which dominated Chechnya and Dagestan at the end of the eighteenth and the beginning of the nineteenth century, was preached by a series of *imams*, who were also political leaders, notably Imam Shamil, and was evidently attractive to the independent-minded Chechens. According to the two leading experts on Sufism in the former Soviet Union, it 'is a highly decentralized order, which maintains its unity only through a community of purpose and the practice of a simple ritual'.[11] Naqshband prayer is in the form of the so-called silent *zikr*. Worshippers gather in a private house and sit in a circle. They whisper or mutter the same holy phrases again and again until they attain a kind of holy trance. This ceremony requires no mosque and can be performed at home. It was a mystery the Soviet authorities found almost impossible to penetrate and break up.

There are still many Naqshbands in eastern Chechnya and Dagestan but they are now outnumbered by adepts of the Qadiriya, which swept through Chechnya in the middle of the nineteenth century. The Qadiriya originated in Baghdad in the twelfth century and was brought to Chechnya by the Dagestani shepherd Kunta Haji. Qadiri worship is more dramatic; its adepts perform the loud *zikr* in which they rush round in a circle, shouting the holy prayers ever louder and louder in an ecstasy of clapping and stamping. When Jokhar Dudayev seized power in 1991, the *zikr* became a political spectacle, and dozens of dancers gathered in the central square in Grozny and danced more and more furiously. When the Russians were poised to invade, it became an independence dance as one desperate dancer ran around the circle brandishing a Chechen flag, pressed in by a crowd of rhythmically clapping people.

The Qadiriya order is more centralized than the Naqshbandiya, but it is split into different sub-orders, known as *wirds*, some of which have gone off at radical tangents. One of these, the Vis Haji, created in the Chechens' exile in Kazakhstan in the 1940s and 1950s, introduced several new elements to the *zikr*. The dancers wear white fur hats, drums and even violins accompany the *zikr*, and women are allowed to join in. A surprising semi-Communist sub-order briefly took hold after the revolution in the village of Geldegan in eastern Chechnya and was named after its founder, Yangulbi-Haji. Its adepts fought as partisans in the civil war and wore red bands on their hats because Yangulbi-Haji's son had fought with the Bolshevik army of Nikolai Gikalo.[12]

There is some confusion about Islam's role in Chechnya. It has been so grafted on to local custom that many outsiders have discounted its influence altogether. The geographer Berzhe was one of several outsiders to call the Chechens 'bad Muslims', looking askance at them in comparison to the more pious Dagestanis. It is true that when the Dagestani leader Imam Shamil tried to impose strict Islamic *shariat* law on the Chechens he had little success. Most of them went on smoking, playing music and dancing as before, and Shamil was eventually forced to allow the Chechens more freedoms than his native Dagestanis. But Chechnya became in its own way a strongly Islamic republic and in the 1920s there were an astonishing 2675 mosques and houses of prayer, 140 religious schools and 850 mullahs in Chechnya. The Soviet authorities clamped down so hard that by 1961 every single mosque had been closed. Sufi worship carried on, however. Said-Hasan Kaimov, the custodian of the shrine outside Vedeno, said that they managed to keep up the *zikr* during the worst times: 'It all continued despite prohibitions, all the time in

Kazakhstan, in Grozny and here.' They would meet at home and tell any inquisitive outsiders that it was just a social gathering.

Willi Weisserth, a German who grew up with the Chechens when they were exiled to Central Asia by Stalin and converted to Islam, says the Chechens he first knew in the 1940s and 1950s stood out for their dignity and religious feeling. 'It was a very difficult period, but the Islam there was of very high quality,' he said. 'It was very just. The Chechens especially were of very high quality. Those old men who I managed to get to know then had a prophetic nature, they had justice, correct behaviour and they observed Islam. Despite all their difficulties they submitted completely, 90 per cent I would say, to Islam. There were no distortions.'

Weisserth is now Haj Mohammed, a respected village elder who has made three pilgrimages to Mecca. Only his pink cheeks, blue eyes and neat Teutonic style reveal his origins. He thus has a unique outsider's perspective on the Chechens. He castigates the attacks on religion and society of the Soviet era and his message is that traditional Chechen culture has decayed since the 1950s as traditional values have been lost and the Chechens have become secularized and urbanized. The Chechens he talks about seem to have been of a different era, more akin to current-day Afghans with their long beards than to modern Chechens and completely alien to Russian ways.

In 1978 the first mosque was reopened in Chechnya and after 1989 more and more were built in every village. But the Soviet years had done enormous damage, wiping out a lot of tradition, and there are now very few Islamic teachers. Islam was not a big factor in the 1991 nationalist movement and there is huge ignorance about it. Irreverent Chechens tell the story of how President Jokhar Dudayev supposedly urged all devout Muslims to honour the Koran and pray three – and not five – times a day.

During the war more and more Chechen fighters started wearing green headbands with Arabic inscriptions and said they were fighting a *ghazavat*. Then after the euphoria of defeating the Russians in August 1996, there was talk about imposing *shariat* law. There was a brief fashion for *shariat* justice but the strength of the secularized society beneath quickly showed itself. The courts were often ignored and kept up only by the zealous fighters. Within a few months the main remaining feature was the absence of alcohol from the kiosks in Grozny.

In October Jumbulat Samkhatov appeared to be the only man left running a *shariat* court in Grozny. In a former school for the deaf he kept a basement full of drink and drug offenders coughing in Dantesque gloom. He had had them beaten with sixty strokes of the rod and left them to dry out until he saw fit to release them. Samkhatov, a neat man with a trim red beard, added that he had shot two people who had been caught trading hashish. But Samkhatov, only twenty-eight, was also a product of his times. He used to be a footballer with the Grozny team Terek Grozny before sewing a Chechen wolf badge on his green felt cap and joining the fighters. Partly his austere views were those of the fighter down from the hills who was disgusted by the decadence of the big city. 'Allah punished us once,' he said. 'People died. It was punishment for the way we were mad before the war.' Even Samkhatov himself was not the fanatical Muslim he supposed himself to be. He apologized for smoking Marlboros as he enthused about the *shariat* and the militant Afghan Islamic movement, the *taleban*, oblivious to the fact that a Western woman was taking his photograph.

The cigarette-smoking *shariat* judge is evidence of another influence in Chechen society, Russification. From the 1950s Soviet ways made big inroads into traditional Chechen culture as village people moved into the big city, Grozny, or to Russia, where they assimilated the urban lifestyle of the Russians. The biggest Chechen city after Grozny is now Moscow, with some 50,000 Chechens resident there. Almost every Chechen under sixty is bilingual in Russian and Chechen and scatters his conversation liberally with Russian words. The women wear short-sleeved dresses and go to work. Chechen men, including most of the fighters in the recent war, served in the Soviet army. During a lull in the fighting in the summer of 1996 Chechen fighters had no problem about cheering the Russian team in the European Championship football tournament on television.

Russification means that Chechens live parallel lives. The Chechen businessman who works in Moscow will have kept his house in a village in the hills. At home he may say his prayers more readily than when he is in Russia. He can both drive a car and ride a horse, use a computer and fire a hunting rifle. The Chechens can see both sides of the cultural divide and they understand the Russians much better than the Russians do them.

3

Conquest and Resistance

The Chechen President Jokhar Dudayev liked to talk about 'three hundred years of struggle with Russia'. It was an exaggeration, but not so far from the truth. Since the end of the eighteenth century there have been literally dozens of Russian military campaigns in Chechnya fought over the same ground and the same place-names. The recent war was a modern conflict arising out of a new crisis of power, but it was also just the latest chapter in a long story.

In the eighteenth century Chechnya fell victim to the Russian empire's laws of expansion. In the south, that meant the empire advanced until it came up against the natural sphere of influence of the nearest great power, the Ottoman Empire. Other aims were to gain access to the warm-water ports of the Black Sea, link up with the Christian kingdoms of Georgia and Armenia, and eventually open up trade routes to the British Empire and India. The North Caucasus was simply the region in between. The only question was how quickly the mountain tribes could be overcome.

Following the end of the Northern War with Sweden in 1721, Peter the Great led an expedition southwards against Persia. He landed in Dagestan on the shore of the Caspian Sea on 27 July 1722. The water was too shallow for his barge to reach the shore and he was carried ashore by four boatmen. The spot where he landed became the town of Petrovsk, later renamed Makhachkala and made the capital of Dagestan. When a detachment of troops travelled inland into the mountains they were pushed back by a group of armed natives. This was probably the first encounter between a regular Russian army unit and the Chechens.

Russian expansion rolled southwards with the help of a demographic tide of Cossacks, the runaway serfs and free settlers who formed a semi-independent frontier army. Thousands of them settled by the River Terek. The Cossacks helped build a new chain of forts along the Terek, called the Line, consolidating their expansion into new territory. The fort of Kizlyar downstream on the Terek was built in 1735. A fort was built at Mozdok, higher upstream, in 1763 and later settled with Cossacks. Vladikavkaz ('Rule over the Caucasus') was constructed in 1783 at the beginning of the new road south into Georgia, the Georgian Military Highway. Gradually the Line was extended and strengthened until in 1832 it extended from the Caspian to the Black Sea.

At this time many Chechens were resettling in the plains. In 1796 there were 1000 Chechens living in Kizlyar alongside the other nationalities, but the two migratory currents could not coexist peacefully. In 1785 a tall Chechen called Ushurma, dressed in a long green cloak, appeared in the village of Aldy, preaching the Naqshbandi form of Sufism and holy war against the Russians. The origins of Ushurma, the mountain tribes' first organized leader, are obscure, and there is indeed no proof that he was actually a Chechen. He was, however, a decisive military leader who had the confidence to rename himself Mansur ('Victor') as he began to fight the Russians. Count Pavel Potyomkin, Catherine the Great's chief minister and lover, sent Colonel Pieri to Aldy to capture the new rebel and in July 1785 he burned the village to the ground. Sheikh Mansur escaped and counter-attacked. He surrounded the Russians in a dense forest and almost wiped them out. Pieri and more than 600 men were killed in one of the most catastrophic military defeats of Catherine's reign.[1]

This was to be Sheikh Mansur's only famous victory. After six years of dogged warfare he was captured by the Russians in 1791 and sent north for inspection by Catherine the Great, before being imprisoned in the Schlusselburg Fortress, where he died in April

1794. Mansur set a precedent by combining religious teaching and military leadership and his short campaign of resistance made him a folk hero. He is still a propaganda symbol amongst the Chechens and his name is used liberally on streets, banknotes and Grozny's civilian airport.

The pivotal figure in Russian strategy in the North Caucasus in the early nineteenth century was Alexei Yermolov. A hero of the Napoleonic Wars, Yermolov was named Viceroy and Commander-in-Chief of the Caucasus in 1816 when he was already entering middle age. He made a tremendous impression on anyone who met him – Pushkin likened his physical bulk and mane of white hair to 'the head of a tiger on a Herculean torso'. He kept the spartan lifestyle of an ordinary soldier, sleeping wrapped in his military cloak and living in an earth dug-out. He boasted of his own cruelty and famously declared: 'I desire that the terror of my name should guard our frontiers more potently than chains or fortresses, that my word should be for the natives a law more inevitable than death.' He displayed contempt for the Muslim tribes he was fighting and called the Chechens variously 'treacherous', 'villains' and 'robbers', good only for complete subjugation. 'Gentleness in the eyes of the Asiatics is a sign of weakness, and out of pure humanity I am inexorably severe,' Yermolov said. 'One execution saves hundreds of Russians from destruction and thousands of Muslims from treason.'

The Caucasian Wars against the mountain tribes were divided into two theatres. In the western theatre the main adversaries were the Circassians or Cherkess. In the middle were the mostly neutral or pro-Russian Ossetians and Kabardians and the Ingush, who did little fighting. The eastern front consisted of Chechnya and Dagestan. The separation of the two fronts made the task of the Russians much easier as they never faced a concerted resistance movement.

Yermolov decided he would subdue the eastern front first and in 1817 he set about conquering Dagestan and Chechnya. He started building a second line of fortresses that advanced the Russian forward line to the Sunzha. In 1818–19 he erected the fortress of Grozny, then called Groznaya, on the site of six Chechen villages which he had levelled. The name ('Terrible' or 'Menacing') was a token of his flamboyant self-advertisement. The new fortress was followed by Vnezapnaya ('Sudden'), built on the border of Chechnya and Dagestan in 1819, and Burnaya ('Stormy') by the Caspian Sea, which completed the line in 1821.

Yermolov attempted to hem the Chechens into the mountains and intimidate them into surrender. The commander and his subordinate General Nikolai Grekov threatened 'to destroy *auls*, hang hostages, and slaughter women and children'.[2] In September 1819 they carried out the threat and destroyed the village of Dada-Yurt on the Terek, killing 300 families. The aggressive campaign Yermolov waged in Dagestan in 1819–20 was outwardly successful but it planted the seeds for the coming Islamic resistance movement. Yermolov was the first, but not the last, Russian commander in the Caucasus to believe in the inevitability of his military success. In 1820 he declared: 'The subjugation of Dagestan, begun last year, is now complete; and this country, proud, warlike and hitherto unconquered, has fallen at the sacred feet of your Imperial Majesty.'[3]

For all his optimism, Yermolov faced a full-scale rebellion in Chechnya in 1825–6. In 1826 he moved across the country and 'punished the rebellious Chechens, burning their villages, destroying their forests, beating them in skirmishes that never developed into battles, and, occasionally, even seeking to win them over by an unwonted display of clemency'.[4] Yermolov was eventually brought down by political intrigue in St Petersburg. He left the Caucasus in April 1827 and spent the next two decades bitterly criticizing the campaigns of his successors.

Yermolov set a precedent of total warfare which prevailed for the next thirty years and beyond. Outright conquest was not the only way of absorbing the region into the empire. Divide-and-rule tactics and political methods which were successful in other parts of the Caucasus sometimes worked with the Chechens in lulls between the campaigns. John Baddeley, the best historian of the Caucasian Wars, says of Yermolov:

> 'It is abundantly evident that to him the complete and permanent conquest of the Caucasus was a matter of a few short years at most, so overweening was his belief in his own power and genius, so blind his ignorance of the latent forces that even now were gathering head against him, gaining strength, indeed, with every seeming success of his vaunted policy, every step in advance of his victorious armies. The mighty edifice he was rearing had its foundations in the sand and before long was to come tumbling about its builder's ears.'[5]

The Chechens' attitude to Yermolov has never been in doubt. In the 1970s and 1980s they kept blowing up his statue in Grozny until it was eventually thrown in the river once and for all. In Russia, for some reason, Yermolov is honoured more than any other general of the Caucasian Wars. This may be the result of Alexander Pushkin's youthful romantic poem 'The Caucasian Captive', which contains the famous line, 'Bow down, Caucasus, Yermolov is coming!' A village outside Grozny was named after the general and in Moscow there is still a street bearing his name adjoining the prestigious Kutuzovsky Prospekt. Incredibly in 1995 the Russians gave permission for a group of armed Cossacks to take up arms and form a Yermolov battalion in Chechnya.

*

Even the mighty Yermolov was overshadowed by the mountain leader who emerged in his wake: Imam Shamil, who led resistance to the Russians for more than twenty-five years. He built a mini-Islamic state, defied death and capture countless times, and fought possibly the longest guerrilla campaign in history.

Imam Shamil was born in 1796 or 1797. He was called Ali at

birth but as he was sickly and ill for the first six years of his life his name was changed. On acquiring his new name, Shamil (Samuel), he became strong and athletic. He was exceptionally tall and grew a long beard that stayed thick and black well into old age. Shamil was a close comrade of the 'first *imam*' of Dagestan, Kazi Mullah, and was one of only two survivors of Kazi Mullah's last stand at the mountain village of Gimry in 1832. It was the first of several escapes which became legendary among Shamil's followers. On that occasion Shamil leapt over the stockade that surrounded the village, cut down three Russians with his sabre and was bayoneted in the chest before making his escape. In 1834, on the death of Kazi Mullah's short-lived successor, Khamza Bek, Shamil was nominated to be the third *imam* of Dagestan and the combined religious and military leader of the region.

The siege of Gimry was repeated five years later in even more dramatic form at Akhulgo. Following a trip to the Caucasus, Tsar Nicholas I had appointed yet another commander to the region, Baron Pavel Grabbe. In 1839 Grabbe launched his strike against Shamil. Shamil conducted a scorched earth policy, destroying all cultivated crops and emptying villages in the path of the Russians, whilst his Chechen lieutenant, Haj Tasho, was entrusted with harrying the Russians in the rear.

The Russians advanced deep into the mountains and began to lay siege to Akhulgo on 12 June. Shamil was shut inside with a population of 4000 men, women and children but for two months he refused to surrender unconditionally and on 22 August the Russians forced their way into Akhulgo. The last battle was a bloodbath:

'Every stone hut, every cave, had to be taken by force of arms. The mountaineers, though irretrievably lost, refused all surrender, and defended themselves fiercely – women and children, with stones or *kinzhals* in their hands, threw themselves on the bayonets, or in despair flung themselves over the cliffs to certain death. It is difficult to imagine all the scenes of this terrible, fanatical struggle; mothers killed their children with their own hands, so that they should not fall into the hands of the Russians . . .'[6]

This seemed to be the end of Shamil but he made another miraculous escape. He slipped away with his infant son down a ravine, sending a raft with dummies strapped on to it downstream as a decoy, then crossed the pass over into the hills of Chechnya. 'Once more the Russians triumphed; once more the Government in St Petersburg congratulated itself on the destruction of Shamil's influence and the extinction of Muridism; and once more they were fooled,' comments Baddeley. Within a year Shamil had reconstituted his movement and within three years he was back in control.

The Russians' mistake was to follow up their victory at Akhulgo with a new crackdown in Chechnya. They imposed direct rule in the region and allowed rumours to spread that the mountain people were about to be conscripted into the Russian army. General Pullo made things still worse by allegedly uttering the careless words, 'Now that we have taken away their arms, we have only to take away their women's trousers.' Shamil had settled in a mountain village in western Chechnya with only seven followers, but when the Chechens invited him to lead their rebellion, he succeeded in raising most of Chechnya behind him, punishing those villages which refused to join him.

A legendary episode from 1843 is an illustration of Imam Shamil's brilliant powers of leadership. A deputation of Chechens went to Shamil asking him to give them either proper protection against the Russians or permission to sue for peace. They were afraid of what the *imam*'s reaction would be and so they interceded with him through his mother. Shamil was angry with the delegation but did not want to alienate the Chechens, so he publicly retired to the mosque for three days of prayer and fasting to consider his verdict, ordering the population to gather in front of the mosque. When he re-emerged he gravely announced that the Prophet had answered him that the Chechens' request was shameful and that the person who had transmitted it should be given 100 lashes. That person was his own mother! Despite protests, he ensured the sentence was carried out, but his mother passed out after the fifth lash. Shamil stripped off his cloak and received the remaining ninety-five strokes himself. The deputation begged for mercy but was sent away unharmed. After that there was no more suggestion of surrender.

*

By the 1840s Russia was bogged down in an endless war in the Caucasus which it was still far from winning. The main theatre of operations on the eastern front was eastern Chechnya and western Dagestan. The Russians preferred to campaign in the Chechen forests in winter when the ground was hard, the rivers low and the trees bare, and in the Dagestani mountains in summer when they were passable. It was a contest between mismatched enemies. The cumbersome Russians had strength in numbers and firepower but they were clumsy and exposed in the mountains, where they had to drag their cannons up the steep mountain paths. Whenever they had the chance of a pitched battle in an open space their artillery usually won them the day, but most of the time they were forced to fight in treacherous conditions better suited to the guerrillas. Shamil's fighters had an invaluable ally in the Chechen beech forests, where some trees were so huge that thirty or forty men could take cover in them and pour fire down on the advancing Russians. The Russian commander Tornau describes the ferocity of a forest battle:

> Small columns were sent out on all sides to ravage the enemy's fields and dwellings. The *auls* blaze, the crops are mowed down,

the musketry rattles, the guns thunder, again the wounded are brought in and the dead. Our Tatars [native allies] come in with severed heads tied to their saddle-bows, but there are no prisoners – the men take no quarter; the women and children are hidden beforehand in places where none care to seek them. Here comes the head of a column returning from a night raid; its rear is not yet in sight; it is fighting in the forest. The nearer it comes to the open space, the faster grows the firing; one can hear the yells of the enemy. They surround and press on the rearguard from all sides; they rush in, sword in hand, and wait only the moment when it debouches on the clearing to pour in a hail of bullets. A fresh battalion and several guns have to be hurried forward to disengage it; the running fire of the infantry and canister from the artillery arrest the onslaught, and enable the column to emerge from the forest without useless sacrifice. Men are sent out to cut grass and at once a fresh fight begins. Fuel for cooking purposes or for the bivouac fires is only obtained by force of arms. If on the far side of the rivulet there is brushwood or any semblance of a hollow the watering-place must be covered by half a battalion and artillery, otherwise the horses will be shot down or driven off. One day is like another, that which happened yesterday will be repeated tomorrow – everywhere are mountains, everywhere forests and the Chechens are fierce and tireless.[7]

Shamil had all the advantages of the guerrilla commander: speed, surprise and closeness to the land. The Chechens had to be prepared to flee from attack at any moment and grew maize because it was easy to cultivate in remote spots. Shamil's crack soldiers were his horsemen, who must have been a terrifying sight as they thundered down from the mountains dressed in long felt coats with cartridge belts wound round them and long sabres at their sides. Velyaminov, the great Russian strategist of the Caucasian Wars, was awestruck by their skill.

They are all but born on horseback and being used to riding from their earliest years, become extremely expert in this art, and accustomed to covering great distances without fatigue.

Having an abundance of horses not pampered in stables, they choose those only which are noted for their swiftness, strength and activity. Amongst them animals are by no means rare that on a summer's day can carry their riders 150 versts [about 100 miles] between dawn and sunset. In Europe, of course, this will sound untrue, but throughout West Asia it will surprise no one. Selecting one horse out of many, the native takes care of him when on the move; never employs him on any considerable journey (i.e. other than raiding), and for a raid uses absolutely no animal under eight years old. The mountaineers' weapons are their personal property, handed down from generation to generation. They value them very highly, carefully preserve them, and keep them in excellent order.

The Chechen horsemen carried out ruthless raids, called *nabegi* by the Russians. Originally these were sorties against their neighbours in which they carried off cattle and sheep, but as the Russian colonizers moved southward, the main target became the Line and Cossack settlements. The essence of a *nabeg* was in its speed; the riders did not use roads and attacked without warning, striking terror into the hearts of the peaceful population. A small raid could be over in a couple of hours as a group of horsemen descended on a Cossack village, looted and took a few hostages. In a big raid a large and fearsome troop of horsemen descended on a whole town. Such was the raid by Kazi Mullah on Kizlyar on the Terek in 1831 in which he carried off dozens of hostages and thousands of rubles' worth of booty. In January 1996 the Chechen fighter Salman Raduyev launched what was essentially a modern *nabeg* on the helicopter base in the same town.

The young Leo Tolstoy, who served in Chechnya from 1851 to 1853, was fascinated and horrified by this vast colonial war and felt sympathy for everyone except the generals and politicians conducting it from afar. In *The Cossacks* Tolstoy says that the Cossacks along the Terek actually had more in common with the Chechens they were fighting than with Russians to the north.

To this day Cossack families consider themselves to be kin of the Chechens and the main features of their character are love of freedom, idleness, robbery and war. The influence of Russia is only felt in a negative way: in restrictions on their elections, the taking down of bells and troops which are stationed there and pass through. A Cossack has less hatred by inclination for the mountain *jigit* [hero] who has killed his brother than the soldier who is standing next to him to defend his *stanitsa* but who has filled his house with tobacco smoke.

The bulk of the Russian army consisted of peasant serfs conscripted for up to twenty-five years. Even more than the teenage recruits of the recent war, they were expendable cannon fodder. Tolstoy measures the huge gulf between the ordinary fighting men and their far-away leaders in his late novella *Haji Murat*. The peasant conscript Avdeyev is killed in a senseless chance skirmish in the woods and the report back inflates the enemy's casualty figures and glorifies the action. After an attack by mountaineers and a brave charge by the soldiers, the report declares, 'Two soldiers were lightly wounded and one killed in the action. The mountaineers lost around one hundred men killed and wounded.'

Tolstoy's empathy extends to the illiterate mountain people being conquered and he has a famous description of an attack on the village of Makhkety in January 1852. The soldiers burn hay and houses, shoot the chickens and bayonet a child. They uproot trees, burn the beehives and defile the fountain and the mosque. When the raid is over, the Chechens sit in the ruins of their village and discuss what to do next:

No one spoke of hatred for the Russians. The feeling which all Chechens felt, both young and old, was stronger than hatred. It was not hatred but a refusal to recognize these Russian dogs as people and such a revulsion, disgust and bewilderment at the senseless cruelty of these beings, that the desire to destroy them, like a desire to destroy rats, poisonous spiders and wolves, was as natural as the instinct of self-preservation. The villagers faced a choice: they could stay where they were and expend terrible effort to restore what had been created with such labour and destroyed so lightly and senselessly, while waiting for the repetition of the same thing at any minute; or, in spite of their religious law and their feeling of revulsion and contempt for the Russians, they could submit to them. The old men prayed and unanimously decided to send envoys to Shamil to ask him for help and immediately set about rebuilding what had been destroyed.

In the mid-1840s Shamil had created a mini-state with its own tax and legal system. He made a strong effort to crack down on some of the *adats* of the Chechens, forcing them to lower the level of their bride-price and giving out benefits for widows and orphans. Essentially it was a state at war. He had a reserve army of 30,000–40,000 people – one man from every household – and a standing army of 5580 cavalry and 8870 foot-soldiers, including a whole battalion of deserters. The harshness of the imamate was matched only by that of Russian rule. The Russian captive Belyayev saw the *imam* ride severely through Chechnya with a long troop of warriors; one of them demonstratively carried an axe as a symbol of the necessity of obeying the law. Shamil forcibly bought up the Chechens' produce at low prices, had troops quartered in the *auls*, and removed villagers to the mountains. It is possible his imamate would have collapsed through internal dissent if it had not fallen to military conquest. 'The tough military discipline prevailing in the imamate was unusual for the mountain people of Chechnya; the excessive regulation of private and public life, the arbitrary actions of the naibs, of the Shamil administration as a whole, caused protests that ranged from simple flight to armed uprisings,' says the Chechen historian Yavus Akhmadov.[8]

The resistance of the mountain tribes was doomed to failure sooner or later. In 1846, following a crushing victory the year before at Dargo, in the mountains, Shamil rode several hundred miles to the west in an attempt to link up with the Right Front of the Caucasian campaign, but the expedition only proved that the whole Caucasus was not behind him. Nor did he get any substantial foreign aid despite letters to Queen Victoria. The British did send some help to the Circassians, but never supported Shamil.[9]

In the 1850s the Russians finally subdued Shamil's imamate. They began in earnest to implement the 'system of the axe' and started clearing the forests. Passages wide enough for a musket to be fired on either side were cut through the trees. They also constructed the 'Advanced Chechen Line' of fortresses in the foothills of the Caucasus at Vozdvizhenskoye ('The Elevated') on the upper Argun in 1844, Achkoi-Martan in 1846 and Urus Martan in 1848.

In July 1856 the intelligent Prince Alexander Baratinsky was made Viceroy and Commander-in-Chief of the Caucasus. He made full advantage of the new campaigning conditions and cut avenues deeper into the forests. One of them led the Russians right through to Vedeno, Shamil's headquarters. Vedeno fell in the spring of 1859 and Shamil retreated to the rocky village of Gunib in Dagestan, where he made his last stand.

On 25 August 1859 – the Tsar's birthday – Shamil was surrounded and finally compelled to surrender. The 'Lion of Dagestan' rode out with fifty *murids* and personally handed over his sword to Prince Baryatinsky. He was sent to St Petersburg, where he became a national celebrity and later retired with his family to the provincial town of Kaluga, He lived in some comfort and late in life was finally allowed to make a pilgrimage to Mecca. He died in Medina in 1871 and was buried there.[10]

By the time of his surrender Shamil was famous across Europe. Karl Marx in his polemical works attacking the Tsarist empire called him 'a great democrat' and exhorted the oppressed peoples of Europe to emulate his courage. Historians have argued that by

laying down the first proper kind of statehood in Chechnya and
Dagestan, Shamil actually made it easier for the Russians to
impose their authority, once they had conquered these countries;
but he also established a precedent of self-determination, which
encouraged the mountain peoples to continue resisting.

In fighting the Caucasian Wars the Russians committed many
of the mistakes which have characterized them in the region
before and since. One general succeeded another and each had
different orders and different ambitions. Above all there was a
constant underestimation of the people they were fighting against.
The policy chosen was consistently one of total attack, leaving
the natives no option but to resist as desperately as they could.

The Chechen Chief of Staff Aslan Maskhadov felt there were
many similarities between the Caucasian Wars and his own
campaigns in the Chechens' latest conflict with the Russians in
1995–6. Many of the routes and the battle-sites were identical
and often the tactics were the same too. 'They took the most
terrible things from those wars. They struck at population centres,
tried to set the population against the Chechen army, created
intolerable conditions for resistance fighters, made traitors and so
on,' he said, sitting on a tree stump in one of the surviving beech
woods in eastern Chechnya. But the nineteenth-century war was
also quaintly slow in comparison to the horrors of modern
warfare. Maskhadov said the vast technological superiority of the
modern-day Russian army had made his task much more difficult:
'In Imam Shamil's time it was much easier for our grandfathers
to fight because the difference in strength was maybe ten times
greater. But today the enemy outnumbers us thousands of times
over in troops and equipment, aviation, artillery, tanks and so on.
We have grenade-launchers and nothing else.'

For all the limitations of the weaponry, the Eastern Caucasus
was devasted by thirty years of war. Chechen historians have
calculated that a population of almost 200,000 in the North-East
Caucasus in the 1820s had been reduced to 130,000 twenty-five

years later. Resistance to Russian rule in the western theatre of the Caucasus did not last much longer. After total defeat some half-million Circassians were expelled from their native lands and deported by sea to the Ottoman Empire.

On 20 February 1860 the Terek Province was created, comprising Chechnya, Ingushetia and modern-day North Ossetia. The mountain tribes were allowed special terms of submission, including the right to practise Islam and the *shariat*, bear arms and not to be conscripted into the Russian army. Even so, serious unrest of some kind in Chechnya erupted every few years. In April 1877, during the Russo-Turkish war, the whole of Chechnya rose up again. A force of 24,000 men was mobilized to put down the rebellion, which stretched from Ingushetia in the west to Vedeno in the east. The rebellion was finally put down in November 1877 and its leaders were hanged.

*

The October Revolution was only a brief interruption in patterns of conquest and resistance in the North Caucasus. If the placenames of Akhulgo, Dargo and Gunib symbolize Shamil's nineteenth-century resistance to the Russians in the mountains, then the name of the village of Tsotsin-Yurt in the plains stands for yet more bloodshed early in the twentieth century. A huge granite obelisk stands on the spot where the village was slaughtered resisting attack by the pro-Tsarist White General Anton Denikin. In 1919 Denikin, fearing that the North Caucasus would support the Bolsheviks, sent his army on a rampage through Chechnya. Tsotsin-Yurt, a village south-east of Grozny, refused to surrender and was surrounded by Denikin's forces. More than 500 Chechens died in hand-to-hand fighting as Denikin stormed the village.

At first the Bolshevik seizure of power seemed to promise tranquillity. The Council of People's Commissars of the RSFSR addressed an appeal, signed by Lenin and Stalin, to 'All Muslims, Toilers of Russia and the East' on 3 December 1917:

Muslims of Russia! Tatars of the Volga and the Crimea! Kyrgyz
and Sarts of Siberia and of Turkestan! Turks and Tatars of
Trans-Caucasus! Chechens and mountain people of the Caucasus! All you whose mosques and prayer houses used to be
destroyed, and whose beliefs and customs were trodden underfoot by the Tsars and oppressors of Russia! From today, your
beliefs and your customs and your national and cultural
constitutions, are free and inviolate. Organize your national
life freely and without hindrance. You are entitled to this . . .
Comrades! Brothers! Let us march towards an honest and
democratic peace. On our banners is inscribed the freedom of
oppressed peoples.

Chechnya had become an important region after the town of
Grozny (renamed as such in 1870) was found to contain large oil
reserves. After the first oil wells were drilled in 1893 Grozny
became an important railway junction and the most important oil
centre in the Russian empire after Baku. When the North Caucasian tribes appeared to be natural allies of the Bolsheviks, the
White Army of General Denikin marched into Chechnya. In his
memoirs Denikin called Chechnya a 'seething volcano' and said
that the North Caucasus had kept one-third of his troops pinned
down, sabotaging his attempts to build a new state to the north.
The Reds were delighted. At the end of January 1919 the
Georgian Bolshevik in charge of the Caucasus, Sergo Orjonikidze,
gave a glowing report to Lenin on the fight against Denikin:

> Battles around the town of Vladikavkaz and in Ingushetia are
> continuing for a seventh day. All of the Ingush, as one man,
> have risen to defend Soviet power . . . Chechnya together with
> the Red Army soldiers is repelling the bands around the town
> of Grozny. The Cossacks of the Sunzha Line under the com-
> mand of Comrade Dyakov are firmly holding their support for
> Soviet power and battering counter-revolutioary settlements
> with artillery. There is a remarkable lifting of spirits amongst
> the Ingush.[11]

In August 1919 the Bolshevik 5th Red Army of Nikolai Gikalo and an Islamic force led by the militant Dagestani *imam* Uzun-Haji jointly destroyed the garrison and fort at Vozdvizhenskoye. Uzun-Haji had all the White officers hanged. By the beginning of 1920 the Red Army had the upper hand over Denikin and the order was given to attack Grozny on 12 March. On 28 March Lenin demanded to know why the city had not yet fallen: 'We urgently need oil. Devise a manifesto to the population that we will slaughter them all if they burn and damage the oil and the oil fields and, on the contrary, we will spare the lives of everyone if they hand over Maikop and particularly Grozny intact.'[12] Grozny fell a few days later. Denikin was beaten and he had his army evacuated on British ships across the Black Sea. The Bolsheviks deported Cossacks who they said had supported Denikin from Chechnya and resettled Chechens in their place.

These allegiances were only temporary, however. The Bolsheviks were just as interested in keeping the Russian empire to its broadest possible extent and using many of the same old tactics to achieve that aim. In 1920 the outrages of the 11th Bolshevik Army provoked a new rebellion in Dagestan and eastern Chechnya with Said Bek, great-grandson of Imam Shamil, as its symbolic leader. The two sides fought over some of the *auls* celebrated from the Caucasian Wars – Gunib, Gimry and Gergebil. The rebels, heavily outnumbered, were defeated in May 1921.

On 20 January 1921 the Bolshevik Commissar on Nationalities, Stalin, spoke to the Mountain Peoples' Congress in Vladikavkaz. The mountain peoples said they wanted autonomy and a legal system based on the *shariat*. Stalin promised an amnesty for participants in the Said Bek rebellion if they recognized Soviet power. A deal was struck and the Mountainous Autonomous Republic was created, covering all the North-East Caucasus except Dagestan. The new republic, which had both a constitution based on *shariat* law and a flag with a Soviet emblem, lasted only five years.

The Caucasus became a battlefield for the differing conceptions of nationalities policy of Lenin and Stalin. Although both were in effect set on rebuilding the Russian empire, Lenin favoured a more equitable relationship between Russia and the other republics, whilst Stalin, although an ethnic Georgian, was implacably in favour of centralization and keeping a tight rein on the regions. The milder Leninist model broadly prevailed until the late 1920s. The Party cadres were staffed with many natives and no attempt was made at the redistribution of land. There was the beginning of the policy of *korenizatsiya* or 'indigenization'. For the first time the policy explicitly linked ethnicity and boundaries with an administrative system. It had some positive effects: books and newspapers were published in written Chechen, in a new script formed from the Latin alphabet in 1924, and literacy rates, which had been below 2 per cent before the Revolution, jumped enormously.

Chechen resistance was sparked again in the mountains with Stalin's efforts to collectivize agriculture. In 1929 Red Army units were sent to put down a rebellion in eastern Chechnya and in 1930 there was a crackdown in Ingushetia. The new Party Secretary, an ethnic Russian named Chernoglaz, was a chauvinist and zealot. He launched a campaign against religion and tried to recruit the Ingush into the Union of Unbelievers. The local head of the secret police, Ivanov, who tried to enforce the new policy, was murdered, and a provocateur's plot instigated by a certain 'representative of Japan' who was actually a secret police agent was uncovered. The cycle of repression, resistance and repression intensified. The Party boss went on a tour of Ingushetia. In the village of Galashki an old man got up and said Chernoglaz reminded him of the Tsarist governor, Colonel Mitnik. The old man's speech has been retold by the Chechen historian Abdurakhman Avtorkhanov:

'Mitnik himself was a good man, but the Tsar's government was bad,' the old man said. 'That is why I killed him on this same spot with a dagger like this one. I was sentenced to penal servitude for life, but twelve years later the Revolution liberated me. The Soviet government is good, but you, Chernoglaz, are a bad man. I do not want to kill you. Instead, I am giving you wise advice: go away from Ingushetia while you still have a head on your shoulders. People here are furious with you. I swear they will kill you.'[13]

The response of Chernoglaz was to order the arrest of the 'old bandit'. That evening the Party leader was murdered and his head was indeed cut off. A new wave of arrests and shootings followed.

On 5 December 1936 the region of Chechen–Ingushetia was upgraded to become an 'autonomous republic'. As part of the official celebrations in the spring of 1937 a women's delegation from the Chechen–Ingush republic visited Stalin's mother, Keke Jugashvili, in Tbilisi to express their gratitude for his 'fatherly attitude to the Chechen–Ingush people'. She gave them a lavish reception and said: 'My wish is that every mother should have such a son.' She promised that she would ask her son to continue his 'caresses' to the 'brothers Kistebi' (the Georgian name for the Chechens and Ingush).

Stalin proved less than fatherly. In a lightning operation launched on 31 July 1937, 14,000 Chechens and Ingush – around 3 per cent of the population – were rounded up, arrested and shot. After mass executions the bodies were dumped in a huge common grave at the foot of the Goryachevodskaya mountain. This was only the prelude to a much greater crime.

4

The Deportations

Vakha Akhmatov is now a flourishing businessman in the capital of Kazakhstan, Almaty, 1300 miles from Chechnya. His easy manner and smart suit and the leather furniture in his basement office tell you he is a successful post-Soviet businessman. That is true, but appearances can be deceptive: scratch any Chechen of middle age and you find a childhood of great deprivation underneath. Kazakhstan was and is Akhmatov's second homeland only because of the deportation of the entire Chechen people to Central Asia in 1944. He was born just outside Almaty in 1946 in destitution.

'I was born in a dug-out,' he says. 'My parents dug out a mud hut and then they put a roof on it. The Kazakhs helped them. It was only in 1947 that they found work in a collective farm and then the farm gave them two sheep, a donkey and a cow.'[1]

Akhmatov's parents were among some half a million Chechens and Ingush deported from the North Caucasus in 1944 as part of Stalin's hidden genocide of Soviet nations singled out for punishment. The Chechens and Ingush were disgorged in places like Pavlodar and Petropavlovsk in northern Kazakhstan, low-slung towns in the featureless steppe, where there was almost nothing to eat and winter temperatures sank to −30 degrees. At least 100,000 of them died of sickness and hunger in the first two years of the forced exile. The survivors were called 'special deportees' and were denied elementary rights.

'In 1953 I was too young to go to school and besides we had no money,' says Akhmatov, who owed his education to a stroke of good luck. 'But I saw other children with their files going to school and I wanted to go too. So I went with these kids into school and sat down at a desk. One lesson passed, two lessons and I had no books, nothing. Then I saw my father glance into the classroom and the teacher called me out. I was afraid he was going to punish me. But my father bought me a file, a satchel and books and they let me go to school.'

The exile in Central Asia left deep wounds and made a new generation of Chechens, whose grandparents had died fifty years before, that much more prepared to go to the edge in conflict with Russia. Deportation also unwillingly dragged thousands of Chechens into the modern era, transforming them from a mountain farming people into a scattered diaspora. Akhmatov, like most of his fellow-countrymen, went back to Chechnya in 1957 when the thirteen-year banishment was overturned by Nikita Khrushchev. But he eventually resettled in Kazakhstan and started his own import business, one of more than 50,000 Chechens who still live in Central Asia. In August 1996 he was anxiously watching the news of the fighting in Grozny and waiting for members of his family to make – irony of ironies – a long voluntary trek to Kazakhstan, to safety.

Stalin decided to deport the entire Chechen and Ingush people in the middle of the Second World War as the Germans retreated from the North Caucasus. On 11 February 1943 the Politburo discussed the idea of 'liquidating' Chechen–Ingushetia and expelling all the Chechens and Ingush. According to the archives, four of the men present argued that Chechen–Ingushetia should be abolished and the population expelled immediately. Five others were in favour of deportation, but only once the Germans had been completely driven out of the region. Amongst this group were Stalin's chief henchman and fellow-Georgian Lavrenty Beria, the man who carried out the deportations, and Nikita Khrushchev, the man who eventually reversed them. Their view was supported by Stalin. Only the Armenian Anastas Mikoyan had words of caution. He did not oppose the deportations but said they might damage the Soviet Union's reputation abroad.[2]

The idea of mass deportations on ethnic grounds was a new escalation of Stalin's terror tactics, which had hitherto been applied on a class or political basis. The first group to be deported was more than a million Germans from the Volga and Ukraine who were shipped to Siberia and Central Asia for alleged collaboration – or the thought of it – with the invading Nazi army. Then attention shifted to the complex ethnic mosaic of the Caucasus and to 68,000 Karachais, a nomadic Turkic people living in the mountains around Mount Elbrus, who were rounded up and expelled in November 1943. In the New Year of 1943–4 some 93,000 Buddhist Kalmyks were deported from their republic by the Caspian Sea. They were scattered in isolated homesteads across vast swathes of Siberia, a blow from which Kalmyk culture has never recovered. Two months later it was the turn of the Chechens and the Ingush, then of the Balkars, the close ethnic kin of the Karachai, the Muslim Meskhetian Turks from Georgia, all the Crimean Tatars – the indigenous inhabitants of the Crimean khanate – Pontic Greeks, Kurds and Koreans. The expulsions went on long after the war was over, and as late as 1949 whole communities of Greeks from the Caucasus and citizens of the Baltic Republics were being deported.

The expulsion of half a million Chechens and Ingush was the most ambitious operation after the deportation of the Germans. Taking place at the height of the war with Nazi Germany, it required a huge redeployment of resources from the front. The operation cost an estimated 150 million rubles, a phenomenal sum which could, at the height of the war, have bought the Soviet government 700 new T-34 tanks.[3] The first soldiers of the NKVD, the forerunner of the KGB, were sent into Chechen–Ingushetia the previous autumn for 'training exercises' or on sham geological expeditions in the mountains. By February 1944 there were 17,698 'special operatives' and 83,003 ordinary soldiers in place and more than 12,000 train carriages had been commandeered.

Every Chechen of late middle age can recall 23 February 1944 with great clarity. Abdullah Muzayev, a devout man who worked as a janitor in the mosque in Grozny and was nine at the time, repeated the folk belief that the day had been predicted by the elders. Spring was beginning and then there was a sudden snowfall that confirmed an old legend: 'It was a summer's day, the flowers were blooming in February and it was predicted a hundred years ago that there would be "snow at our backs". And that night snow fell, which our clever sheikhs, our leaders, foretold a hundred years ago,' he recalled.[4]

On the night of 22–23 February all the villages were sealed off and communications were cut. American-supplied Studebaker lorries, delivered to the Soviet government on lend-lease through Iran, were drawn up outside the villages and hundreds of freight trains were deployed in Grozny station. The operation began at 5 a.m. when flares were fired into the night sky. Deception was helped by it being Red Army Day, a national holiday (Beria had a penchant for organizing the deportations on Soviet holidays). Mairbek Mugadayev, who later became a minister in the Dudayev government, was a confused child that day.

'The whole male population of our village above fifteen years old were invited deceitfully to one of the buildings in the village supposedly to select dancers for a party. When they had all been collected, the doors and windows were boarded up and they brought the Studebakers into our courtyards. They gave us twenty-five minutes to get ready, then they loaded us up and set off. I remember there was no snow in our village. I took a kerosene lamp with me. I was very upset when they shot my blind dog. It was obvious that the soldiers and the officers were drunk. School had just opened, we were sitting in class and our teachers were taken away, and as he left our teacher managed to say that we were being taken to Siberia.'

Fifty years later three old men sat in the back room of the mosque in the village of Noviye Atagi and shared their memories of how they were sent to Kazakhstan and came back. In the tape of their conversation the cackling laugh of the oldest man, Suleiman Usmanov, cuts through like a rusty gate. The Russian of the two brothers Aziz and Abdullah was still broken despite all the years of Soviet rule.

'I was sixteen years old,' said Aziz Jebrailov. 'One day the soldiers came and said you have two hours, we're taking you to warm lands. Take only clothes and food for a week. We took a few stores of flour, what quickly came to hand, blankets. We were loaded up into the cattle wagons, there was a stove and we were fed once in a week. The snow was a metre deep and we were from warm parts, unknown people in an unknown land-scape. There had been propaganda work done so we weren't accepted. They were told cannibals had come to drink their blood. They looked at us with astonished eyes.'

The Chechens and Ingush were shipped at the rate of 80,000 a day and within a week there were virtually none left in their republic. 'By 29 February 1944 478,479 people, including 91,250 Ingush and 387,229 Chechens, have been deported and loaded into troops trains,' reported Beria, the mastermind of the oper-ation, in a telegram to Stalin dated 1 March 1944. 'One hundred and eighty trains have been loaded up, of which 159 have been sent to their place of new settlement. Today the troop-trains with former workers from the leadership and religious authorities from Chechen–Ingushetia, who were used in carrying out the oper-ation, were dispatched.' Beria reported that only 6000 people in the Galanchozh region had not yet been deported and that 2016 'anti-Soviet elements' had been arrested. Finally he reported that he was leaving Chechen–Ingushetia to go and supervise the next deportation, that of the Balkars.[5]

The Kafkaesque logic of total deportation required that every-one had to be sent away. Thousands of soldiers fighting at the front were demobilized and then packed off to Kazakhstan. The Chechen Party officials who had collaborated in the deportations were themselves sent away, as were 4000 qualified oil workers, without whom productivity in the Grozny oil fields never recovered for the rest of the war.

Thousands of people died on the three-week journey to Kazakhstan. A chilling declassified memo dated 18 March 1944 reported that 12,525 railway carriages had been dispatched to Central Asia, fewer than anticipated, because it had been possible to pack the deportees in very tightly and because so many of them were children: 'The required number of carriages was reduced by 2652 carriages or forty-one trains (with sixty-five carriages in each). The "compression" of the cargo of the special contingent from forty to forty-five persons in a carriage taking into account 40–50 per cent children is completely expedient.'[6] On board the trains men and women were crammed together without any toilets or washing arrangements – a terrible humiliation in the traditional Vainakh society and the cause of a typhoid epidemic that raged through the carriages. Anyone who ventured more than five metres away from the trains could be shot and the dead had to be left unburied in the snow by the railway tracks.

But the heaviest death toll came afterwards, when the unprotected North Caucasian peoples perished of hunger and cold in the Kazakhstan winters. According to official statistics given in an Interior Ministry report in 1949, of 608,749 Chechens, Ingush, Karachais and Balkars deported 'by 1 July 1948, 144,704 had died'.[7] In other words, a quarter of the deportees had died in five years.

After the Chechen and Ingush had been sent away, Chechen–Ingushetia ceased to exist. Parts of it were transferred to neighbouring republics and what was left was transformed into the humble Grozny Region within the Russian Federation. On 26 November 1948 the Supreme Soviet of the USSR decreed that the deportation was permanent without right of return.

Russians and Dagestanis moved into the Chechens' houses and Ossetians were resettled in the Prigorodny Region of Ingushetia. A systematic programme to eradicate Chechen and Ingush culture completely began. Old Chechen village names were changed and books in Chechen and Ingush were swept off the shelves of the Republican Library in Grozny to be burned, despite the efforts of the Russian librarian who hid many of them at home. The long gravestones in Chechen cemeteries were uprooted and used to pave roads and construct walls. To cap the extinction of the Chechens, a statue of General Yermolov was erected in Grozny in 1949 and one of Yermolov's quotations was inscribed on the base: 'There is no people under the sun more vile and deceitful than this one.'

The official justification for this huge programme of ethnic cleansing – punishment for mass collaboration with the invading Nazi forces – was only published two years later. A decree published by the Presidium of the Supreme Soviet of the RSFSR on 25 June 1946 alleged that 'Many Chechens and Ingush, incited by German agents, entered voluntarily into formations organized by Germans and, together with German armed forces, rose up in arms against the Soviet army.'[8]

The evidence adduced for this 'mass collaboration' was slight and tendentious. Many Chechens had indeed deserted from the Red Army. They had been conscripted into Russian units, where often they did not speak the language and were forced to eat pork. Hundreds of North Caucasians also fought with the Nazis in detachments recruited by the Dagestani Osman Gube, but as such they were no different from any other nationality – some 300,000 Russians and 700,000 non-Russians, mainly prisoners-of-war, fought on the Nazi side against Stalin in the Second World War. Equally, some 30,000 Chechens and Ingush served at the front and several were made Heroes of the Soviet Union. The famous cavalry commander Movlid Virsaitov was one of the first men to reach the Elbe in 1945, and Chechens speak with pride of the Chechen defenders of the Brest Fortress on the western frontier of the Soviet Union, where in June and July 1941 a small garrison died withstanding a massive German assault.

Another pretext for deportation was the latest Chechen mountain rebellion led by the writer Hasan Israilov and the lawyer Mairbek Sheripov which began in 1940 and led in the spring of 1942 to the use of Soviet aircraft to bomb Chechen mountain villages. Around the same time the German army made a push towards Chechnya, heading for the oil fields of Grozny, a major strategic objective. They got only as far as Vladikavkaz before they were halted on 25 October 1942. Israilov declared that 'if the liberation of the Caucasus meant the exchange of one colonizer for another, the Caucasus would only consider this a new stage in the national liberation war'. By the end of 1942 the rebel bands consisted of at best a few hundred men and possibly far fewer.[9] The mountain rebellion was snuffed out by early 1943 and by the time of the deportations fourteen months later Chechnya was a long way from the battle zone.

The deportations are better explained as an attempt to destroy the troublesome Chechens once and for all. They were the most numerous as well as the most militant people in the North Caucasus and had put up a stiff resistance to Stalinist collectivization. Mass deportation of the Chechens deprived the mountain peoples of a natural leadership in any future insurgency.

It was an old strategy in the Caucasus. Six thousand Karabulaks, a western Chechen people who lived in what is now the borderland between Chechnya and Ingushetia, were deported to Turkey in 1865 and their lands were settled by Cossacks. In 1856, when the Russians appeared to be winning control of Chechnya, they provoked the Chechens into renewed armed resistance by a plan for mass deportation to the Manych basin east of Rostov. 'For the pacification of the Caucasus it was necessary to transfer the submitting population to Vologda Province or any other empty land ... and it was decided, in the council in Stavropol, to send all the Chechens to Manych,' it was reported.[10]

The tactic was one of gradual genocide. A whole ethnic group was selected for punishment but the homeland, rather than the people, was abolished. Stalin merely brought this tsarist policy to a new level of sophistication. But ultimately the whole project defies rationalization. There is no explanation, for example, of why Stalin chose not to deport the warlike Avars of Dagestan but did punish the tiny Balkar people. The deportation of an entire people on racial principles has a strong echo of Yermolov's visceral hatred of all Chechens; and Stalin and Beria, both natives of the Caucasus, shared deep hatreds which are hard to fathom.

*

In February 1944 heavy snow fell in the mountainous Galanchozh area, an inaccessible region of valleys of oak woods and old fortified towers near the border with Georgia. Soldiers had been deployed there for at least six weeks under the command of General Mikhail Gvishiani of the NKVD in the Russian Far East.

There were no roads in the region and Gvishiani's orders were to dispatch the inhabitants on foot on a two-day trek down the snow-covered mountain paths to be loaded on to the trains. By chance he had a young local Chechen deputed to work with him. Dziyayudin Malsagov, then aged thirty, was a commissar in the Ministry of Justice. He thought of himself as an 'honest Communist' and had taken part in Stalin's policy of collectivization with enthusiasm. He stares out of an old black-and-white photograph with the pleasant zeal of a young convert.

On 26 February Gvishiani collected together several thousand people from the surrounding region, including the village of Yalkhoroi, where, as it happened, the infant Jokhar Dudayev had been born only a month before. They were to spend the night in the hamlet of Khaibakh in the LP Beria Collective Farm. Gvishiani decided that more than 500 people – old folk, the sick, pregnant women and young children – were 'untransportable' and should stay behind. He told them that they would be taken down to the plains on horses, in cars or even by aeroplane. Many able-bodied relatives of the 'untransportables' chose to stay behind as well. More than 600 people were herded inside the stable-block at Khaibakh.

In fact Gvishiani had other plans. He had had the windows of the stables stuffed with straw and the whole building doused with kerosene. When the rest of the people had left the village, Gvishiani suddenly had the doors to the stables boarded up. He shouted 'Fire!' and soldiers torched the building. The earth-and-wooden stables were engulfed with flames and the air was filled with the screams of people being burned alive.

As the flames took hold, Malsagov and a Russian captain named Gromov rushed up to Gvishiani and shouted at him to put out the fire. Gvishiani said he was acting on the orders of Beria and told them not to interfere or else they would be arrested. Some people managed to break down the door and scramble out but Gvishiani gave the orders for them to be machine-gunned down. Malsagov said that the doorway was 'piled with corpses'. He saw how one young man managed to break free into the open air and run 20 metres from the stables before he was shot down.

The burning of the innocents at Khaibakh altered the life of Dziyayudin Malsagov. Fifty years later, a frail and bed-ridden old man, he still wept and shook with emotion as he told the story and remembered the cries of the burning people. After he and Gromov protested, Gvishiani had them sent away down the mountain under armed escort. On the way they came upon corpses every few yards and realized that the NKVD had ordered mass killings in the entire region. Two days later the two men managed to go back to Khaibakh, where they found that no one had survived the massacre. A group of Chechens who had been hiding in the woods had come down and started furtively burying what was left of the bodies. They immediately ran off, but one of

them, Zhandar Gayev, came back after Malsagov called out to
them in Chechen. Gayev said they had managed to bury 137
bodies, but it was mostly a matter of picking up charred limbs
and pieces of jewellery. The only figure who could be identified
was the 110-year-old bearded patriarch Tuta Gayev, who was
lying face-down buried in the mud. Another significant detail
emerged only years later. Among the dead were relatives of the
later President of Chechnya, Jokhar Dudayev: his mother's
mother, his aunt and two of his first cousins aged eight and
eleven.[11]

Malsagov at first believed that Gvishiani had carried out the
massacre on his own initiative, but when he went to Grozny and
told the NKVD commissar Ivan Serov what he had seen, Serov
was furious and told him to keep quiet. It later transpired that
Serov was one of those who had authorized the killings. Malsagov
was then sent to Kazakhstan himself but allowed to keep his job
as a commissar. From there he wrote a letter directly to Stalin in
January 1945, recounting what had happened. For this he was
sacked from his job and warned that if he protested again he
would 'lose his head'.

Eight years later, after the death of Stalin and the arrest of
Beria, the indefatigable Malsagov tried again and this time he was
summoned to Moscow to give testimony. He noticed that his
evidence on Beria was taken down zealously by the investigators
but that they paid little attention to the other names he mentioned. Beria was shot in December 1953 but the matter went no
further. When travel restrictions were lifted on the deportees in
Kazakhstan, Malsagov made two trips to Moscow in 1954 and
in March 1955 to seek an audience with Khrushchev, but to no
avail. The turning-point came with Khrushchev's celebrated
'secret speech' made at the 20th Party Congress in February 1956,
when he mentioned Stalin's deportations before a large audience
for the first time. In July of that year Khrushchev went to
Kazakhstan and gave a speech at the Almaty opera house at

which Malsagov was present. The head of the local KGB guards protecting Khrushchev was a friend of Malsagov and he allowed him to go up to the Soviet leader in the opera house foyer, introduce himself and personally place a letter about Khaibakh in Khrushchev's hands. 'Khrushchev received me well,' Malsagov said in 1994. 'He invited me into his room and read my statement attentively. He asked me if I knew what a responsibility would fall on me if the facts I had set out in my statement were not confirmed. I replied that these facts could not not be confirmed and I fully vouched for my actions.'

Khrushchev set up a commission to investigate the massacre, which spent several months carrying out dozens of interviews. The head of the commission, Tikunov, wrote a detailed memo to Khrushchev confirming that the massacre had indeed taken place and that the evidence for the Chechens' culpability of 'mass treason' was flimsy. It was a contributory factor to the decision Khrushchev soon made to rehabilitate Chechen–Ingushetia and allow the Chechens and Ingush to return.[12]

Despite his success, Malsagov went on protesting. As a Party member he was one of the first Chechens allowed to return to Grozny in 1957 and he immediately started arguing with the local Russian Party leadership about the rights of the returning Chechen population. In March 1959 Malsagov was arrested on a ludicrous charge of distributing anti-Soviet leaflets that supposedly contained attacks on Khrushchev as well as 'praise of the members of the Molotov–Malenkov anti-Party group and of the Tsarist General Yermolov, insults against Chechens and Ingush'. In September 1959 he was sentenced to five years' imprisonment and his Russian wife Valentina was turned out of her job. He served time in two camps and was then transferred to a psychiatric hospital in Leningrad and pronounced insane – a classic method of persecuting dissidents, who were treated with mind-bending drugs if they protested their sanity. He was released on 31 December 1963.

The first published material about Khaibakh, including an article by Malsagov, appeared in Grozny only in August 1989, though not without a crude attempt by the local KGB to destroy all copies of the newspaper concerned. In 1990 a now elderly Malsagov took part in an expedition that went up to Khaibakh. They dug up evidence of the massacre, including skulls with bullet-holes and the bones of children. The regional prosecutor rather optimistically opened a criminal case on the evidence.

In 1994 Malsagov, white-haired, hoarse and bed-ridden, came to life at the mention of the story and leafed through a stack of papers addressed to each successive Soviet leader. He was still demanding justice for the victims of Khaibakh, for himself and his family and for individual Chechens. In some of the letters he continued to say he had been a loyal Communist. This fighter for justice died in April 1994 and fortunately probably did not see his house and orchard destroyed by Russian bombing. 'It is just as well he did not live to see the war,' said Valentina Malsagova. 'He would not have borne it.'

Khaibakh is now deserted and hauntingly quiet, its farms and houses in ruins. In the autumn of 1996 the oaks and beeches were turning gold and yellow and moss had gathered on the simple graves in the old Muslim cemetery overhung by a damson tree laden with ripe fruit. The only intact building is the square seventeenth-century tower soaring 100 feet up and topped by a beehive roof. There is no monument to the massacre.

No Chechens resettled high in the mountains after they returned from Kazakhstan in the 1950s, but five hours down in the valley there are still witnesses to Khaibakh, like Said-Hasan Ampukayev, who lives in the village of Gekhi-Chu. Ampukayev's face has been worn into a thousand creases but his voice remains firm. His Russian is still shaky despite years in exile and Siberian prison camps. He was about eighteen in 1944, although his passport puts his year of birth at 1920; something, he says laughingly, that has allowed him to outwit the Soviet pension authorities by a few years.[13]

In February 1944 Ampukayev was out tending the animals when the soldiers came. He hid in the woods and watched for three days as his fellow-villagers were taken off, the cattle were driven away and homes looted. He teamed up with other farmers who were also hiding: 'We got together and began a fight for existence, not knowing what we had to do. We lived like wild animals since we were separated from the rest of the world. We knew and felt that if we fell into the hands of the soldiers they would shoot us.'

On the fourth day of the deportations Ampukayev heard about the massacre at Khaibakh and went down to look. He became the youngest member of the grisly burial party. The embers of the stables were still burning and there were charred corpses everywhere. They made improvised stretchers of branches to carry the pieces of body away for burial. Almost no one was identifiable: 'Of the dead I recognized only Tuta Gayev. He lay face-down and so his body was preserved and I recognized him by his distinctive beard.' They spent three days burying what they could find and sleeping in the woods. It was more a matter of collecting bits of people, bones and fingers, and putting them in graves: 'There wasn't a whole person there.' He can still remember that the children's skulls had been softer and burned right through: 'They were burned alive. A living person burns faster.'

Ampukayev was amongst a group of desperate Chechens who camped in the hills for the whole spring and summer of 1944. They lived in twos and threes, sleeping in caves, eating berries and killing wild goats. Search parties of soldiers came looking for them and shot anyone they found. Sometimes they set mines and left poisoned food and gingerbread for the runaways. Eventually, in the late summer of 1944, two Chechen mullahs, Abdul-Khamid Yandarov and Baudi Arsanov, were persuaded to return from

Kazakhstan and go into the hills offering an amnesty to the runaways in return for surrender. Ampukayev gave himself up. He was sent to Pavlodar in northern Kazakhstan, but within a year he was arrested on a charge of abetting banditry. He spent eight years in the camps and goldmines of Magadan and Komsomolsk-na-Amure before he was released in 1954 and allowed to come home in 1958. Why was he arrested? Ampukayev gave an irritated and mischievous look. 'There was no reason,' he muttered. 'Because I stayed alive, that was the reason.'

*

In exile the Chechens and Ingush were among the most troublesome deportees. Many of them did not speak Russian and years of Soviet rule had not made much of an impression on them. There were several instances of Chechens and Ingush rebelling en masse.[14] In Part 5 of his *Gulag Archipelago* Alexander Solzhenitsyn gives a grudgingly sympathetic portrait of how the Chechens responded to the rebellion in the Kengir camp where he was living in May–June 1954:

> The Chechens cannot be reproached for ever giving in to oppression. They understood the meaning of the Kengir uprising beautifully and once they brought a vehicle full of baked bread to the zone. Naturally they were driven away by the troops. As for these Chechens ... They were difficult people for the inhabitants of Kazakhstan around them, rough and insolent, and they openly disliked the Russians. But as soon as the people of Kengir showed independence and courage they were immediately at their disposal. If we feel that we have not earned the respect of others we should ask ourselves if we live like them.

It was as though the Chechens were a whole nation of outlaws, a classification they themselves took some pride in. The old man Suleiman Usmanov recalled with a laugh: 'In 1953 when they announced that Stalin had died there was mourning, the Russians were crying, but we Chechens, we secretly danced for joy.'

All deportees were treated as third-class citizens, good only for cheap labour. They had to register with the police once a week and the punishment for straying out of your registered area was up to twenty years' hard labour. This was especially bitter because a Chechen's place of exile was entirely arbitrary and depended completely on which of 200 trains he or she happened to end up in in February 1944. Relatives who had by chance been apart on the day of deportation were separated and some people spent years and risked jail terms looking for each other.

In the first years living conditions were so poor that thousands simply died of hunger and cold in makeshift homes in the Kazakh steppe. A report by M. V. Kuznetsov, head of the 'Department of Special Deportees' for the NKVD dated 5 September 1944, notes laconically that many deportees were at risk of dying of cold, something that might affect their usefulness to the state: 'The majority of the special deportees banished from the North Caucasus, former Kalmykia and Crimea, do not have shoes or warm clothing. The necessity is arising to provide especially needy deportees with the appropriate amount of cotton to sew winter clothes and to provide them with basic footwear. The absence of clothes and footwear in winter could have a fatal effect on special contingents and their ability to work.'[15]

Children ran wild and survived on what scraps their parents could find them. Salambek Khajiev, who became the first Chechen minister in the Soviet government in 1991, grew up outside the town of Jambul in southern Kazakhstan.

'The first three or four years were the hardest because in 1946 and 1947 there was a bad harvest and famine. I remember how when people had nothing to eat they ate grass. But for some reason they swell up from grass. A person has a swollen stomach, but it is almost transparent, his skin becomes transparent and sooner or later he dies. We went to school and the town was next door, six kilometres away, and children went to look at the museum, but we Chechens could not go there, we did not have the right to leave the confines of the village. So we hid and went by other small roads to the town and there we caught up with our group. We already understood that something was not right.'[16]

After Stalin's death in 1953 restrictions on deportees were slowly lifted. They were allowed to travel freely around Kazakhstan and they no longer had to register with the authorities. A Chechen newspaper and Chechen and Ingush radio stations were opened. Khrushchev's secret speech in February 1956 mentioned the deportations but did not specifically refer to the Chechens and Ingush. Party officials debated what to do with them. One plan was to create an 'autonomous Chechen–Ingush region' in southern Kazakhstan. However, thousands of Chechens and Ingush forced the issue by heading back to their homeland and camping out near their old homes. Attempts were made to stop them returning, such as a ban on selling them rail tickets, but they kept on coming. The decision was made to let them all go back.

On 9 January 1957 Chechen–Ingushetia was officially re-instated and the Chechens and Ingush were officially free to return home. In the same decree the Balkars, Karachai and Kalmyks were also given their republics back, but the Volga Germans, Crimean Tatars and Meskhetian Turks, although rehabilitated, were not allowed to leave Central Asia.[17]

The official plan was for a phased return of the Chechens which would last until 1960, but many people left as soon as they could, buying tickets first to Moscow and then on to Grozny. The historian Viktor Listov remembers travelling on a train from Almaty to Moscow in 1959 in which there were three wooden bunks in the carriage and the top shelf was occupied by boxes that emitted a horrible stench. The Chechens were carrying the bones of their relatives back to Chechnya for burial in their ancestral graveyards.

Just as every Chechen can remember the day he was deported, every Chechen can remember the miraculous day of return. Mairbek Mugadayev was nineteen when he came back. 'I got to Moscow, more than five thousand kilometres, without a ticket, fare-dodging. In Moscow I naturally got a ticket to Grozny, arrived in Grozny. For two days before we arrived we could not sleep, we simply embraced this land, kissed it, honestly asked God that he never again tear us from our native land. I don't have God's gift to recount all these emotions.' 'It was as though the dead had been resurrected!' said Suleiman Usmanov, who was reunited with people he had not seen since February 1944.

However, there were no regulations about the rights of returnees. Grants of 1000 rubles were handed out which Chechens typically used to buy back their houses from the Russians and Dagestanis who had moved into them. The housing crisis was a major reason why the Soviet government allocated the new Chechen–Ingushetia three sparsely populated regions of Stavropol Region in the north, which had historically been Cossack lands and which are now a political issue on the agendas of various Russian nationalist groups.[18] In the west the Ingush lands of Prigorodny Region on the right bank of the Terek stayed within North Ossetia, creating a long-running dispute between the Ingush and Ossetians that later erupted into violence.

The Chechens were the largest nation on a compact territory to be deported and then allowed to return. The experience of deportation was thus a collective experience based only on ethnic criteria – something which had far-reaching political consequences a generation later. In 1991 other small deported nations, such as the Balkars, tried to mobilize themselves, but the Chechens had force of numbers as well as the fresh historical grievance that pushed them into open separatism.

Thirteen years of exile arguably gave the Chechens a sense of
a common national identity as Chechens – as distinct from
belonging to a certain *teip* or village – for the first time. The
closeness of the Chechens in deportation has become legendary
to themselves. 'We were welded together,' said Aziz Jebrailov.
'We survived because we were friends to each other. If one of us
was offended we never forgave it, so they barely touched us. Not
like other peoples, the Kurds, Turks, Azerbaijanis . . . We always
struck back.'

After the 1950s no public discussion of the deportations was
allowed and it became a kind of clan secret festering beneath the
surface. During the anti-Chechen campaign at the end of the
Brezhnev era the authorities made the hidden grievance even
worse by propagating the false notion that the deportations had
actually benefited the Chechens by giving them 'technical education'. 'There was an attempt at the beginning of the 1980s to
promote the idea that, although at the 20th Party Congress
Khrushchev supposedly rehabilitated you, in actual fact you were
not rehabilitated but only pardoned,' Magomed Muzayev, Director of the Chechen National Archive in Grozny, recalled. 'And
there was the idea that you were really bandits and counter-
revolutionaries. You weren't grateful, Soviet power had pardoned
you and so you should constantly be praying to Soviet power,
pray to the Communists, sometimes they said – to the great
Russian people.'

The collective anger about the deportations broke to the
surface only in 1989–90. It was the most emotive element in a
rich brew of nationalism as the Chechens started to invent
themselves as a nation. Jokhar Dudayev used the issue as the
touchstone of his political ideology and periodically he raised the
fear that Russia was planning to deport the Chechens all over
again. For the old men and the mountain villagers who were the
core of his support, it struck a deep chord. In 1994 Dudayev's
Vice-President Zelimkhan Yandarbiyev cited the deportations as

a reason why Russia could never be trusted. 'Over the last two or three hundred years we have always acted on the assumption that Russia is acting out of a wish to occupy Chechnya and expel the Chechen people from its territory,' he said ominously. 'This factor is constantly present, consciously or unconsciously it is present.' As in Armenia and Israel, a common memory of attempted genocide underlay the process of the Chechens' nation-building. It added an extra fear to their mistrust of the outside invader and gave them a kind of recklessness as they defied Russia.

5

Dudayev's Revolution

In November 1990 a unique event occurred in Chechnya. The Congress of the Chechen People gathered more than 1000 Chechen delegates together in Grozny. The Congress was convened to put pressure on the local authorities to speed up political change and to celebrate Chechen history and culture in a way that had never been possible before. Among the guests was a man who a year before had become 'the first Chechen general', Jokhar Dudayev. Dudayev, then forty-six, and the commander of an air force division in the Estonian city of Tartu, was a striking man. There was something rather old-fashioned in his neatly combed pencil moustache, his taste for 1920s-style fedoras and well-tailored suits. He had a proud military bearing, a strong gaze and a captivating musical voice that commanded attention as he spoke to the Congress. The man who later became Chechen Vice-President, Zelimkhan Yandarbiyev, recalls:

'It was a short but very striking speech. He effectively said then that declaring an independent state was an act of great responsibility, something very difficult, but once we had declared it, we should go to the end. He said, using a saying we have, do not draw your *kinzhal* from its case, do not draw it without cause, but if you draw it, do not put it back without doing battle.'[1]

The Congress had been organized by Lechi Umkhayev, who ran the road-building company in Chechnya. Umkhayev was a small, neat, quick-witted man and an able administrator but he was not going to be – nor did he intend to be – the leader of a new Chechen national movement. The Congress elected Umkhayev to the No. 2 job on the executive committee, a post that gave him the powers to run the Congress, but the post of Chairman was kept empty for someone who would symbolize more aptly the national awakening of the Chechen people. Almost unanimously it was decided that the Chairman should be General Dudayev, the honoured guest from Estonia.

The Congress dispersed, having forced the Supreme Soviet of Chechen–Ingushetia to pass a dramatic-sounding 'declaration of sovereignty' and Chairman Dudayev returned to Estonia. Unbeknownst to most of the delegates, the combination of events had set in motion a small revolution.

Less than a year later, in the autumn of 1991, the old regime in Grozny fell in dramatic scenes unprecedented in the Soviet Union, and Dudayev took power. There were differing interpretations of how the precipitate collapse of Communism in the republic came about. Some saw the overthrow of the old government in Chechnya as the delayed result of the Stalinist deportations. This was the reaction of the Chechen historian Abdurakhman Avtorkhanov to events in Grozny in late 1991.

What is happening now in Chechen–Ingushetia is, in my opinion, a revolt by the children in revenge for the deaths of their fathers and mothers in the hellish conditions of the deportations in distant, cold and hungry Kazakhstan and Kirgizia. It is a protest by the whole people against the continuing supremacy of the old power structures in Chechen–Ingushetia.[2]

Others emphasized that it was a revolt by the poor and disadvantaged. As the Chechen political analyst Timur Muzayev put it: 'In Chechnya economic growth had contrasted with great poverty in the villages. In the mountains the poverty and unemployment were appalling. The political explosion combined with a social explosion. The spring was released.'[3]

For the intellectuals who opposed Dudayev the seizure of power was performed by a revolutionary movement that had been hijacked by the radical fringe. The history professor Jabrail Gakayev, one of many intellectuals opposed to Dudayev, said: 'Our tragedy was that we did not have an intelligentsia, only isolated individuals. If in somewhere like the Baltic States the Popular Front was led by the intelligentsia, with us it was led by people from the margins of society.'[4]

Chechnya had long been ripe for some kind of political uprising. In the late 1950s after the restitution of Chechen–Ingushetia, ethnic relations were extremely tense between Russians and the returning Chechens and Ingush. One of the worst instances of social unrest in the post-war Soviet Union occurred in Grozny in August 1958. After a young Ingush killed a Russian at a dance in a fight over a girl, the friends of the dead Russian carried his open coffin through the streets and his funeral became a big political demonstration. The protesters distributed leaflets and made speeches demanding that the Chechens and the Ingush be sent back to Central Asia. An angry crowd stormed into the local government headquarters and there were clashes on the streets. An elderly peddler from Urus-Martan was killed by the mob. Only on the third day of the disturbances when shops were being looted were troops called in to restore order.[5]

Again in February 1973 one of the largest political demonstrations of the Brezhnev years took place in Grozny when a crowd of Ingush demanded the return of the Prigorodny Region from Ossetia to Ingushetia. Shop windows were broken and the police and fire brigade broke up the demonstration with truncheons and high-pressure hoses. Hussein Iskhanov, who later became aide-de-camp to the Chechen Commander Aslan Maskhadov during the war with Russia, said that seeing the suppression of the rally as a young man opened his eyes to the brutality of the Soviet regime: 'The Communists were firmly in power then and I met such courageous people there. It was winter and I saw how they were dispersed. They attacked them with water and batons and beat them like cattle.'[6]

The Soviet authorities made sure Chechen–Ingushetia remained a backwater of deep political conservatism and thinly disguised Russian chauvinism. Official policy required that the First Party Secretary, the local head of the KGB, the local police chief and all the top administrators in the oil industry should be ethnic Russians. Despite this, Leonid Brezhnev's ideologist Mikhail Suslov launched a campaign against 'anti-Russian' sentiment in the press and academia in Chechnya in the early 1980s. Suslov sponsored the ideas of the Russian historian Vitaly Vinogradov, who said that the Chechens and Ingush had willingly joined the Russian empire in the reign of Catherine the Great in an act of 'voluntary union'. Six Chechen historians who contested this point of view were harassed. In 1982 the republic had to go through the charade of official celebrations of the 200th anniversary of the 'voluntary union'.

The Chechens and Ingush were second-class citizens who found it extremely hard to get higher education or advance in prestigious professions. The pilot Hussein Khamidov got his flying licence only after studying in four different institutes and taking correspondence courses: 'If there was the slightest flaw or the smallest obstacle they didn't let you in,' he said. 'They didn't even make Chechens bus drivers, especially on important routes.'

It was a time of social upheaval. The Chechens had one of the highest birth-rates in the Soviet Union. In 1953 only 316,000 of them were registered in Central Asia as special deportees. By 1989 there were 958,309 Chechens, of whom 734,501 lived in Chechnya, and by 1991 there were already a million Chechens in the Soviet Union. Most of them still lived in the villages. In the 1970s the Chechen workers at the sewing factory in central Grozny still lived in the villages and were bussed into the city to work, and in 1989 only a third of the population of Grozny, a city of 400,000 people, was Chechen or Ingush. The apartment blocks in central Grozny were mainly reserved for Russians –

something which later ensured that thousands of Russians died in the bombing of the city at the beginning of the war.

Despite the income from the oil industry, Chechen–Ingushetia was one of the poorest regions in Russia and regularly in last or second-to-last place on a series of economic indicators. Unemployment was particularly bad: up to 200,000 people, mainly young men, were out of work and tens of thousands of Chechen men were forced to work as seasonal cheap labour in different parts of Russia. They went to northern Russia and Siberia to work on collective farms and building sites in the summer and returned home for the winter, effectively *gastarbeiter* in their own country.

In the spring of 1989 the frozen political landscape in Chechnya began to thaw. After the Russian Party boss Vladimir Foteyev had left, the Politburo in Moscow put forward the name of Nikolai Semyonov, a former head of the Grozny Party Committee, to replace him. The local committee objected and said it was time to have a Chechen as Party boss, and Moscow backed down. Lechi Magomadov, who was then the second most senior Chechen in the Party, says it was he who proposed Doku Zavgayev, his immediate superior, for the job. 'We forced them to elect Zavgayev,' said Magomadov.[7] In June 1989 Zavgayev became the first Chechen ever to be put in charge of the region and there were festivities everywhere. 'We had a big celebration not because of Zavgayev, but because of a Chechen becoming First Secretary,' said Magomadov. Zavgayev was later elected as head of the new regional legislature, the Supreme Soviet.

Zavgayev failed to live up to expectations, however. A sleek man with probing, hooded eyes, he was a born back-room manipulator, not a politician with the popular touch. Not for nothing had he managed to hold on to the job of Second Secretary of the Communist Party in the republic for fifteen years, throughout the deepest stagnation of the Brezhnev era. When he came to power, members of the two powerful *teips* of his parents, the

gendargeno and the *beno*, and friends from northern Chechnya
followed him into top jobs; the practice whereby everything was
for sale – from Party cards to jobs in the local administration –
thrived with new vigour.

Zavgayev helped further the careers of two Chechens in a way
he later regretted. In October 1989 it was agreed that the
appointment of a first Chechen general in the Soviet army was
long overdue. Zavgayev helped nominate Jokhar Dudayev to
become a major-general and he was soon followed by seven other
generals. Just as significant was the elevation the following year
of the Chechen economics professor Ruslan Khasbulatov to
become First Deputy to the then Speaker of the Russian parliament, Boris Yeltsin. Khasbulatov was another child of the
deportations era. He was born in 1942 and grew up in
the Petropavlovsk region of northern Kazakhstan. Against all the
odds he went into further education and eventually became a
professor of economics at Moscow's Plekhanov Institute. Then in
1990 he was elected to the Russian Parliament from a Grozny
constituency. Khasbulatov's pallor, watchful eyes and pipe-
smoking habit made him an untypical Chechen and he proved to
be a born political manipulator, who took swimmingly to Moscow's political intrigues. According to Zavgayev: 'I personally
recommended him to Yeltsin. I literally insisted. I asked him a
first time, then a second time.'[8] When Yeltsin became President of
the Russian Federation in 1991, Khasbulatov first became acting
Speaker and then Speaker of the Parliament and the second most
powerful politican in Russia.

Political liberalization took hold in Chechnya. The press
started criticizing the authorities and religion was unbanned.
Dozens of mosques were built. Zavgayev now likes to take the
credit for this, but his critics say he was merely running with the
times. In the summer of 1990 a group of Chechens, led by Lechi
Umkhayev, started organizing the Chechen National Congress,
with the aim of pulling together the different nationalist groups

in Chechnya and putting pressure on the local leadership to claim more autonomy from Moscow for the republic.

The Congress which met on 23–25 November 1990 was the biggest event in Chechnya in years. There were 1000 delegates, each one of whom nominally represented 1000 Chechens. Guests came from Jordan and Turkey, reminding the locals of their forgotten diaspora, and there were long, impassioned discussions about the deportations and Chechen history. Delegates to the Congress remember it as a time of euphoria but there was also a note of stridency. They resolved that Vitaly Vinogradov, author of the concept of 'voluntary union', should be stripped of all awards and titles and citizenship of the republic. Moreover, only Chechens were invited and it set the precedent of excluding the Ingush from the nationalist movement.

The Congress was split between different political groups and different *teip* lobbies in Chechnya. To balance interests, Dudayev, a radical but also an outsider, was given the No. 1 post in the congress, Chairman of the Executive Committee, with an honorific role. Umkhayev, the moderate organizer, was given the No. 2 job, First Deputy Chairman, and most of the responsibility.

The Congress achieved its immediate aim. The morning after it closed, the Supreme Soviet met. There was only one item on the agenda, a resolution declaring Chechen–Ingushetia a 'sovereign republic'. Debate raged all day and the resolution was finally passed in the small hours of the morning. The phrasing of the document was radical. The Russian Federation does not even get a mention and the Soviet Union is mentioned only in passing in a reference to 'the act of genocide perpetrated against the Chechens, the Ingush and other peoples of the USSR'. Article 1 states that 'The Chechen–Ingush Republic is a sovereign state, created as a result of the self-determination of the Chechen and Ingush peoples.' Article 18 states that: 'The Chechen–Ingush Republic has the attributes of a sovereign state: citizenship, a crest, a flag, a national anthem and a capital.'

The declaration was not meant to be taken at face-value, however. It was fashionable at the time to talk loosely about 'sovereignty' and 'independence' after the Russian Parliament, chaired by Boris Yeltsin, had passed a declaration declaring Russian 'sovereignty' in 1990. Yeltsin himself, as he travelled round Russia in 1990 and 1991, uttered the famous phrase, 'Take as much sovereignty as you can swallow,' inspiring what became known as the 'parade of sovereignties' by Russia's autonomous republics. The Chechens' proclamation was in this spirit, a declaration of intent to lay claim to more economic and political power as the hold of Moscow over the regions dwindled. It was a foretaste of Chechen radicalism but the local leadership had managed to keep the challenge to Moscow within official channels.

*

A revolution needs a leader and Dudayev fitted the role perfectly. This was not obvious at first, however. Dudayev later so dominated Chechen politics that it is hard to believe now that he was a little-known figure when he came to the Chechen National Congress in 1990. But at the time most delegates regarded him as, in the Russian phrase, a 'wedding general', an honoured guest who lent grandeur but no substance to the proceedings. Outwardly Dudayev was much more a product of the Soviet system than a budding Chechen nationalist. He had spent his childhood in Kazakhstan and lived in Chechnya only briefly as a teenager before making his career in Russia. He had had little contact with his homeland for thirty years, during which time he only came home occasionally to visit his family. He was married to a Russian and spoke Chechen haltingly and in a mountain dialect.

Dudayev was born in early 1944, just a few weeks before the deportations, in the mountain village of Yalkhoroi in southwestern Chechnya. He was the youngest of fourteen children, seven boys and seven girls, born to his father, Musa Dudayev, from two marriages. The elder Dudayev was a veterinary surgeon and an old Bolshevik. His *teip* was an obscure mountain one, the *yalkhoro*, descended from the semi-Ingush people, the Karabulaks, and with little influence in Chechnya.

Dudayev's almost satanic pride in later years emerged from a childhood of great hardship and humiliation. In 1992 he said: 'I lived with one dream: to escape the shameful condition of my people in which human dignity was humiliated.'[9] In 1944 Jokhar was a babe-in-arms when the Dudayevs were dumped in the snow outside the north-eastern Kazakh city of Pavlodar. The family spent its first winter picking potatoes in the Proletarsky Collective Farm and trying not to die of hunger. A brother who had fought at the front died of his wounds only five kilometres away but they were not allowed to visit him. Dudayev recalled being sent away from school because he could not prove he was the right age: 'We had no documents of any kind left. We had to go to school and they told me, "You're not seven – we won't take you in the first class." They told me to run off and prove it.'[10]

After the first two hungry years of the deportations, Dudayev's family moved to a one-storey wooden house in the middle of Pavlodar. It was here that Musa Dudayev died in 1951. A year after Stalin's death they moved again to the city of Chimkent in southern Kazakhstan before they were allowed to return to Grozny in 1957. The young Jokhar Dudayev was restless and ambitious. His elder brother Bekmurza remembers him as 'rebellious, quick-witted and able'. He studied in night school and then studied physics and maths at the university in North Ossetia.

After a year's studies Dudayev left abruptly, without telling his family, and transferred to the Tambov Higher Military Aviation College, where he studied to be a pilot. He managed this only by covering up that he was a Chechen. He had applied the year before but had been turned down because he wrote 'Chechen' in the box for 'Nationality' on the application form. This time he wrote 'Ossetian' on the form. Apparently he concealed his true nationality for several years because, according to his father-in-law, he only revealed he was a Chechen just before his graduation ceremony to become a pilot. His confounded teachers agreed to overlook the deception.

In 1966 the twenty-two-year-old Dudayev was one of ten young lieutenants transferred from Tambov to fly at the airbase at Shaikovka near Kaluga, south-west of Moscow. The commander of the garrison was Fyodor Kulikov, who now recalls: 'They were all good lads, good pilots, but he stood out as being more serious than his friends, he was the unrecognized leader in this group of young lieutenants and I paid a lot of attention to him as he was spending time with my daughter. He made a good impression on all the bosses in the regiment, he flew well.'[11] The dashing young Chechen began a long romance with Kulikov's pretty nineteen-year-old daughter Alla, who was studying to be an artist. In 1969 they were married. Alla was even more romantic than her husband and became a devoted officer's wife. As they moved around the Soviet Union she wrote poetry and painted sweeping landscapes in oils.

Dudayev's marriage to a Russian officer's daughter boosted his career prospects, which were still limited by his being a Chechen, but he had cut himself off from his family for the sake of his career and rarely saw them in those years. His brothers say they were hostile towards him marrying a Russian and he did not even tell them he had got married. Bekmurza Dudayev only found out when he went to visit his brother outside Moscow in 1971. 'He hid from us. They already had a son when I visited them.'[12] The birth of a male child reunited Dudayev with his Chechen relatives and he went to Grozny for a reconciliatory visit.

The paradox of Dudayev – which comes up in almost every conversation with those who knew him – was that he was a model Soviet officer who later fought the Russian army. 'I declare with full responsibility to my fellow-countrymen as to all young men: there is nothing more honourable than to be a defender of the Motherland,' he said in 1989.[13] Until the very end of his career nothing in his behaviour smacked of unconventionality and he was highly praised for his military professionalism. He served in Irkutsk in Siberia and the Ukrainian city of Poltava and loyally commanded a bomber fleet destroying villages in the war in Afghanistan for which he was awarded the Order of the Red Star and the Order of the Red Banner. Even after he became Chechen President he still talked with pride and nostalgia about the values of the Soviet army.

People also spotted an old-fashioned code of values in him, which made him more akin to an officer of the nineteenth century. Educated in Russia, he had formed his picture of Chechnya and the Caucasus mainly through the prism of the romantic Russian authors. He adored reading the poets Pushkin and Lermontov and their works about the Caucasus. More than one observer has commented on Dudayev's physical resemblance to the proud romantic poet and officer Lermontov, who also had a neat black moustache and intense eyes. The oriental history professor Linnart Mall, who got to know Dudayev in Estonia, commented: 'He was like an officer of the Tsarist Army ... He wrote verse himself in Russian and Chechen. In Russian it is very similar to Lermontov. Heroic themes and lines about how he was born in the Caucasus. It was already evident what was beginning.'[14]

The key shift inside him came in 1988 when Dudayev was promoted to be commander of a division of long-range strategic bombers in the Estonian city of Tartu. It was a very prestigious job: the bombers were equipped to carry nuclear weapons, which were stored in a silo not far away. Dudayev had some 6000 men under his command and commanded two regiments, one of transport planes, one of thirty-two long-range bombers.

As commander of the airbase, Dudayev had a high profile in local society and was a member of the town soviet. He discovered that Tartu, Estonia's second city and an old university town, was convulsed with political debate. Estonia and the other Baltic countries, Latvia and Lithuania, were beginning the campaign for the independence they had lost with Stalin's occupation in 1940. The nationalist movement was gaining strength and even in the supposedly Communist town council in Tartu there was discussion about how to regain Estonia's independence.

Colonel Ants Laaneots was head of the local military district in Tartu. He was slowly being converted to the new political ideas and he began to discuss them freely with his new friend, Colonel Dudayev: 'We found that we had many similar views, that we supported the movement for independence in Estonia and the other Baltic republics,' said Laaneots.[15] They met to talk in cafés, wearing civilian clothes in order not to be conspicuous, and had long discussions about the future of Estonia, the cool, blue-eyed Laaneots playing the pragmatist to Dudayev the idealist. Laaneots passed on documents from the emerging Estonian nationalist movement and had them translated for Dudayev.

Dudayev took inspiration from the Estonian model and started believing his native Chechnya could also militate for independence from Moscow. It was a dangerous temptation because Estonia, in contrast to Chechnya, had been a state before 1940 and had all the structures for potential independence in place. At the same time, Dudayev started to rediscover his buried Chechen roots. He read widely about Chechen history and the Caucasian Wars and talked constantly about Imam Shamil and Sheikh Mansur.

Laaneots stresses that Dudayev's mindset was still that of the rigid disciplinarian fashioned by years in the cruel school of the Soviet armed forces. 'He was not such a kind or good person,' Laaneots remembers. 'He was a strong-willed man, a purely military man.' He distrusted liberalism and his fondness for Estonia did not extend to the West, which was still the presumed target of his strategic bombers: 'When there was the war in the Gulf, when Iraq seized Kuwait, then there was the Desert Storm operation for the liberation of Kuwait, he was of course strongly on the side of Iraq as an Islamist. He was very optimistic that in the end Saddam would win. I tried to persuade him otherwise many times, but he did not believe me until it was all over.'

As the nationalist movement in Estonia grew in strength, Dudayev helped it more overtly. He ordered the men under his command to stay out of sight and not to interfere in any political activity in Tartu. He wooed the local population and organized an unprecedented 'open day' at his base in the summer of 1990 at which ordinary citizens were allowed to come and see the bombers.[16] In November 1990 Dudayev, now a major-general, went to Grozny and was elected Chairman of the Chechen National Congress. From that moment his ambition blossomed. 'Especially when he came back after the Congress, when he was elected, he was walking on air,' recalls Laaneots. 'He was full of optimism. We will throw out the Communists, the imperialists, he said.'

At this time Dudayev publicly supported Boris Yeltsin, the leader of the Russian democratic movement. 'I declare that were it not for the civic courage of Boris Yeltsin who saw the danger of the further unfolding of events, had he not spoken up in good time in the Baltic States, then the balance of forces and the situation today would be completely different,' Dudayev said in an interview in April 1991. He was referring to the dramatic events of January 1991 during which the two men never met, but were linked by a curious incident. Soviet troops had just killed demonstrators in clashes on the streets of the Lithuanian capital, Vilnius, and then again in Latvia, and there was a fear that the same scenario would occur in Estonia. Dudayev declared that he would not let Soviet planes land on Estonian soil. Yeltsin flew to Tallinn for a one-day visit to sign a pact of friendship with the Estonian Parliament and try to avert another crackdown. When he was in Tallinn, Yeltsin was warned that there might be an 'accident' with his plane on the flight back to Moscow. Eventually Yeltsin left Estonia for Leningrad by car and flew to Moscow from there. It was Dudayev who supplied Yeltsin with the black

Volga in which he drove to Leningrad, says Galina Starovoitova, who was Yeltsin's nationalities adviser at the time. This is confirmed in Tartu, with the added detail that the man behind the wheel driving Yeltsin out of Estonia was a Chechen. Neither man acknowledged the incident afterwards.

After Dudayev's stand during the Vilnius events he had burnt his boats with the Soviet military and could easily have been sacked for political subordination: he was now set on a political career in Chechnya. When this became clear, Lechi Umkhayev, the moderate organizer of the Chechen National Congress, and his political opponent, the radical nationalist Zelimkhan Yandarbiyev, flew to Tartu to talk to Dudayev. They had completely opposing aims. Umkhayev hoped to persuade Dudayev to stay in Tartu, while Yandarbiyev wanted him to come back and join the opposition movement. Dudayev had already made up his mind. In March 1991 he resigned his commission and moved back to Grozny and began to work full-time for the Chechen National Congress.

*

As Dudayev settled back in Grozny, Chechnya started to become one issue in the tussle for power between Mikhail Gorbachev and Boris Yeltsin.

By mid-1990 the architecture of Stalin's Soviet Union had started to fall apart. Different lobbies had different conceptions of whether the union should disintegrate altogether or be redesigned in a new way. Yeltsin, who was pushing to undermine the authority of Gorbachev and the Soviet power structures, became the ally of the leaders of the fourteen other 'union republics', many of whom were demanding secession from the centre. Under a little-noticed article in the 1922 treaty forming the Soviet Union, these republics had nominally joined the USSR voluntarily and therefore had the right to secede. This was the fault-line down which the Soviet Union eventually cracked apart. Gorbachev was working in the other direction, to keep the union together in a redesigned form and to weaken Yeltsin. He therefore sought the support of Russia's twenty 'autonomous republics', such as Chechen–Ingushetia and Tatarstan, and promised them more rights within a revamped union. Gorbachev invited the Chechen leader Doku Zavgayev and the Tatar Party boss Mintimer Shaimiyev to play an active part in the discussions for a new 'union treaty' that went on at Novo-Ogarevo outside Moscow in 1991.

Yeltsin was soon to regard Zavgayev as a political opponent, but in March 1991 on his first trip to the North Caucasus, to drum up support for the Russian presidential elections in June, he was given a lavish welcome by the Chechen leader. Galina Starovoitova, an expert on the North Caucasus, went with him:

'Zavgayev behaved exactly . . . like an Oriental party boss. They were all playing a double game . . . They put us up in the best palaces outside of town, there was a huge guard, plentiful food, a lot to drink, they tried to stop us from encountering ordinary people and speaking at rallies. They were like normal Soviet functionaries.'[17]

Yeltsin had no contact with the Chechen opposition on his trip to Grozny but he ran straight into graphic evidence of public discontent. As Yeltsin talked to Zavgayev at the top of the nine-storey concrete Communist Party headquarters in the centre of the city, in what was later to be Dudayev's office, they could hear shouts from a large crowd outside demanding a meeting with the man from Moscow. Demonstrators surrounded Yeltsin's car and threatened to stop him leaving until Starovoitova took their petitions and persuaded them to let him go.

Yeltsin's trip attained its short-term effect. In the presidential election in June Yeltsin received a massive 80 per cent of the vote in Chechen-Ingushetia, one of his best results in the whole of Russia. In Ingushetia the level of his support was the highest in Russia: 99.7 per cent. Despite this Yeltsin was out of his depth in a rally in the Ingush city Nazran, according to Starovoitova:

'On the road I reminded him that with these people their God is Allah, don't forget that . . . He didn't make that mistake, but they didn't react so strongly. For example, when Yeltsin said that Russia would no longer help foreign countries, like Cuba or other places, it was met with ovations in Moscow, but here there was an uncertain silence because they were worried about relations with Ossetia, not Cuba. It was too far away for them. He felt that it was a different people and was rather disappointed. His populism did not encounter support. And he left with the feeling of confusion that he did not know how to communicate with that people and that psychological residue stayed with him after that trip. And I think in a subconscious way that residue played a role at the beginning of the Chechen war.'

*

Dudayev's first aim in Chechnya in the spring of 1991 was to turn the Chechen National Congress into a radical political movement. He worked with four men, none of whom had a savoury reputation. The chief ideologist of the Congress was Zelimkhan Yandarbiyev, a schoolteacher and writer who was a member of the Russian Writers' Union. A tall man with a bushy black beard, Yandarbiyev was eloquent in spoken Chechen and a skilled political operator, but his slippery political tactics and shady contacts meant that he never became a popular figure. His strength lay in the Vainakh Democratic Party he had created in 1990 and which was Chechnya's first political party, with branches in almost every village.

Yaragi Mamodayev, a wealthy oil businessman, bankrolled the new movement. In the spring of 1991 he provided a house and later rented the former headquarters of the city Communist Party for the Congress to use as its base. A chubby man who looked much older than his thirty-eight years, Mamodayev never presumed to a public role and was content to hold the purse-strings. Later on he was accused of massive corruption. Beslan Gantemirov, who came from the same *teip* as Mamodayev, the *chinkho*, was a twenty-seven-year-old former policeman turned black marketeer. He had also formed a 'party' called Islamic Path, which was in fact a paramilitary organization. The fighters of the Islamic Path formed the core of the 'National Guard' that roamed the streets of Grozny in August and September. The fourth man in this disreputable group, Yusup Soslambekov, had served time in prison for rape when a student in Moscow. A born orator, he was the people's tribune in Grozny in 1991 and skilled at whipping up a crowd.

Very probably the four envisaged Dudayev as no more than a figurehead for their revolutionary movement. They reckoned that he had not lived in Chechnya for thirty years and did not have influential *teip* connections behind him. But Dudayev ended up outgrowing them all. Three of the four – the only exception was Yandarbiyev – later broke with Dudayev, and Gantemirov took up arms against him.

Dudayev took a radical approach. On 8–9 June he claimed his right as Chairman to convene a new session of the Congress. This time it was an overtly political occasion. The radicals, many of them drafted in specially, now formed the majority. The gathering renamed itself the National Congress of the Chechen People and proclaimed the formation of the republic of Nokhchi-Chu, a Chechen state outside both the Soviet Union and Russia. The Executive Committee of the new Congress was declared to be the only legitimate organ of power in the republic. Three radicals, Soslambekov, Yandarbiyev and Hussein Akhmadov, were elected to be Dudayev's deputies. The organizers of the first Congress, a large group of intellectuals and moderates led by Umkhayev, saw they had been outmanoeuvred and walked out, never to return.

The political manoeuvring in Chechnya might have continued for a long time without incident but for the global crisis that hit the Soviet Union when the disgruntled hardliners in Moscow attempted to overthrow Gorbachev in August 1991. The defeat of the putsch resulted in victory for Yeltsin and defeat for both

Gorbachev and the hardliners. The local Chechen Party leader, Zavgayev, was in Moscow as the coup began and, like many regional Communist leaders, he decided to sit on the fence and did not publicly condemn it. He only returned to Grozny on the third day, 21 August, at which point he finally denounced the coup plotters.

Dudayev and the Congress leaders had been quicker off the mark and immediately organized a protest rally on the square in front of the Party headquarters in Grozny. On the first day of the coup attempt, 19 August, only a few dozen people gathered. Three days later, when the coup had collapsed, it had turned into a huge and militant crowd. A volcano had been awakened and the 'Chechen Revolution' had begun. People remember events unfolding with extraordinary speed. Communism had collapsed and any building could be seized, any Soviet institution disbanded.

The vanguard of the revolution – the role played by the Bolsheviks in October 1917 – was taken by the armed wing of the Congress, Gantemirov's National Guard. Paying homage to Lenin's dictum to 'seize the telegraph', armed men seized the television centre on 22 August. They soon took over the radio station and the building of the Council of Ministers, hoisted green Islamic flags above them and threw up barricades on the streets. With every day more demonstrators poured in from the villages; they were mainly young men, and old men with lambskin *papakhas* and staves of the generation that had survived the deportations. Soon the centre of Grozny was filled by a vast permanent crowd. They shouted anti-Communist slogans and danced the *zikr* all day long, stamping and clapping. The rallies developed a dangerous edge. Men produced weapons – evidence that the Chechens had never actually disarmed fully in the Soviet era. Prisoners broke out of jail and looted warehouses. The businessmen Mamodayev and Gantemirov ensured that truck-loads of food were on hand to feed the crowds.

It is quite likely that the Congress would have taken power anyway. Soviet Communism was disintegrating and discredited and the Congress leaders had the support of the most mobilized part of the population and an armed wing. All the same, in August 1991 they had to face down the apparatus of the Soviet state. The republican Supreme Soviet was increasingly powerless, but there were still the police and the KGB, and there was an army garrison stationed outside Grozny. However, the state apparatus either gave up without a fight or simply stood by and did nothing. This was because it had been specifically told by Moscow not to put up any resistance.

The feeling in Yeltsin's team was that now was the moment to get rid of Zavgayev. Not only was he an old Communist, but he had supported Gorbachev against Yeltsin over the new Union Treaty. The two Chechens in Yeltsin's team, Ruslan Khasbulatov, who was now acting Parliamentary Speaker, and Aslanbek Aslakhanov, actively pressed for him to be removed.

Two senior KGB officers in Chechen–Ingushetia have testified that at the end of August and the beginning of September 1991 they monitored telephone calls between Khasbulatov and Aslakhanov in Moscow and Dudayev in Grozny about his plans to remove Zavgayev. According to Magomed Zaugayev, who was in charge of the KGB's Organized Crime Department: 'On 26 August Dudayev rang Khasbulatov's office and asked hysterically if the tanks of the Grozny garrison would be brought out if the Supreme Soviet was dissolved. And Dudayev received serious assurances that there would be no tanks. And a second time Aslakhanov, who was at the time a member of the presidium of the Supreme Soviet of Russia, assured Dudayev that force would not be used and that he could act boldly and decisively.'[18]

Any evidence from the KGB should be treated cautiously, but this version fits with the pattern of events which followed. On 26 August Aslanbek Aslakhanov arrived in Grozny and publicly told Zavgayev not to use force to suppress the demonstrations. With him came Salambek Khajiev, who was Soviet Minister of the Chemical Industry and an ally of Khasbulatov at the time. Khajiev had been one of only two Soviet ministers to condemn the 19 August putsch. A thoughtful man with greying temples, he was a respected academician and considered by Yeltsin as a possible leader for Chechnya, but he advised on his return to Moscow that Yeltsin's team should back Dudayev. Dudayev, Khajiev argued, would be a good ally for the Yeltsin administration. He was an outsider, who was not mixed up in the corrupt Soviet politics in Chechnya and not dependent on one influential *teip*; he was a respected general and he talked like a democrat. Khajiev, who later regretted his judgement, now recalls:

'I was struck by the way [Dudayev] took a very firm line and his declarations at least were democratic. He was the first Chechen general and not just a general but an air force general, which suggested a high level of development. His family was Russian – his wife was Russian – which I thought meant that he would not shout extremist slogans against Russians. So it seemed to me he was definitely a serious and heavyweight figure. The only thing that I didn't like was that around him there were already a lot of armed men in military uniforms. But back then unfortunately I just put that down to the mentality of a general, that he liked people to be well turned out and spruce. But in the back of my mind I had the feeling that this had happened before in history when the Germans created their SS. But I did not take that seriously and put it down to the weaknesses of a general.'[19]

The official organ of power in the republic, the Supreme Soviet, was still sitting, although no one paid much attention to it any more. It did little to avert its impending demise and when on 3 September it belatedly declared a state of emergency the decree was simply ignored. The demonstrators now ruled the streets of Grozny. On 6 September a crowd burst into the building where the Supreme Soviet was sitting. Doku Zavgayev was physically dragged out of the building and forced to sign an 'act of

abdication'. Several deputies were beaten up by National Guardsmen. Vitaly Kutsenko, the elderly First Secretary of the town
soviet either was pushed out of a first-floor window or tried to
clamber out to escape the crowd. In any event he fell and was
killed. Zavgayev fled to his home village in northern Chechnya.

Ruslan Khasbulatov was publicly delighted by this violent end
to the Supreme Soviet and described it as 'a victory of democratic
forces over the Party bureaucracy'. On 14 September, he flew into
Grozny and addressed the demonstrators, reputedly telling them
he would 'bring Zavgayev to Moscow in an iron cage'.

Khasbulatov's deviousness as Speaker of the Russian Parliament became legendary and his position on Chechnya has
changed so many times that it is hard to keep track of him. He
now says he was distant from events in Grozny in 1991 and that
he knew very little of Dudayev. 'I saw him in 1991 for just fifteen
minutes,' Khasbulatov says of Dudayev. 'He gave me his word
that he would be governed by the law.'[20] In fact Khasbulatov
appeared to be trying to mastermind the whole process. On 15
September he was in the chair when the Supreme Soviet held its
last meeting in a building ringed by National Guardsmen. The
Supreme Soviet agreed to dissolve itself after voting to form a
new 'Provisional Supreme Soviet' of thirty-two deputies, which
would operate only until new elections were held on 17
November.

It now seems clear that Khasbulatov and Dudayev had in fact
made a power-sharing deal, and Dudayev simply outmanoeuvred
Khasbulatov and decided to take power on his own. After
Khasbulatov went back to Moscow, Dudayev ignored the agreement he had signed and announced he was dissolving the new
Provisional Supreme Soviet and that the Executive Committee of
the Congress took upon itself the functions of a 'revolutionary
committee for the transitional period with all powers'. Beslan
Gantemirov's guardsmen seized the KGB building in Grozny and
captured a huge cache of weapons. By Gantemirov's own account:

'We had thirty-three fighters. We trained for a long time. We took it in exactly forty seconds. We wounded one lieutenant colonel, but otherwise there were no losses.'[21]

The Russian leadership was now starting to get worried by events in Chechnya, but as they tried to reel back the rebellious Chechens, the line snapped. When Viktor Ivanenko, newly appointed as head of the Russian KGB with a reforming mandate, heard about the seizure of the KGB building, he decided to go to Grozny. The Russian Vice-President, Alexander Rutskoi, offered to go with him. The bluff Rutskoi was a former fighter pilot in Afghanistan and not known for his political subtlety. 'When we were in the air we discussed the situation and our plan of action,' Ivanenko said in a newspaper interview. 'I said that I would try to free the building peacefully, meet with elders, I explained the complexity of the situation in the Caucasus. Rutskoi in reply told me how he solved problems in Afghanistan. "A *kishlak* [village] fires at us and kills someone. I send up a couple of planes and there is nothing left of the *kishlak*. After I've burned a couple of *kishlaks* they stop shooting." That is more or less, he says, what we need to do here. I began to feel unwell.'[22]

The visit only aggravated relations between Grozny and Moscow. Dudayev refused to give up the KGB building and the blunt-talking Rutskoi angered the Chechens with the phrase 'This is not democracy, it is banditry.' On Tuesday 8 October Rutskoi gave an emotional report back to the Supreme Soviet in Moscow after which the chamber voted through a statement giving Chechen 'illegal armed formations' an ultimatum to disarm by midnight on Thursday. As no one has succeeded in disarming the Chechens in 200 years it was a clear threat to use force. It was the signal Dudayev had been waiting for and he issued an order for the 'mobilization' of all males between fifteen and fifty-five. Several thousand men had soon signed up to join a voluntary defence force.

Dudayev was by no means in full control of Grozny and his

imperious style and fondness for armed guards increasingly disturbed some Chechens. An opposition group calling itself Round Table was formed and demanded that Dudayev cede control of the media and disband his armed groups. A rival permanent opposition rally began to meet on Lenin Square only two minutes' walk away from the pro-Dudayev demonstration on Victory Square.

On 19 October Yeltsin spoke for the first time on Russian television about Chechnya. He said the situation had become intolerable and condemned the 'openly anti-constitutional and provocative actions of the Executive Committee of the All-National Congress of the Chechen People and its leader, who are striving to destabilize the situation in the republic and to seize power through the organized armed detachments of the so called "National Guard".' Yeltsin insisted that the elections for a new Supreme Soviet on 17 November must go ahead as scheduled as well as a 'referendum on the state structure of the Chechen–Ingush republic according to the existing legislature of the RSFSR [the Russian Federation].' If the Congress did not go along with this, he would be forced to 'defend constitutional order'. It was much too late and the Congress ignored the threats. One of Dudayev's deputies, Hussein Akhmadov, called Yeltsin's speech 'the last belch of the Russian empire'.

The Chechen presidential and parliamentary elections went ahead for 27 October, as the Congress had planned. Dudayev was the only credible candidate for President, although he did face three opponents. He campaigned not only as the candidate for an independent Chechnya but as the champion of social justice for the poor. The elections were entirely run by the Congress. It appointed the Central Electoral Commission and drew up an electoral law which barred some Communist officials from taking part. The electoral commission did not solve the question of where Chechnya ended and Ingushetia began. An arbitrary dividing line was drawn across Chechen–Ingushetia and two Ingush regions did not vote.

The elections were chaotic. Many people did not know where to cast their votes even if they wanted to and almost none of the large Russian population voted. The official turnout figure – 458,144 people or 72 per cent of the electorate – seems far-fetched. None the less whole villages in the mountains turned out enthusiastically for what they saw as their first-ever free all-Chechen elections, and the claim by the anti-Dudayev opposition that only 15 per cent of the electorate voted is also implausible.

The election commission announced Dudayev had won with 90.1 per cent of the vote. One of four 'international observers' who pronounced the vote free and fair was Prince Peter Volkonsky from Estonia. Despite his distinguished Russian ancestry, Volkonsky, who is half-Estonian and a theatre director, musician and psychologist, was an active supporter of the Estonian nationalist movement. Volkonsky now says of the elections: 'It was hard to check, to be honest, because many people did not have passports, especially the women. They didn't know, it was their first elections. For them it was a matter of honour. I even told them openly there had been infringements but I believed in the Chechen people's respect of the concept of honour – but this should not happen again next time!'[23]

The bearded bohemian Volkonsky captures the pulse of excitement running through Chechnya at the time: 'After the election I was at a meeting of old men. I did a V for victory sign and shouted "Marsho" ["Freedom" in Chechen]. These old men stood up, like at a rock concert, and shouted "Marsho". I am an old hippie but I have never experienced such a response.'

In his first decree as President on 1 November 1991 Dudayev declared Chechnya an independent state. The following day Ruslan Khasbulatov was formally confirmed as Speaker of the Russian Parliament. One of his first acts as Speaker was to sponsor a resolution that declared the Chechen elections invalid. Moscow and Grozny were now on collision course.

Rutskoi now drew up plans to overthrow Dudayev by force. Moscow was to declare a state of emergency, land troops and arrest Dudayev and the leading members of the Congress. The first flaw in the plan was revealed almost immediately when the decree imposing a state of emergency was signed on 7 November, the October Revolution public holiday. None of the Russian leadership was at work. Yeltsin was at his dacha at Zavidovo outside Moscow and – on the first of several occasions in his presidency – could not be located, even by telephone. He had evidently disappeared into one of his occasional bouts of drinking or periods of black depression. Rutskoi took charge. According to the KGB chief, Ivanenko, Rutskoi summoned himself, the Interior Minister Andrei Dunayev and the Prosecutor General Valentin Stepankov to a late-night meeting and threatened to have them put on trial if they 'sabotaged' the decree.

At this point interests in the Gorbachev–Yeltsin power struggle had shifted. The Soviet President Gorbachev, whose power-base was dwindling, was only too happy to see Yeltsin humiliated by a rebellion inside the Russian Federation. Yeltsin had not yet created any Russian armed forces and so the assent of Gorbachev was needed for Soviet troops to be sent in as reinforcements. Gorbachev flatly refused to help, saying the whole plan was misconceived and chaotic. When two ministers rang up asking him for orders, he told them on no account to give any troops to Rutskoi. Gorbachev recalls:

'Everyone was playing some kind of game. Rutskoi, brandishing his sword, said, "Give me several divisions and I'll put it down and crush all the separatists and Dudayev" and so on. Suddenly Shaposhnikov, the Defence Minister, and the Interior Minister Barannikov ring me up and say, "Mikhail Sergeyevich, Rutskoi is asking us for troops." I say, "No decisions without my agreement, absolutely none." I ring Khasbulatov and say, "Have you gone mad?" Khasbulatov was against [sending in troops], I have to say objectively. So I say, "Why are you dragging me into this? Where is your President?" Khasbulatov said, "I'd also like to know where he is." '[24]

The following evening, 8 November, Russian television announced the declaration of a state of emergency in Chechnya. The new Chechen Parliament, elected on the same day as Dudayev, met in emergency session and voted Dudayev powers to 'defend the sovereignty of Chechnya', a role he felt he had been born to play. He scoffed at the Russian threat, started mobilizing fighters and appointed Yusup Soslambekov his 'Minister of War'. That night 600 Russian Interior Ministry troops landed at the military airbase at Khankala outside Grozny. They received no backup and attempts to reinforce them went comically wrong. Extra weapons were sent to Mozdok and reinforcements went to Vladikavkaz (whether by accident or by deliberate design of the Soviet leadership is not clear). By the morning of 9 November the airbase had been surrounded by Chechen fighters. Meanwhile hundreds of thousands of people gathered in the centre of Grozny for the biggest rally yet seen in Chechnya. Faced with the Russian threat, the big opposition demonstration on Lenin Square dissolved and melted into the bigger rally.

From the threat of tragedy the whole thing had turned into farce. At midday Dudayev, now a national hero, took his oath as President in the Lermontov Theatre. In an emotional ceremony he laid his hand on the Koran brought to him by the Chairman of the Council of Elders, then he went out on to the balcony and addressed an ecstatic crowd. That afternoon the Russian Deputy Interior Minister, Vyacheslav Komissarov, flew in to meet Dudayev and agreed to pull out the troops. They skulked out of Chechnya in buses, having suffered no casualties. In Moscow the Supreme Soviet met and, despite the pleadings of Rutskoi and Khasbulatov, voted to revoke the state of emergency.

Dudayev emerged from the whole fisaco as the general-

liberator of Chechnya. Opposition to him had completely evap-
orated. 'Before 9 November Dudayev was zero', complains one
of his opposition critics, Jabrail Gakayev, bitterly. 'Afterwards he
became a national hero.'

Since then many Russian commentators have regretted that the
bungled operation was not carried through more decisively, but
in fact its bungling may have averted a bloodbath. Dudayev had
already won the legitimacy of an election victory and many
Chechens were in euphoria from the presidential election.
Dudayev already had a large crowd of fighters at his disposal and
although it was a much smaller fighting force than three years
later, it was enough to put up a determined resistance. Moreover,
Moscow had no political plan to put into action. After killing or
arresting members of the Congress, the Kremlin would have been
hard-pressed to find a government capable of taking power. The
net result of the events of 9 November was that Jokhar Dudayev
had won a popular mandate as the man leading Chechnya's
breakaway from Russia.

6

Independent Chechnya

Grozny was cold in January 1994. The streets were deserted after dark and people sat in their kitchens with all the gas rings on the stove lit to keep warm. The night was punctuated by gunshots. It was probably just the playfulness of armed men but it was best not to check.

In the third winter of Chechen independence the Chechen capital had become the most extraordinary city in the former Soviet Union. There were abundant symbols of Chechen independence. In what was now Sheikh Mansur Square, Lenin's statue had been toppled and a Chechen flag planted on the pedestal. It had a wide field of green (for Islam) crossed by two narrow strips of white and one of red. In the middle of the green field was a Chechen wolf growling out from under a full moon. But in no other way did Chechnya look like a state. The black market was booming – the new Chechen rich drove their Mercedes and BMWs at speed around the streets of Grozny, and a rash of red-brick villas was being thrown up in the suburbs. But ordinary civic life had collapsed. The government was spending no money on public services and people working in schools or hospitals had not been paid for months. If they went to work, they sat at their desks in their overcoats because there was no heating.

Dissent was widespread, although you had to seek it out because people were reluctant to speak publicly against President Dudayev. Salam Khamsat, the *imam* of the mosque in central Grozny, was an exception in agreeing to see a foreign reporter at his home. Almost the entire opposition had scattered after armed men had dispersed demonstrations on the streets of Grozny the summer before. The *imam* estimated that one-third of Chechnya supported the President and two-thirds were against him. He listed a long catalogue of grievances about what Dudayev had done or failed to do. 'He has done nothing for the republic,' he said. 'He hasn't built a single school or hospital.' Dudayev had not even built a single mosque, he said, and respect for religion and for mullahs had fallen away.

The Dudayev regime was tottering and increasingly robbed of public support. How long could it last? The Presidential Palace in the middle of Grozny was gripped more by idleness than by agitation. 'Palace' was rather an ambitious word for the nine-storey echoing slab of concrete overlooking the central square. The wind howled in through the front door, annoying the bored men with Kalashnikovs who queried each visitor as they went in. Officials in their bare offices had plenty of time to talk and not much to do. Only Dudayev was too busy to be seen. Dudayev began his working day in the late afternoon and worked until dawn, receiving large delegations or recording long television addresses when he talked about the deportations and Russian aggression, and sometimes working out in his gym. On this occasion he was said to be receiving a large Lithuanian delegation. Otherwise the Information Minister, Movladi Udugov, was watching videos, and Zelimkhan Yandarbiyev, now Vice-President, had an almost instant gap in his not-so-busy schedule. The bearded Yandarbiyev sat in an office that was also unheated at a large desk with a Chechen flag draped behind him. A parrot in a cage chirped in the background.

Yandarbiyev spoke in a sarcastic tone that implied nothing here was as it seemed. He said the disorder in Chechnya was 'temporary' and blamed the collapse of the economy on Russia's economic blockade. He escaped from concrete examples into dialectic and quoted Hegel to the effect that 'A people cannot develop if it has enough to eat but does not have a political, psychological and philosophical base for its development.' The chaos in Chechnya, Yandarbiyev said, was part of an 'inevitable process' of nation-building: 'A nation should by itself construct its social and state psychology and philosophy in relation to the world and in relation to its own statehood and out of that is constructed the economic base of this nation.'

At the end of the interview Yandarbiyev, a poet, presented a poem written in Russian in which Russia was the 'scourge', the imperial devourer of nations. Russia was the hidden mover shaping all their designs, if only as a negative force. The Russian threat was still the Chechen leadership's trump card and it was a message that still had a sympathetic audience. The nearer you got to the mountains, the more people you found ready to defend Chechen independence. In Yandarbiyev's home village of Stariye Atagi visitors were invited into an Arabic school in the mosque as a sign that Islam was now freely practised in a free Chechnya. Young boys sat in patient lines being given instruction in the Koran. In the back room of the mosque, as Aziz Jebrailov told the story of how he was deported to Kazakhstan, he said life was no harder now than it had ever been. At least, he said in a robust voice, the Russians had gone and Chechens were free. 'It is better to die than lose your freedom!' he declared.

Attitudes like this put the moderate opposition to Dudayev in a quandary. If they suggested doing a deal with Russia they were accused of being 'traitors'. Their tactic was just to wait and hope change would come of its own accord. Said-Khamzat Nunuyev, a young writer who was elected to the 1990 Russian Parliament, said the logical thing was for Chechnya to accept a settlement with Moscow that granted it 'special status' within the Federation. The tragedy, he said, was that the republic was, in the Russian phrase, 'caught between two fires'; Russia in the form of 'a new empire according to a new constitution [recently adopted in December 1993] and on the other side this bandit super-radicalism'. The urban middle class was powerless to do anything about it because Dudayev was surviving on the credit he had earned in the countryside by proclaiming Chechnya an independent state. 'After suffering Tsarism and Communism the people haven't breathed the air of freedom enough,' he said.

Chechnya was not so much an independent country as a twilight zone, neither inside Russia nor outside it. The republic had definitely fallen out of the Russian political space. Nameplates outside ministries told you you were now in the 'Noxchijn Respublika' and there was not a Russian flag or symbol to be seen. From the summer of 1992 there were no Russian troops in the republic – something that was not true of any other part of the former Soviet empire, even East Germany, at the time. Instead, there were plenty of gunmen in camouflage who could have belonged to anyone, but appeared to be defending President Dudayev.

On the other hand, Chechens kept the Russian ruble and their Soviet passports. Any resident of the 'Republic of Ichkeria' could leave Grozny and the flag with the wolf and the full moon in the morning and be in Moscow in the afternoon, after flying on an air ticket bought in rubles. There were no signposts announcing that you were entering the territory of a new state. There were no checks on the borders of Chechnya – none at any rate that could not be overcome with a small bribe. Russian television still broadcast to Chechnya and was the main source of evening entertainment. The Chechen football team, Terek Grozny, continued to play in the Russian league.

In 1992 there were some modest attempts at building a Chechen state. The Parliament elected on the same day as Dudayev proved a lively debating chamber and the press was vigorous and uncensored. A report by the organization International Alert in October 1992 concluded that 'The Chechen Republic has made impressive beginnings in creating a state and government structure. Chechen society is characterized by a remarkable degree of political openness and freedom of expression.'

In fact 'openness' increasingly meant chaos. The ever more eccentric President Dudayev seemed much more interested in the idea of calling Chechnya independent than in the practicality of making that idea work. From the first Dudayev failed to create a proper government or devise an intelligent economic policy. In January 1992 he had invited Salambek Khajiev to take the job of First Deputy Prime Minister and head the government. Khajiev's job as Soviet Minister of the Chemical Industry had been disbanded with the end of the Soviet Union and he had just settled back in Grozny. He and Dudayev met in the house of Dudayev's elder brother on Ulitsa Shekspira (Shakespeare Street) in Taskhkala on the edge of Grozny. After a conversation that lasted three and a half hours Khajiev turned Dudayev's offer down. Dudayev was insisting on keeping all the levers of economic power firmly with the state, he says, and they could not understand each other.

'I told him I wouldn't take part in this because he had a typically stateist conception of things. He was a typical military man: force, order and submission! ... I said we should reassure the people that we are heading for independence and that we had in the first place to deal step by step with the economy but not in the way that he wanted, keeping everything in the state sector. I said that the only way ahead was to liberalize the economy very quickly and switch on all the energy locked up in the people in the private sector ... But he had a typical old way of thinking, that everything should be firmly in the hands of the commander of the division. I said that was not realistic.'[1]

Shamil Beno came up against the same problem. One of the few intellectuals who agreed to work in the new government, Beno was a historian who was born in Jordan and spoke Arabic. In fact he looks more Celtic than Middle Eastern, with a hearty laugh and a reddish scruffy beard. Now, at the age of thirty-three, he was made Foreign Minister. Beno remembers the early months of Chechen independence as 'a complete mess'. On one occasion he, the Foreign Minister, and the presidential aide Ramzan

Gantemirov were called out to go to the barracks of the Interior Ministry troops, the OMON, and help find mattresses for the men. They were sleeping on their bed-frames because no one had bothered to allocate them any mattresses.[2] Beno had growing clashes with Dudayev about how and whether to negotiate with Moscow. He resigned in protest in July 1992 and later joined the Daimokkh Party, an opposition movement led by Khajiev.

Beno says he finally decided to quit when Dudayev made Yaragi Mamodayev, the businessman who had financed the Chechen Congress, Deputy Prime Minister in charge of the economy. Mamodayev and his fellow *teip*-member, the paramilitary leader Beslan Gantemirov, had a hold over Dudayev. They felt they had financed the 'Chechen Revolution' with large amounts of money and now it was pay-back time. At first Dudayev, who had a streak of pure naïvety to him, seemed not to notice them. Mamodayev was given overall control of the economy. Gantemirov, who was still only twenty-eight, was made Mayor of Grozny and simultaneously head of the city police with control over city property and, according to one source, a personal oil quota of 100,000 tonnes.

Mamodayev and Gantemirov epitomized what some called a 'mafia government'. It did not last long. Mamodayev later abandoned Dudayev and there is evidence that Gantemirov was working only for himself from the very beginning. Documents from a commission investigating the theft of weapons seized in the KGB building in October 1991 by Gantemirov and his National Guardsmen ended up in the hands of the Russian newspaper *Izvestia*. In the transcripts of a commission hearing, the guardsman Shamil Basayev, then subordinate to Gantemirov, said Gantemirov had arranged for a big cache of weapons from the KGB building to be taken away by lorry to a secret location outside the village of Gekhi without Dudayev's knowledge.[3]

*

Dudayev enjoyed striking extravagant poses. Soon after taking power, he offered political asylum to the former East German leader Erich Honecker. The offer was not taken up. Undeterred by Honecker's refusal, he then gave a haven to the ousted President of Georgia, Zviad Gamsakhurdia, who had been toppled from power in the New Year of 1992. Like Dudayev, Gamsakhurdia was a romantic nationalist who had come to power on a wave of popular support but became increasingly eccentric and dictatorial. By giving a home to Gamsakhurdia, Dudayev only succeeded in angering the new regime in the only other country with which he shared a frontier: Georgia.

Dudayev decided to try to ignore Russia and to reach out to the outside world for international recognition, in the first instance in the Arab world. It was a tactic strongly opposed by his Foreign Minister Shamil Beno, himself Jordanian-born. 'Our main problem was in the north, not in the south,' he said. None the less the President set off on a series of high-profile foreign trips. In 1992, as well as visiting Turkey, he travelled to Sudan, Jordan, Saudi Arabia and Kuwait. The pilot Husacin Khamidov flew him on a Tupolev-134 on three of these trips, where he was given a warm reception. 'In all the countries we flew to Dudayev was received very well and on the highest level, with red carpets,' Khamidov recalled.

Dudayev subsequently squandered a lot of this goodwill. Mairbek Vachargayev, his Foreign Ministry representative in Moscow in early 1992, despaired of his President's impetuous stabs at diplomacy: 'He repeated everything that was done on the level of personal diplomacy ... "This is what the representative of the President of Turkey said. He promised that. The Iranian said this. The Libyan said this." What I told him in secret he retold on television. The next day I was forced to explain to the ambassadors why President Dudayev was speaking on television about what was confidential.'[4]

On another occasion Dudayev was interviewed by a Palestinian journalist and, to the latter's evident satisfaction, told him that 'I have a plan to destroy the Israeli state.' Vachargayev recalls: 'I was rung up by the consular section of Israel and asked: "Can you explain what the matter is? We have given no grounds for him to express himself so insultingly." I said he didn't understand. Dudayev was joking. He was mistranslated. It ended at that.' Vachargayev resigned in May 1992 and no state, even Jordan and Syria with their large Chechen diasporas, ever came near recognizing Chechen independence.

Flying abroad was absurdly easy. Friendly contacts in the host countries arranged visas and the Chechens' Soviet passports were still valid at the borders. As an ex-pilot Dudayev still had influential friends in air traffic control and knew the right air codes needed to enter Russian air corridors. On one occasion at the end of 1992, travelling to Vilnius to meet the Lithuanian President Vytautas Landsbergis, he himself sat at the controls of the Tupolev plane and flew the most direct route straight across Russia and Ukraine, having evidently cleared his air corridor in advance with old comrades.

In late 1992 Dudayev went to Britain and the United States, where his oil industry attracted considerable interest. Mystery surrounds a trip he apparently made to Sarajevo about the same time. According to some sources, he went there from northern Cyprus, where he had met the separatist Turkish leader Rauf Denktash. In Bosnia Dudayev is said to have promised President Izetbegovic 40,000 Chechen armed volunteers, but he did not say how they were supposed to cross all the borders needed to get to Bosnia.

In September 1993 Dudayev appointed Charles Tchokotoua, a cultivated American Georgian with a Chelsea address, as his 'Ambassador to the European Community'. Tchokotoua helped organize a trip to France in June 1993. It was a whirl of top-level engagements. They went first to Istanbul and had a meeting with the Turkish President, Turgut Ozal. They then moved on to

Paris, where they stayed in a smart hotel near the Champs-
Elysées, and to the South of France. Usman Imayev, the bright
young Chairman of the Chechen Central Bank, was on the trip:
'The President had a lot of military men with him,' Imayev
recalled. 'We went to the Base Orange and the President did a
mock battle on a Mirage 2000, which had only just begun to be
issued. He won the battle and he was included on the pilots' list
for France. Then there was a meeting at the Russian Officers'
Club, there was a reception. We visited Le Bourget, looked at all
the hardware.'[5]

The reception in France, Imayev said, was very positive and
included a meeting with the Deputy Interior Minister. The
delegation then went on to Bonn, Munich and Vienna. In
Germany they did a deal with the firm Rohstoff Handel GmbH
for the delivery of 100,000 tonnes of heating oil in return for new
oil equipment and signed a contract with a firm called Veba for
the supply of oil. In Austria they had a meeting with the Deputy
Chancellor. All of this was a tonic for President Dudayev's pride
and possibly gave a small boost to the Chechen budget, but
probably the main effect of it was to deeply irritate the Russian
Foreign Ministry. According to Andrei Kozyrev, who was Foreign
Minister during the whole period, the first reports that Dudayev
was travelling came from Russian embassies, not from intelligence
services: 'We never had information before he appeared in a given
country and knocked at the government's door,' he said. 'And
that became quite an irritating factor.'[6]

*

In 1992 the newly formed Russian state was so weak that the
Kremlin paid little attention to the breakaway regime in
Chechnya. Those who wanted to resolve the issue merely concen-
trated on more pressing problems and hoped that it would sort
itself out. In retrospect this was unfortunate because in 1992
Yeltsin briefly had a team of professionals competent to deal with

nationalities policy. The formidable anthropologist Galina Staro-voitova remained his nationalities adviser and Valery Tishkov, a respected academic with a professional interest in conflict preven-tion, was Nationalities Minister. By the end of the year both had resigned – as he did so, Tishkov complained that Russia 'has no nationalities policy' – and more traditionally colonialist minds had taken over the running of Moscow's policy towards the regions.

The drama of the break-up of the Soviet Union in December 1991 gave Dudayev a breathing space and he dealt deftly with Moscow's efforts to reel him in. Soon after he was elected, his old acquaintance General Pyotr Deinekin, the head of the Russian air force, was dispatched to Grozny and offered Dudayev three posts in the air force, including promotion to the rank of Colonel-General. Dudayev publicly proclaimed that he preferred to be 'an ordinary Chechen'. Chechen television exploited to the full the propaganda effect of Deinekin's begging mission. Deinekin, whose bombers were later to massacre the citizens of Grozny, started to play down his connection with Dudayev. He now says that apart from once in Grozny 'I never once drank a glass of vodka with him.'[7]

There were still Soviet military bases in Chechnya stacked with weapons, and Moscow and Grozny played a discreet game over who would get control of them. In fact the answer was clear from the start, for the Soviet military, in transition to becoming the Russian armed forces, could not remove the weapons without provoking bloodshed. Throughout the former Soviet Union local leaders were calmly laying claim to Soviet bases and taking them over. Dudayev did the same. He sent crowds of ordinary Chech-ens and fighters to surround the bases, applying pressure on Moscow to give up the weapons.

In Moscow the issue was the responsibility of first the Soviet Defence Minister Yevgeny Shaposhnikov and then his Russian deputy and eventual successor Pavel Grachev. The Kalmyk air force general, Valery Ochirov, who had served with Dudayev, was deputed by Moscow to negotiate over the weapons. As a native of Kalmykia, another deported nation, Ochirov found he got on well with Dudayev and there may have been secret dealings between them. He was a frequent guest in the Dudayev home and has fond memories of Alla Dudayeva. He later worked in the Kremlin and became one of Dudayev's lines of communication to top Russian officials.[8] Ochirov reported in the spring of 1992 that 'Provocations against military garrisons and the personal staff of parts of the Grozny garrison began in October 1991 and have not stopped. At the current time 80 per cent of the heavy equipment and 75 per cent of the small arms have been stolen.'[9]

On 28 May 1992 Grachev signed a directive agreeing to divide the weapons fifty-fifty between the Russian military and Dudayev. It was actually an attempt at a dignified cover-up of the fact that almost all the weapons had been lost. Many people believe Dudayev simply bought them. Eleven days later, on 8 June, the last Russian troops pulled out of Chechnya.

According to official lists, 226 aeroplanes, forty-two tanks, thirty-six armoured personnel carriers and 29,000 machine-guns were left behind in Chechnya. In this single fact many members of the opposition to Boris Yeltsin in 1994 chose to see the reason why the Russian army did not win a quick military victory over Dudayev. They blamed Pavel Grachev for losing Chechnya twice – once by arming Dudayev's fighters and once by conducting a botched invasion. The truth is probably far more dirty. Dudayev had nothing like those amounts of weapons and armour at the beginning of the war. There is some evidence that he was doing good business in exporting arms, including arms from outside Chechnya, abroad to the Muslims of Bosnia, among others. Most of his planes were light Czech aircraft, which were destroyed before the ground invasion began. Much of the weaponry the Chechen fighters used in the war was probably acquired subsequently from abroad or through corrupt elements in the Russian armed forces.

Dudayev easily saw off the first attempt to overthrow him by

force. On 31 March 1992 armed men tried to take over the
television centre in Grozny. There was shooting in which five
people were killed and the clumsily organized operation soon
collapsed. It seems certain the operation was inspired in Moscow,
although no definite proof emerged to confirm this. The Chechen
Parliament declared a state of emergency and awarded Dudayev
emergency powers. Dudayev himself declared he was disbanding
the local police force for its association in the 'coup'. He pointed
the finger at Ruslan Khasbulatov.

Khasbulatov's attitudes deeply complicated Russian policy
towards Chechnya. After helping Dudayev come to power and
then being outwitted by him, Khasbulatov had become deeply
hostile to the Chechen President. The two men traded insults.
Khasbulatov called what was going on in Chechnya 'a senseless
and shameful witches' sabbath'. Dudayev retorted that Khasbulatov should come back to Chechnya so they could put him on
trial: 'We demand from him that he be handed over to face the
courts, he and his political vagrants.' The Chechen authorities
taunted him, saying that his election to the Russian Parliament
was no longer valid, since his constituency in Grozny was now
part of an independent country.

Just as Chechnya had been a hostage to the Yeltsin–Gorbachev
power struggle, it now became tied to the power struggle between
Yeltsin and Khasbulatov. In early 1992, as the second most
powerful politician in Russia, Khasbulatov was turning the
Supreme Soviet into the centre of opposition to his former ally
Yeltsin. He regarded Chechnya as his own fiefdom and blocked
attempts by others to negotiate with Dudayev. When for instance
the Nationalities Minister Tishkov expressed an interest in visiting
Chechnya in 1992, Khasbulatov vetoed his visit. On another
occasion at the beginning of 1992 Starovoitova said she telephoned Dudayev directly from the Russian Parliament building.
She said Dudayev was pleasantly surprised – no one had yet taken
the initiative to get in touch with him. They discussed a location

for possible talks. Dudayev suggested Tartu, but Starovoitova insisted they should be in Russia and said she would guarantee his security in St Petersburg. The conversation ended on a hopeful note, but Khasbulatov launched a savage attack on Dudayev two days later, and when Starovoitova tried to call Dudayev back, government lines to Grozny had been switched off.[10]

On the whole Chechnya was simply ignored in Moscow. A symptom of the lack of attention paid to the republic was that the nationalist opposition in the Russian Parliament did not make an issue out of the plight of the ethnic Russians in Chechnya. While they were making loud noises about alleged infringements of the rights of ethnic Russians in the Baltic States, they ignored Chechnya. The Slavic community (Russians, Ukrainians and Belorussians) in Chechen–Ingushetia in 1989 was just over 300,000, one-quarter of the population, the overwhelming majority of whom were in Grozny. In the first year of independence an estimated 50,000 Russians left. In a poll of Russians outside Russia in 1992, the highest percentage wishing to emigrate from their current place of residence was in Chechnya – 37 per cent. They left because the official economy in which Russians used to work had collapsed and because they were suddenly second-class citizens in a society where they had once been the privileged ones.

Russians were also the most vulnerable group in society to the lawlessness gripping the republic. There was a big increase in robberies, burglaries and murders. The Russian Interior Ministry claimed there were as many as 600 murders in Chechnya in both 1992 and 1993. A particularly ugly practice was that of forcing people to sell their apartments at gunpoint. Russians were especially prey to this because they did not have large extended families – what might be called the extended revenge network – who could come to their defence. But the other nationalities in Chechnya – Chechens, Ingush, Dagestanis, Jews and Armenians – also suffered from the crime epidemic.

A so-called 'White Book' has been compiled chronicling instances of crime against the Russian population under Dudayev. It is a depressing catalogue of muggings, kidnaps and murders but it is an insidious document because it misleadingly presents the crimes as having been a deliberately targeted anti-Russian policy by the Dudayev government. The White Book was handed out to Russian soldiers during the war. Almost all the incidents in the book probably occurred, but its unbalanced focus on the sufferings of Russians as an ethnic group consolidated the image of 'cut-throat Chechens' and helped to legitimize atrocities by those same soldiers against the local Chechen population.

*

The Ingush, the Chechens' ethnic cousins, had been left behind by the Chechen revolution. Historically they had felt badly used by both the Russians and the Chechens in the Soviet republic of Chechen–Ingushetia – rather as the Slovaks did by the Czechs in Czechoslovakia. When Chechnya declared independence, the Ingush decided to go their own way. In a referendum on 30 November 1991 the Ingush voted to form their own republic within Russia, and in June 1992 a republic of Ingushetia was formed. In the same referendum the Ingush voted to demand the return of the lands on the right bank of the Terek – Prigorodny Region, which Stalin had awarded to North Ossetia in 1944 – and the part of Vladikavkaz on the right bank of the Terek which had been part of Ingushetia until 1934. It was an emotional issue. Many ancestral cemeteries and the village of Angusht, which gave birth to the Russian name for the Ingush, were in the region, and thousands of Ingush were living unregistered in their old homes in the Prigorodny Region.

By the end of 1992 the area had become a tinderbox and the Ossetians were amassing weapons in anticipation of violence. The spark was struck on 20 October 1992 when an armoured car crushed an Ingush schoolgirl to death. The following day two more Ingush villagers were killed. Armed Ingush men poured into Prigorodny Region, overrunning their old villages and expelling the Ossetians. Moscow then sent in troops, which stopped the Ingush offensive. It was widely perceived that Moscow was favouring its traditional ally in the North Caucasus, Ossetia; at any rate Moscow's intervention swung the initiative back in favour of the Ossetians, and despite the presence of federal troops the Ingush came off worse in brutal fighting. Within a few days some 30,000 Ingush had been expelled over the border into Ingushetia. By the end of the year the number of officially registered refugees had reached 65,000. According to the Russian Provisional Administration 419 Ingush, 171 Ossetians and sixty others died in the fighting and 3397 homes were burnt, of which 3000 were Ingush.

The Chechen government watched developments over the border with alarm and officially declared neutrality in the crisis. The stance was condemned in Ingushetia, but it helped save Chechnya from invasion. On 10 November federal forces occupied Ingushetia and moved towards the Chechen border. Dudayev declared a state of emergency and said that if the Russian troops did not pull back, 'Both Nazran and Vladikavkaz will be blown sky-high.' Chechens blocked the roads into their republic with petrol lorries.

On 11 November Yegor Gaidar, Yeltsin's acting Prime Minister, flew down to Ingushetia. He now admits that the Russian military was on the verge of invading Chechnya: 'The idea was a very simple one,' Gaidar said. 'There were simple people in power at the time. As troops had been sent into the Ingush–Ossetian conflict and the border between Chechnya and Ingushetia was not demarcated, where should they stop? ... So "with a single blow, swiftly, in two hours with a parachute regiment" and so on ...'[11] In Nazran Gaidar met a Chechen delegation headed by his opposite number Yaragi Mamodayev. Gaidar remembers that the Chechens were 'very afraid'. An agreement was reached whereby a demarcation line was drawn as a provisional border between Chechnya and Ingushetia. Both sides pulled back and the Russian hawks were restrained from doing what they eventually did two years later.

*

In 1993 the fragile political stability in Chechnya disintegrated. In January the highest-level Russian delegation yet, led by the new Nationalities Minister and Deputy Prime Minister Sergei Shakhrai, came to Grozny. They negotiated with the Speaker of the Chechen Parliament, Hussein Akhmadov, and Yusup Soslambekov, who was now Chairman of the Parliament's 'Foreign Affairs Committee'. The two sides worked out a document that was a basis for a treaty between Moscow and Grozny to be called 'on the delimitation and mutual delegation of powers'. Both sides were treated as equal partners and there was deliberate ambiguity about Chechen's international status. The protocol noted the 'vital need for a normalization of relations between the Russian Federation and the Chechen Republic in preserving a single economic, defence, information and cultural space'. The two sides were to start working on the treaty at the end of January, but the day after the meeting Dudayev condemned the idea of a treaty and said the meeting had occurred without his approval. Later he said, 'No political agreements with Russia are possible.'

Dudayev was falling out with most of his former allies. In many ways he was too much of a general to understand the intrigues raging around him. Probably he had expected that being Chechen President would be much easier than it was. Aiza Abasova, who was his aide and interpreter, remembers him on one occasion in March 1993 disconsolate and depressed. He said he had quarrelled with half his aides and did not trust the other half: 'He said, "I have no one at all. I have no one I can trust. I am the President and I cannot believe anyone!"'[12]

Lechi Umkhayev, the organizer of the first Chechen Congress, says he was offered the vice-presidency by Dudayev more than once during this period. One of their conversations lasted four hours after which Umkhayev decided he could not work with Dudayev: 'He said, "We have everything, we have nuclear weapons, we have rockets, we will fight with Russia." I said, "OK, fine, if they come we will fight, but let's talk about those problems which we will solve without fighting." In the course of four hours' conversation in his flat when Alla Dudayeva was serving us and Gantemirov and his personal guard stood watch, in the course of those four hours he could not say two sentences about his programme of normal economic activity in the republic.'[13]

There was an uncanny parallel between events in Chechnya and in Russia. Just as Yeltsin did, Dudayev fell out with a once-friendly Parliament and used violence to suppress his opposition. On 15 April the opposition openly challenged Dudayev and held a huge rally in central Grozny. On that day, Lechi Umkhayev says, Dudayev offered him the vice-presidency for the last time. When he again refused, the poet Zelimkhan Yandarbiyev was appointed Vice-President. Two days later Dudayev declared presidential rule and a curfew. He dissolved Parliament and the Town Assembly, headed by Gantemirov, who had gone over to the opposition. The next day the defiant Parliament met and voted to start impeachment proceedings against Dudayev. They also voted to make Mamodayev Prime Minister. On 19 April the Chechen Constitutional Court declared Dudayev's dissolution of Parliament unconstitutional. The court was itself dissolved on 3 June.

As in 1991, two permanent rallies formed in Grozny. The pro-Dudayev rally met on Freedom Square in front of the Presidential Palace while the opposition met in front of the Lermontov Theatre on Teatralnaya Square. The opposition said it wanted a referendum to be held on 5 June. There were to be three questions: Do you trust the Parliament? Do you trust the President? And should Chechnya be a presidential republic? Scuffles and fights broke out. Beslan Gantemirov handed out arms to the demonstrators and made his Town Assembly building available for the planned referendum. Shamil Dudayev, a nephew of the president, was killed in one clash, and a popular pro-Dudayev Member of Parliament, the physicist Isa Arsemikov, died in another.

On 4 June, the day before the opposition's referendum, Dudayev struck. Armed men led by the fighter Shamil Basayev shot up the Town Assembly building where the electoral commission was located and dispersed the demonstrators on Teatralnaya Square. At least seventeen people were killed. The opposition puts forward a figure of sixty. Whatever the real death toll, it was the first mass bloodshed in Chechnya and destroyed the hope of democratic dialogue. From now most overt opposition to Dudayev was violent. Dudayev had control of Grozny but large areas of Chechnya fell out of his control. Gantemirov retired to Urus-Martan and began plotting armed resistance to Dudayev.

The second anniversary celebrations of Independence Day in Grozny showed how bizarre independent Chechnya had become. In a military parade Dudayev had the empty cases of SS-20 missiles transported several times around Freedom Square, as if to demonstrate that he was armed with nuclear weapons. One of the guests for the independence celebrations was the Russian ultra-nationalist and presidential hopeful Vladimir Zhirinovsky. When Zhirinovsky sat down for dinner with Dudayev, Zviad Gamsakhurdia and the President of Ingushetia, Ruslan Aushev, it was dubbed 'the dinner of the four Presidents'. Zhirinovsky pleased his hosts by drinking a toast to Chechen independence.

For all his anti-Russian rhetoric, there were signs that Dudayev was actually prepared for real compromise with Moscow if only he would be the one to strike a deal and would be treated with proper respect by Moscow. In the interludes of his darkest anti-imperialist rhetoric he would suddenly allow himself positive phrases about Russia and the Soviet Union. The Soviet patriot in him was still there under the surface. 'He did not change in one thing,' comments Shamil Beno, 'in his directness and both love and hatred – paradoxical as it sounds – for the Communist system and the country to which he belonged. He hated and simultaneously loved this country, not only Chechnya but the Soviet Union.' This helps to explain Dudayev's sudden professions of friendship to Boris Yeltsin and the Russian people. During the referendum called by Yeltsin in April 1993, for example, Dudayev unexpectedly told the Moscow radio station Ekho Moskvy that he would 'not obstruct citizens of Chechnya who have not lost their Russian citizenship who want to take part in the referendum on 25 April. I too am ready to cast one vote. I have not yet lost my Russian citizenship.'[14]

Two weeks before the Russian referendum, on 11 April 1993, Dudayev sent an extraordinary telegram to Yeltsin expressing solidarity with him in his struggle against their common enemy, the Russian Supreme Soviet, and its Speaker, Ruslan Khasbulatov. Dudayev offered the advice to Yeltsin that the 'lesser of two evils' was 'the dissolution of the Supreme Soviet and the calling of elections to Parliament with the simultaneous holding of a referendum on the adoption of a new Constitution in September 1993'. Yeltsin, knowingly or not, followed Dudayev's advice almost to the letter. In September 1993 he dissolved the Supreme Soviet. In October his tanks pounded the Supreme Soviet building, the White House, into submission and Khasbulatov was thrown into prison. In December he simultaneously held new parliamentary elections and a referendum on a new constitution.

With Khasbulatov out of the way, the autumn of 1993 appeared to be a good season for compromise and the long-mooted meeting between Dudayev and Yeltsin, in which they would strike a deal on Chechnya's status. Dudayev again made overtures of friendship in an undated telegram to the Russian Prime Minister Viktor Chernomyrdin, which appears to be from the beginning of October 1993, just after the storming of the White House: 'We consider that at the current moment all the necessary conditions are at last in place for the renewal and successful conducting of negotiations with the government of Russia on a whole package of problems which concern our relations on the basis of principles of multilateral cooperation, friendship and mutual help. Moreover we do not see strategically a place for the Chechen Republic outside the single economic, political and legal space which covers the current Commonwealth of Independent States.'[15]

The meaning of the telegram beneath this Soviet-style verbiage appears to be that Dudayev was ready for compromise if a meeting could be agreed. Later Dudayev was to say that he needed only 'half an hour with Yeltsin' and all problems could be solved. In many ways the characters of the two men were more alike than either of them would care to admit. Both were impulsive, impressionable, very reliant on personal communication, quick to offence. Above all both were extremely proud. That meant that Dudayev would never agree to making concessions to anyone but Yeltsin personally. Many people believe that he would have made those concessions – but the intrigues that characterized Kremlin politics at the time never allowed a meeting to happen.

Ruslan Aushev, the famous Afghan veteran who had been elected President of Ingushetia in March 1993, appeared to be an ideal intermediary for such a meeting. As a military man and an Ingush, he enjoyed the trust of Dudayev, but he had also chosen to keep Ingushetia within the Russian Federation and remained loyal to Moscow. However, the meeting he almost arranged got cancelled:

'Dudayev was ready for a meeting with the President and the President was ready to receive him,' Aushev said over two years later. 'The only thing was to name a day when he could fly to meet him. But one of [Yeltsin's] advisers said that he should not meet with an illegally elected president. It was in December 1993. I said to the President that Dudayev will fly in on the appointed day and you can solve the controversial questions with him existing between Chechnya and Russia. I said he was ready for constructive dialogue and you can restrict his authority to a kind of special status. I was sure that Dudayev would have agreed to that, we only needed for him to come here. But someone in his entourage did not want that.'[16]

7

A Free Economic Zone

A famous fictional Russian fraudster said that he needed just one kilometre of the Russian frontier to become a millionaire. Chechnya's indeterminate status following the collapse of the Soviet Union made his dream come true. Here were more than 300 kilometres of frontier open for trading!

A short walk through the Grozny bazaar was graphic evidence that literally anything could be bought in Chechnya. It was as packed and as strictly regimented as a London department store. In the centre of the covered section the shopper could pick up Italian dresses, French perfume or Japanese electronics. Further down, at the north end of the market, were the money-changers, men with prowling eyes, holding wads of $100 bills. Nearby, on the gun traders' corner, Ruslan, an unshaven young man in a Hawaiian shirt and reflector sun-glasses, pulled from his pocket a Polaroid photograph of a pistol with a gold-inlaid handle. 'It's a Mauser we worked on specially,' said Ruslan. 'Sorry about the picture quality. The price is 6000 dollars.' Asked where he bought the gun, Ruslan answered: 'You don't have to leave the former Soviet Union to get hold of this stuff.' He said he could supply a Makarov pistol for $600 or a Kalashnikov machine gun for $500.

The business opportunities afforded by Chechnya's outlaw status were a major reason why the Dudayev regime survived as long as it did. All over the former Soviet Union the command economy had crumbled, the Communist Party's monopoly on ownership had been removed and the new elite was setting the rules of the economic game. The scope for corruption and enrichment was phenomenal and in Chechnya, outside Russia's legal and customs space, this was true ten times over. As one wing of the Russian government gradually cut Chechnya out of the official budget as part of a 'blockade' intended to break the separatist regime, other corrupt officials and businessmen were working in the opposite direction, helping Chechnya to become the former Soviet Union's biggest black market emporium.

Sergei Shakhrai, the Deputy Prime Minister dealing with Chechnya, frequently complained that it was impossible to control the Chechen 'free economic zone'. Asked how much this zone was nurtured in Moscow, Shakhrai answers unhesitatingly, 'One hundred per cent.'[1] This was sometimes quite overt – long after other ministries had pulled out of Chechnya, the Russian Foreign Trade Ministry kept a representative in Grozny. The true nature of this relationship will probably never come to light as most of the evidence, including all the oil refineries' archives, was destroyed in the bombing of Grozny.

Russia's 'blockade' cut Chechnya off from the federal budget, but only gradually. The last federal payments for pensions and salaries were given to Grozny in March 1993, and about the same time Chechnya was excluded from the central banking system. But the republic still remained fully accessible: its borders with the rest of Russia were never closed and Grozny airport handled flights to Baku and the Middle East. The effect was to make Grozny a perfect place through which to channel dirty deals. The same process happened with other 'unrecognized republics' in the former Soviet Union, which faced political isolation, such as Abkhazia and the breakaway part of Moldova, Transdnestr. Cut off from central budgets and without proper banking systems but with porous frontiers, they also became black market economies.[2]

Chechnya's official economy gradually came to a halt. In January 1992, when prices on consumer goods were freed throughout Russia, Dudayev did not follow suit and kept price controls on key goods, although Chechnya remained in the ruble zone. As a result, enterprising traders simply bought up a lot of goods in Chechnya and resold them outside its borders. For a long time Dudayev insisted that bread cost the symbolic price of one ruble, a policy which ate a large hole in the state budget. Only in July 1993, when Dudayev was away, did his government secretly put up the price. He was angry on his return but did not reverse the decision.[3]

Many people doubt Dudayev was personally corrupt – at least to begin with. His first Foreign Minister, Shamil Beno, remembers him living in down-at-heel disorder in his brother's house in Grozny in his first months in office. Eventually he acquired a house just down the road. Apart from a love of karate and smart suits, the Chechen President displayed no obvious extravagances. Dudayev was too caught up in his romantic project of Chechen independence and too much of the army officer to bother himself with personal enrichment. Many or most of his government got very rich indeed, however. A kind of clan warfare developed as to who would control what, and officials started appropriating different sections of the economy.

When suspicions arose that Yaragi Mamodayev and Beslan Gantemirov were helping themselves to a large slice of the oil revenues, Dudayev appointed the businessman Ruslan Utsiyev to be a counter-influence and his 'adviser on foreign economic relations'. Utsiyev was a talented businessman who had become a millionaire on the profits of a Moscow insurance company. He had two powerful allies in Salman Albakov, the Interior Minister, and his brother Adam, who controlled oil distribution, probably the most lucrative job in the republic. They too started living the high life. According to one story, Adam Albakov was stopped for drunken driving in the southern Russian city of Pyatigorsk and tried to give the traffic policeman a $10,000 bribe. Dudayev had in fact only exchanged one set of privateers for another.

*

Oil accounted for around two-thirds of revenue in Chechnya. It briefly kept the cash-starved official budget afloat, but it also fostered corruption on a huge scale. Oil was first discovered in Chechnya in the early nineteenth century but not extracted commercially until the 1890s. By the turn of the century Grozny was the second oil city in the Russian empire after Baku and a magnet for British and American oil workers. The Grozny oil yield gradually fell and in 1980 Chechen–Ingushetia was producing just 7.4 million tonnes of oil a year, only 1.5 per cent of Russia's output. The yield kept falling, but Grozny still kept providing the Soviet Union with a large degree of its quota of special aviation oils. More importantly, the three Grozny oil refineries meant the city remained a major refining centre, and Grozny was at the centre of a pipeline network that branched out to Kazakhstan and Siberia, Baku and the Black Sea port of Novorossiisk. In 1991 the refineries were processing 16–17 million tonnes of oil a year. About a quarter of the oil was local, the rest came from the North Caucasus and Western Siberia.

When Dudayev seized power, the Russian government announced a blockade of Chechnya and made an official decision to shut down oil deliveries. However, Moscow kept on sending oil to the refineries in 1992 and 1993. The official reason for this was that the deliveries could only be reduced gradually because the rest of the North Caucasus was supplied with fuel from Grozny and could not be cut off; so exports to Stavropol ceased only in August 1993 and to Dagestan in November 1994, one month before the war began.

This decision meant that ample oil revenues kept coming in to independent Chechnya, making a mockery of the officially proclaimed Russian blockade. Moreover, after the middle of 1992 the trade was entirely unmonitored by Moscow because Chechnya was outside the Russian banking system. Officially 23 million tonnes of oil were exported from Chechnya between 1991 and 1994, mainly through the Black Sea ports. According to one estimate, the profits to be made on sale of oil from Chechnya in 1993 were $800–900 million.

Possibly the oil trade was bigger than advertised. That was the conclusion of the Russian parliamentary commission on Chechnya, which reported that more oil than was recorded in the official quotas was actually being refined in Grozny.[4] In other cases the murky status of Chechnya was a cover for dirty business elsewhere in Russia. According to Valery Draganov, Deputy Chairman of the State Customs Committee, 'Chechnya was used not only for the export of oil but more than that – as a cover for illegal Russian operations. In a series of cases oil was exported from eastern regions of Russia but according to the documents it was registered as having come from Chechnya.'[5]

The Grozny government used the money to keep the budget afloat and to try to attract foreign investment with oil swap deals. There were also barter deals with Ukraine for metals and Estonia for butter, but a lot of the money did not get back to the budget at all. In 1992, when the Chechen press and parliamentary debate were still relatively free, the findings of a parliamentary commission into the oil business were published in the newspaper *Ichkeria*. The newspaper tabled the sale of 3.5 million tonnes of oil for which no money at all had been received by the budget. Government officials were simply putting their personal signatures to oil sales to individual clients and a large cut of each sale was presumably coming back to the signatory concerned. Powerful interests made sure the full truth did not emerge: an oil industry official working with the parliamentary commission, Gennady Sanko, was murdered in the street on 12 March 1993.

Towards the end of Dudayev's time in power, the Chechen oil system was breaking down completely. Oil was syphoned from the Chechen pipelines and stolen. Private deals were struck by junior oil officials. Equipment was stolen from the refineries. According to Timur Muzayev, the political analyst: 'At first there was centralized distribution. Dudayev signed everything. Gradually it went to smaller officials, lower and lower. At the end everyone had started to steal.'

*

Oil was just one item among many being traded in this fantastic customs-free zone. Chechnya also became a centre of the arms trade. Small arms were freely available in Chechnya and could be bought openly at the bazaar. Larger weapons, it seems, were only slightly more difficult to obtain. One witness tells the story of sitting in Dudayev's outer office when a man appeared with two heavy plastic bags. 'Do you want to look inside?' he said. There were $2 million in new dollar bills still shrink-wrapped from an American bank. This, apparently, was the payment for an arms deal.

It was a period when rogue elements in the Russian armed forces were selling off weapons and it is logical to presume that the former Soviet general-turned-president Dudayev was buying. Only one source of arms sales to Chechnya has been pinpointed – the Estonian firm Koneston.[6] Dudayev's former miltiary colleague in Tartu, Ants Laaneots, hints that this was not an isolated case, however. For three years Chechen transport planes flew back and forth from Chechnya to Estonia, he said, with heavy cargoes on board. 'What goods we won't say, eh?' he adds.

The deals with Russia are still murkier. Dmitry Kholodov, an investigative reporter for the Moscow daily newspaper *Moskovsky Komsomolets*, was following up one line of enquiry. He had collected documents on the disappearance of arms from the notoriously corrupt Western Group of Forces stationed in Germany and headed by Matvei Burlakov, an old crony of Pavel Grachev, the Defence Minister. Kholodov also spent a lot of time in Chechnya. He was killed by a booby-trapped bomb in a suitcase on 17 October 1994. His killers have not been caught.

Dudayev's Chechnya was a mafioso's dream. Many of them could not care less about politics or Chechen independence and if they backed Dudayev it was because he was the gamekeeper who kept the Russians out and let them get on with their own business. Once Chechnya became independent these spivs and crooks moved to Grozny and flaunted their luxury cars on the mountain roads. Once the war started most of the cars disappeared, although one patriotic Chechen tried to sell his Rolls-Royce to a group of Western journalists to raise money for the war effort and was disappointed when there were no takers.

For obvious reasons 'the Chechen mafia' is an understudied phenomenon. Little is known about its members, apart from a half-dozen flamboyant godfathers, but Chechens certainly had the strongest ethnic mafia in Moscow for their size. The leaders were all in their thirties and forties, members of the rootless post-deportations generation and exceptionally disciplined and ruthless. The peak of their influence was the first two years after the collapse of the Soviet Union, when they were also sustained by the safe haven of independent Chechnya. In Moscow Chechens still control several big hotels, the second-hand car market and drug rings, and Chechen businessmen of dubious provenance are still linked to the city government of the mayor, Yury Luzhkov.

Some mafiosi did invest in politics. The most famous, Suleiman 'Khoza', who made a fortune in stolen cars, was a friend of the gangster Ruslan Labazanov and close to the anti-Dudayev opposition. 'Khoza' was murdered in Moscow in December 1994. Khozh-Akhmed Nukhayev, head of the Lazanskaya gang based in Moscow's Lazania Restaurant, was close to the Dudayev government. Zelimkhan Yandarbiyev appointed the fabulously wealthy Nukhayev, who divides his time between Grozny, Moscow and Turkey, First Deputy Prime Minister in his government in the autumn of 1996.

Chechen mafiosi artfully exploited Chechnya's ambiguous status to make the republic a big centre for the famous bank frauds of 1992. This was the case of the so-called *avizo* promissory notes from the Russian banking system. It was discovered that by bribing bank officials or forging promissory notes it was possible to get a spurious slip of paper in one part of the former Soviet Union and cash it in in another for huge amounts of money. The practice was especially rife in Chechnya, and some Chechen *avizovshchiki* brought home literally lorry-loads of rubles. The Central Bank only managed to stop the practice in July 1992 by re-regulating its payments system, but by then the damage to the state was estimated at trillions of rubles. One Chechen gang netted 60 billion rubles (then worth $700 million) in the biggest bank fraud in Russian history.

Meanwhile, ordinary people lived off the scraps that were left over from this mass plunder. Not much of the immense wealth earned by some Chechens trickled back to the mountain villages and the collapse of the official economy forced ordinary Chechens to turn to trade, something that had traditionally always been despised in a society of horsemen and farmers. Now widespread poverty, lack of government regulation and the customs-free borders soon conspired to create a whole new class of traders making their money from 'shop tours'.

The scheme went as follows: a group of individuals formed a 'tour company' and leased an aeroplane, often from Ukraine or Azerbaijan; they then advertised for customers and flew them to Turkey, the Middle East, even as far as China. The 'shuttles', as the traders were known, would buy up consumer goods, bring them back to Grozny, dodging Russian customs, and resell them in the Grozny market, undercutting average Russian prices by about a third. The tour company paid dues to Grozny airport of about $20,000 a month and cleared the way with Russian air traffic control, presumably for bribes. Once out of Russian airspace, the flights were the responsibility of the country receiving them.

About two flights a day left Grozny airport on these tours. An advertisement in the government newspaper *Ichkeria* in 1994 offered trips to Dubai, Iran and Syria with a firm called Mona

Lisa. 'In the Emirates you will be met and seen off by our representatives,' the firm announced. 'They will help you buy the goods you need, make business contacts,' the advertisement said. The cost of a week-long trip was $400 plus 150,000 rubles, with the first 50 kilograms of luggage transported free.

In 1994 as much as half the adult population had something to do with the 'shop tours' business. Khalik and Malika, a brother and sister in their twenties, were trained oil engineers but had been forced into the shop tour business by the slump in the oil industry. They now bought and resold electronic goods, mainly from Dubai, in a kiosk in the market. Khalik said he could buy a Shivaki television set for $230 and resell it for $300. 'Some of them are probably not the best quality,' he said with a laugh. 'Not all our buyers know that of course.'

The 'shop tour' business shored up the Chechen economy, and the whole of the North Caucasus descended on the 'big bazaar' in Grozny. The Chechen government earned no customs duties from the trade but it softened the wrath of the population and kept ordinary people from destitution. The Russian government knew it was losing millions of dollars in lost customs duties but it also calculated that the business was easing poverty in the North Caucasus, one of the poorest and most heavily subsidized regions of Russia.

*

In 1992 President Dudayev had ambitious plans to circumvent the Russian economy and do business deals abroad. Even as the economic situation in Chechnya deteriorated, he talked more and more about making the republic a 'second Kuwait'. Americans expressed business interests in Chechnya despite the objections of Moscow. According to one Dudayev aide, half a dozen Texan oil experts came to Grozny in the spring of 1992. However, a certain William Andersen III from the American Embassy in Moscow flew down to meet them and persuaded them to go home.

In the autumn of 1992 Dudayev went to America and, after marathon all-night discussions, signed a $200 million deal with the Texan company EnForce. EnForce would provide oil equipment in return for crude oil and dollars. There was talk about building a huge new oil complex in Grozny to house 200 American workers, but the political instability in Chechnya in 1993 meant the deal fell through.[7]

Dudayev's trips to Britain, France and Germany were commercially motivated. He went to London in October 1992, accompanied by his wife Alla, his new Foreign Minister Shamsudin Yusef and his English-speaking foreign trade adviser Eduard Khachukayev. Dudayev stayed at the Dorchester Hotel and had a number of meetings with businessmen and politicians. He went to the House of Commons, where his hosts were Den Dover, the Conservative MP for Chorley, and Gerrard Neale, another former Conservative MP. Dover had links with the construction industry and saw possibilities for business in Chechnya.[8]

The London trip had a lurid sequel that exposed the criminalized connections of the Dudayev regime. Ruslan Utsiyev, Dudayev's 'economic adviser', and his younger brother, the twenty-one-year-old Nazarbek, arrived in the capital around the same time as Dudayev and stayed on for several months. They first stayed at the Royal Lancaster Hotel before buying a luxury penthouse flat in Birkenhall Mansions in Marylebone for £750,000 in cash. The brothers lived a riotous lifestyle and brought home expensive call-girls. Harrods delivery vans came to the door with pricey furniture and gym equipment for Nazarbek.

Ruslan Utsiyev was nominally in London to sign eight contracts with the reputable British firm Thomas de la Rue. The contracts were for new banknotes, passports, coins, medals and lottery tickets for Chechnya. He also began negotiating a £173 million loan-for-oil deal with the American Joseph Ripp, a convicted fraudster with links to the Mafia.[9] On 26 and 28 February 1993, first Ruslan and then Nazarbek were found dead, one in his bedroom, the other packed into a large fridge freezer. Both had been shot. Two Armenians, one of whom had been working as their interpreter, were arrested. One of the Armenians later hanged himself in his cell.

The reason for the Utsiyevs' murders has never been pinpointed. The Chechen authorities alleged they were murdered on Russian orders to scupper the passports and currency contracts. Others said the Armenians had been trying to stop the brothers selling Stinger missiles to Armenia's regional enemy, Azerbaijan. The former wrestler Salman Khasmikov, who became head of Dudayev's security service, the DGB, had a third explanation; he told the investigative reporter Andrew Jennings he thought the murders were linked to oil sales and the murder of the oil official Gennady Sanko: 'I believe the murders of the Utsiyev brothers and Sanko were all links in one chain. If there had been proper accountability of our oil sales, these killings would not have happened. Sanko was killed by the very people involved in the theft of the nation's oil wealth.' Later Dmitry Krikoryants, a Grozny-based journalist who had helped Jennings investigate the story, was murdered too.

Whatever the motive for the killings, the revelations about the Utsiyev murders made Dudayev's regime a pariah state overnight. The deaths spawned lurid newspaper stories about the 'mafia state' or 'the land where the gun is king'. One Chechen observed bitterly: 'It was as though they had murdered half of London and not been murdered themselves.'

The Thomas de la Rue deal was called off. The loss of the contract cost the Chechen government several million dollars which they had already paid up front and the Chairman of the Central Bank, Usman Imayev, decided to try to recover the money. Imayev was an ambitious Moscow-educated interpreter, who was then only thirty-five. One of the few Chechens to work abroad, he studied Spanish and Portuguese and worked as a trade representative in Angola. He set off for London alone. When he arrived, Thomas de la Rue refused to see him. Then, he says, he used the threat of the press and legal action to force a meeting. The firm finally agreed to pay what was owing to the Chechen government and was even forced to add on a hefty fine for cancellation of contract. Imayev was given a Barclays Bank cheque for $8,108,112.

He tells the story with a mixture of self-deprecation and Chechen panache. After receiving the money, Imayev spent a sleepless night in his hotel holding the cheque, thinking about the Utsiyevs' murders and wondering how to get it back to Grozny: 'In the morning I came out of my hotel. I didn't see anybody, but as a Russian I felt that someone was breathing down my neck . . . I was carrying a large sum. Imagine, I am carrying a cheque for eight million dollars and three months ago two Chechens were murdered in London. My nerves lasted out till lunch-time. At twelve o'clock in the hotel I booked a ticket to France, then my helper from the law firm rang and ordered a ticket for Istanbul. And in actual fact I went to the airport and bought a ticket to Germany, to Munich, so they didn't know where I was going. I went to Munich. I waited literally two hours, and from there I went on to Istanbul.[10]

In Istanbul Imayev found a 'shop tour' flight back to Grozny. Arriving home, he presented the cheque personally into the hands of President Dudayev, who had completely run out of budget funds. The next headache was banking the cheque. First Imayev went to Switzerland, where he was not allowed to open an account; finally he found a bank in Turkey willing to accept it.

On another trip to Istanbul in September Imayev managed to withdraw $4 million in cash for a 1 per cent 'commission'. Chechnya's Central Banker then travelled back to Grozny with his hoard of cash on an ordinary shuttle flight full of tourists: 'I took all the money, four million dollars, in a cardboard box used for household soap. I put two million in each of two boxes. The boxes were dirty and I carelessly kicked them across the floor of the airport. I was rather disreputably dressed as I went through the hall, that's what I agreed with the lads. I arrived back and it saved the situation. One million went on workers in the oil industry, one million went to pensioners, one million went to the budget, one million was kept in reserve.'

8

A Small Victorious War

In August 1994 Chechnya had turned into a Shakespearean kingdom – armed groups roamed the country at will and there were no fixed borders or front lines.

Moscow believed the death-throes of the Dudayev regime had begun, but it seemed to have a little life left in it. In Grozny on 3 August a lone armoured car stood in front of the Presidential Palace and a few armed men milled about. The lazy atmosphere was in contrast to the triumphant declarations about Chechnya pouring out of Russian television. The day before, Moscow had finally declared its public support for the opposition. The opposition group the Provisional Council had declared Dudayev's regime overthrown and that from henceforth it was the only legitimate authority in Chechnya.

Dudayev was sitting in his office on the ninth floor of the Presidential Palace, flanked by the symbols of his bid for independence – the green, white and red Chechen flag and a bound Koran. On the wall was a full-length portrait of Sheikh Mansur holding a curved *kinzhal*. As ever, Dudayev, dressed in a neat grey suit, bore himself proudly in military manner and radiated energy. 'All is calm,' he said. He was angry but also delighted. After all, what he had been saying for three years was now coming true before his eyes – Moscow-backed forces were actively seeking to destroy him.

It was more a monologue than a conversation. Dudayev started on a theme and then wandered off in improvisation, enjoying the melody of his words. He talked about a Turkish tiger cub he had been given, called Raja. 'He is three months old, he has real claws so that we are fighting a tiger,' he said. Only progressively did he come to the subject in hand. What did he make of the pronouncements coming out of Moscow? 'Lies, threats, blackmail, lies,' he lilted.

Dudayev predicted quite plausibly a gradual escalation in plans to overthrow him. 'For the third year Russia is fighting a war with us,' he said. 'The idea is clear. A terrorist act against me and then it gets turned up a notch: passions at rallies, a strike by oil workers, riots in Grozny. Then the farce of holding a congress in the Nadterechny Region is played out because they cannot hold one in Grozny. That is the selection which will probably be used in different combinations.'

The Chechen President liked producing an effect on his listeners and it was hard to tell how much his fanatical statements were an act, an imitation of demonic anger, or the real thing. On this occasion, coming away from the interview, it was hard to convey anything but the impression of a man possessed. His declarations were a deliberate mirror-image of everything that was said in Moscow. In Russia they accused the Chechens of banditry and organized crime. Here it was the other way round: 'They have trained bandits of all nationalities – Koreans, Karelians, professional criminals.' In Moscow people were suggesting Dudayev was crazy, but he turned the accusation round on Yeltsin: 'If God wants to damage a person who has offended him, imagine what happens if that person is head of a major state.'

The Provisional Council were also dismissed as madmen: 'Today or tomorrow if Russia continues to support these paranoid people one of them will declare himself President of Russia, another Emperor of Japan,' he said with a high-pitched laugh. He began listing his enemies. The list had got very long and now ranged from Khasbulatov to Zavgayev to Khajiev to Mamodayev to Gantemirov to Avturkhanov.

Outbursts like this were part of the reason Moscow found it so hard to talk to Dudayev. Sometimes, when he softened his tone, the demands he was asking for seemed quite acceptable. But then the flights of fantasy, the accusations and the threats persuaded Kremlin politicians they could not talk to him.

Dudayev was unpopular in Chechnya by now, but not as unpopular as might have been supposed. He was still able to catch the mood of many Chechens and to address their fears of Russia. In the streets of Grozny people were angry at the presumption of the Provisional Council claiming power. Nurli, a pilot, was walking through the bazaar. 'His position is much weaker,' he said of Dudayev. 'People are fed up, especially in the villages, but they don't like hearing on TV that someone is claiming power.' He added: 'I don't like the mess we're in but I don't want Russia to come in and impose order.'

The opposition to Dudayev was scattered and disorganized – an assortment of ex-Communists, intellectuals and gangsters; some had been plotting against the Chechen President for years, others had worked with Dudayev and fallen out with him. They had virtually nothing in common except a desire to get rid of the existing regime.

Two hours to the north of Grozny in the dusty plains by the River Terek, Umar Avturkhanov, a former policeman, had set up the headquarters of his Provisional Council in the old Party offices in the village of Znamenskoye in the Nadterechny Region adjoining Russia. This was the man who had declared that he was claiming power and was the 'only legitimate authority' now in Chechnya, but if this was the beginning of an attempt to overthrow Dudayev, it was unimpressive. By Chechen standards the crowd of armed men jostling each other outside the Provisional Council headquarters was tiny.

The ex-Party headquarters was one of thousands of such buildings across the former Soviet Union, a two-storey concrete box with bare walls and plywood furniture. Avturkhanov was a lean, angular man with thick charcoal eyebrows and a ponderous, extremely cautious manner. 'Was he prepared to use force to oust

Dudayev?' we asked him. He said no: 'The conditions have been
created as never before to resolve the Chechen issue without an
invasion from outside.' Avturkhanov did his best to sound
conciliatory on every subject, even Chechen independence, which
he said should be decided by a referendum. He did have weapons,
he conceded, but they were purely to defend the Provisional
Council against attacks by Dudayev: 'We have enough equipment
and arms to defend what we've won.'

What was Avturkhanov's main strategy then? Money, came
the answer. He had just come from Moscow with two billion
rubles of Russian budget money owed to the local population in
pensions and salaries that had not been paid for three years. Two
old women in the street outside the opposition headquarters said
this was what they wanted to hear. 'We've just recently been
paid. Things are good for us now that Avturkhanov is helping
us,' said Fatima. 'My mother just got her pension for January and
February,' said Roza. 'It makes no difference if we have Avturkhanov or Dudayev as long as we're getting money.'

Avturkhanov was conspicuous among the politicians on the
Dudayev side for making thoughtful statements and avoiding
words like 'genocide', but behind the cautious phrasing there
soon turned out to be a hidden agenda, a thrust for power that
was as brutal as anyone's. As we stood outside, the dust swirled
up in the field next to the Provisional Council building as a
military helicopter rattled in to land. It attracted a wave of
curious onlookers and village children and the tracksuited
gunmen staked around the field whooped cheers of welcome. The
camouflaged man who got out, they said, was a 'colonel'. This
was the clue to what the Provisional Council stood for: it was
Russia's new front line in Chechnya.

*

In another part of the Chechen battlefield sat Ruslan Labazanov,
a gunman who affected to despise Avturkhanov but also wanted

to kill Dudayev. Visiting Labazanov was an education in how a Chechen gangster lived – crime, politics and business all blended together seamlessly.

Labazanov had been a leading member of Dudayev's body-guard. He had been driven out of Grozny and had sworn blood revenge against the President, and was now hiding out with three dozen fighters at his mother's house in the town of Argun, only 10 miles out on the road east. In the compound of Labazanov's house there were a couple of jeeps and knots of unshaven men in denim jackets and camouflage fatigues lolling about. They had rocket-launchers and machine-guns and were eating soup. Some wore black bands on their arms to signify that they were involved in a blood feud, but their main inspiration appeared to be Jean-Claude Van Damme and Arnold Schwarzenegger. In the front room a group of fighters were squashed up on a sofa watching a loud war video called *Triple Blow*.

Labazanov himself was stretched out on his bed barefoot and playing with a pistol between his bandaged toes. He was clearly weapon-mad – moving back the stool you were sitting on sent dozens of rounds of ammunition suddenly slithering on to the floor. He was also very rich. A fighter came in and whispered something to him. He lazily took out a thick wad of 100-dollar bills, peeled off fifteen of them and gave them to the supplicant.

Labazanov was twenty-seven and a convicted murderer. In August 1991 during the chaos of the collapse of the Communist regime in Grozny, he sprang himself from jail and formed an instant gang from his fellow-escapees. Later he went to work in Dudayev's Presidential Guard and Dudayev called him 'my little bandit'. He liked to compare himself to Robin Hood and rode around Grozny in an armoured car, ostentatiously doling out money to destitute Russian pensioners.

When he talked about his quarrel with Dudayev, Labazanov's blue eyes grew dull and he rattled out five- or ten-word answers: 'We had good normal relations, then Dudayev spoiled it all.' In the early hours of the morning of 13 June 1994 Dudayev sent in a column of men and armoured cars to wipe out Labazanov's base in an apartment block in the east of the city. The two sides pounded each other with all the weaponry they had, paying no regard to the residents of the densely populated area. Labazanov escaped the firefight, but later that day someone grotesquely exhibited in a Grozny square three severed heads of his dead fighters, one of them his cousin Arbi. He swore a blood feud against Dudayev and launched a war by video, distributing tapes about how Dudayev had become a dictator.

Labazanov was a gangster pure and simple who later calmly traded in his threats to fight for Chechen independence and started working with the Russian intelligence services. He was interested in one thing only, killing Dudayev. All the rest was empty talk. 'If Hitler came and said he was here to help the Chechen people we would welcome him,' said Labazanov.

Back in Moscow there was one more piece in the opposition puzzle. The former Prime Minister Yaragi Mamodayev had settled into a two-floor suite at the top of the Intourist Hotel just along the corridor from a popular Tex-Mex restaurant. He sat at the top of a little spiral staircase, barely squeezed into a large suit. He was about forty, but already balding and running to fat. Mamodayev's business card said 'Prime Minister of the Chechen Republic, Grozny' but gave no address or telephone number. He liked to remind visitors that he had been elected by Parliament and was therefore the only legally elected official in the opposition. Others pointed out that Mamodayev had no party and that his 'Government of National Trust' did not extend beyond his Moscow hotel room.

Mamodayev was cynical about both Dudayev and the new Provisional Council. Both of them, he said, were playing games with Russia's new imperial policy – Dudayev was gambling on being a national hero by playing up the Russian threat, and the opposition was cooperating with Moscow to make that threat real. Mamodayev quoted General Yermolov to the effect that Russia was hoping for the help of 'one Chechen' in order to subdue the North Caucasus. 'They have found their one Chechen who represents no one but himself,' he said, referring to Umar Avturkhanov.

*

In the New Year of 1994 Kremlin politicans were exasperated that the rebel regime in Chechnya had lasted so long, but they also had more and more grounds to believe that Chechnya might be 'solved' by the end of the year. The Kremlin signed a power-sharing treaty with Russia's only other rebel region, Tatarstan, in February after two years of negotiations, which gave the Tatars broad economic and political rights but kept them within the federation. A change in the political tide had freed President Yeltsin's ability to conduct policy the autumn before when he had literally destroyed the federal parliament and had had his bitterest political opponents, Khasbulatov and Rutskoi, thrown into jail. Yeltsin had then held elections to a new parliament, and forced through a new constitution that gave him strongly enhanced presidential powers. The Kremlin was now the only centre of major policy-making in Moscow.

Many people believed at the time that Chechnya would sort itself out if only Moscow was patient. Yegor Gaidar lists the arguments for this in the spring of 1994: 'Khasbulatov was no longer in high office and no longer had opportunities for dialogue and manipulation from his side – oil deliveries had been cut off, Russian authority had been consolidated, the conflicts between different branches of power were no longer possible, Dudayev's regime had sunk to its lowest level of popularity and was beginning to collapse before our eyes, people were running from Dudayev, Dudayev no longer controlled the situation in Chechnya and naturally there were attempts on his part to start negotiations. What was so distressing was that in 1994 there was the chance to bring a gradual settlement of the problem on a plate. And at this moment the most crude and unforgivable mistakes were made.'

Despite the gradual changes, many Moscow politicians were impatient for the Dudayev regime to fall as soon as possible and ideally by the end of the year. Presidential elections were now only two years away and Boris Yeltsin's popularity rating was below 10 per cent. The old opposition had been replaced by a new threat – the rise of the extreme nationalist Vladimir Zhirinovsky, who had won the largest share of the vote in the December 1993 parliamentary elections. Zhirinovsky's victory shifted Russian politics to the right; it put on the agenda the issue of a revivalist Russia and 'defence' of ethnic Russians living outside Russia itself, and it coincided with an upsurge of racism in Moscow against 'people of Caucasian nationality'. Chechens, Georgians, Armenians and Azerbaijanis were routinely harassed by the police. Some Kremlin advisers reasoned that a decisive strike against the Chechens would steal the nationalist vote from Zhirinovsky.

There were also geopolitical reasons to sort out Chechnya. A multi-billion-dollar deal to exploit new oil fields in the Caspian Sea was due to be signed in Azerbaijan in 1995 by an international oil consortium that included the Russian firm Lukoil. There were a number of pipeline routes that could take the oil to the West and all were problematic. The least costly route was to the Russian Black Sea port of Novorossiisk down an existing pipeline, which unfortunately went through Chechnya – another reason to bring the rebel republic to heel.

One more factor was probably even more important for top politicians: the man who sorted out Chechnya, Russia's trickiest political issue, would earn high political laurels. He could become Boris Yeltsin's heir apparent or win high office. Yeltsin ran the Kremlin on a 'divide-and-rule' principle, allowing different factions to lobby him with different policies. This old Soviet political tactic of playing off one group against another ensured maximum loyalty from courtiers who were always anxious about their own future. It also meant that there were almost as many Chechen policies as there were presidential advisers. On the liberal wing was a team of academics and analysts such as Emil Pain and Arkady Popov, who had a professional knowledge of the North Caucasus. Their first premise was that force must on all accounts be avoided to solve ethnic problems. Their idea in 1994 was to make the north of Chechnya a 'shop window' by supplying the pro-Moscow administration in the Nadterechny Region with the money it was due from the Russian budget. Schools would be opened, pensions and salaries paid. After a suitable lapse of time – up to two years – the rest of the Chechen population would reject independence and poverty and beg to be reunited with Russia. 'The task was to give people a choice. Here is a school, a hospital, some kind of civilization, while outside this region is destruction, cholera, and so on. So that was the straightforward idea,' said Pain.[1]

The professionalism of men like Pain was matched only by their lack of political weight. Other more influential figures were itching to deal with Chechnya sooner. There was one lightning-rod of contention – should Dudayev be invited to meet Boris Yeltsin? Some, like Vladimir Shumeiko, the Speaker of the upper house of Parliament, the Federation Council, openly said that Yeltsin should acknowledge Dudayev as the legitimate leader of Chechnya and hold talks with him. Others were strongly against a meeting with Dudayev, most notably the Nationalities Minister Sergei Shakhrai, who was the most influential voice on Chechen policy in early 1994. Shakhrai had been one of Yeltsin's chief strategists since 1991 and had helped him find a way out of more than one tricky political situation. Short and swarthy, with a sharp legal mind and hard black eyes, Shakhrai came from a Cossack family from the village of Soldatskaya in the Russian plains north of Chechnya. His ancestors had helped build Grozny in the early nineteenth century. Shakhrai was by no means a hawk and tried different tactics on Chechnya, but he was unmovable on two issues. He strongly opposed what he called the 'virus of separatism' and was implacably against any concessions to Chechen demands for secession; and he insisted that Yeltsin should on no account meet an illegally elected leader.

In February 1994 Ruslan Khasbulatov returned to complicate Moscow's Chechen policy. Under an amnesty passed in the State Duma, all the leaders of the parliamentary resistance to Yeltsin from the previous autumn were freed from prison. Khasbulatov immediately returned home to Chechnya, where he was greeted by crowds of thousands as a national hero and martyr. His triumphant progress through Chechnya worried Yeltsin and Dudayev equally and members of the Kremlin inner circle grew alarmed at the prospect of Khasbulatov, Yeltsin's *bête noire*, seeking a route back to power through Chechnya.

Fear of Khasbulatov's ambitions in Chechnya was a spur for those who wanted Yeltsin to meet Dudayev and reach an agreement that way. Yeltsin appeared to heed their words. On 22 March the Kremlin announced that there would be a Russian–Chechen summit, then the presidential Press Secretary, Vyacheslav Kostikov, said that Yeltsin had agreed to meet Dudayev. Yeltsin still dithered and on 23 May a presidential spokesman said a meeting was still 'being discussed'. Four days later a meeting looked out of the question once again. As Dudayev was driving through Grozny with his wife and son and a group of top officials, a car packed with explosives blew up on their route. Two top police officials and their driver were killed. Dudayev emerged unhurt but fulminating against Russia. On 1 June he imposed a curfew in Grozny and, in a statement bizarre even by his standards, accused the Kremlin of planning to stage a nuclear explosion over Chechnya.

Despite this, Yeltsin was still thinking about a meeting, and on 10 June he told the President of Tatarstan, Mintimer Shaimiyev, that he was still ready to negotiate with Dudayev. But after the car bomb, Dudayev's position had hardened. In an interview relayed on Russian television the quick-tempered Dudayev referred to Yeltsin as a 'drunkard'. This was the last straw. In Shakhrai's words: 'Dudayev simply insulted the President, called him a sick man, an alcoholic. After that a personal meeting again failed to happen.'[2]

Other Chechen lobbyists now seized their chance. Avturkhanov had been touring the offices of Moscow officials trying to drum up more support for his Provisional Council. Eventually he found two patrons. One was Sergei Filatov, President Yeltsin's moderate Chief of Staff, the other was Shakhrai. Shakhrai was losing favour with Yeltsin and had lost his job as Nationalities Minister on 16 May although he stayed on as Deputy Prime Minister with some responsibility for Chechnya.

The man appointed to succeed Shakhrai as Nationalities Minister was a fateful choice. Nikolai Yegorov was a Cossack-born former collective farm boss from the traditionally conservative Krasnodar Region north-west of Chechnya. As governor of Krasnodar Region he was an implacable hardliner who had refused to register any refugees from the conflicts of the Caucasus in his region. The thickset Yegorov was a protégé of two increasingly important men: Yeltsin's chief bodyguard, friend and closest confidant, Alexander Korzhakov, and the conservative No. 2 in the government, the inscrutable Oleg Soskovets. They thrust Yegorov forward as a new regional super-boss. His staff in the Nationalities Ministry was expanded and he was given a direct telephone line to Yeltsin. Yegorov too liked the idea of backing the anti-Dudayev Provisional Council. And his imperial cast of mind meant that he was categorically against negotiating with Dudayev.[3]

*

The conflict in Chechnya started imperceptibly. First, Moscow supplied the opposition with a few arms, then stepped up support with the delivery of helicopters and tanks. Next, Russian service-men were recruited to help the opposition. Finally, the army was sent in. The failure of each successive stage might have persuaded the strategists in Moscow to abandon military methods altogether, but instead they escalated the armed strategy. There was no sign that the process had been thought through. 'Russia in general got drawn into all conflicts. First there were actions, then decisions,' said Emil Pain.

On 28 July 1994 four hijackers seized a bus near the town of Mineralniye Vody in the North Caucasus. They demanded $15 million in ransom and two helicopters to flee to Chechnya. When a special police unit tried to raid the bus and one of the hijackers detonated a grenade, five women hostages and one hijacker died. It was the fourth hijacking incident involving people from or trying to flee to Chechnya in seven months and it was more proof that Chechnya was a haven for criminals. The official media began a propaganda blitz on the evils of the Chechen regime. A police official showed a photograph of the three severed heads of Labazanov's gang exhibited in the Grozny square in June – except that he said they were the heads of Russian police officers. On 2 August television broadcasts led with the news that the Pro-visional Council had declared that Dudayev had been 'removed from office' and that it was now the only legitimate organ of power in Chechnya. Avturkhanov, given plenty of airtime to put forward his views, said he had the support of 80 per cent of the Chechen population.

This was the start of an autumn campaign in which the Russians tried to use the Chechen opposition to overthrow Dudayev. The official position in Moscow was to treat it as an 'internal Chechen matter'. The model was two other Caucasian republics, Azerbaijan and Georgia, where in 1992 two anti-Moscow presidents had successfully been overthrown with covert Russian help, while Moscow officially stayed on the sidelines. On 11 August Yeltsin conceded that Moscow had an 'influence' on the Chechen opposition but he was absolutely categorical that there would be no Russian military intervention. 'Armed intervention is impermissible and must not be done. Were we to apply pressure of force against Chechnya, the whole Caucasus would rise up and there would be such turmoil and blood that no one would ever forgive us. It is absolutely impossible,' Yeltsin said in unusually perspicacious comments. He went on: 'However, the situation in Chechnya is now changing. The role of the opposition to Dudayev is increasing. So I would not say that we are not having any influence at all.'

The two Russian institutions exerting this 'influence' on the opposition were the Nationalities Ministry, supposedly responsible for regional policy and Russia's ethnic minorities, under its new minister, Yegorov, and the counter-intelligence service, the FSK. Different federal security structures were more interested in working against each other than coordinating their tactics, and the operations in Chechnya were kept secret from the Defence Ministry. Boris Gromov, the Deputy Defence Minister, later complained that he learned about what was going on in Chechnya from the media. 'Where did they acquire all of that [equipment]?' he asked rhetorically. 'Maybe the helicopters flew in from Brazil? I, who was Deputy Defence Minister, do not know this.'[4]

Moscow's troubleshooter on the ground was the Deputy Nationalities Minister Alexander Kotenkov, an old Yeltsin loyalist and an ex-colonel, who had served in the 'political organs' of the Soviet army, teaching Communist Party propaganda.[5] From his base in Mozdok just across the border from Chechnya, Kotenkov flew around by helicopter ferrying equipment and large bags of cash to different Chechen opposition groups. Dmitry Balburov of *Moscow News* remembers him landing in Znamenskoye by helicopter in September: 'He personally flew in for a personal conversation with Avturkhanov for five minutes and then flew off again. They obviously didn't trust conversations by telephone.' The FSK, the successor to the domestic arm of the

KGB, was for obvious reasons less conspicuous, but it supplied Avturkhanov with six permanent guards and kept an office in his Provisional Council building.

There was one big flaw at the heart of the policy of supporting the Provisional Council: Avturkhanov, a middle-ranking police-man who had spent most of his career in Georgia, was a person without any standing in Chechnya. Chechen society respects ancient family roots and big achievements – Avturkhanov had neither.

One Chechen did have that commanding authority in society, but he lacked what Avturkhanov had: the trust of the Kremlin. After his spell in prison, Khasbulatov had added authority in his homeland because no one could accuse him of being a stooge of the Kremlin. On 8 August he again muddied the waters of Chechen politics and returned to his homeland. Wherever he went, rallies of tens of thousands of people turned out to listen to him. He met most of the influential people in the republic, except Dudayev but including – if he is to be believed – top Dudayev officials such as the security chief Sultan Geliskhanov. The Dudayev regime was visibly worried. Khasbulatov said that he had come as a 'peacemaker' and soon set up a 'peacemaking mission' with a group of Muslim clerics in the village of Tolstoy-Yurt, north of Grozny. Most people believed this was just a cover for a bid for power: Khasbulatov now says the Kremlin was terrified of him coming to power. 'They were very afraid that Khasbulatov would come to power in the republic. I think that's why they started this war, out of fear that Khasbulatov would come to power.'[6]

Interestingly, the Chechen policy-maker Shakhrai shares the same view and believes the war might have been averted if his Kremlin colleagues had bitten the bullet and acknowledged that their old enemy Khasbulatov was capable of bringing down Dudayev: 'On 25 August 1994 there was a chance to take power from Dudayev in Grozny in a peaceful way, when Khasbulatov called a rally of 100,000 people and we had to do just one thing – recognize Khasbulatov in Moscow. I spoke at a press conference and said that what is important for Moscow is not a name, but a figure who can in one way or another keep Chechnya in the Russian Federation. This figure is now Khasbulatov. We have to keep up a dialogue with him, we have to attract him to this. I immediately received a memo from the first aide of the President [Viktor Ilyushin] that "Yegorov has been appointed instead of you and you are forbidden to talk about Chechnya, do anything about Chechnya, be involved in this business." '7

So most Russian aid continued to be channelled to Avturkhanov and to Dudayev's former paramilitary leader, Gantemirov, and Khasbulatov, the most credible opposition figure, remained in the background. In September he tried to bolster himself with the help of a new and dubious ally, the gang leader Ruslan Labazanov, who had been driven out of Argun in a big gun fight. Labazanov asked to become bodyguard to Ruslan Khasbulatov. Khasbulatov agreed – an association with a convicted murderer that was to severely embarrass him later.[8]

The pretence that the opposition was non-violent was soon discarded. At the end of August a column of fighters moved on Grozny but was routed; only the intervention of Russian Mi-24 helicopters from Mozdok prevented a much bigger defeat. Russian involvement became more explicit with each new operation. On 28 September Dudayev's forces attacked Avturkhanov's headquarters at Znamenskoye and again Russian helicopters helped the opposition repulse the attackers. The next day's edition of the military newspaper *Krasnaya Zvezda* announced that a Russian officer stationed at Mozdok had died when his helicopter was hit over Chechnya. The following day the newspaper was forced to print a retraction that 'the helicopter did not belong to the Russian army and it was unknown whom it belonged to'.[9] An aide to Avturkhanov was pressed to say how the opposition was obtaining helicopters, if not from Russia. 'If we want to, we'll find cosmonauts,' he snapped back.[10]

On 4 October Yeltsin told a press conference he was pleased with the existing Chechen strategy. 'A process that we welcome is taking place there,' he said. Yeltsin again explicitly ruled out the use of force by Russia and declared that 'in no circumstances' would Russia intervene: 'This is a Chechen question and it is they who must resolve it,' he insisted.

Throughout October the opposition tried and failed to dislodge Dudayev. After another unsuccessful sortie on Grozny a bloody battle was fought at Urus Martan between Dudayev's forces and his ex-comrade Beslan Gantemirov. After this, as Gantemirov himself noted, Moscow began giving the opposition heavy weapons, and this fighter, who had never renounced his support for Chechen independence, was supplied with eleven helicopters and several dozen tanks. The more arms the opposition got, the more incompetent they proved to be, however. A lot of the weapons went astray and were resold. At best they could muster little more than a few hundred fighters between them, who were no match for Dudayev's much better-trained National Guard. So in Moscow they decided on a new degree of escalation: the decision not to invade, but to allow Russian soldiers to help the opposition fighters.

*

The face of Moscow politics changed rapidly over the summer and autumn of 1994. Yeltsin himself had visibly degenerated from the vigorous politician of 1990–1 and had become a remote, tired-looking figure, who rarely appeared in public. He was now in the grip of a hardline group who were increasingly winning the battle for access to him and his thoughts.

The central figure in the group was Korzhakov, who had become Yeltsin's chief bodyguard and head of the Presidential

Security Service. Korzhakov had been with Yeltsin since he became head of the Moscow Communist Party in 1985. He was a former KGB guard in both physical build and authoritarian outlook. He stayed at Yeltsin's side through his period of political exile and sat up with him during nights of depression and insomnia. In October 1993 it was he who helped coerce Defence Minister Pavel Grachev to storm the White House building. Pain observed how 'in the spring of 1994 not a single appointment, even the tiniest personnel change, could be made without Korzhakov . . . And everyone knew it. And anyone who wanted to get something in the Kremlin first had to go and bow before him.'

Korzhakov's cronies were Mikhail Barsukov, a fellow ex-KGB officer whom he had known for fifteen years and who became head of the Kremlin guard; the poker-faced First Deputy Prime Minister Soskovets, who was later described as the 'spiritual father' of the group and who was a patron of the arms industry; the Sports Minister and presidential tennis partner Shamil Tarpishchev; and – from May 1994 – the Nationalities Minister, Yegorov. Their outlook was authoritarian and nationalist. They were a collection of Russian *muzhiki*. That meant that they swore heavily, drank heavily and went to the steam baths together. Increasingly Yeltsin joined them.

Korzhakov had a host of enemies: he was hostile to the Mayor of Moscow, Yury Luzhkov, despised Grachev and disliked the Prime Minister, Chernomyrdin, whom he dreamed of replacing with Soskovets. But his main foes were the surviving group of reformist advisers in the Kremlin who had been the core of Yeltsin's administration in 1992. This group included Pain, Yeltsin's Press Secretary Vyacheslav Kostikov, his chief political adviser Georgy Satarov and his foreign affairs adviser Dmitry Ryurikov. In many ways their intellectual mentor remained Yegor Gaidar, Yeltsin's acting Prime Minister in 1992, who had retained influence over the President after he was forced to relinquish him at the request of a hostile parliament. Gaidar, a Moscow intellectual who is tougher than his mild, cultivated manner suggests, felt that the Kremlin was turning into a Byzantine court with fawning courtiers and an ailing monarch: '[Yeltsin] is a man who communicates very well. For him live communication is a much more important source of information than any documents or papers. And if he is constantly talking to people who say, "Yes, we have to do this," even with his fairly subtle ability to analyse the situation it can have an effect.'

In the late summer of 1994 Yeltsin's principle of 'divide-and-rule' politics broke down and the hawks all but took over the Kremlin. The trigger for this was a ridiculous incident. On 31 August, when Yeltsin was attending the ceremony in Berlin to mark the withdrawal of the Russian armed forces from Germany, he appeared to be drunk. He stumbled down some steps after the champagne lunch, then seized the baton from the conductor of a police band and started to conduct it exuberantly. Then he grabbed a microphone and began loudly and tunelessly to sing the Russian folk song 'Kalinka'. This apparently drunken behaviour by the Russian head of state mortified the liberal aides in the Kremlin and several of them wrote a letter remonstrating with Yeltsin about his behaviour. The letter had the opposite effect to the one intended: the President took offence and stopped talking to them. Kostikov, Ryurikov and others were pointedly left behind when Yeltsin flew to the United States on 24 September.

While Yeltsin was away in America, Kostikov dared to make the Kremlin power struggle public, declaring that 'A struggle is on for the President as a democrat and for Russia's foreseeable future.' Two days later his point was underlined. Flying back from the United States, Yeltsin was due for a stopover at Shannon Airport and a meeting with the Irish Prime Minister, Albert Reynolds. Yeltsin did not get off the plane. The supposition was that he was again drunk. Just as interesting was the choice of man deputed to get off the plane to talk to Reynolds. It was Korzhakov's friend Soskovets.

October weakened the influence of the Prime Minister, Chernomyrdin, and correspondingly strengthened his opponents. On 11 October or 'Black Tuesday' the ruble suddenly crashed against the dollar and lost 27 per cent of its value in a single day. There were calls for the resignation of Chernomyrdin, who unexpectedly did not return from holiday to meet Queen Elizabeth II at the airport as she arrived to make her historic trip to Russia: his place was taken by Soskovets. In November two more moderates, Kostikov, the presidential Press Secretary, and Alexander Shokhin, the Economics Minister, lost their jobs. On 15 November the centrist Shakhrai was formally removed from Chechen policy-making, although he stayed a member of the Security Council. This was the political climate in which the decision to invade Chechnya was made.

*

In mid-November the Chechen opposition had proved so weak in its efforts to topple Dudayev that the decision was made to supply them with Russian manpower. The FSK under the direction of its Deputy Director Yevgeny Savostyanov signed secret contracts with forty-seven tank crews from the Kantemirov and Taman Divisions outside Moscow. It was an entirely secret operation and the head of the Kantemirov Division, General Boris Polyakov, later resigned, saying that his men had been recruited behind his back. The plan was for seventeen tanks to move on Grozny from Urus Martan in the south-west under the command of Gantemirov, while another thirty would roll in from the north from Tolstoy-Yurt, escorted by Labazanov, and from Znamenskoye with Avturkhanov.

On 22 November the leading opposition figure, Salambek Khajiev, who had stayed on the sidelines for a long time, finally decided to get involved. He flew down to Znamenskoye to help organize the attack. The tank columns moved into Grozny at dawn on 26 November. It was a fiasco. The opposition commanders had been supplied with 100 walkie-talkies but the frequencies did not match and they were forced to relay instructions and news across the front line by car. Khajiev followed the Znamenskoye column by car: 'I arrived in Grozny about twelve and what I saw there was of course a shock. I saw that there had been a real battle and moreover that the men on the opposition side were not real fighters. They were afraid to shoot. They had never shot in their lives.'

The opposition fighters turned out not to be genuine fighters at all: as soon as they reached Grozny many of them broke ranks and started looting kiosks and shops. Dudayev's most hardened fighters soon surrounded the tanks in the streets and blitzed them with rocket-propelled grenades. Those of the tank crews who were not killed fled or were captured. A few days later one of the captured Russian soldiers told his story to reporters under the watchful eye of his Chechen captors in the basement of the State Security building. Andrei Chasov, twenty-one, a small, frightened, sandy-haired boy, said he was a conscript who had served seven months in the Kantemirov Tank Division outside Moscow. Two days before the attack he was sent down to Mozdok and told only that they were being sent to control a demonstration. 'They told us nothing, they do everything in secret,' he said. When they reached the edge of town his comrades fled and Chasov was captured, still having only a vague idea where he was.

Once the battle was lost, the opposition leaders retreated, distraught, to Tolstoy-Yurt. Their whole autumn campaign was now in ruins. The débâcle was made worse by the official Russian news agency Itar-Tass and the First Channel of Russian television, which had been primed to release news of the attack. They flashed up the news that the fight had reached the Presidential Palace and

Dudayev was fleeing, then they were forced to make a humiliating retraction.

*

The failure of the 26 November attack on Grozny was a humiliation for the whole autumn strategy of arming the Chechen opposition. Twenty-one Russian servicemen were now in captivity in Grozny, although it took a week for Moscow to acknowledge that they were indeed its soldiers. Dudayev used the propaganda value of this to the full. He declared that if Moscow acknowledged that they were its own soldiers they would be treated as prisoners-of-war; if not, they would be shot as mercenaries.

A day after the débâcle Pavel Grachev, the pug-faced Defence Minister, was questioned about Chechnya. He was extremely cheerful. First of all he said that he had for a long time taken 'no interest' in Chechnya, underlining that he had nothing to do with the arming of the opposition. He washed his hands of the captured men, saying they were not his but were probably mercenaries. Then he mocked the incompetence of the attack on Grozny and said, 'If the army had fought, we would have needed one parachute regiment to decide the whole affair in two hours.' The remark about 'one parachute regiment in two hours' became legendary and made Grachev a hostage to expectations.

The decision to send in the army to Chechnya was probably made on Monday, 28 November. On that day Yegorov drafted an 'appeal' from the leaders of the North Caucasus to Yeltsin, asking him 'swiftly to stop the bloody conflict in Chechnya and take all measures for the imposition of constitutional order'. It was blatantly a device to legitimize a coming invasion. Ruslan Aushev, the President of Ingushetia, says he was summoned that evening by Chernomyrdin to his office in the government headquarters in the White House and asked to sign the appeal. Seven leaders of the regions of the North Caucasus had already signed. Aushev says he was appalled and refused to sign: 'I said, "Viktor Stepanovich! This is war!" He replied, "Not at all. They will just impose constitutional order." '[11]

That same evening Chernomyrdin met the 'Power Ministers' – the Defence Minister Pavel Grachev, the Interior Minister Viktor Yerin, and the head of the FSK, Sergei Stepashin – to discuss the use of force. According to Andrei Kozyrev, the then Foreign Minister, 'I was invited a little bit later than the others. So when I arrived it was something like late evening and I found the Prime Minister presiding over a meeting mostly of the Power Ministers, the Ministers of Defence, the Interior and Security. And my understanding was that they had already made up their minds and after a very brief introduction I was asked what was my opinion: whether force should be used, (a), and (b) what the international reaction to that would be.'[12] Kozyrev said that in answer to the first question he backed the military option – although he added that he thought it should be 'quick, decisive and limited' – and that he then answered, correctly as it turned out, that the international community would treat the use of force in Chechnya as a strictly domestic Russian affair.

Whenever the decision was made to invade, Boris Yeltsin was, according to two witnesses, already committed to sending in the army the following day. On the morning of 29 November Aushev says he rang Yeltsin's office. 'His aide Viktor Vasilyevich Ilyushin helped me to be put through to the President fairly quickly and I appealed to him with literally the following words: "Boris Niko-layevich! Receive me. Give me just ten minutes. You have incorrect information. And if this decision is taken it will lead to bloodshed and deaths." But he replied that his information was complete.'

Then the Security Council gathered in the Kremlin. This was the gathering of fourteen men, including the President, the Prime Minister and all the Power Ministers, which met periodically to discuss issues of national security and defence. The Council Secretary was Oleg Lobov, an old Party comrade of Yeltsin's from the Urals.

Yury Kalmykov, the Justice Minister, was a Cherkess from the North Caucasus. A distinguished lawyer in late middle age who was already suffering from heart illness, he was a professional in Yeltsin's team with no political ambitions. Kalmykov was a slow, cautious man with old-fashioned, gentlemanly manners and was something of a misfit in the Kremlin team. He arrived a little late at the Security Council meeting, which was held in a grand chamber on the fourth floor of the so-called '14th Corpus' in the Kremlin behind the Spassky Gates on Red Square. He was immediately told that all the members of the Council were about to vote on the use of force in Chechnya. Yeltsin was at his most gruff and bearish. 'From the President's tone of voice I understood that he had already decided on force to resolve the question and that it was useless to discuss it,' Kalmykov recalled almost two years later.[13]

Kalmykov said he tried to object but was told that he had to vote first: 'It was done in the following way. They laid out papers. The President said, "Let's vote." I said, "I want to speak." "No, we vote without discussion." . . . I was not allowed to speak and we voted. I had to vote. I said, "If that's the main thing. If I have to vote, I'll vote." It is a purely Soviet system. The Security Council almost always took decisions unanimously. And the President could not tolerate any discussion or any actions that looked as though they were directed directly against him. So I said, "OK, let's vote."' There was only one way to vote – in favour of the use of force. They all, including Kalmykov, voted yes.

Then Yeltsin allowed the meeting to proceed. Grachev 'hung up all these maps, with arrows showing how to take Grozny, which detachments should go into Grozny and into Chechnya. I little understood this and I was so agitated and upset, the more so because the President hadn't let me speak at first. I demanded that discussion could start and he said, "No, wait, wait, wait." Then he let me speak. Maybe I spoke sharply. Maybe I spoke too hotly. I said that by using military means in the Caucasus you only achieve the worst result. That's how it turned out.'

The two most enthusiastic supporters of the invasion at the meeting, Kalmykov said, were Grachev and Kozyrev. Parallels were drawn with the Americans' lightning operation to overthrow the military junta in Haiti two months before, a comparison that horrified Kalmykov. The only person who supported him was Yevgeny Primakov, who was then head of the Foreign Intelligence Service and later became Foreign Minister. 'I said that you can't solve things in the Caucasus that way, it's not Haiti,' Kalmykov went on. 'Someone said that in Haiti the Americans had come in and imposed order and left again. I said that kind of thing is more complicated in the Caucasus, there's a completely different mentality, different rules, different people, different nations. And I spoke out against the use of force. And Primakov said we should support Yury Khamzatovich and try peaceful means of resolving the conflict.'

After the meeting Kalmykov handed in his resignation and flew to Grozny to talk to Dudayev. But their talks produced no result. The only minister who resigned over the Chechen invasion, he died of a heart attack in January 1997.

Even before the Security Council had met, Yeltsin had issued an ultimatum. It gave all the Chechens forty-eight hours to disarm. Otherwise, the ultimatum said, 'All the forces and means at the disposal of the state will be used to put a stop to the bloodshed.' Effectively, it was a call for unconditional surrender.

The ultimatum alarmed Russian liberal politicians, people like Sergei Yushenkov, a former colonel and dissident who was now Chairman of the parliamentary Defence Committee. Yushenkov was strongly opposed to the use of force in Chechnya. He had already started planning a trip to Grozny to try to free the prisoners from the 26 November expedition after the Defence Ministry had renounced them.

The following day, 30 November, Yushenkov was making last-minute arrangements to fly to Chechnya. There was confusion about whether Yeltsin would impose a state of emergency in Chechnya, something that would heighten the tension. To clarify what was happening, Yushenkov called Oleg Lobov, the Secretary of the Security Council. Lobov told him that there would be no state of emergency. But then he added that yes, there would be a war: 'On the telephone Lobov used the phrase that "It is not only a question of the integrity of Russia. We need a small victorious war to raise the President's ratings." There was the comparison, the parallel that Clinton in Haiti could perform a successful operation and his ratings immediately jumped up. I was not able to convince Lobov that Chechnya was not Haiti.'[14]

*

The decision to invade Chechnya was made very quickly and there is no easy answer to the old Russian question: 'Who is to blame?' The fateful decision was taken in great secrecy in a Kremlin that was impenetrable to the outside world, and as with some of the most critical decisions of the Soviet era, such as the order to invade Afghanistan or to attack demonstrators in the streets of Tbilisi in April 1989, there was no single written order or command to which the decision can be traced. It was underwritten with collective responsibility by the Kremlin Security Council, which had become a kind of Politburo, and the presidential powers set out in the new constitution were so strong that Parliament need not be consulted.

Most of those who were involved keep silent on the issue and those who do speak about it now all distance themselves from the decision to embark on an adventure that was planned in great haste. Asked if there were other methods he believes they should have tried, Sergei Stepashin, head of the FSK at the time, and one of the few top figures willing to comment on the issue, now firmly says there were. 'Both [methods] using force and ones avoiding force, but definitely not the one we ended up with,' he says.[15]

In his only recorded public outburst on the issue, Yeltsin blamed Sergei Shakhrai for getting him into the mess. Valery Borshchyov, a liberal Member of Parliament, was witness to the scene. 'There was a meeting in 1995, I think in April. I was a representative from the Yabloko faction [in Parliament] and I then said to Yeltsin that the war in Chechnya was a crime, that he had to stop it immediately, that our fellow-countrymen were dying there, our citizens, women, children, elderly people, that the war was a crime, that he had to sack Yerin, Grachev and Stepashin. Yeltsin tried to speak up for Yerin and Grachev, but weakly. At that moment Shakhrai broke in and started to speak and Yeltsin shouted him down and said, "You be quiet! You yourself cooked up all this business, so you should keep quiet." So he laid responsibility for what had happened on Shakhrai. He shut up Shakhrai rudely, very rudely.'[16]

This should probably not be taken too literally, however. By the end of November Shakhrai had lost influence over Chechen decision-making. He remained a member of the Security Council and voted for the invasion, but he was no longer powerful enough to be the main ideologue for the war. Yeltsin evidently was angry about Shakhrai's earlier policy-making and quite probably about his insistence that he should not meet Dudayev. Shakhrai helped make the fuse that sparked the war in Chechnya but he did not light it.

What stands out in the sequence of events following the botched 26 November operation is the sudden escalation in the speed of decision-making. Many media reports at the time used stock phrases such as 'the Kremlin's patience was wearing thin' in late November and early December. That is highly misleading. On the contrary, there was suddenly a great impatience to throw aside all other strategies and use force against Dudayev, who after

all had been in power for three years. As late as 4 October Yeltsin
had spoken categorically against Russian intervention. In late
November the decision was made within three days, and two
weeks later a 40,000-strong army rolled into Chechnya. What
had changed in the meantime?

Clearly the 26 November operation was a catalyst that persuaded many people who had formerly been against military
intervention to support it: principally Stepashin, whose FSK had
been embarrassed by the botched attack on Grozny. Stepashin, a
former policeman from Leningrad, had been associated with the
generation of reformist politicians in 1991 and kept open his line
of communication with them even as he hardened his political
beliefs. He took over the FSK with a mandate to reform it, but
the organization got the better of him. On Chechnya, bolstered
by reports from the opposition, Stepashin's agents supplied
Yeltsin with highly misleading intelligence information about the
state of Dudayev's defences. Stepashin now says the intelligence
he was receiving led him to believe a small show of military force
would be enough. 'It was reported to the President that it would
need only two or three hours of military pressure, not even
military force, to change the situation radically,' he said.

The other key figure to back the use of force after 26 November
was Grachev. No decision to start the biggest Russian military
operation since Afghanistan could have been taken without the
support of the Defence Minister. It was he who made the arrogant
boast that Dudayev could be overthrown 'in two hours'. It was a
barbed comment fired off in the war of rivalry between the
different Russian security structures, but it was also a bid for
the limelight. Grachev was enjoying the discomfort of his rivals
after 26 November and evidently saw political dividends in the
prospect of a swift military campaign against Dudayev.

Stepashin – who is of course an interested party in this debate
– now says that it was Grachev who insisted on the strategy of a
massed invasion. 'I was never in agreement with the way they

went in,' Stepashin said. 'I thought it was possible to use other methods of pressure on the hardliners on Dudayev's side. It was a decision made by others, in the first place by the Defence Minister.' Stepashin's assertion gains more weight from the testimony of the unbiased witness, Kalmykov, who saw Grachev enthusiastically talking about a lightning campaign in the Security Council on 29 November.

But there is also evidence that Grachev was converted to the cause of military action only belatedly at the end of November after his rivals had so conspicuously failed. Most analysts agree that the Defence Ministry was uninvolved with Chechnya until late November. Senior army officials, such as Eduard Vorobyov, the First Deputy Commander of Russian ground forces, said they learned about the order to invade literally days before it was due to happen. Most opinion in the army, drawing on the lessons of Afghanistan, was said to be highly sceptical about starting another mountain war with an overstretched army in the dead of winter.

Grachev has portrayed himself in two interviews as just the general who carried out orders. 'Now that a year has passed I can say that I was never a supporter of armed action and especially in such a quick way as was planned in Chechnya,' he said in December 1995. 'As a soldier I was compelled to carry out an order.'[17] In another interview he said he was in favour of postponing the invasion till the following spring. Whatever one makes of these assertions, it seems plausible that Grachev was the willing executor rather than the author of the idea of sending in the troops to Chechnya. Grachev had stayed in his job for so long only by displaying an almost servile loyalty to Yeltsin. He was not a political heavyweight in Yeltsin's entourage and his subservient role meant that he was probably ready to submit to any orders from Yeltsin, even the most stupid. In searching for the roots of the military adventure it makes more sense to look for a political context and for a source of advice closer to the heart of the Kremlin.

The firm conviction of some Kremlin advisers is that someone had been praising the merits of a military intervention in Chechnya to Yeltsin for some time. 'We sent in documents with our own plans,' said Mark Urnov, the reformist head of the Kremlin Analytical Centre at the time. 'I find it impossible to believe that alternative plans proposing the use of force were not landing on the President's desk.'[18]

In November 1994 pro-Yeltsin liberals like Gaidar, Kostikov and Satarov were in disarray. They found it hard to gain access to Yeltsin and complained that Korzhakov was keeping him in an 'information blockade'. Here, in the view of many political insiders, is the key to the start of the Chechen war – not in oil or a radical change in the situation on the ground, but in a shift in the balance of Kremlin politics combined with poor intelligence from Chechnya. The hawks would have approved of a military intervention in Chechnya as their way of remaking Yeltsin in their own image and stealing the rhetoric of the nationalist opposition. In the words of Gaidar: 'I have said more than once that the "Zhirinovsky effect" played a big part because of his rhetoric, his "last march to the south", and so on. It seemed that a victorious war would be very helpful.' A small war against the 'mafiosi' Chechens would go down well with the electorate, the argument went, and Yeltsin would enter the lists for the 1996 presidential elections as a tough ruler whose flirtation with Western liberalism was finally over.

In interviews given since his removal from office, Korzhakov has denied that he supported the invasion of Chechnya.[19] That may be so, although it seems unlikely Yeltsin would have made such a crucial decision without the support of his most trusted aide. Korzhakov may just be lying. Whatever the truth, Korzhakov's personal position is almost irrelevant because his group took complete command of the political scene once the decision to invade had been made. His close ally, Yegorov, who had drawn up the 'appeal' to Yeltsin to be signed by the leaders of the North Caucasus, was now made Yeltsin's 'special representative to Chechnya' and promoted to become Deputy Prime Minister, while Soskovets was made head of the 'Government Crisis Committee' on Chechnya. When Yeltsin went into hospital shortly before the invasion, the only man who had full access to him was Korzhakov – even Viktor Ilyushin, Yeltsin's aide of twenty years, kept in touch only by telephone. Prime Minister Chernomyrdin was allowed to visit Yeltsin, but only in the company of Soskovets.

Korzhakov flaunted his arrogance in other ways. On 2 December guards from his Presidential Security Service put on a bizarre show of raw muscle in central Moscow. Armed men in ski masks raided the headquarters of the powerful MOST Bank and forced the guards to lie face-down in the snow. It was a public spectacle intended to humiliate Korzhakov's foe, the patron of MOST and Mayor of Moscow, Yury Luzhkov. Yevgeny Savostyanov, who had been the mastermind of the 26 November operation and headed the Moscow branch of the FSK, called his men out to intervene. A few hours later Savostyanov received a call from Korzhakov and Barsukov in the Kremlin, telling him he was being sacked.

All the thick fog of Kremlin intrigues should not disguise a central fact: Yeltsin himself, who had spoken against the use of force in October, had now come out in favour of it. On 29 November he firmly backed the use of force and demanded a unanimous vote in favour at the Security Council. The following day he signed a secret decree authorizing an invasion. It was a clear, calculated and ruthless decision made by a politician who, in the final analysis, always made up his own mind. Once his mind was made up, the military machine was set in motion and there was no turning back. It exposed the lack of any proper

decision-making mechanisms in the Kremlin. The Security Council merely endorsed a decision taken privately by Yeltsin and a
few advisers and there was no mechanism for dissenters to register
their objections. The former dissident Sergei Kovalyov saw it as a
purely Soviet chain of events in which the most important thing
was not to make the best decision, but to ensure that the boss
was always right: 'It is a law of Soviet politics. Not a single
adviser in the Soviet system can allow himself to say something
different from what the boss wants to hear. That means he falls
out of the system, he is not playing by the rules ... Of course a
nomenklatura politician, if he is dealing with the Chechen issue,
of course he thinks about solving it, but the main thing for him is
not that problem at all. The main thing is to coincide with the
opinion of the boss.'[20]

*

On 30 November Grozny was still shaking off the effects of the
tank assault on the town four days before. On Prospekt Pobedy
trolleybus wires were dangling in the air and trees were jagged
and split where tanks had tried to burst through to the Presidential Palace. The market was a deserted mess. Twice a day jets
roared over the city and bombed the city's two airfields, destroying Dudayev's embryo air force. A long black column of smoke
rose from the northern airport, hit in an air raid the day before.
But some bombs landed in the city too. A crowd of people waiting
for a bus were sprayed with metal and one woman died. The air
raids had been authorized as soon as the Security Council met to
discuss Chechnya. The Kremlin refused to acknowledge that the
bombers were Russian, just as it still refused to admit that the
captives from the 26 November operation were Russian soldiers.
It was a bad omen for standards of truthfulness as the country
went to war.

It was as though something ancient had been awakened among
the Chechens. A rally of old men with staves and young men with

guns had gathered in Freedom Square outside the Presidential Palace. As the road out of the city was full of cars taking Chechen families to safety in their villages, men were arriving in buses from those same villages carrying hunting rifles and pistols. Fighters in the State Security building, where the Russian captives were being held, were signing up volunteers and handing out weapons. Suddenly a Russian jet screamed overhead. The crowd whooped and cried out and the men fired looping rounds from their Kalashnikovs in the air at the smudge of the disappearing jet.

The whole of Grozny was bracing itself for war. As with the last attempt to overthrow Dudayev three years before, the Russian threat spontaneously rallied Chechens, whatever their former allegiances, behind the existing regime, represented by Dudayev. A restaurateur who usually lived in Moscow and was more interested in money than politics, said that he would take up his gun and fight if there was a Russian invasion: 'I am against Dudayev, I am against the opposition, but if the Russians come in I will go and fight.' There was no middle way any more. Khasbulatov, who had spent the whole autumn trying to overthrow Dudayev, now pulled out of Chechnya. He soon condemned his former allies in the opposition and denied his involvement in the armed insurgency campaign.

Just occasionally on the edge of a crowd it was possible to hear someone express fear that a war was starting. The opinion usually came from a woman, who melted away as soon as the curious onlookers came over to see the foreign reporter. Otherwise there was a lot of bravado and slogans: 'We will fight to the last Chechen' or 'If Grozny falls we will fight in the mountains.'

The biggest show of bravado was from Dudayev. At a press conference in a musty bunker of the Presidential Palace he sat at a table in a forage cap and camouflage fatigues, lapping up the attention, his eyes flashing with anger. He had taken Russia to the brink and, in public at least, was enjoying the game. 'We have been waiting for the invasion for four years,' Dudayev said, waving his index finger, and then, 'After my death I will achieve the aim that events will finally destroy Russia, the evil empire.' There then followed a stream of Dudayev invective. Russia was spreading 'propaganda, propaganda, lies, lies' and Russia was 'an aggressive, aggressive, unbridled Satanic force, a Satanic force'. He quoted Harry Truman to the effect that Russia could never be trusted. He then read out a typically flamboyant telegram to his former comrade, Pyotr Deinekin, the head of the Russian air force: 'I congratulate you, commander-in-chief and the valiant air force of Russia, on your success in winning supremacy over the air of the Chechen Republic Ichkeria. We shall meet on the ground!'

In private Dudayev was more worried, according to the Russian Members of Parliament who arrived to negotiate the release of the Russian soldiers. Yushenkov, the leader of the delegation, says that Dudayev was trying to play games with Russia: 'I know that he was a person who tried to exploit contradictions within the Russian leadership. He was a Communist with the Communists, he was a democrat with the democrats, and so on.'

Pain says this was symptomatic of Dudayev right up until the assault on Grozny. One moment he seemed ready to make terms, the next he would take a hard line, utterly confusing Moscow policy-makers. But always he was keen to have an interlocutor in Moscow, someone to put his point of view to. 'Telephone contact did not break off for a single hour, even when the war started,' said Pain. 'And before it all the more so. There were often mutually exclusive calls and information . . . One intermediary brought one version and another brought a completely contradictory one. I was a direct witness to this.'

Dudayev was still holding out for a meeting with Yeltsin, Yushenkov said, but when he was pressed on his terms of agreement they were actually quite reasonable. 'He was ready . . . to sign an agreement on the principle of Tatarstan,' Yushenkov said. 'Moreover, he said that Chechnya would not break away, it could not do that. He imagined the independence of Chechnya in a very idiosyncratic way. There should be common armed forces, a common currency, a shared frontier and border guards. Effectively he was saying that he was part of Russia. He agreed that the status could be deferred and a special commission could work on it.' By this time, however, there was no one in Moscow to negotiate with.

The deadline for the first ultimatum passed and Grozny breathed a little more freely. Yushenkov's delegation flew out, having obtained the release of two of the Russian prisoners. At this point Pavel Grachev flew down to meet Dudayev and Dudayev suddenly swept out of Grozny in a column of cars and drove to the Ingush border at Sleptsovskaya. The two men talked for over an hour. When they emerged from the meeting Dudayev was smiling as usual, while Grachev looked in a sour mood. They declared it was a 'meeting of two generals' and said 'there will be no military option'. 'Of course there won't be a war, for what reason would there be war?' said Dudayev. He agreed to release the remaining Russian prisoners.

The substance of the Sleptsovskaya meeting is a mystery. Very possibly Grachev, who like Dudayev had fought in Afghanistan, was having doubts at this eleventh hour and was trying to persuade Dudayev to back down – but whatever assurances he won out of the Chechen leader were not enough. Dudayev's widow, Alla, says that her husband did not blame Grachev for the war, evidently basing his judgement on their meeting. 'He felt sorry for Pavel Grachev,' she said eighteen months later. 'He told me that Grachev started this war against his will and it was not in his power to stop it.'[21]

Grachev returned to Moscow, and on 7 December the Security Council gave the final go-ahead for the invasion. According to a source at secondhand – a conversation between Sergei Kovalyov and Kozyrev – Grachev was now arguing that the invasion should be put off, citing his meeting with Dudayev, but was overruled. Yeltsin rebuked him for being a 'coward' and Grachev buckled under. He cancelled plans for a second meeting with Dudayev in Chechnya. A statement issued after the Security Council session said that 'all constitutional measures must be taken to disarm and liquidate illegal armed formations'. Opinions differ with regard to Dudayev. His chief of staff Aslan Maskhadov said later that Dudayev still did not believe Russia would go to war. Others say he was still striking a proud stance at the meeting with Grachev, as though anticipating the battle he had been predicting for three years. Dudayev seemed to be incapable of making the public climbdown that was necessary if he were to strike a deal with Russia.

Yeltsin himself now decided to disappear and let his ministers take the heat of the 'lightning operation'. It was announced that he had gone into hospital for an operation on a deviated septum. It is a completely routine operation to the nose which is usually performed with a local anaesthetic and the patient discharged immediately. But the President stayed out of sight for more than two weeks.

In Moscow, Yegor Gaidar heard from a reliable source that the invasion was about to happen. On 9 December he tried to call Yeltsin to voice his objections. Although he had left the government in December 1992, he had stayed in Yeltsin's confidence and called the President occasionally to discuss important issues. Without fail Yeltsin would either speak to him or ring him back later. Now, for the first time, he was not put through. 'I tried to get in touch with him and it didn't work,' Gaidar said. 'It was the first time ever. He was in hospital, it's true. None the less, he didn't ring me back. I called Chernomyrdin and told him that as far as I knew the decision had been taken, and if it had been taken it was a terrible mistake, which could destroy all that I had done and everything that, as far as I understood, he was trying to do.'

Chernomyrdin replied evasively and Gaidar realized that the invasion would go ahead. But even at this late hour the picture was confused and Yeltsin's real intentions had been kept secret. Senior figures in the Kremlin were still in the dark about what was going on. Mark Urnov, head of the Kremlin Analytical Centre, wryly recalls: 'I well remember how on the eve of the invasion late in the evening . . . we in the Analytical Centre wrote our latest document, sent it off, and there was a sensation that it had a good response, that we should not send in forces en masse. I remember a feeling of happiness, late in the evening. I left at about 10 p.m. and I said to my secretary, "Thank God, there won't now be a war in Chechnya." A day later it all started.'

9

Russia Invades

A group of Western journalists were listening to the opposition leader Umar Avturkhanov speaking at a rally in Znamenskoye in northern Chechnya on the morning of 11 December, when a great rumbling noise drowned out his words. Running towards the road, they saw a huge column of armoured vehicles rolling across the plains. 'It stretched off to the horizon, rumbling along and raising huge clouds of dust,' remembers American journalist Bill Gasperini.[1] Without fanfare and apparently without opposition, the tanks had rolled across the border into Chechnya. Tanks, armoured personnel carriers, supply trucks and even pontoon bridges on flat-bed vehicles drove by, heading along the northern road that would bring them out on to a ridge of hills just north of Grozny.

Some 40,000 Russian troops, on alert all night, were ordered in that morning at 7 a.m. Three columns converged on Chechnya from different directions, one from the huge army base at Mozdok on the north-west border of Chechnya, another from Vladikavkaz, the North Ossetian capital, to the south-west, and a third from Dagestan, to the east. It was a menacing display of force, the biggest Russian manoeuvre since the war in Afghanistan. Helicopters clattered overhead as hundreds of heavy guns and pieces of armour moved through the snow-bound countryside.

Within hours, though, the Russian invasion force was floundering, attacked by protesting crowds, the soldiers unsure of what to do in the face of civilian opposition, drawn to a halt. By the end of the day there were casualties among both soldiers and civilians and forty Russian soldiers taken prisoner. It was a messy beginning that boded ill for the whole campaign.

In Dagestan, a crowd of civilians stopped the tanks before they even reached the border, begging the soldiers not to go on. Men in the crowd quickly disarmed the soldiers and took them prisoner. The column never advanced further. On Chechnya's western border, things rapidly turned nasty. The troop column from Vladikavkaz had to travel through the slender republic of Ingushetià to reach the Chechen border, a drive of no more than a couple of hours. Before it even came to the border, a crowd of civilians was blocking its path, protesting at Russia's use of force against their Chechen 'brothers'. Several people were crushed in the mêlée as they massed on the road in front of the tanks. The Ingush Health Minister, driving back from Grozny, climbed out of his car to talk to the soldiers. He was promptly arrested, searched and roughed up, and as tempers rose he collapsed and died from a heart attack.

What started as a peaceful demonstration rapidly degenerated into a fight. The crowds smashed the windscreens and set fire to some of the troop trucks. Shooting broke out and soon five Ingush civilians were dead and some fifteen wounded. The army barely came off better, with one soldier killed and fourteen wounded. It sealed the road and set up outposts on all approaches. Soldiers were towing away the burnt-out and smashed wrecks of twenty military trucks two days later; two heavy vehicles carrying a pontoon bridge had been pushed off the road, their axles and wheels twisted and broken.

The troops were supposed to blockade the city of Grozny from three sides and encircle Dudayev's forces, but the plan was already falling apart and any advantage of surprise was completely squandered. Only the northern column came anywhere close to Grozny, and it too was halted three days later at the village of Dolinsky, still 15 miles from Grozny. The massive display of force, intended to force Dudayev to negotiate on Moscow's terms, was suddenly looking uncertain.

The army was floundering because of its vague orders and an even less clear sense of purpose. In a statement, Yeltsin as their commander-in-chief ordered the troops to protect Chechnya's civilians against the threat of full-scale civil war. They were to use all necessary means to put an end to the bloodshed and restore 'constitutional order'. To the soldiers on the ground, who instead of a civil war found the popular anger aimed directly at them, the orders were meaningless.

For many officers the situation was dangerously familiar. Barely five years before, the Soviet army had extricated itself from a debilitating ten-year war in Afghanistan, where in the name of 'international communism' they had tried to impose Soviet rule. Thousands of Russian soldiers died in the face of determined Afghan resistance and morale plummeted as men began to question the point of a war they could never win. Chechnya, with its mountainous terrain and history of resistance to outside rule, promised a similar type of war and filled many Russian officers with deep foreboding.

Thick, damp fog hung over a lonely stretch of road leading west out of Chechnya through dense woodland. Out of the mist loomed the stranded hulk of an Mi-8 Russian military helicopter, crash-landed, its long metal blades dipping down on to the road. A bullet had pierced its windscreen, and blood stained the cockpit floor. Fuel flooded across the road from its bullet-ridden tanks. Chechens had already hauled off the crew, but a few others stood around triumphant that the symbol of Russia's military superiority had been downed by rifle shots.

Several miles down the road the Russian western column was stalled for the fourth day near the village of Davydenko, still 30 miles west of Grozny. Three tanks were spread across the road, cumbersome rollers pushed out in front to protect against mines.

Dozens more tanks fanned out across the snowy fields. Then slowly, one by one, they lumbered backwards, withdrawing 100 yards back down the road. It was a gesture of goodwill to the local civilians, who were still demonstrating on the road, and part of a deal in which the Chechens returned the Russian helicopter crew, two of whom were dead. More than anything, though, the Russian retreat reflected the unhappy mood of the soldiers.

'We are not doing anything good by being here,' said a Russian captain, a doctor who stood at the head of the column waiting to collect the third injured helicopter crew member. 'We are fighting civilians, it would be better if we left. Almost all the officers think the way I do,' he added. Asked if they were heading for Grozny, he said, 'It would be senseless to attack Grozny, it would lead to a guerrilla war. It would be like a second Afghanistan and it would end the same way.'

The general commanding the column seemed to think much the same. The next day Major-General Ivan Babichev stood on the road in front of his tanks and promised the crowd of hundreds of Chechens that he would not use armed force against civilians. 'They [Russian leaders] may condemn us, but we are not going to shoot. We're not going to use tanks against the people. We are not going any further,' he said. 'If they give me such an order I would treat it as a criminal order. The military must execute only legitimate orders, and the order to crush villages with tanks is not a legitimate order.'

Elderly women in overcoats and wollen headscarves pushed forward to hug and kiss the general as several hundred men continued chanting and praying on the road. Babichev went on, 'It is not our fault that we are here. We did not want this. This [operation] contradicted the constitution. It is forbidden to use the army against civilians. It is forbidden to shoot against the people.'

The general was not mutinying since he was quoting Yeltsin's initial decree on the crisis saying that force would not be used against unarmed civilians. He was calming the crowd in the hope it would disperse, and looking to avoid any clash that endangered the lives of his men. Soon after, he pulled his tanks off the road and headed north through the fields on to a ridge of hills that gave him a clear run all the way into Grozny. By the end of the month they were poised to take the city. But his week-long dithering on the foggy road highlighted a debate that was convulsing the armed forces at all levels.

*

Opposition to the deployment of the army in Chechnya went much higher than Babichev, in fact right to the top. Colonel General Eduard Vorobyov, First Deputy Commander of Russia's Ground Forces, one of Russia's most senior military commanders, resigned rather than take command of the invasion that he concluded was criminal in both conception and execution. A week after Russian tanks moved into Chechnya, Vorobyov was sent down to help administer the huge, sprawling Russian military base at Mozdok in North Ossetia, on the north-west border with Chechnya. Mozdok was a fortified town often described as the corner-stone of the Russian conquest of the Caucasus. Now it provided the operational headquarters for Russia's latest war in the region.

Vorobyov spent two days at the base and satisfied himself that everything was in order. He had had no part in the planning of the operation, only learning about the build-up and invasion from the press. He imagined, though, that it was largely an elaborate game of bluff, that Grachev was massing the tanks for their frightening effect, to pressure Dudayev into backing down. Vorobyov was also confident that Yeltsin would do a deal in the end.

It was only on his third day at the base that he learned by chance from an old acquaintance that he was to take over command of the operation in Chechnya.

'I met a general of the Cossack forces. We knew each other

from when we studied together at the Academy. It was a chance meeting and he said: "Thank God, finally there is someone here who will bring order." In my two days there I was sure everything was already in order. I meant order in the administration, and he said; "No, order in operations in Chechnya."[2]

'"What do you mean?" I said. "We already know that they have sent you to take over the main command and that you are going to be in command," he said. I thought at first it was a joke but he said that according to their information it really was so. Then, through my own channels, I made enquiries, and in the end through other channels I was told that it could not be ruled out.'

It was the morning of 19 December, and Vorobyov started looking into the real state of affairs in Chechnya. He met the heads of every unit from intelligence, air force, paratroopers, interior and army troop commanders to logistics and medical staff, as if he were going to take command.

Sitting in the State Duma a year and a half later, a neat, dapper man in a grey civilian suit to fit his new life as a parliamentary deputy, the former general ran through a detailed list of things he checked, from the number of forces and armour of each fighting unit down to the quality of personnel and the number of boots and ammunition supplied.

'When I heard all these people, and met them personally, I decided that the operation was not prepared. There were no reserves organized, which is the most important part of an operation. They had not considered weather conditions, the snow, rain, mud, slush. The strength of these forces was based on aviation, which could not operate in such conditions, they could not work in the fog, and could not use their laser weapons. They could only drop bombs. Helicopters could not fly and could not provide the corresponding support.'

The weather was so bad and the mud so thick, Vorobyov said, that a few days earlier on 17 December, every single unit in Chechnya in every direction, except one north-east of Grozny, ground to a complete halt. Even worse, personnel, the bulk of them raw conscripts, were inadequately trained for the task.

Basic skills aside, Vorobyov also realized that no one had properly studied the enemy they were facing. 'No one had assessed or appreciated Dudayev's fanaticism,' he said. Still more importantly, no one had stopped to think how the civilian population would react to the intervention of troops or how the troops would handle orders to move against their own people, he said. He felt uneasy about the legal position of the troops. No state of emergency had been declared which would allow the use of the army inside Russia and no media campaign had been launched to prepare the population. The morale of the troops would be affected, with dangerous results, he warned.

On the night of 20 December he sat up alone in his quarters in a railway carriage, thinking. 'I did not eat, did not go out. I sat all night without turning on the light, without undressing, weighing it all up,' he recalled later. 'I did not consult anyone. I did not call home or talk to my comrades. I did not want to ask anyone's advice so that later, when the investigation began, I could say that no one had persuaded me, it was my personal decision.'

He came to the conclusion that the lack of preparation of the military operation verged on the criminal. He was also troubled by the moral implications of using the army against their own people. 'I would say that the use of troops was a crime. To send the army against its own people. It was stupidity, the most real stupidity of people who are not capable of organizing the most elementary affair.'

The operation in Chechnya threatened to be the latest abuse of the army by Russia's political leaders who had used it to crush popular dissent in the dying days of the Soviet Union and then made it a scapegoat, he said.

'The army is brought out and then when it is comes to responsibility, the investigation begins, all those who gave the orders for the attack, all hide their heads and are silent,' he said.

'And all those people's deputies who cried "Murderers, murderers," and all those who sat on the praesidiums, remained silent. Exactly the same was going to happen now,' he said.

The following day Vorobyov spoke to Russia's Chief of the General Staff Mikhail Kolesnikov and told him that no change of commander could rescue the faltering military operation. Moreover, whoever ordered the operation to take Grozny should be investigated for criminal irresponsibility. 'The military operation would go in two parts: first, a widespread use of aviation, and with the weather conditions that would mean widespread destruction and civilian deaths, and second, military combat relies on the men, and these had just stepped off their transport vehicles and were not ready. Both seemed like crimes.' Nevertheless, he said he would take command if he was given the time to train and prepare for it. He said he needed three months.

'What, will you say all that to the Minister?' Kolesnikov asked him. Vorobyov told him yes. A request went through to talk to the Defence Minister and Grachev called back.

'The Minister called me and said, "This is the situation. Colonel-General Mityukhin has fallen sick and must go and be treated. Take over command of the operation." I said, "Comrade Minister, I have laid out my position in a report to the Chief of the General Staff." And that was it . . . There was no written order, no verbal order, the word order did not even come up, it was just a thirty-second talk on the phone. He understood my position and said, "Very well, I will fly down this evening."'

Grachev arrived that evening with a large group of officers, and immediately dismissed all the commanders of the operation, advising them to think of resigning from the army. He announced that he was personally taking command of the operation and appointed a new staff, naming his deputy as Lieutenant-General Anatoly Kvashnin, who as Deputy Commander of the North Caucasus Military District had already worked on the plan.

Then he turned to Vorobyov. 'To me he said literally just one phrase: "I am disappointed in you, Comrade Colonel-General, I think you should submit your resignation." I replied, "It is ready." And that was it.

'I left by plane at 2 a.m. It was already the 22nd. I went home and at 10 a.m. on the 22nd I handed in my resignation to the main commander of my regiment.' It was the end of a thirty-eight-year career in the army. A strange footnote to Vorobyov's story is that in May the following year he was awarded an order for personal courage and a weapon engraved with his name.

Vorobyov was not alone in having serious doubts about the war. The first person to call him in support was General Alexander Lebed, the outspoken commander of Russia's 14th Army in the breakaway region of Transdnestr in Moldova. Also an Afghan war veteran, Lebed criticized his military colleagues for sending 'untrained kids' into Chechnya and vowed that none of his troops would go there 'under any circumstances'. He would only go there himself to withdraw troops, or to lead a unit made up of the sons of goverment leaders, he said. 'Step by step the Afghan war experience is being repeated in Chechnya,' he declared. 'We risk getting involved in a war with the entire Muslim world. Individual guerrillas will indefinitely shoot at our tanks and pick off our soldiers with single bullets.'

Three of the Defence Ministry's top generals, Boris Gromov, Georgy Kondratyev and Valery Mironov, all Deputy Ministers, also spoke out against use of the army in Chechnya. Kondratyev, a former close comrade of Grachev's, described Dudayev as a 'legitimate' leader, and called for the President to find a political solution, not a military one. Gromov, one of the army's most popular generals, who in 1989 led the troops out of Afghanistan, warned that Chechnya would be a repeat of that costly and disastrous war.

'No one is drawing the right conclusions from the experience we had fifteen years ago,' he said. 'The main thing I do not understand is for what reason our young and not so young people have to die,' he told a meeting of Afghan war veterans. The warnings from such senior military men seemed to go unheard, and within weeks all three generals were dismissed. The faltering military operation was ordered on.

*

Political efforts to head off the disaster eventually gave way under the momentum of the military machine. Deputy Nationalities Minister Vyacheslav Mikhailov flew down for peace talks to Vladikavkaz on 11 December, only learning of the invasion as he boarded the plane in Moscow. He met a Chechen delegation, headed by Finance Minister Taimaz Abubakarov, who drove slap into an invading Russian column as he travelled out from Grozny. The two sides decided it was worth pursuing discussions anyway, Mikhailov recalled. Even at this stage there was a chance of bringing Yeltsin and Dudayev or at second-best Chernomyrdin and Dudayev together to avert a full-scale war. Mikhailov says he understood the Vladikavkaz peace talks were a preparation so that he could hand over to someone more senior, 'on a level with Dudayev'.[3]

Mikhailov understood that Dudayev was ready to negotiate with Chernomyrdin, in place of Yeltsin, and that Chernomyrdin was also ready for a meeting. Yeltsin seemed to confirm the plan the following day in a statement, saying the federal side was ready to meet Dudayev at a high level.

This was the meeting Dudayev had been waiting for. He later told the Russian negotiator Arkady Volsky that he had had a new uniform made specially and a new forage cap with a special insignia embroidered by hand depicting the Chechen emblem of the wolf.[4] 'I got ready, I shaved, I washed, and then they said no,' Volsky recalled Dudayev saying.

Mikhailov expected Chernomyrdin to come to Vladikavkaz to meet Dudayev, but then someone changed their mind because Moscow announced the meeting would be in Mozdok, and not with Chernomyrdin but with the three hawks Yegorov, Grachev and Yerin. 'I replied that Dudayev would never go to a meeting like that, all the more so in Mozdok, which was crammed full of armed detachments. So it happened, as was obvious, that Dudayev refused to go to Mozdok, and simultaneously the negotiations were effectively stopped,' Mikhailov said. The invasion rolled on.

Meanwhile, the Russian political scene was in turmoil over these events. The only supporters of the invasion were the ultra-nationalist Vladimir Zhirinovsky and a small group of authoritarian-minded free marketeers, led by the former Finance Minister, Boris Fyodorov.

A line of politicians right across the spectrum sat together at a chaotic press conference on 12 December to condemn the invasion. Ironically, it was the first anniversary of the adoption of Yeltsin's super-presidential new constitution. That constitution meant that Parliament had almost no checks on the Presidency. It was almost impossible to impeach the President and no decisions had to be ratified by the legislature.

The most outspoken opponents were the Western-leaning liberals who now declared that they had finally broken with the President. 'Yeltsin no longer listens to us. He does not need our advice, so it's time to move into opposition,' said Sergei Yushenkov. Gaidar warned that an assault on Grozny could be a pretext for a wider political crackdown in Russia. 'If this button is pressed we will, with absolute certainty, see the collapse of democratic institutions in Russia within a few months,' he said.

The media took up this line, showing that *glasnost* had come a long way since the war in Afghanistan. The independent television station NTV provided no-holds-barred reporting from Grozny of the devastation.

When the former Soviet dissident Sergei Kovalyov, now a deputy of the State Duma and head of the presidential commission on human rights, heard that troops had moved into Chechnya, he decided to go to Grozny at once. He had repeatedly warned against a military solution in Chechnya and now that the war had begun, feared the worst. Imprisoned in a Soviet labour camp for seven years and exiled for another three for disseminating anti-Soviet propaganda, Kovalyov was seen by many as the heir to the legacy of his old friend, the famous physicist and human rights activist Andrei Sakharov, who suffered years of exile in the town of Gorky for his opposition to the Soviet invasion of Afghanistan.

A frail, bespectacled man, his health battered by his time in prison and his chain-smoking, Kovalyov became the most tireless campaigner against the war in Chechnya, risking his life and incurring the wrath of his old enemies in the security services. Almost immediately he came up against obstacles that he recognized for the Soviet blocking tactics of old. Yeltsin, Kovalyov was told by presidential aide Georgy Satarov, would be in hospital for eight days. 'I then understood that those eight days were set by for the military operations. And lying in the hospital meant naturally refusing admittance to anyone,' Kovalyov recalled later.[5]

Kovalyov instead tried to reach Soskovets and the Chief of the General Staff Mikhail Kolesnikov, the only two men who could authorize a plane to take him to Chechnya. He used a special government telephone in the Duma, with a direct link to the corridors of power in the Kremlin and the White House. There were only two special phones in the Duma, one in the office of Yushenkov, Chairman of the Duma's Defence Committee, and one belonging to Mikhail Poltoranin, a former Yeltsin confidant and then Chairman of the Duma's Press Committee. Yushenkov's phone was cut off after he put a call through to Dudayev's aides in Chechnya on the day of the invasion, so Kovalyov used Poltoranin's. Within hours that too went dead.

'Someone listened into a government conversation, on a government line, a deputy's conversation, and decided whether it was a good conversation or not, whether to leave the telephone or disconnect it. And he decided it was necessary to disconnect it. This is the basis of our politics, such is our politics,' Kovalyov explained. He then decided to send the President a fax. 'I called reception to ask for the fax number. "There is no fax," [he says] "How can you not have a fax?" "We don't." "What do you mean, the President does not have a fax?" He says, "No,"' Kovalyov recounted, laughing. 'It was nonsensical. "So, how can I communicate with him?" "I do not know," he says.'

Kovalyov told the story to friends and colleagues gathered in honour of the fifth anniversary of Sakharov's death, two days later on 14 December. 'I told them all that had happened on the phone, that the President does not have a fax, and I said, "Come on, let's get together, maybe we can buy him a fax." And the first who came up and gave money was Kozyrev,' he chuckled.

He told Kozyrev how he had to go down to Chechnya but could not reach anyone in the government to agree it. 'My place is there, I need to go there. If Andrei [Sakharov] was the commissioner for human rights, he would be there, not in Moscow, he would be in Grozny,' he said. And then it could not have been simpler. Kozyrev called up Soskovets from a pay-phone in the House of Physicians where they were gathered and Soskovets agreed as if nothing could be more normal.

'The Deputy Prime Minister said, "So do you believe him or what?"' Kovalyov said. It turned out to be another blocking tactic. Told he could only take a group of five people, Kovalyov arrived at the military airport of Chkalovskoye the following day to find a huge empty plane waiting for them, and two generals saluting them at the gangway steps. They took off, but after several hours' flying were denied permission to land and had to return. 'Already there is no one there, the generals have gone. There is even no tea, I ask for some tea and they say, "No, and the biscuits are for tomorrow,"' Kovalyov remembered.

The following day they were told they could not fly since their names were not on the list. Without saying so, the authorities were doing everything to prevent the human rights commissioner from doing his job. Eventually Kovalyov gave up and joined an ordinary passenger flight to the southern Russian town of Mineralniye Vody, making the long journey into Chechnya by car.

*

The Western reaction to events in Chechnya was, apart from a few carefully phrased comments about 'excessive use of force', silence. Spokesmen and ministers said that this was an 'internal matter of Russia'. Chechnya was barely discussed at the Budapest summit of the OSCE a week before the invasion, which was dominated by discussion of NATO and Bosnia. 'It was not a topic there,' said senior Hungarian diplomat Istvan Gyarmati, who later led the first OSCE mission to Chechnya.

Once the invasion started, reassurances from the Foreign Ministry that it would all be over quickly kept the sting out of any Western reaction. Kozyrev, one of the warmest supporters of the invasion, said publicly that Moscow still wanted a negotiated end to the crisis, 'but in any event, it will be solved within the next few days'. Western embassies waited and watched without comment. The reaction of one Western ambassador in Moscow in a private conversation to a correspondent was typical: 'It's the choice between slapping them on the wrist once or twice.'

President Clinton's first publicly reported telephone call to Yeltsin on Chechnya came only on 13 February, two months into the conflict, and was exceptionally bland, even at that late stage. 'President Clinton reiterated the importance of an end to the bloodshed and the start of a process leading to a peaceful settlement of the dispute,' White House Press Secretary Mike McCurry said afterwards. 'He stated once again that Chechnya is part of Russia, but noted the legitimate international concern over the humanitarian toll the fighting has taken.'

This low-key reponse infuriated the Russian opponents of the war, who were also the most pro-Western political camp in

Moscow. The rug had been pulled from beneath their feet. Speaking two years later, Kovalyov stormed against 'senseless diplomatic steps in the Western tradition counting on cultivated partners. We are not cultivated partners. We are not! When you criticize us politely, we perceive it as a compliment.' Gaidar says he had 'no illusions' that the West would take a forthright stand, but he regrets that there was no pressure to rein in the military operation. The West ignored the political subtext of the invasion and helped untie the hands of the hawks:

'I am convinced that in December, right up to 31 December, the beginning of the assault on Grozny, everything hung in the balance. It was possible, by coordinated force of pressure, to change the course of events to one of negotiations on the basis of a demonstrated threat. It was the moment when we had to, and we could have used all channels and levers of influence to convince Yeltsin that he had made a mistake – as they say, it was worse than a crime, it was a mistake. And at that moment the West was silent.'[6]

*

In Grozny, with tanks on the horizon, residents packed up and fled to villages in the mountains or the neighbouring republics of Ingushetia and Dagestan. By now Dudayev's blood was up. Angry at Moscow's latest rebuff, he called off any further efforts for peace talks, contemptuously denouncing the negotiations in Vladikavkaz as a 'farce' in a television address to the Chechen people. 'I call on the population to wage war with Russia until it leaves the territory of Chechnya ... The earth should burn under the feet of the Russian occupiers,' he said. 'It is a war for life or death. The current Russian regime has left no other option for the citizens of Chechnya.'

Moscow again extended the deadline for the Chechens to disarm by forty-eight hours, but already the first shells had landed within the suburbs, and the city shook to a heavy bombardment as Russian tanks blasted outlying villages from positions just 5 miles north of Grozny. Groups of men stood hunched on street corners watching, and children hung over apartment balconies pointing at the sky. Military jets screamed low over the village of Pervomaiskaya, unleashing a string of explosions. A trail of fire streaked across the sky from the hills to the east, landing with a flash and a crunch, smoke marking the shell's impact. Villagers now fled in panic as mortars exploded around them, pitting the snow with deadly shrapnel. They passed Chechen fighters pouring into the village in cars and buses to take up the fight.

Facing the 40,000-strong Russian invasion force was a make-shift army of barely 1000 Chechen fighters, according to the Chechen Chief of Staff Aslan Maskhadov. Volunteers soon flocked to increase that number several times over, but the number of trained men under arms at the beginning of the war was only in the hundreds, some 500 belonging to the National Guard led by Shamil Basayev, another 200 in the Presidential Guard, and a few more in special forces and security service units.

Maskhadov had only been Chief of Staff for a matter of months. He had resigned from the Russian army and returned to Chechnya in 1992, when the Ingush–Ossetian conflict threatened to spill over into Chechnya. He was immediately appointed Deputy Chief of Staff of Chechnya's forces. Maskhadov, like all of his generation, was born in exile in Kazakhstan in 1951. He says his family were always fighters, his father and his uncle both fought in their time. At the age of seven he returned with his family to their home village of Zebir-Yurt in northern Chechnya. He joined the Soviet army at the age of eighteen and moved all over Russia and Eastern Europe, passing through Leningrad Academy in 1981 and then serving in Hungary for five years. His last post was commander of a Soviet artillery division in Vilnius, Lithuania, from 1986 to 1992. He was regarded as one of the best artillery officers of his year. His men remember him as strict but fair. They noticed he improved the quality of the food, as well as the fitness of both officers and soldiers, joining them on runs and training exercises himself, unlike any other commander.

As with Dudayev, the break-up of the Soviet Union and independence demonstrations in the Baltics brought an awareness of nationalism. He was in Vilnius when civilians were killed as KGB troops stormed the television centre. 'I was in Lithuania, in Vilnius during those events. I also thought at that time that the Lithuanians were allowed to do what they wanted, to live under the wing of Russia, they lived normally there. And today it is shameful for me that I had those views and I think differently.'[7] In July 1994 as the clashes against the Chechen opposition grew more serious, Maskhadov took over as Chief of Staff of Chechen forces.

'We did not have a regular army, we did not manage to create one. All those parades, it was for show. When I came back from the Russian army, I knew that Russia was preparing to fight us, I quickly began to bring them up to strength, to prepare, but I did not succeed,' Maskhadov said later.[8]

Hussein Iskhanov, Maskhadov's aide-de-camp from autumn 1994, managed to laugh at their early naïvety and lack of preparation as he looked back. 'Maskhadov sometimes says, "If I recount how we fought the war, with what forces and with what means, firstly no one will believe it and secondly it would be shameful to admit that we were not ready and how we fought."' he said.[9]

To all appearances the Chechen preparations were shambolical, their mission suicidal. As the Russian tanks ranged across the hills to the north of Grozny, attacking a line of villages, Dolinsky, Pervomaiskaya and Petropavlovskaya, the Chechens appeared to be doing little to prepare defences. Along the main street running out north of the city windows were taped with white crosses, to give some small protection against flying glass when the shelling came close. A single cannon stood in the centre aisle under a camouflage net. A bulldozer was digging shallow trenches alongside.

A group of a dozen Chechen fighters armed with a collection of rifles stood on guard on one road leading north-east out of the city. Many were only eighteen or nineteen with no battle experience at all. Beside them on the ground stood two milk crates full of home-made Molotov cocktails. They had filled any bottle to hand – Russian champagne bottles, vodka and beer bottles – with a mixture of petrol and fuel oil, stuffing old rags in the top.

'These are our strongest weapon. We have no aviation, no tanks like the Russians. We will jump under their tanks together with these,' one young fighter, Mairbek Bokhacheyev, said. 'God gives and God takes life. I have no fear of death, it comes only once.'

'If we are all honest we are all *smertniki* [suicide fighters]. If we feared death we would not be here,' another said. Then, in a comment that summed up the irrepressible Chechen optimism and hospitality, he added, 'When we are free we will invite you and kill a sheep.'

Another group of a dozen men were staked out in a building beside Staropromyslovskoye Chaussee, the main road running north-west out of the city, some armed with rocket-propelled grenades, but most just with automatic rifles. A couple of fighters stood look-out on the roof of a five-storey building.

The fighters wore green headbands, some inscribed with Arabic script, to mark their commitment to Islam as well as independence. It was a holy war, or *ghazavat*, in the tradition of previous Caucasian wars against Russia, they said. They would fight to the death, and if they died in the battle for freedom and Islam, they would go straight to paradise, martyrs of the faith. 'If we win we will become wealthy in the future. If we die we will join Allah and be happy,' one of the fighters, Naib Idigov, said. They had gone to the mosque, repeating prayers after the *imam* in Arabic, and received his blessing to fight to defend their land and their faith, he said.

It seemed reckless talk amidst so little practical preparation for defence of the city. But the lack of fixed defences and the mobility of the small groups of fighters were in fact their strength. This group was watching for any movement of Russian tanks on the city, their commander said. 'A tank is a moving coffin. I say that as a tank specialist who once served in the Soviet army. One hit is enough,' he said, holding up an anti-tank grenade. In fact these men were in deadly earnest and were to prove highly successful when the Russians eventually moved on the city. The older ones had trained in the Soviet army, and served in Afghanistan or more recently in the separatist wars that had wracked the Caucasus region since the break-up of the Soviet Union. The best commanders to emerge in the course of the war were almost all fighters with recent battle experience in Nagorno-Karabakh, the enclave fought over by Azerbaijan and Armenia, and in Abkhazia, the North Caucasian region which fought successfully to break away from Georgia in 1992–3.

Men in the Chechen Presidential Guard, which was formed with one or two men from villages all over Chechnya, often had no more training than their two-year conscript service in the Soviet army and a lifetime of experience hunting and shooting. Virtually every Chechen learns to use a gun at an early age, and most households possess at least a hunting rifle. Modern weapons were rare, though, and many of the hundreds of volunteers who flocked from the villages to fight did not even have weapons. One young volunteer joined the fighters and carried ammunition for six months before he succeeded in capturing a Kalashnikov for himself in battle. Many were not supporters of Dudayev, some had even been in the opposition, but the majority were villagers with little previous interest in politics who were angered by Russia's use of tanks and bombers against Chechnya.

Many men said they had offered their services to the main

command, only to be told there were no spare weapons. Some were trading at Grozny's famous gun bazaar: Said Udùgov was selling a 9mm Makarov pistol for $600 so that he could buy something bigger. A Kalashnikov was going for the same sum at the time, although six months later the price dropped to a third of that. Another young man said he was trying to trade a radio for a box of grenades. Even the armed fighters were short of the necessary gear. One commander had come in from his positions in the north-east of Grozny to buy five home-made waistcoats sewn with special pockets for the curved magazines for a Kalashnikov rifle.

The Chechens had some tanks at the beginning of the war, although probably no more than a dozen, far fewer than the Russians claimed they had and most of which were showing signs of wear and tear from two years of skirmishing with the opposition. They were put into action in the battle for Pervomaiskaya in mid-December and Russian soldiers came up against Chechen tanks later in Grozny, but for the rest of the war they played no part.

A single armoured personnel carrier often roared through the ice-rutted streets of Grozny in December, flying the Chechen flag, along with a truck bearing an anti-aircraft gun, which was posted at times on the central square. The Chechens also had Grad multiple rocket-launchers and mortars, which they used very effectively in the early days of the war, moving them around between strikes to avoid detection.

Yet the overwhelming firepower of the Russian forces was obvious, not least to senior officers like Dudayev and Maskhadov, who had served most of their lives in the Soviet and then Russian army. To resist looked like dangerous recklessness, although naïvety may have been closer to the mark.

Iskhanov, Maskhadov's aide-de-camp since the previous autumn, said they never thought Russia would attack with such force but, rather, expected some sort of police operation. 'We thought the borders would be closed, like in Dagestan when there was cholera there, and soldiers with automatic rifles started to keep people out. We thought they would do the same here. Even when they started bombing we thought it was to frighten us.'

Akhmed Zupkukhajiev, a commander of the Chechen Presidential Guard, who escorted Dudayev to his meeting with Grachev, said that although they all knew it would come to war, 'No one expected it to be like it was. Dudayev himself did not expect that it would be so large-scale, with such quantities of armour.' Akhmed anticipated more of a quick assault by Russian special troops. 'Personally I thought if there would be a war it would be shooting with automatic rifles and grenades. But aviation, mortars, artillery, everything they had, thrown all at once, aimed at the civilian population . . . No one thought that would happen.'[10]

By many Chechen accounts Dudayev believed that Russia was trying to frighten him into submission but would baulk at full-scale war. He persisted in trying to contact Yeltsin. In the last week of December, shortly before the assault on Grozny, Dudayev called his old friend the Kalmyk General Valery Ochirov, who worked in the Kremlin, and said that 'if only Yeltsin calls' he would be prepared to make terms. This threw a team of small-time aides into a frenzy of activity trying to reach Yeltsin, according to one Kremlin source. They finally reached his first aide, Viktor Ilyushin, only to be told it was 'too late'. Dudayev reacted with more threats that left him no room for manoeuvre. 'This is a war of life or death. All our citizens must know that we have to defend our country and our lives,' he told his nation. Chechen pride demanded that once a challenge was made, honour required a man to meet it.

*

Five days into the war, Ayub Khansultanov came home from the battlefield, dumping a whole arsenal of weapons on the kitchen floor. A big, taciturn Chechen dressed in combat fatigues, he looked older than his thirty years, dark circles ringing his eyes. He sat down silently, looking hard at the three foreign journalists he found in his kitchen. 'My grandfather was shot by the Cheka [secret police], Russians who wanted his horse. It was a good horse, he loved it as much as his wife, so they shot him.'[11] They were his first words, his way of explaining the weapons on the floor.

He unpacked four grenades as he talked, lining them up on the kitchen counter. One by one he unscrewed their tops and inserted new silver pins. 'This one's for Yeltsin,' he said, laughing, showing a glint of gold teeth. 'Yeltsin himself made bandits out of us.'

Ayub came from Benoi, a village high in the southern mountains. His forefathers fought alongside Imam Shamil in the last century when they slaughtered whole battalions of the Tsar's army in the woods near Benoi. Ayub had been fighting for a week already around Grozny and now his group of 150 fighters had been ordered to head into the mountains. He had sent his wife and three children, along with all their valuables, ahead to the safety of their village. 'If I die my son will need something,' he said.

Orphaned at an early age, Ayub had been a trader since he was thirteen, later travelling to China, Pakistan and Turkey when the borders opened up under Gorbachev. Life had been good until the Russians came. 'They are uninvited guests; they do not let us lead our lives in peace,' he said. 'We have a saying: An uninvited guest is like a Tartar. Here, the Mongol Tartars are remembered.'

He prepared his stash of weapons, a Kalashnikov assault rifle, a shoulder-held grenade-launcher with several anti-tank grenades, and a big-calibre machine-gun with a roll of armour-piercing bullets, captured from the Russians, he said. In his car outside, lying across the hand-brake were two Russian-made ground-to-air missiles. Ayub had returned just two months earlier from a

Right: Imam Shamil, the Dagestani warrior and religious leader, shortly after his surrender in 1859.

Below: Murids crossing a river during the Caucasian Wars. A drawing by Prince Gagarin.

Left: Ruslan Khasbulatov, speaker of the Russian parliament 1991–3.
Right: Pavel Grachev, Russian Defence Minister 1991–6.

Jokhar Dudayev on the terrace of the House of Commons in October 1992 with adviser Eduard Khachukayev (far left), Foreign Minister Shamsudin Yusef (third from right), Gerrard Neale (second from left), Den Dover MP (fourth from right).

Jokhar Dudayev at a rally in 1994.

Men performing the *zikr* in the village of Itum-Kale on the third day of mourning after Dudayev's death, April 1996.

A Chechen fighter standing over the bodies of Russian soldiers after the New Year's Eve battle, 5 January 1995.

Russian conscript prisoners in the bunker of the Presidential Palace in Grozny, 5 January 1995.

Chechen fighters moving through the city, January 1995.

Russian soldiers camped in the heart of Grozny, February 1995.

Central Grozny, February 1995.

A mother searching for her missing son in a mass grave at the Orthodox cemetery in Grozny, February 1995.

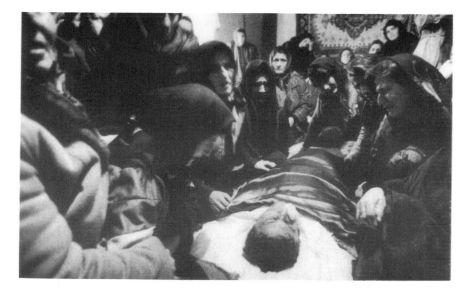

The wake for Falkhadrin Azizov, a Dagestani hostage killed during the siege of Pervomaiskoye, January 1996. Relatives retrieved his body from the ruined village days after the battle.

Thousands of Chechens rallied for days outside the ruined Presidential Palace in February 1996, calling for the withdrawal of troops.

Shamil Basayev, top field commander, with his fighters in Vedeno, summer of 1996.

At a joint peace ceremony on 24 August 1996, Aslan Maskhadov, the Chechen chief of staff, berates the Russian soldiers for staining the honour of the Russian army after their conduct in the Chechen war.

period training in guerrilla warfare in the remote mountainous border region between Pakistan and Afghanistan. Along with a couple of hundred Chechens, Uzbeks, Tajiks and others at a training camp, he learned how to use different weapons, lay mines and plan ambushes. He watched idly as a Chechen fighter on local Chechen television read from an instruction manual how to knock out a Russian tank, describing the weakest points. Another bearded fighter told all civilians to leave the city to the fighters and said those blocking the tanks on the roads should move out of the way of the fighting.

Ayub's eyes barely flickered. Like most of the other fighters, he was not paid and supported himself. There was no doubting his readiness to fight the Russians, and he knew what to expect. 'First they will bomb with planes. That will be very tough. The rest will be rubbish. We will come at them from all sides, shooting them like partridges,' he said. 'The day may be theirs, but the night is ours.'

*

The Presidential Palace already had an air of civil emergency, its nine floors of windows shattered from the bombing, its offices empty. The Chechen leadership had moved down into the warren of underground rooms in the basement. Fighters in fatigues guarded the head of the stairs as civilians in fur hats and sheepskin coats milled around the freezing, marble-clad foyer. Someone delivered great sides of fresh beef, dumping them on a table along with loaves of bread. Large glass jars of pickled tomatoes were stacked on the floor beneath. Nurses in army jackets brought in a bale of cotton for bandages and a pile of army winter coats. Outside on Freedom Square a constant throng of people ignored the cold to demonstrate against the war, dancing the traditional *zikr*, praying and chanting. It was invariably led by Mansur, a seventy-year-old descendant of Sheikh Mansur, sporting a long flowing white beard, a tall red hat and carrying a staff, playing up to the television cameras. Others came dressed in long Caucasian coats, decorated with loops across the chest for rifle cartridges, half their faces hidden by woolly sheepskin hats almost as imposing as English guardmen's bearskins.

A group of Russian parliamentarians emerged from a meeting with Chechen ministers expressing the bleak hope that by their presence in Grozny they might force the Kremlin leadership to back off from the war. The message from Moscow was, however, increasingly stern, and the tactics were ever more brutal. 'Grozny will shortly be encircled and only capitulation of Dudayev's forces would stop bloodshed,' said Yegorov, who was now to be seen wearing camouflage fatigues.

Yeltsin's deadline was due to expire at midnight on 17 December. It was the signal for military jets to bomb Grozny. They struck minutes after midnight, roaring low over the city and waking residents with heavy explosions as they demolished a factory on the edge of town. They returned the following night and ran sorties until dawn, hitting more targets in the suburbs.

The Security Council resolved to step up operations even further. 'Today, Russian troops will continue delivering missile strikes on the most important objects and will conduct decisive offensive actions,' a Russian government statement said on 20 December. The nightly bombing grew noticeably heavier and closer to the city centre, each morning revealing huge craters and destroyed buildings.

Casualties were rising daily on both sides and already dozens of civilians had been killed. Refugees started pouring out of the city, a solid stream of cars, bumping along the icy roads. The streets were deserted as families still in Grozny moved down into their cellars for protection. In the Leninsky district across the river from the Palace, a fire roared from a broken gas main where a bomb had flattened several houses. A Chechen family sifted through the rubble of what had been their home, the grand-mother, speechless, clutching two cooking pots she had rescued from the debris. The city was now without water, and people were gathering snow for drinking water. Kovalyov, still in Grozny, said his team had seen forty-two bodies of civilians killed in the conflict, and appealed to Yeltsin to halt the bombing. 'These pilots and gunners do not know where they are aiming,' he said.

'It's our own troops who are killing here,' shouted Tanya Yemelina, a blonde forty-year-old Russian woman hovering in the entrance to her apartment block. Several Russian families came out of the communal cellar, angry, frightened and bewildered. One of the children held a thick, ragged piece of shrapnel from a missile that had just landed in the courtyard. It was still hot. It had gouged a deep crater in the ground and torn chunks out of the wall of their building. The bombing had already knocked out the electricity, water and gas supplies to the suburb where mostly Russians lived, all workers at the nearby electricity station. Yet with the war on their doorsteps they still did not plan to leave. 'I have nowhere to go,' Yemelina said. 'All I have is my two children, nothing else. Everything I have is here.' It was a common cry among the Russian residents of Chechnya, estimated at some 200,000 at the beginning of the war, the majority of them living in Grozny. Unlike the Chechens, who could rely on their extended family networks and find shelter with relatives in the villages or elsewhere outside Chechnya, many of the Russians literally had nowhere to go. Some simply did not want to leave the apartment that they had spent a lifetime acquiring, but those who stayed were invariably the ones who were too poor or too sick to leave.

Polina Shakhayeva, a tiny, bird-like Russian pensioner, wrapped in a grey woollen headscarf against the bitter cold, was selling three loaves of bread on a cardboard box on the side of the street. She had bought the bread from the state bakery that morning and was selling it at a mark-up, hoping to earn enough to buy some food. 'I cannot go. My husband is at home, he is paralysed. I cannot leave him and I cannot move him,' she said, tears welling up in her eyes. Her children were living far away in the Siberian city of Novosibirsk. 'They cannot come, they have their own problems,' she said simply.

The Chechens and fellow-North Caucasians were more energetic about helping themselves. Umar Galaborchev, a thirty-three-year-old Ingush businessman living 1000 miles away in Kazakhstan, dropped everything when he heard of the Russian invasion. Jumping into his car, he drove day and night to Grozny to take his relatives out of the city to safety, returning the following day to help their neighbours.

Hundreds of reporters had arrived in Chechnya when the tanks rolled in. They encountered reckless acts of nobility and generosity on the part of ordinary Chechens at the height of the bombing. One group of French journalists took a taxi to observe the first fighting north of Grozny at Petropavlovskaya. Didier François of the French daily *Libération* left all his belongings, including his computer and satellite telephone, with the driver as they headed on foot over a bridge towards the front line. They were suddenly overtaken by advancing Russian troops and forced to return to Grozny by another route but the driver waited for them by the bridge all day, even when shellfire came in close and the Russian troops advanced around him. As the Russians searched his car, the driver insisted they not touch anything that belonged to the French journalists. He then spent two days searching the city to return François's belongings. 'When he found me, he apologized that there were two Snickers bars and an apple missing. "I promise you I did not take them. It was the Russian soldiers who took them." This guy we hardly knew, he risked his life for us and he was apologizing for two Snickers bars.'

The bombing escalated sharply with the first daytime raids on the city on 22 December. It was mid-morning when seventy-five-year-old Alexander Shevchenko ventured outside for a breath of fresh air. The Russian pensioner moved carefully over the ice on his walking stick towards a few stalls where women were selling bread and chocolate. Traffic was moving along the street, crossing the river to the main square just 100 yards away.

The apartment next to Shevchenko's had been bombed in the night. He stared in disbelief at the mound of rubble and broken rafters sticking skywards that was all that was left of his neighbours' building. The earsplitting blast had rocked his own building and his neighbours had urged him down to the basement. 'It was terrifying, terrifying,' he said, his whole body shaking, still in his pyjamas under his coat. 'They are not people who are doing this, they are wild beasts, savage.'

As he spoke, the sound of jets sent the crowd of people running for cover. The planes came out of nowhere, suddenly diving right overhead, the roar of the engines escalating to an urgent scream. People fled in panic, not knowing where to run, bumping into each other as they scanned the skies and looked round for friends. Two huge explosions shook the ground with a deafening bang. Then followed a moment of complete silence as debris, bits of branches, brick dust rained down on figures crouching on the ground. The sound of falling glass tinkled to a stop. Then people were shouting. The women running the kiosks were hurriedly packing away their chocolate bars and sweet drinks with shaking hands. This was the first time planes had bombed in daylight hours, and suddenly no one felt safe. A column of black smoke rose above the trees. A truck and car on the bridge just 300 yards away were on fire, the bodies still inside. More mangled bodies lay in the street. The missiles had blown a huge crater in the black earth of the river-bank and sliced into the trees of a small park. A man's body lay where he had been walking, a red stain in the snow where his head should have been. The death toll was at least six; the bridge, presumably the target, was untouched.

Across the city at a crossroads in the Mikrorayon district half a dozen cars and buses were blazing after another terrifying bombing raid. People were out clearing the debris from the previous night's bombing when the jets returned. At least twenty people were killed, including American photographer Cynthia Elbaum, a young freelance. It was the first war she had covered and she had not even told her parents she was going to Chechnya. Like many of the Chechens at the bomb site, she had absolutely no warning and no chance to take cover. That day the planes ran sortie after sortie on the city centre, flattening houses and apartment buildings, rocketing major intersections and roads. The city centre now looked, felt and smelled like a battlefield. Ash from the burning fires and explosions turned the snow black, broken glass crunched underfoot and torn-down trolleybus wires trailed in the streets. Trees snapped off by the explosions left ragged, gleaming yellow stumps and the acrid smell of burning and explosives hung in the air. Incredibly, the Russian government press office denied there had been any bombing or any damage to apartment buildings. Kovalyov sent Yeltsin a telegram from Grozny, calling on him to stop 'this crazy massacre' and pull the country 'out of this vicious circle of despair and blood-stained lies'.

*

Yeltsin emerged from his seclusion to chair a Security Council meeting on 26 December, his first public appearance since the war began, and moved to quiet his critics with a promise to stop the aerial bombing. He even suggested peace talks could be resumed. Yet behind closed doors he delivered a scathing rebuke to Grachev and Yerin for not bringing events in Chechnya to a close sooner.[12] Perhaps the most revealing comment was made by the arch-hawk Yegorov after the meeting. 'It is imperative that gangs in Chechnya be disarmed and Grozny taken quickly,' he said. 'Any delay will be viewed inside and outside Russia as a sign of the nation's weakness.'

The following day Yeltsin gave a national address on television. He took a tough line on Chechnya, insisting that troops were defending Russia's integrity and constitution. 'No territory has the right to leave Russia,' he said. Sending in troops had been a difficult decision but long overdue, he said, justifying it by describing Chechnya as a breeding ground of crime and a threat to the nation's security. Some of his comments blatantly contradicted the situation on the ground. Russia's troops would restore peace and order soon and help the Chechen people escape their misfortune, he said. He also made the fantastic claim that Chechnya was awash with 10,000 foreign mercenaries. Nevertheless the military was doing a good job, had now surrounded Grozny and blocked the 'armed bands', he said. It seemed he was ignoring all the alarm signals.

He repeated his previous day's promise that the bombing would stop. 'The Gordian knot posed by the Chechen crisis can be cut. But the cost is too high – the cost of the lives of Russian citizens. In order to save lives, I have ordered that there be no air strikes that could lead to civilian casualties in Grozny.'

The very next day the bombers were back in the skies. Kovalyov reported that no bombs dropped on the city for two days, but they returned with a vengeance on 29 December, hitting an orphanage among other buildings. Amazingly, the children escaped injury, all crammed, wide-eyed and silent, in the underground basement. Across to the west of the city, the bombers had also hit the oil refinery, where dense black smoke started to fill the sky. Another bomb fell close to the Presidential Palace but Dudayev's stronghold still stood untouched.

Heavy fighting was concentrated east of Grozny, as Russian troops took control of the village of Petropavlovskaya and moved down the ridge across the snowy fields to the military base at Khankala. Planes and artillery battered the fields and settlements, forcing back Chechen fighters dressed in white snow-camouflage suits who fought back ferociously, bringing down a helicopter and inflicting heavy casualties on the Russian units.

But there was something inexorable about the Russian operation now, despite the blundering and botching of the previous weeks. The sheer firepower and massed serries of tanks gave the Russians a huge advantage in the open spaces around Grozny. They took Khankala on 29 December, gaining control of the eastern approaches to Grozny, and manoeuvred around Pervomaiskaya, the village to the north, to move in on the Rodina collective farm much closer to the city.

The same day Grachev, Yerin and Stepashin flew back down to Mozdok, where the Defence Minister told journalists his forces would advance on Grozny to seize weapons but would not storm the city with all-out force. 'We do not intend anything of the kind, since there are civilians in the town,' he said. 'But we will continue to advance deep into the town with a view to confiscating weapons and eradicating gangs.' His underestimation of the Chechen resistance in Grozny, coupled with a complete misunderstanding of the military task of capturing a city, was to prove catastrophic for his soldiers.

Grachev was ignoring not only Russia's experience in Afghanistan but also lessons from the historic battles fought on Russian soil in the Second World War. The epic struggles of Stalingrad and Leningrad had shown more than anything in military history that a city can only be taken with enormous cruelty and passion. Tanks were no good in a city, it needed a ruthlessly enforced blockade, and then very determined infantry. Grachev had neither. His army had omitted to seal off the southern part of Grozny and was looking very reluctant.

It was a mixture of personal inexperience and racial arrogance that made Grachev overconfident. Vorobyov argues that Grachev was simply not qualified to be Minister of Defence. He had served in Afghanistan but had only ever been a divisional commander, and lacked the organizational experience and strategic thinking necessary to mastermind a large campaign. Grachev neither had the courage to tell Yeltsin he needed more time to prepare, nor did he understand what he was letting himself in for, Vorobyov said. 'Why does a little child put its tiny fingers in an electric socket? Because he does not know that there is a current and it will kill him.'

Russian television, in derogatory manner, had already shown a video clip of Dudayev telling his people how to fight. 'This is the centuries-old tactic of the mountain people,' he said. 'Strike and withdraw, strike and withdraw . . . to exhaust them until they die of fear and horror.' The Russian presenter dismissed it as more of Dudayev's wild talk, showing the sort of historical ignorance that dominated much of Russian official thinking.

To many people even in government, though, the next step in the ground assault seemed self-evidently a bad idea because Grozny was also populated by a large number of ethnic Russians. Government spokesman Valery Grishin said on 14 December, 'There will be no storming of Grozny . . . It is a densely populated Russian city.' The decision to do just that was taken in the end, with the same secrecy and lack of consultation as the decision to start the war. In Mozdok, Grachev gathered his friends and generals to celebrate his birthday.[13]

10

The Battle for Grozny

The battle for Grozny only really began several days after the disastrous incursion on New Year's Eve. As the Russian generals slowly comprehended the scale of that defeat, they pulled back the surviving troops from the centre and unleashed a heavy air and artillery bombardment on the city. It was a critical moment for them. There was very nearly a complete breakdown in morale in the Russian forces and many senior officers were on the verge of disobeying orders. Several generals had been sacked and two were accused of cowardice for their performance on New Year's Eve. Only after a few days, under the command of Afghan war veteran General Lev Rokhlin, did they begin a purposeful assault.[1]

They blasted the city block by block, building by building, with mortars, tank and cannon fire, Grad missiles and bombs and then sent in troops in small groups, spearheaded by special forces units, who inched forward carefully on the ground, taking one building at a time. More wary of their Chechen opponents, they made massive use of sniper teams and torched whole streets of buildings to flush out any resistance. It was to take them two more months of grim fighting to clear the city of Chechen fighters and establish Russian control. In the process they ground up thousands of lives, the vast majority of them civilian, as well as acres of homes and public buildings.

Their first aim was the Presidential Palace where Maskhadov was still directing the defence of Grozny, but it took three more weeks of heavy fighting for Russian troops to reach it. The dead bodies of their comrades lay on the streets all that time. The battle for control of the railway station raged on for days. Basayev recalled how his fighters repelled Russian advances again and again around the station. Fierce fighting also engulfed the area just east of the centre around Pervomaiskaya Street, which was already strewn with the wreckage of a Russian armoured column. Some Russian soldiers, who had escaped their burning armour and dived into nearby buildings, were still holding out in tiny pockets in the centre, shooting at anything that moved.

Russian troops had already established strong positions in the north part of Grozny in early January. The Chechens had lost ground on the east side of the city where Russian forces had moved in from Khankala. Now they had also lost Karpinsky Hill, the strategic high ground on the west. Major-General Babichev, last seen on the western road promising not to advance against civilians, had moved his troops into a park just half a mile from the railway station. General Rokhlin had occupied the canning factory and the airport in the north-east.

The Chechens still held much of the city centre, and were in good spirits, flush with weapons and new volunteers. They gathered in and around the circular conference hall at the back of the Presidential Palace and even danced their traditional *zikr* while the anti-aircraft guns turned slowly watching the skies. On 3 January they were still milling around when Basayev strolled up in relaxed fashion, a rifle in one hand, in the other a plastic bag full of the documents of captured and dead Russian soldiers.

Basayev was the commander of the 500-strong Chechen National Guard. The title acknowledged his experience leading a battalion of volunteers in Abkhazia for a year in 1992–3. His fighters now formed the hardcore of the defence of Grozny and, along with those of commanders Ruslan Gelayev and Umal Dashayev, also veterans of Abkhazia, were known as the Abkhaz Battalion. Young and fit, they were mostly still in their twenties, but old enough to have completed military service in the Soviet or Russian army. They were battle-hardened and organized, and moved around the city as a mobile force, taking the fight to the Russians.

The photographer Patrick Chauvel saw them in action in Grozny. They would arrive in a group 200 strong, usually on foot but sometimes in a couple of tanks, to sort out any fighting. Spreading out, they would leap straight over the barricades where other fighters were crouching. 'They were really tough commando fighters, completely purposeful and not friendly at all,' he remembered. 'As soon as they went in all hell would let loose, the fight would suddenly escalate. They were like firemen. Then they would move on to the next place.'[2]

The Russians also had their crack commandos. Chauvel was with a group of Chechen fighters sloshing through the city sewers, one of the safest ways to cut through the city on the way to an ambush, when the commander in front pushed him down and opened fire into the darkness. A furious gun battle lit up the pitch-black tunnel, as half a dozen rifles opened up and bullets ricocheted off the roof, killing the man behind Chauvel. They had walked slap into a Russian patrol group. The Russians took off, vanishing easily in the black passages, leaving two of their own dead, their faces blackened with greasepaint, their uniforms marking them as special forces.

The Chechens were at a huge advantage fighting on home ground in a city most knew from childhood. They worked mostly at night, laying mines and carrying supplies and ammunition to forward positions. Their mobility was their great strength. Using back alleys and the sewers, slipping through basements and destroyed buildings, they danced around the Russians, who still often clung to the dubious safety of their armoured vehicles.

Very resourceful, they were also cheeky. Resting up in one of the many underground cellars, they would listen in to Russian units on a captured radio set. When a unit sounded as if they were in trouble and calling for instructions, one of the Chechens would grab the receiver and shout commands in Russian to retreat. When the Russians rumbled them, one of the commanders rained curses on them, vowing personally to string up the culprit. The euphoria from early success, however, soon dissipated under constant bombardment. The Chechens began taking heavy casualties and within ten days were running short of ammunition, Basayev says, forcing them to economize and opening up what was to be his biggest problem throughout the war.

*

Even when the Russian generals began the serious assault on Grozny, their armed forces were beset with problems. Units came under 'friendly fire' as poorly trained and equipped units were sent in unsure of their target and with the vaguest of orders. Communications and logistics were so poor that officers complained their desperate signals or requests for support went unanswered. The casualties kept mounting.

Vladimir Povetkin, a nineteen-year-old conscript with the 503rd Motor Rifle Regiment, was sent into Grozny in the early hours of New Year's Day in a small unit of eight armoured troop-carriers and immediately fell into a furious firefight with the Russian unit they were meant to be reinforcing. 'In Grozny the first thing we fired on was our own troops,' he said. 'When we went in we met an armoured vehicle and they told us that ours were standing on this side, and the Chechens over there. When they started to hit us, we were given an order by radio to open fire.'[3] It took an hour and a half of heavy shooting before the message got through that they were both on the same side. Suddenly the others held their fire. As they savoured ten minutes of quiet, Povetkin's unit was told over the radio they had killed five men and wounded seven, two of them badly.

It was only one of countless fatal mess-ups. The Russians' communications were so basic that units could often only talk to their base command and not to other groups around them. The Defence Ministry, Interior Ministry and FSK all sent their own units into Grozny with dangerous results. The lack of coordination between the different services was aggravated by an extremely cumbersome command structure. All three Power Ministers, Grachev, Yerin and Stepashin, were directing operations in person from Mozdok. Yegorov was also there in his role as special representative to Chechnya. There was no combined joint headquarters set up in Moscow specifically for the operation where instructions could have been coordinated by one staff and one commander. 'How could they communicate when they are all in different buildings?' asked one Western military analyst.

One of the most glaring failures was that of Russian intelligence-gathering. The Russian leadership and military chiefs had certainly vastly underestimated the strength of the Chechen fighting force. There has since been a lot of buck-passing as each ministry disowned responsibility. Technically the job lay with the counter-intelligence service, the FSK, since by law the Defence Ministry was not entitled to conduct military intelligence inside Russia. The Interior Ministry at the time did not have an intelligence-gathering unit at all, so did nothing, according to Anatoly Kulikov, who was a deputy Interior Minister at the beginning of the war. Stepashin later admitted 'shortcomings' in the intelligence-gathering. He said they estimated Dudayev had a fighting force of 5000–7000 men but clearly they miscalculated the more important question of how capable and determined that fighting force was. The FSK's information was undoubtedly fatally flawed since its main source was the self-serving anti-Dudayev opposition. Grachev was a fool to trust it.

If the poor intelligence cost lives, the lack of organization and preparation of troops cost many more. One staggering statistic showed that for every Russian soldier killed by the Chechens, five died in Chechnya due to carelessness or other reasons.[4] 'We were just thrown into Grozny right into the heaviest fighting,' Povetkin recalled. Within four days his unit, isolated and outnumbered at the train depot, without food and with only their automatic rifles left, surrendered to the Chechens.

One Interior Ministry unit from Sverdlovsk, in the Ural mountains, was so angered by the lack of military command and the inhuman conditions in Chechnya that they packed up and went home in disgust. 'We were poorly armed. We did not have enough food or heat. We had to sleep in trenches, and finally we were given no specific orders,' one of the 100 OMON police officers said on his return home.[5] They had not been told they were heading for Chechnya until they arrived. The unit, which specializes in riot control, was given five old APCs and told to guard a road north of Grozny. They were then ordered to repulse an attack of Chechen tanks. 'My heart sank. We just had to let the tanks pass by, without trying to stop them, because we had no anti-tank weapons,' the officer said. Finally a senseless attack by Russian helicopters on a nearby village convinced him there was 'no centralized control over the military operation'.

Logistical backup was so abysmal, there was not even enough drinking water for soldiers in the first month. Denis Fedulov, who drove a truck ferrying in supplies and wounded out of the city, remembers they were only given 250 millilitres of water each a day. In the bitterly cold winter conditions few men had good boots and none had gloves. One Interior Ministry officer cursed Grachev for treating his Defence Ministry soldiers so badly. 'He should be strung up on Red Square. They were starving. They had one tin of meat each for a whole day. And nothing else, no bread, nothing.' Some resorted to killing and eating stray dogs, he said.

The conditions and the enormous casualties Russian soldiers were taking was catastrophic for morale. Slava Naumov, a deputy commander of reconnaissance even though he was only nineteen, was sent into the city at night on patrol. Almost two years later he said he could not remember anything about it. Sitting in the

Rus sanatorium for war veterans outside Moscow, his eyes dark holes of despair, he began shivering despite the greenhouse central heating in the sanatorium. Goose-pimples rose along his well-muscled arms and shoulders.

Piled into a light tank, his unit would inch their way down side streets, looking for evidence of fighters. They came upon dozens of pieces of wrecked Russian armour, and bodies of their own soldiers. They did not dare step outside the protection of their armoured vehicle for snipers lurked everywhere, but they saw at every turn of the street what would happen to them if caught by the Chechens.

'I do not think about it. It was the mood. Many thought they would not get out alive from that. We all felt the same,' he said. 'We thought there would simply be guards protecting the President. It turned out the opposite: there was a whole army of Chechens there.'[6]

Fedulov roared around the battle-strewn streets at top speed. 'It was essential not to stop, because they said if you ever stopped anyone could fire on you, from a grenade-launcher or a sniper, so if I stopped I would be a dead man. And there was no way to avoid them, because if they saw Russians they came running for you.'[7]

He said he was most scared of air and rocket fire from his own side, the jets that never let up with their bombing raids and the 'Grad' rockets, which take their name from the Russian for 'hail'. Launched from a multiple rocket system, the Grads would fall in a thick wall of explosions, with a deafening roar. The Chechen side had Grads too, hitting Russian positions in the hills to the north of Grozny, making the Russian soldiers freezing in their trenches wonder what the hell they were doing there.

A column of battle-weary troops of the Interior Ministry Dzerzhinsky regiment pulled a dozen tanks and artillery pieces out of the village of Dolinsky on the north of Grozny after a month of fighting. Filthy from living in trenches for weeks, they were heading back to base in Mozdok for a few days' rest. The fighting was not getting any easier, a senior lieutenant said, embarrassed to shake hands since his were so dirty. Casualties were high among their own and among civilians in the north part of the city, he said, and morale was rock-bottom. 'No one wants the war at this point.'

They were days of senseless fear and horror. 'Right from the beginning we were saying, "Why are we fighting?" No one knew what we were doing there. No one was fighting for anything concrete,' Fedulov said.

Sergei Kovalyov returned from Grozny to Moscow in early January and demanded a meeting with Yeltsin as his human rights commissioner. He had heard Yeltsin announce an end to the bombing but had seen no let-up in Chechnya. He wanted to report to the President what was really happening and beg him to order a ceasefire. Finally the Kremlin aides relented. The two men talked for forty minutes, although it was Kovalyov who did most of the talking. Yeltsin listened in grim silence. It was 6 January, the day before Russian Orthodox Christmas. 'Boris Nikolaevich, I entreat you, tomorrow is Christmas, tomorrow is the 7th, Orthodox Christmas, let them use it as an excuse for a ceasefire, even just to gather up the bodies and wounded, maybe we can save someone,' Kovalyov remembers saying. Yeltsin was unmoved. 'He did not say no, he said, "It is not time yet." That is, tomorrow is too early. But why did he say that? Because he had calculated on a crushing defeat.'[8]

The very next day, Orthodox Christmas, Russian forces moved in on the Presidential Palace in the most concerted assault since New Year's Eve. The seventh floor of the Palace caught fire but the Chechens once again repelled the Russian attack.

A few days later an extraordinary meeting took place in the half-built twelve-storey hotel on Orjonikidze Prospekt, just 500 yards from the Palace. Fighters had trapped sixty-five Russian paratroopers on the top floor and threatened to blow the building up unless they surrendered. Meanwhile Maskhadov had proposed a ceasefire to the Russians. Saying he was concerned that the hundreds of dead bodies lying around the streets would spread disease, he suggested each side gather up the dead bodies in the area they controlled. Through a Russian radio operator taken prisoner with his radio, they contacted the Russian command and agreed to a meeting. The Russians sent an armoured vehicle to the Presidential Palace and Maskhadov and a couple of body-guards climbed in and travelled the short distance from the square to the red-brick skeleton building of the hotel.

There, on the third floor, with the paratroopers trapped above them, he met Babichev. The Russian General told Maskhadov to send his fighters out along Rosa Luxembourg Street, stripped to the waist, their arms up, Kalashnikovs in their right hands, the magazine in their left. 'They thought that when we proposed a ceasefire to collect the bodies it was a sign of weakness, that we were close to defeat,' said Iskhanov, Maskhadov's aide-de-camp, who accompanied him. 'We were in fact much more concerned about an epidemic.'[9]

The meeting between the two generals came to nothing. The bodies lay there for weeks more, until Russian firepower eventually forced the Chechens out of the city centre. Maskhadov and Babichev did not even resolve the immediate dilemma of the paratroopers. Cold, thirsty and hungry, the Russians were growing desperate as the Chechens stood guard on the floor below. Maskhadov recalled that his Russian counterpart did not seem to care about their fate. 'Babichev just waved his hand, saying do as you want,' Maskhadov recalled in his book. 'Babichev was simply not interested in their fate.'[10]

In the end the Chechens let them go, making them hand over their weapons. One Chechen officer was bright enough to check the weapons as they gave them in and noticed they had removed the pins from inside. 'He ordered them back up to find the pins, shouting "We will kill one man for each pin missing." They were crying, they said they had thrown them away. One soldier broke down sobbing, he never found his but in the end they let him go,' Iskhanov recalled.

That meeting was a one-off. Maskhadov spoke several times to Babichev and Rokhlin over the radio but always met a blank wall of stubbornness. He remembers warning them that persisting in the war would bring humiliation and shame upon the Russian army, but the generals, desperate to avenge their early defeat, were not in a listening mood. By 10 January two tanks were placed on the north corners of the square and a third in the market, and were firing on the Palace.

The Chechen fighters were losing ground, largely through lack of manpower and firepower. Some units were remarkably organized for a volunteer guerrilla force, signing for heavy weapons as one shift took over from another. But lack of discipline lost them key areas. Posted to one place, fighters were easily diverted or bored, and would abandon their post when they heard shooting elsewhere, joining other fighters who came by and often leaving a crucial position unguarded without telling their commander. Other volunteers were simply operating on their own, and took no part in a coordinated defence.

The command in the Presidential Palace stayed on for ten more days but was critically low on food and water, and reduced for the last week to drinking water trickling from broken drainpipes. Iskhanov remembers people coming in begging for more ammunition and only having five anti-tank rockets left under the bed. Somehow, someone, usually Basayev, would turn up with more when it seemed they were finished. With the shelling growing heavier and deadlier by the hour, it was becoming increasingly difficult to fight. They lost eleven men of the Presidential Guard in the last week, recalled the commander Akhmed Zupkukhajiev.

Looking back, Maskhadov described it as the most dangerous time of the war for them. 'We were tightly encircled. Just 50 metres away Russian forces had blockaded us with tanks, and they were firing point-blank at the building,' he recalled.[11] 'We were practically suicide fighters then, we never thought we would get out alive, we were ready for that, to stand to the end.'

*

It was then that Valentina Krayeva, a school headmistress from Volgodonsk, a minor provincial town in the rolling Russian farmlands of the Don valley, turned up looking for her son Alexei. He was one of the dozens of Russian conscript soldiers taken prisoner and lying in the Presidential Palace. Chechens had called her from the Palace in late December to tell her where he was. 'They said, "You know your son is with us. He is alive, and everything will be fine but you must demand an end to the war,"' she recalled.[12]

A dynamic forty-five-year-old, director of a 2000-pupil co-ed school, Krayeva organized meetings and fired off telegrams to Yeltsin, Ivan Rybkin, the Speaker of the Russian Parliament and others. She then travelled to the Russian base in Mozdok but they told her to go home since for the moment they could not do anything. Instead she took a bus and turned up in Grozny at Basayev's headquarters on the evening of 17 January to plead for her son's release. That night she met not only Basayev but also Dudayev, who arrived to wild shouts and cheers from the fighters. Summoned to meet Dudayev, Krayeva sat at the table with him, staring down at her plate of potatoes and meat. 'I remember that because I did not look anywhere, I only looked at the table. I was scared to look at anyone, because I did not know what to do or where to turn. I had already started to reproach myself that something would happen to my boy because I had come here.' Dudayev ranted feverishly at Moscow for bringing the war to Chechnya and at the Russians for allowing it to happen. 'You do not even dare come to Grozny and get your sons, and they say there are forty mothers who are coming. I do not see any of them. I see only one who is sitting at this table who did not fear to come. So give her back her son.'

A dozen armed fighters set off with the blonde, plump school-mistress in the dead of night, first driving and then running on foot into the thick of the battleground. 'There was one Chechen, a scout, Alik, he was like so many ordinary Chechens who consantly helped me. I was carrying a bag with clothes, water and sweets for them [prisoners]. I already cannot keep up, we are running and I am forty-five and they constantly carried that bag for me. They see I am struggling, they snatch the bag, run ahead with it fifty metres, put it down, I again run to it. Then Alik, this tall Chechen, like my Alyosha, I say to him, Alik, you are my little son, you won't leave me. They all come to me, these young men, "Don't worry, you will get to your son, don't be upset,"' Krayeva recounted.

'They were like that the whole way, here jump up, there lie down.' They ran through a burning city, artillery shells slamming in close, under a sky lit up by flares, until they were within 150 yards of the Palace. 'We wait a minute, then they say, now you must run fast, bend low, do not straighten up, run as fast as you can.' Once inside she searched for Alexei with a torch through the pitch-black maze of rooms underground. Within half an hour she was heading out with another group of Chechens carrying her wounded son and another Chechen on stretchers.

'Boom! And they have only just started to carry him out, at the door, when "Get back!" Then after a few awful moments while they calculate the chances, he shouts "Go!" Across those 150 yards, I thought I had gone mad, how they began, boom! boom! boom! Those with the stretcher hurled themselves forward, I completely lost the stretcher because they were running like rabbits, I huddled in some sort of crater, there were such huge craters, I huddled down, I do not know what flew by but something flew by my head,' she said. 'There is no one, I cannot see anyone, not Alyosha, no Chechens. And with this massive boom, and everyone scattering I thought, oh my God, now they are going to kill me, and only Alyosha will be left, or maybe he is already dead and why did I bring him out of there, he would have been better off inside. Then I look and I see a Chechen and say, "I'm here, I'm here, where should I go?" He says, "Run! Run! what you are sitting there for – run!"' They reached a ruined house and Krayeva was just beginning to fear the worst when feet came running up behind and the exhausted Chechens put down Alyosha. He looked as if he was dead but bleated 'Mam' when she spoke to him.

Back at the base, Basayev was sleeping but got up when Krayeva came in, and on inspecting the shivering Alyosha, gave her a kettle and fruit preserve and told her to prepare him a hot drink. Then he gave them a talk. 'I immediately said to Shamil, "I am very grateful to you," and he says to Alyosha, "Do you understand what a heroic mother you have? You know, you are still growing up, but if you ever say a word against your mother then you are not worthy son of your mother." He said it like that!' It was only on the way home that Alyosha turned to his mother. 'He said, "You cannot imagine what sort of hell you got me out of,"' she remembered. 'The boys were frightened of what would happen to them, the Russians were closing in, there was constant firing at that building and who knew what was going to happen?'

Krayeva was soon followed by dozens more soldiers' mothers looking for their sons who had fallen prisoner to the Chechens. Encountering indifference and helplessness from the Russian military, they ended up searching for their sons themselves. They were in an extraordinary situation, travelling behind Russian lines, under fire from their own armed forces, dependent on the assistance and hospitality of the Chechens who were supposed to be their enemy. They became a fixture at the gates of the Russian bases and at the doors of the Chechen leadership. Some lived in

Chechnya for over a year, searching all over the republic for news or information about their sons. Many are still looking.

*

The very next day after Krayeva's bolt into the Presidential Palace, Russian planes dealt the final blow to the building. They hit it with two deep penetration bombs that crashed through all nine floors of the strong concrete building, right through into the reinforced bunker. Iskhanov was on the ground floor when it happened. 'I heard the plane, I thought they were probably going to fire. Then everything went black.' He ran downstairs, choking on the thick dust, unable to see in the murk and chaos. 'You could not see anything. A torch was useless because the air was completely black and opaque. We tied wet cloths over our faces against the dust, but you could not breathe,' he said.

The hospital had been hit, and two of the wounded killed. One bomb tore a hole two or three rooms wide down the whole building. The second knocked out the stairs at the centre back. It was obvious the Palace was no longer tenable, and at lunch-time on the 18th Maskhadov gave the order to evacuate. They waited until night-time and then left in three groups. A forward group of fighters left at 11 p.m., taking the fifty-odd prisoners and carrying the dead and wounded. Maskhadov and Yandarbiyev headed out an hour later with a small group of bodyguards, running down to the river-bank and heading west, past the circus, where the bridge was still held by Chechen fighters. Iskhanov followed behind, weighed down with the headquarters documents and carrying a dead fighter in a blanket. 'We were exhausted. We were so weighed down and the dead man was so heavy. When a shell came in close and we all hit the ground I could barely stand up again,' he said. Akhmed and a group of twenty-three fighters were the last to leave in the early hours of the 19th. The Russian snipers seemed to let them go, perhaps reluctant to get into a fight. 'They were tired too,' Akhmed said.

The following day Maskhadov and Iskhanov set up a new headquarters in Hospital No. 2, several kilometres south of the Palace. It was the beginning of a life constantly on the move for the Chechen military leadership. Over the next six months they packed up their front-line headquarters half a dozen times, constantly pushed back by the overwhelming firepower of Russian artillery and aviation. The way the Palace fell, with the Russian forces having to destroy it with ferocious air and artillery power and the fighters slipping away into the night, was to become a pattern for the whole war.

The Chechen fighters put on a brave face at the loss of the Presidential Palace. 'It's just a skeleton,' said one. It remained, however, the lasting symbol of their resistance to the Russian invasion and its loss was a major blow to morale. The fighters, whose efforts had been concentrated in the last days on supplying and defending the Palace, suddenly lost their focus in the city. For some, like Akhmed, the battle for Grozny was over, and they were ordered to their home towns and villages to prepare for the battle for the countryside.[13]

For the Russian army, it was an important and much-needed victory after their dismal performance in previous weeks. Troops moved in to claim the ruined carcass of the building and raised their flag over the square. Yeltsin, under growing pressure from critics of the war at home and abroad, declared with evident relief that the military phase of operations was effectively over, adding that the next task of restoring law and order would be handed to the Interior Ministry. Grachev was congratulated for the job done and on 26 January Deputy Interior Minister Colonel-General Anatoly Kulikov was appointed commander of troops in Chechnya, to run what was now termed a 'police operation'.

Russian forces controlled half of Grozny now, a deserted, blitzed landscape north of the river, where the streets were invisible under bomb debris, mud and ash, and the buildings bombed or burnt-out skeletons. It had taken over a month to dislodge Dudayev's regime from the Palace and they had reduced the city to ruins and killed thousands of civilians in the process. It would take another month to wrest control of the remainder of the city from rebel hands.

*

The battle changed as it shifted south of the river. There was a distinct front line again, and no Russian troops in the southern districts. Russian artillery and air force units could now release a barrage of mortars, Grad missiles, rockets and bombs, destroying houses, trees, roads and whole blocks of flats. Tank gunners on the hills to the north fired rounds every three minutes for days on end. Incoming shells smashed on to the city every few seconds for hour after hour. One observer counted 4000 detonations in a single hour.[14] It was the heaviest artillery bombardment that anyone had seen since the Second World War.

There were still as many as 100,000 civilians in Grozny, thousands of them sheltering in bunkers in what had been the densely populated city centre, thousands more dying in the rubble of their apartments. Two middle-aged Chechen women, crazy with fear, screamed for help as they struggled up the hill with their belongings after enduring three weeks under bombardment in a cellar. Shell-shocked civilians, their faces black and grimy from days in bunkers and the smoke from wood fires, staggered out, all telling the same story. Their house had been destroyed, bombed or gutted by fire, everyone had been killed and all they had left were the clothes they stood up in. Larissa Timurbulatova, a twenty-four-year-old nurse, sweating and bloodied but her make-up still intact, slumped against the wall of a building as she described how her hospital was wrecked and she and a surgeon and one other nurse had tended fifty wounded civilians in the hospital cellar.

If the Russian bombing campaign needed a symbol of its own futility, it was the destruction of the Orthodox church on Lenin

Prospekt. The plum-red belfry stood out in the heart of the city, just across the bridge from the Presidential Palace. The mild-mannered parish priest, Father Anatoly, and some of his parish-ioners spent six weeks in the cellar of the parish house next door, saying services by candlelight. On 26 January the bell-tower was decapitated by Russian artillery and the church went up in flames. They rushed in to try to save the icons, but only managed to salvage about a fifth of them. Every morning Father Anatoly led his parishioners out under shellfire to collect water, vainly holding up a cross to try to still the guns. Valentina Rudakova, who sold candles in the church, said she lost 'dozens' of friends and acquain-tances as well as her own home and possessions in the fighting. 'The Russians didn't care what they were hitting,' she said.

Two blocks away from the church Yelena Andrianova, assist-ant professor of English at Grozny University, had, like many other Grozny professionals an apartment in a prime central location. When daylight bombing raids started, she descended from her book-lined flat to the dark basement of School No. 22 on Lenin Prospekt. She spent forty-five days there. When she and her companion, the Siamese cat Mishka, emerged in the first week of February, her flat was in ruins, her books burnt and the poems of her late husband destroyed. The apartment building, just across the bridge from the Presidential Palace, was first hit by Russian bombs. Then it became a stronghold for Chechen snipers and was ravaged by artillery fire.

Fifty people, the majority Russian, took shelter in the dank basement of School No. 22, with only two candles to see by. They were mostly elderly or single people who had not managed to escape before the bombing started. A school tuba lay in the corner. To keep off the damp, Andrianova slept on a portrait of the poet Nekrasov while her neighbour lay on Lenin. It was safe to venture out only between 7 a.m. and 8.30 a.m. when there was usually a brief lull in the raids. Andrianova is lame and walks only with the aid of two walking sticks, but she scuttled crab-wise across the rubble of ruined apartments scavenging for food in bombed kitchens and larders.

'I'm not afraid, by the way,' said fifty-nine-year-old Andrianova, a small, indomitable woman with slightly old-fashioned but perfectly accented English.[15] 'I found that the men who lived with us were very afraid living in the cellar. My friend only left if he held my hand. There were some bullets but I never thought they were aimed at me.' The worst thing, she remembers, was not the cold or the dark, but the constant bickering and quarrels of the frightened and bewildered people in the bunker. At first the Chechens in the bunker defended President Dudayev and there were big political dissensions.

'Everyone agreed that Yeltsin is a good-for-nothing,' she said. 'As for Dudayev, most thought he was no better than Yeltsin but there were some who thought he was better. By the end of our stay our political views changed and everyone agreed that Dudayev is a good-for-nothing too.' Her own view of the warring parties was expressed crisply: 'Both sides are barbarians.'

Six of her fellow bunker dwellers died from the cold and 'catacomb cough' in the six weeks underground. One or two left and never came back, possibly becoming victims to falling bombs and shrapnel. But when the battle had passed over them and the shooting died down, the longed-for deliverance from the ordeal was not what they had prayed for. The first Russian soldiers who came into the basement were 'very pleasant', Andrianova said. They said they would be back in a few days to evacuate them. But the troops who came back were 'very young, very drunk conscripts who threatened us'. Other soldiers, meanwhile, ran amok looting what was left of the apartments.

Andrianova left the town she had lived in for ten years in a convoy of emergency trucks. She was carrying only five bags and Mishka, who had survived unscathed but with his silky fur blackened with soot. She joined over a quarter of a million refugees from the war, who only ever received minimal compensation for the destruction of their homes and lives.

*

The continued bombing, as well as news of the Chechen early successes, had spurred huge popular resistance across the republic. Chechen fighters and volunteers poured into the city, arriving from villages in open trucks, some of them carrying old rifles and ancient-looking gas masks and steel helmets. Support for Dudayev came second to the desire to protect their homes and land. 'We are here because this is our fatherland,' said Apti Vasarkhanov, one fighter heading in with a small group from his village. 'We have no choice, we have nowhere else to go.'

They headed into the city from southern districts on foot, hugging the buildings along the main thoroughfare, Lenin Prospekt, crunching over the shards of broken glass and bomb debris, ducking into doorways when a shell came in close, crouching low as they ran fast up over the railway track and across intersections.

Planes were now dropping lethal fragmentation bombs, filled with ball-bearings or little arrows which caused appalling injuries. Patrick Chauvel saw one fall not far ahead of him. Slowed by a parachute, the bomb fell gently; when still high above the ground, it split into dozens of smaller bomblets which dropped further and then exploded silently. The man in front of Chauvel was hit as if by an electric shock, collapsing like a heap of meat on to the ground. 'There was no noise, then just phew, phew, phew, lots of little arrows shooting by. It was as if he was fried like a steak,' Chauvel said. Doctors were aghast at the terrible internal injuries inflicted by the bombs. The flechettes and ball bearings, aimed at causing maximum infantry casualties in open spaces, were wounding dozens of civilians trying to escape the bombing or fetch water.

The fighters split into smaller group, some heading off down a side street without a glance back. They were still penetrating Russian lines in small groups, mounting attacks and then melting into thin air when the Russians replied with their big guns. Another group sprinted across an open space and into a high-rise apartment block. Climbing the stairs to the thirteenth floor, they slipped carefully into an apartment, hanging back by the far wall. The window, blown out, looked out towards the blackened Presidential Palace and Russian positions along the river. One fighter trimmed his beard in the mirror, another lounged on the sofa, while the third, standing in the far corner of the room, gazed long and carefully down the sniper sights of his rifle out of the window. Despite their overwhelmingly superior firepower, Russian forces were hesitant to push forward, not least because of Chechen snipers. It took them two weeks after occupying the Presidential Palace to take the bridges just yards beyond.

*

Ruslan Aushev, President of Ingushetia, won a momentary easing in the battle when he brought the military commanders of both sides together for talks. Maskhadov and his top two commanders Basayev and Gelayev met Kulikov and Kvashnin several times over the next few days just over the border in Ingushetia. That the Russians had agreed to negotiate with an enemy they had dismissed as 'bandit formations' showed how much they had failed. But the two sides were at their most unyielding and the talks broke up without result. Kulikov says it was clear then that Maskhadov was a man Moscow could deal with, but Basayev was uncompromising.[16]

They drank a toast to the dead, one of the few things they could agree on. Independence was still the main bugbear. Basayev was urging the Russians to give up Chechnya, which was such a tiny spot on the vast map of Russia. Aushev remembers Kvashnin told him that if they gave Chechnya independence all their neighbours would want it too. Aushev spoke up, 'I told them

Comrade Kulikov, Comrade Kvashnin, you give them independence and I promise that we will never ask for independence.'

In Moscow, meanwhile, the Russian leadership was making a
lot of declarations that things were 'normalizing' in Chechnya.
The hawks still seemed to dominate the Kremlin, although
Yegorov became the first scapegoat of the military failure and
was removed from his post as envoy to Chechnya on grounds of
'ill-health'. Soskovets was appointed special representative to
Chechnya on 16 February. With his close ties to the military–
industrial complex and therefore an interest in prolonging the
conflict, it was not a good omen.

Grachev, despite the appalling setbacks the army experienced
under his command, seemed unrepentant. In an extraordinary
outburst at a press conference in Moscow, he called Kovalyov an
'enemy of Russia' and the Duma Defence Committee Chairman
Sergei Yushenkov a 'little reptile'. The two men had been outspoken critics of the military campaign, but Grachev's rambling
monologue, shown on Russian television, stunned even his allies.
Yerin and Stepashin sat silently on either side of him during the
speech, both looking highly uncomfortable. Grachev went on to
utter the now infamous remark: 'Eighteen-year-old boys have
been dying for Russia, they have been dying with smiles on their
faces and we should raise a monument to them.'

*

In Grozny the shelling and bomb and Grad attacks went on and
on, marching through the southern districts of the city throughout
the whole of February. Maskhadov pulled his headquarters out
of Grozny to the town of Argun. On 9 February he conceded that
the city was all but lost. He darted into the village of Goity, 6
miles south of Grozny, in a lightning tour of the front line, and
held a brief conference in the back room of a local culture club.
Within an hour he was off again, investigating reports of tanks at
a nearby crossroads.

Maskhadov faced the increasingly impossible task of plugging a dyke being punctured by a dozen holes. He sat at a desk covered in red baize, dressed in grey camouflage fatigues, stabbing at different points of a map. 'In effect we are pulling back to consolidate and give people access to me without being fired at by the enemy,' he said as fighters craned round to hear his assessment of the fighting. He described it as an orderly retreat into the countryside to regroup. They were simply outnumbered by the Russians' superiority in weaponry, Maskhadov said. 'Someone said I had 150 tanks destroyed near the zoo in Grozny. If I had 150 tanks I would storm the Kremlin! When this is over I'll tell the historians how many tanks I had.'

Maskhadov barely concealed his irritation with Jokhar Dudayev, who was giving nightly interviews to the US-sponsored Radio Liberty that differed from his own assessment of events. The previous night Dudayev, with a peal of high-pitched laughter, had said, 'My mood is excellent' and that he had given orders to withdraw from Grozny. Maskhadov contradicted this and said there was still a 'forward command post' in the city. Asked what his and Dudayev's roles were, Maskhadov said laconically that while he commanded the war effort, Dudayev dealt with 'political matters'.

For all the overpowering might of the Russian army, the Chechens frequently got the better of their opponents through sheer presumption. On New Year's Eve as Russian forces were 'storming' Grozny, an elite group of twenty-five paratroopers were dropped off in the snowy foothills south of the city near the village of Alkhazurovo, ostensibly to cut off the expected rebel retreat from the capital. They spent two days in the hills, setting up camp and laying mines, then, as they began to run out of food, radioed in for more supplies. In answer, twenty-five more paratroopers were dropped in but no food. The situation was growing serious when the paras ran into two Chechen hunters in the woods with their shotguns, and took them prisoner. When the hunters failed to return home, Zelimkhan Amadov, a karate expert and professional athlete, formed a search party of thirty-seven villagers, mostly armed with hunting rifles. They came upon the Russians on the third day and a firefight broke out. After about twenty minutes they heard someone shouting. 'It was one of the hunters, his elder brother was with us and recognized his voice,' Amadov recounted a few days after the incident. 'He came to us and said they want to talk.'[17]

The Chechens suggested the Russians surrender and three officers came out, agreed, and laid down their weapons. They sealed the agreement with a much-needed cigarette. Two Russians had been killed in the shooting and two more wounded. The Chechens marched the Russians down the hill. 'For two days they had eaten nothing. When we gave them food they fell upon it like dogs,' Amadov recalled.

Of the fifty paratroopers, fifteen to twenty were officers, a very high number for a group that only needed three or four officers. 'Half were quite tough and serious, half seemed useless,' said television journalist Peter Jouvenal, who saw them. 'They felt bitter and isolated. In Afghanistan they would probably have fought to the death but the Chechens had served in the army and knew they did not want to fight.' The commander of the group, Major Igor Morozov, from Rostov, said his decision to surrender was purely military. Completely surrounded, they could not have survived. In fact the Chechens treated the paratroopers remarkably humanely; they marched them back up the mountain to remove the mines they had laid, then telephoned their mothers to come and fetch them home.

Basayev fought on with several hundred men in the southern districts into late February. As the end came he organized some sixty men to stay on to fight as undercover hit-and-run units, a tactic they kept up throughout the war. He finally pulled out on 23 February, leaving on foot with his men through the woods of Chernoreche, the suburb on the far south-west of Grozny. He headed for the foothills where Dudayev was based and then turned east to Shali, now the new Chechen rebel capital.

On 7 March Russian forces finally occupied the last parts of Grozny. It had taken nearly three months and is estimated to have killed as many as 27,000 civilians.[18] The sheer scale of the destruction was something that not even the people of Sarajevo would be able to comprehend. The city was not only in ruins but the bombing had destroyed its very foundations, wrecking thousands of miles of water and sewage pipes that reduced a modern city to the level of a Third World shanty-town. Two years later central Grozny remains a desert scene of rubble and burnt-out buildings.

11

War Against the People

On 24 January 1995 two brothers, Magomed, eighteen, and Said-Emir, twenty-one, left their family apartment in Grozny near the old airport in the north part of the city to go and fetch water. They went with a Russian friend, Andrei Tretyakov. The three never came back. The Chechen boys' father, Hussein Khamidov, a professional civil airline pilot, started a long, agonizing search for them in a city that was still at war and extremely dangerous.

Khamidov had told his sons to carry their name and address in a pocket of their clothes at all times – if anything happened to them, they were to throw it out. For two months after they disappeared he combed Grozny for any clue as to what had happened to them. Some neighbours said they had seen them talking to Russian soldiers not far from their apartment block. He badgered the Russian checkpoints and command posts for information, and travelled to the main military base at Mozdok and to prisons in neighbouring towns and republics, drinking vodka with the guards and administrators and bribing them for a look at their lists of inmates. He toured the mass graves at the Russian Orthodox cemetery in northern Grozny where hundreds of unidentified bodies, picked up from around the destroyed city, were spread out in messy lines or dumped in wide trenches in unspeakable testimony to the human cost of the war.

One day at the end of March a woman came to Khamidov's home with a little notebook bearing his younger son's name and address. She had found it in the courtyard of her home on Mayakovsky Street in central Grozny. There Khamidov uncovered five bodies, his sons and Andrei among them. Their hands and legs were tied with barbed wire. Andrei had been shot in the head. Khamidov's sons had been stabbed and slashed with knives and their faces smashed in before being shot. 'They died slowly,' Khamidov said with a deep sigh. His youngest son had somehow managed to throw out his notebook before what was undoubtedly an execution.[1]

They had been caught up in one of the ugliest operations of the war as Russian troops attempted to 'cleanse' Grozny of Chechen resistance. They began by clearing bunkers and houses around their bases in north Grozny, arresting hundreds of Chechens for interrogation and detention. The Russian Interior Ministry set up what it called a 'filtration camp' at the military base in Mozdok to 'filter' out Chechen fighters and criminals from ordinary civilians. The prisoners were held in several disused train carriages in a siding where they were beaten and tortured. Thousands passed through the filtration camps and an unknown number died in captivity or shortly after their release. The overwhelming majority were civilians. Everyone was caught up in the war.

In February the Russian command set up another filtration camp in Grozny in a bus depot, known by its acronym PAP-1, where prisoners were held in dark, airless cells fronted with iron cages or made to stand for hours, shoulder-deep in pools of water. Some 1500 Chechens are listed as disappeared from the early months of the war. Most probably never made it as far as the filtration camps but, like the Khamidov brothers and their Russian friend, were killed and dumped or shovelled up with the rubble. Two years later when Russian troops pulled out of Chechnya, Khamidov, whose experience had led him to set up a Commission for Missing Persons, still had 1500 Chechens on his lists.

Ramzan Lorzanov, director of an industrial complex on the north side of the city, took refuge in a bomb shelter in the compound along with dozens of families on New Year's Eve. On

2 January soldiers banged on the door, ordering them out. 'We opened the door. They had two automatic rifles pointing at us and a machine-gun on a stand,' he recalled. 'I came out first and they said, "Men against the wall."'[2]

Lorzanov addressed the General who was looking on. 'I say to this General, "Listen, commander, what are you doing, these are civilians who ran into the bomb shelter to escape death." He says, "Silence." I take out my keys for the storehouse of my industrial complex, "These are the keys of my complex, these are all people like me, who ran in here from the nearest houses." He said again, "Silence, today it might be keys, tomorrow a grenade-launcher. We know you all."'

The women and children were led away and the thirty-two men were taken to the canning factory nearby and thrown into a bunker with another thirty men picked up from the streets. No weapons were found on them, none of them had been fighting, Lorzanov said. Among them were twelve ethnic Russians, an Ossetian and a sixty-year-old homeless man, Vakha, a harmless soul who was well known in Grozny.

The following afternoon they were loaded into a KamAZ army truck and made to lie face-down, their arms behind their backs, in a row of five. More men were laid on top of them, then more and more in layers. Soldiers then sat on top and ordered them not to move. Lorzanov was the first into the truck, and so lay at the bottom of the pile. As the weight on his back increased he slipped his arms out and braced them on the floor beneath his chin to give himself some breathing space. That action saved his life. As they set off on a long bumpy ride the men alongside him cried out that they were suffocating.

By the time they arrived in Mozdok the four next to Lorzanov were dead. The rest had to run between some forty Interior Ministry soldiers, who formed a corridor from the truck to some railway carriages and kicked and beat the prisoners with rifle butts and truncheons. As Lorzanov climbed into the carriage a soldier hanging from a bar swung both feet at his stomach, knocking him sideways and smashing his wrist against the door post.

Twenty men, all injured, were crammed into a railway cabin built for six people. They were close to collapse but there was only room to stand. Eventually they worked out a system to sit on top of each other. In stifling heat, with little ventilation, they were given just 100 millilitres of water a day. The carriage would rock sometimes as they listened to beatings of prisoners next door. ' "You will live, but not long," the soldiers said, shoving their face in yours. "After our work, people do not live long," ' Lorzanov quoted them as saying.

At intervals the Chechens were pulled out for interrogation. Lorzanov found himself before a team led by a young twenty- to thirty-year-old Interior Ministry officer. 'They put handcuffs around the knuckles of my hand and they began to ask, "Where can Dudayev run to? Where is his bunker? How many lifts are there in the Presidential Palace?" ' he recalled. 'They knew perfectly well, they were seeking an excuse for torture. When they said that, I replied, "If such serious guys as you do not know where Dudayev can go and how many lifts he has, then how should I know?" [The interrogator] said, "Are you joking or what?" He looked at me, took up a truncheon and smashed my hand. The bones were all poking through.'

After five days they were moved to a prison in the southern Russian town of Pyatigorsk. It was a pre-trial detention centre, notorious throughout Russia for appalling conditions and overcrowding. To Lorzanov, coming from the filtration camp, it felt like a Western hotel. It was only after twenty days that Ramzan's brother secured the release of six of them with an order signed by Yegorov himself. Of the thirty-two taken that day from the bomb shelter, six died in captivity and eight shortly after their release.

The railway carriages in Mozdok rapidly became notorious. Kovalyov, who together with the Russian human rights organization

Memorial began investigating the filtration camps as soon as the first reports emerged, called them Stolypin-type rail carriages, a reference to the prisoner transport cars used throughout the Soviet era to take people to the labour camps. Named after the ruthless pre-Revolutionary Interior Minister Pyotr Stolypin, they were used most widely in Stalin's time and are described unforgettably by Alexander Solzhenitsyn in *Gulag Archipelago*.

Memorial documented dozens of testimonies of Chechens arrested and held in the Mozdok filtration camp and others in 1995, and even succeeded in visiting the camp and seeing the registers which recorded the release of Lorzanov's group. The testimonies were all the same: mass arrests from the streets and bomb shelters, irrational and cruel violence, including vicious beatings, mock executions, psychological and often physical torture to obtain confessions, and life-threatening conditions on the way to and in the camps.

Memorial concluded that the mass filtration system had failed in its main objective of sorting out fighters from civilians but formed the 'beginnings of a system of mass terror'. Mozdok and PAP-1 were not the only camps. There were secret detention areas in virtually every Russian base, where prisoners were held in mud pits in the ground, often partly filled with water.

Khaz-Magomed Mosarov, Deputy Mayor of Assinovskaya, was held blindfolded in a prisoner van for five days along with several other men at the Russian base that sprawled in the fields beside the village. 'Sometimes they took me outside and put me in a trench, and beat me there in the trench. And sometimes they took me to a tent for questioning. There were many people there, sitting around, and each would ask me questions. I could not see but there were about twenty men, not old men, thirty to thirty-five years old maybe. They were drinking: without any order, one would shout, then another, each for himself. Sometimes for an hour, for two hours.[3] Mosarov was questioned about the whereabouts and quantities of Dudayev's fighters and given repeated electric shocks to his throat, shoulders and chest and handcuffs that left his entire left side numb and limp for days.

Then eleven of the prisoners, still blindfolded, were loaded into a helicopter. The machine took off, then suddenly the door was thrown open and the prisoners ordered to stand. One by one they were placed in front of the open door and pushed out with a kick from behind. Mosarov reckons he fell some 20 feet, landing on churned-up mud. None of the prisoners broke any bones, but they all thought they were falling to their death. They were then hauled off for the most savage beating session that left Mosarov with broken ribs and fingers and the lower part of his body black with bruising for months.[4]

A Cossack from Rostov, Pyotr Kosov, worked throughout the spring of 1995 to win the release of the 100-odd Russian prisoners held by the Chechens, often negotiating the release of Chechens from the filtration camps in exchange. He says he was ashamed at the state of the Chechen prisoners he handed over, some of whom were near death. By contrast the Chechens treated their prisoners more humanely, although some were beaten up and at least four Kosov knew of were executed. The International Committee of the Red Cross, which works all over the world to release prisoners-of-war, declined to be involved in what it called the bartering of human beings.

*

In Russian-occupied Grozny in February the 'constitutional order' the Russians had promised to impose on Chechnya had turned into a horrible orgy of violence against the civilian population. On 10 February Said Dadayev, an eighty-year-old Chechen war veteran who walked on crutches, was standing at a meagre street market on Tukhachevsky Street when an armoured personnel carrier full of Russian soldiers careered down the street and without warning charged straight into the line of stallholders. Dadayev was struck on the head and killed. The following day a huddle of weeping relatives washed down his bloody body and begged for someone to tell the world how he had died. At the scene of his death, the old man's wooden crutch was still lying in a mess of smashed jars, splintered wood and blood-spattered earth. He was not the only victim. 'There was a girl next to me from my apartment block, Ira, selling cigarettes,' said Madina, a young stallholder, sobbing. 'She thought they were turning round but they drove straight into her. They crushed her legs. They were laughing. It was wild laughter.' Madina and other traders said four people had been killed, including Dadayev. Four others had been carried off wounded.

The Russian soldiers roaming the streets of Grozny were a law unto themselves and many were committing seemingly random atrocities. In a brief twenty-four-hour period in the north of the city, now fully under Russian control, ordinary people of all nationalities came up again and again with tales of atrocities and marauding. The most vulnerable group were Chechen males. One old man literally shook with fear when he saw two foreign reporters on his doorstep, screaming at them to go away. Neighbours of two brothers who lived in a red-brick cottage described how they had been summarily shot by Interior Ministry troops who then threw their bodies into a septic tank in the garden. The concrete paving of the courtyard was still stained with blood.

Even Russian women had cause to be afraid. According to Tanya, a mother, 'Lena, my daughter, was walking along with a friend when some soldiers came up to them, put guns to their heads and said, "They're nice, it's a pity to shoot them." The girls cried out, "We're Russian," and the soldiers went on.'

Natasha, a divorcee, was the only one of fifty inhabitants on her staircase who sat out the battle for the city. She proudly showed off the scorched wall in her flat where a piece of shrapnel had torn through the window. Natasha had hated the Dudayev regime and looked forward to liberation by Russia and when the soldiers first came she brought them food. She said she had not slept for a month after she saw three young Russian soldiers blown to pieces by a rocket-propelled grenade. But Natasha too was threatened by soldiers and when she tried to investigate what had happened at the battered market stall, a soldier shouted, 'Go back into your porch or I'll shoot.' One of Natasha's neighbours simply refused to believe what was going on: the soldiers looting apartments and killing, she said, were actually Chechen fighters dressed in Russian uniforms. Just hours later, a mighty column of more than 100 Russian armoured vehicles crawled out of the city, throwing up a storm of dust. Many of the tanks had chairs, tables and carpets strapped on the top.[5]

*

The National History Museum, already badly bombed, was also looted. Jabrail Chakhkiev, the archaeology curator, a gentle man in pebble-lens glasses, was trying to salvage what he could of the collection when soldiers arrived. 'They burst in and shot off the locks and wounded three people. They said they had been told by their commander to "Go get some souvenirs",' he said. 'They stole the collection of precious metals and antique Chechen swords and also took away stuffed animals which they put on their APC. What can you do when they have guns, we couldn't stop them,' Chakhkiev said. What they did not take they smashed. As he looked down at broken fragments of his archaeological collection, he shook his head: 'The most frightening thing is that you can rebuild a city, and buildings, but you cannot rebuild our culture.'

It was the same story wherever Russian troops went. Assinovskaya came in for violent treatment from the very beginning when the Russians set up their field headquarters on land beside it. The tented camp became known as 'Kulikov's field' after the diminutive and pugnacious General Anatoly Kulikov, now in command of troops in Chechnya. Defence and Interior Ministry troops set up posts around the village, cutting it off from the outside world for the whole length of the war. They were worlds apart in their attitudes. The army soldiers, relaxed and friendly, stood on the road by their tanks and begged matches off a passing car. The Interior Ministry troops, legs apart in an aggressive pose, black balaclavas over their faces, trained their guns on approaching cars.

A Russian woman, Olga Sokolova, mother of two, said she was raped by men from the checkpoint. In a statement to the local authorities, she wrote: 'On 25 December, 1994, at 11 p.m., someone knocked on my door . . . They said, "We are Russian soldiers," and I said that I would not open the door. They said they would throw a grenade. I opened it, and they burst in and started taking groceries and good things. They took my wedding ring, they drank my home-brew. One of them held us at gunpoint. After that they took me into the third room and four of them started raping me. They were in masks. I am forced to leave. I ask you to help me.'[6]

Interior Ministry troops raided the dairy farm in Assinovskaya a few weeks later. They moved in with tanks, firing on the farm workers who fled across the fields. One Chechen tractor driver, a father of four, did not get away. 'We found him lying here, his hat over there. They beat him and dragged him to this point. Then they shot him through the mouth,' said Sulumbeg Osiyev, the farm manager. Osiyev and the others, who lay in the fields for six hours, returned to find the farm trashed. The soldiers had stolen the radio, ransacked the office and sprayed bullets around the living quarters. Outside they burned the hay, shot up the milking machines and killed forty-seven cows. One cow, wounded from a bullet in the leg, lay unable to stand. Osiyev said he did not even had a knife to put it out of its misery. Trying to explain the wrecking of his farm, he threw up his hands in anger: 'We did nothing to them. The cows did nothing to them.'

The looting, rapes, beatings and wanton damage were probably mostly spontaneous, the work of undisciplined, frightened and brutalized soldiers, but their commanders did little to stop it. A document distributed by the command of the Interior Ministry to all its soldiers in February 1995 showed the higher command was aware of the actrocities. The document said that 'Carrying out their military service the warriors of the internal forces are displaying the highest courage and heroism, the best human qualities. None the less cases have begun to occur recently of looting, extortion, and atrocities committed by servicemen with relation to the civilian population.' Kulikov says he twice publicly condemned the practices but this was patently not enough.[7] The attacks on the civilian population formed a hatred of the Russian forces among all Chechens, whatever their political allegiances.

*

The Russian army is a brutal place even in normal times. The raw conscripts come off the worst, subjected to bullying and beating, and even rape and murder. In peacetime some 2000 conscripts die annually in the army, many from suicide or killed by their comrades. Tens of thousands of criminal cases are reported within the armed forces every year but even more crimes go by unnoticed. In wartime the brutality within the army increased and led to numerous desertions among the young conscripts and virtual anarchy in some units. In the town of Gudermes one young officer said soldiers slept with grenades beside them, not for protection against a Chechen attack but in fear of their own side. A few days before, he said, Russian soldiers had shot and killed an old Russian woman outside her home. When one of the soldiers remonstrated, the section leader shot him too. Some officers seemed to do whatever they liked.

Arkady Fedin, an eighteen-year-old conscript from the 503rd Motor Rifle Regiment, was serving at a checkpoint outside the village of Shali on 9 May 1995. Three Chechen men in their twenties disappeared that day. Two, Ayub Damayev and Shamkhan Tashkhajiev, were cousins, and the third was their childhood friend Aslanbek. They were so inseparable that people called them the Three Musketeers. They were driving around in a new white Zhiguli car, just cruising with nothing much to do. They came across Musa Damayev, Ayub and Shamkhan's uncle, in the centre of the town and stopped to chat. Then they took off again, heading west out of town. That was the last time anyone saw them alive.

Musa and his relatives found their first clue at Fedin's post. Someone had written the number of the boys' white Zhiguli on the concrete block of the post. The soldiers said they had written the number themselves to remember the car since they had asked them to bring back some bread. Later in the day the number was scrubbed out. It was at that post that the three men were tortured, executed and buried along with their car, crushed by a tank, in the field beside the camp. The families only found out six weeks later when Fedin deserted.[8]

Fedin made his way into Shali, where a Chechen took him round to the families of the missing three. An ordinary boy from the Russian city of Arkhangelsk near the Arctic Circle, he rapidly found himself out of his depth. He had deserted on a whim, he said. Now he paced the room all night, his head bursting, as they bombarded him with questions.

Slowly the story came out. He told how the three Chechens had driven up to buy petrol from the soldiers. Fedin, sitting at the controls of his APC, remembered them. They were arrested and taken away to the camp and the car was pulled off the road. 'Officers were beating up those guys in a pit, the captain was there himself, and a warrant officer, they did it thoroughly, they beat them, there was a military telephone, and they tortured them hard with the current,' he recalled, over a year later, while living in semi-captivity in Shali.[9]

'Then the next day, during the day, they were there, and that night they shot them,' he said. The commander had ordered the men to be released, according to Fedin, but the captain, an

Ossetian, argued to his soldiers that the Chechens had seen too much and could cause trouble. 'You know how they taught us, fighter or no fighter, every Chechen, from a small boy to an adult, exterminate them all. Even if you find a ring on them, immediately kill them, you know a little ring (from a grenade), it's not important if he is young or old, shoot straight away,' Fedin said.

Three soldiers were ordered to prepare the grave. 'We dug a hole in the field. If they gave us a signal with a rocket or a flare – they were looking out from the block post with binoculars – we were to lie down straight away, so that our own guys did not see us. Then when we took them out we said we are taking you for questioning with the commander of the regiment.' Fedin even led one of them to his death. 'He sat in the pit. I took him, there was no way out, they shot him with an automatic rifle, right there, once. Our morale was such that here every man is an enemy.' It was not the first killing of this sort that Fedin had seen. They had killed another carload of four men before that, he said. 'They ordered us at the beginning, they took us there so that we would not fear to look at blood, there were ten of us there, young guys,' he said. When he showed Musa where to dig for the bodies, they found several more with them, along with several car number plates. One of the bodies was missing all its fingers, according to Musa. Fedin, now twenty years old and a Muslim convert, said he had felt nothing at the time about taking part in the ghastly deed. 'I personally thought then that if it is war, and they tell me to . . .' He tailed off. 'Anyway, I was not very independent-minded. I was eighteen years old, it is two years ago now,' he said. 'To tell you honestly, when it happened there was no pity, no kind of pity, like killing a fly, just like that, I felt no pity, I was not afraid of anything, not blood, not anything.'

Fedin's story that the commander of the detachment did not know about the murders is credible, as is the meanness of a captain to his subordinates. Russian MP Anatoly Shabad has few illusions about the men in the Russian army. 'If an army goes into a populated area there is inevitably going to be brutality. The Americans did it in Vietnam, people go mad in war, even a good man, under pressure of his comrades. A collective effect appears. In any war there is brutality, but of course when an army has no sense, no idea what the war is for, then that army is especially inclined to brutality. This army is completely demoralized and absolutely not fit for war.'[10]

*

The Chechens, many of whom knew the Russian army well from military service, exploited its rottenness to devastating effect. Lomali, a swarthy oil trader, had been living in New York and Moscow before the war and had a Mercedes gathering dust in the courtyard. When he came back to his native village of Achkoi-Martan to command a detachment, he found his hard-currency earnings were even more helpful than his fighting skills. Lomali rummaged through his wardrobe and pulled out a wad of $5000 in $100 bills. It was the payment, he said, for the next consignment of snipers' rifles, grenade-launchers and ammunition he was due to pick up from a Russian soldier in a few days' time. The soldiers only ever took dollars, not rubles. 'American dollars, Russian weapons and Chechen spirit will win this war,' Lomali laughed.

The trade made a mockery of the Russians' declared aim of 'disarming bandit formations'. Lomali said he had been approached first by a local Russian about buying weapons. After two successful transactions he dispensed with the middleman and went to meet the soldiers directly. That night he procured two boxes of ammunition from a couple of nervous Russian recruits and received a picture of his enemy that sent his morale rocketing. 'They were frightened, morally dead, two soldiers of twenty years old, just boys,' he said. 'I had some grenades in my jacket. When I unzipped it, they saw the grenades and ran back twenty metres.'

'It is an amazing army,' he said with contempt. 'The army is selling weapons, which are killing its own men. But the soldiers are fully aware that the top leadership is making huge amounts of money from this war, so they are too.' He said he had the impression that the transactions were being authorized higher up, by captains or majors who were taking a large share of the cut, and that even higher ranks might be involved. The officers would then write off the missing stocks as losses in battle and go home from the war with a profit in their pockets. 'They know that they won't be here for long,' he said.

The best conversation-opener with soldiers in Chechnya was always 'How long do you have left?' It is what they always ask each other. The conscripts often had to serve a whole year in Chechnya, but officers and Interior Ministry units served two-month stints at a time. Designed to give them a break, it was a short-sighted policy that meant troops cared little about the long-term consequences of their behaviour and rarely established any sort of relationship with local residents. Units were boosted with soldiers serving under contract, a system intended to turn the Russian army gradually into a professional one, but which in fact brought in men who were quite literally mercenaries, hired specifically to fight in Chechnya. They rarely had any sense of mission other than looking out for themselves.

The *kontraktniki*, as they were known, soon acquired a bad name. They wore bandanas tight across their foreheads and black sleeveless T-shirts baring their muscles. Not all of them were bad but most of them were angry. One, manning a post in eastern Chechnya, said he had only joined up to earn enough money to buy a fridge, a television and a video for his family. 'I never expected this hell,' he said. Another said he had signed on for twenty-five years on a salary of US$200 a month. When we expressed amazement, he gave a twisted smile. 'It's a job,' he said.

*

The mindless brutality of the Russian army in Chechnya was summed up most starkly by its performance in the village of Samashki in April 1995. The Russian command ordered troops in to flush fighters out from the village. But instead of a battle it turned into a massacre of civilians. As My Lai did in Vietnam, Samashki came to symbolize the senseless horror of a war that was aimed as much at the civilian population as at the rebels. For two days Russian troops stormed through the village, torching houses and cellars with grenades and flame-throwing rockets, burning residents alive or shooting them at point-blank range in the streets and courtyards. Over 100 people were killed, all but four of them civilians. It seemed at first an action of undisciplined wildness. Chechen survivors told stories of soldiers injecting themselves with drugs and laughing as they shot villagers or watched them trying to escape the burning buildings.[11] Subsequent evidence casts a different but even more sinister light. This was an operation ordered from high up, probably to terrorize and so subdue the civilian population of the whole region.

It was an Interior Ministry forces' operation, the first in Chechnya that they performed on their own, independent of regular army troops. The Sofrinskaya Brigade, one of the Interior Ministry's top fighting forces, formed in 1988 specifically to handle internal conflicts around the Soviet Union, led the assault. The brigade had been in Chechnya for several months but had not been involved in any serious fighting and had yet to lose any men.

They had information that there were large numbers of fighters in Samashki. In fact the village elders had persuaded them to leave in early March, but the Russian command issued an ultimatum to the villagers, ordering them to expel any fighters from the village, hand over weapons, and allow Russian troops into the village. If they did not comply, the troops would enter by force.

The village elders tried to stave off an attack, going out to meet

Russian commanders at a post outside the village. They say they were at a loss when ordered to hand in several hundred weapons and an APC. Time was running out. The Sofrinskaya Brigade occupied the high ground just north of the village on 4 April and started bombarding the woods on the southern edge of the village. According to the brigade's military log, a copy of which came into the hands of the authors, reconnaissance teams ventured towards the village from the north-east, attacking a Chechen gun emplacement before running into a minefield and losing a couple of tanks. The elders went out again on 7 April to meet the deputy commander of Russian troops in Chechnya, Interior Ministry Lieutenant-General Anatoly Romanov, but failed to avert the assault. They were given until 4 p.m., a matter of a few hours, to evacuate the village.

Shells started slamming in before 4 p.m. and by dusk they had killed thirteen people, some of whom were still trying to leave. Then several hundred troops advanced on the village, according to S., a senior Russian officer who was there. A short, stocky soldier, S. had served with the Sofrinskaya Brigade in Nagorno-Karabakh and now for several months in Chechnya. Slightly on guard, he talked about the operation on condition his name and rank not be used.[12]

Divided into storm groups of thirty-five men, the Russian troops went in on foot, followed by tanks and armoured vehicles mounted with big guns. Some units encountered no resistance, going the length of the village without seeing any action, but the southernmost units came under fire and suffered losses almost immediately. The level of resistance was nothing like the determined defence that organized Chechen fighters put up in Grozny and other towns but it was enough, under cover of darkness, to shake the Russian troops. According to S., the brigade lost eleven men in the operation, almost half the total they lost in the whole war. Forty-five were wounded and a number of armoured vehicles knocked out. 'It was frightening. The boys came out with their eyes wide and their hair on end,' S. said. Part of the problem was that in the dark they lost their way and could not see what they were doing. 'It was plain stupid to storm the village in the dark,' he commented.

The Chechens who resisted were from the forty-strong village self-defence force, armed mostly with Kalashnikov rifles, but also grenade-launchers. They admit to knocking out a Russian tank and setting up defensive positions in the school, but deny there was any large-scale battle. By dawn they were all gone, they say, slipping away through the woods. Four Chechen fighters were killed in the night's fighting, two of them in the woods as they escaped.

Then the Russian troops started an operation that has become notorious throughout Chechnya, the *zachistka*, a 'mop-up operation', or more literally a 'cleansing'. Officially it is a house-to-house search for rebel fighters and arms caches, but it has become synonymous with looting, violence and mass detentions of the male population. Tense and swearing, the Russian troops screamed at three men who emerged from one house to lie down. They used Salavdi Umakhanov as a hostage to check the rest of the buildings, then forced the three into the garage, pushing them down into the car repair pit before opening fire. Only Umakhanov survived.[13]

The killing and burning continued the following morning. The constant explosions kept most people hiding indoors or in their cellars, but two old Chechen men, Supyan Minayev and Zahir Kabilov, both Second World War veterans, sat on a bench outside Minayev's home. 'They won't do anything to a veteran,' his wife, Malezha, remembers him saying, as he sent her and their daughters away before the storm. He was wrong. Russian soldiers shot the veterans point-blank and dragged their bodies into the house and set it alight. Malezha, still sifting through her fire-gutted house three weeks later with her daughters, held out a tiny pair of scissors fitted with a nail file, charred and rusted from the fire. 'He bought them in Germany in 1944,' where he fought in the Soviet army. 'He was so delighted with them,' she said. They were all she had left. She had buried an unrecognizable blackened skeleton that was her husband in the garden behind the charred ruins of her home.[14]

Many of those killed were shot at point-blank range. Three middle-aged ethnic Russian labourers, living in Samashki, were gunned down in the bedroom of their house.[15] More were killed when soldiers hurled grenades into houses and cellars without warning. S. admitted they burnt many houses that morning, and blamed soldiers from OMON units who were also taking part. Nearly 200 homes were burned and at least 103 people killed, the overwhelming majority unarmed civilians. Over 100 men were arrested and taken away to filtration camps although they were later released without charge. The Interior Ministry denied the civilian casualties, insisting the dead were all rebel fighters. The military log also only registers the killing of 'fighters'. But the men on the ground, shaken and angered by their losses, were just taking it out on anyone they found. There was revenge in the air for those comrades who had been killed, according to S. 'They brought back one APC that was burnt. The men inside were just cinders and pieces of bones,' he said, still angry nearly two years later. He expressed no remorse, just bitterness that the brigade received so much flak for carrying out orders. As he was leaving, he confided, 'It was better in Soviet times, then we just did our job and there was no talk about civilians.'

Anatoly Shabad, barred by Russian troops from entering the village, borrowed a dress, slippers and headscarf and climbed aboard the bus with some women being allowed through just days after the massacre. 'The women knew immediately, they noticed things. There was some detail. I had a woman's coat on and I could never remember which way it was supposed to do up,' he recalled with a laugh. Inside the village he started investigating. What he found convinced him that there had been little or no battle at all.

'As regards the character of destruction, it was evident that it was not from war. For example, you see a house burnt, and the fence shows not a sign of battle, not a bullet-hole or shrapnel mark. The fence is completely intact. So we understood that there was no resistance, they were simply burning. All the destruction was not from artillery nor bombs, it was just houses set alight.'

The operation in Samashki was not a first for Russian troops. The Soviet army had acted with impunity for ten years in Afghanistan, repeatedly marching off the entire male population of villages and probably executing them. In one notorious incident they gassed dozens of villagers hiding in an underground irrigation channel. Shabad says he saw similar operations in Nagorno-Karabakh, the Armenian enclave in Azerbaijan in what was still then the Soviet Union in May 1991. 'It was done to terrify,' Shabad said. 'It was successful because the neighbouring village, Achkoi-Martan, capitulated,' he added.

No Russian officer was tried or punished for Samashki, although a number of those in the Sofrinskaya Brigade were removed to other jobs in semi-disgrace, S. said. 'Some of them had already turned,' he said, twisting his hand against his head to mean crazy. In July 1995 the Military Prosecutor's office declared there was insufficient basis to conclude that the mass killing of civilians in Samashki was illegal. A Parliamentary Commission, chaired by Stanislav Govorukhin, a film director better known for his nostalgic nationalist film *The Russia We Have Lost*, concluded much the same. The commission lost some credibility when four members refused to sign its final report. In an extraordinary scene in the Russian Parliament Govorukhin then publicly denounced his fellow-Duma deputies, Shabad and Koval-yov, for what they had said about Samashki, and called for them to be put on trial for inciting hatred and 'Russophobia'.

Perhaps more than anywhere Samashki showed that the war was against the entire population of Chechnya. Kulikov talks of 'liberating' villages from the fighters but he was really using all means, including terror, to force the villagers to expel the fighters themselves. Samashki is still being torn apart by recriminations between fighters and elders who blame each other for allowing the disaster. As in any guerrilla war, the division between fighters and civilians was vague. Fighters moved among the civilians and often lived at home, inevitably endangering the lives of their own people. Their hit-and-run attacks on Russian posts brought swift retaliation from the Russians on the nearest villages. 'They come and talk to us by day, and then they shoot us at night,' complained one Russian soldier manning a checkpoint. The Russian soldiers began to see every citizen of Chechnya as the enemy.

*

Three months into the war, with Grozny taken, Russian forces could concentrate on a broad push south, spreading out across the plains from the capital to the foothills of the Caucasus. The joint force of Defence and Interior Ministry troops was now 58,000 strong, according to Kulikov. His tank battalions came into their own on the open plain and Russia's overwhelming supremacy in the air played a crucial role, as the planes and helicopters turned their guns on towns, villages, roads and bridges across the republic.

They met a dogged resistance from the fighters who fought them every stage of the way. After Grozny fell there was a lot of talk of fighters going to the mountains to carry on a guerrilla war. In fact they defended every town and village they could on the plains in a conventional front-line war. 'It was essential, because we have too small a territory. If we had not taken defensive positions like that, the Russian forces would have reached [the mountains] in a week,' Maskhadov said.

In a clumsy attempt to persuade the fighters to surrender and to rob them of local support, the Russians dropped leaflets from the air across the countryside. They were in turns threatening and condescending. 'Come to your senses! You are protecting not sovereignty and freedom, but the money of Dudayev . . . that he stole from the people,' one read. Another, headed 'Ultimatum', warned: 'Any provocation against the Russian forces will rapidly be met with all the might of Russian firepower! Those caught with weapons will be annihilated!'

Villagers were caught in a dilemma and different villages adopted different tactics. Most were anxious only to avoid war, and if the Russians had acted with any subtlety they could have exploited this very well, but they seemed to prefer General Yermolov's old tactic of complete 'pacification'. The head of Urus-Martan was on a knife edge. Yusup Elmurzayev, a pale, moustachioed man, was from the first generation of Chechen nationalist intellectuals. He was a founding member of the Chechen National Congress and had split with Dudayev as long ago as June 1991, after which he supported Chechen independence but stoutly opposed the Dudayev regime. Urus-Martan became an island of opposition within Chechnya. During the war the village stayed out of the fighting and kept up its busy bazaar in which weapons frequently changed hands.

'We don't want to fight here,' said Vakha Makhmutkhajiev, a retired policeman in a permanently milling crowd in the main square. 'Only 10 per cent of the population support Dudayev.' But the war had put the village under huge pressure. Makhmutkhajiev was furious at Yeltsin and the Russians. 'You don't disarm bandits with bombs. If they wanted to disarm them they should have removed two people: the President and the Vice-President.'

This was the paradox Elmurzayev was trying to solve. 'We thought the problem could have been solved differently,' he said, sitting hunched in his office. 'We ourselves should have got rid of Dudayev.' He was almost dragged into the war on 27 December when the Russians bombed the edge of the town, damaging thirteen houses and killing eight people. Stepashin flew in personally by helicopter to apologize and promise an inquiry into how the anti-Dudayev stronghold had been bombed. 'We were told it was a misunderstanding, but that won't resurrect the dead,' said Elmurzayev.[16]

Moscow now set up a tame government in Grozny, headed by Salambek Khajiev. The opposition leader, Umar Avturkhanov, was made his deputy and Beslan Gantemirov got his old job back as Mayor of Grozny. At the same time a Russian administration formed in Chechnya which seemed to have more clout and was headed by Nikolai Semyonov, the former First Secretary of the Grozny Communist Party Committee. The Chechens had absolutely no influence with the Russian military and Khajiev says he never even met the commanders.

In March Russian forces turned their attention on the town of Argun, 10 miles to the east of Grozny, settled on the banks of the wide River Argun. Commanding the main railway and road routes across the republic, it was vital for control of the country and supply routes into Grozny from Russia. The Russians unleashed the full strength of their firepower upon the town from tank positions across the river. The nearest district of small one-storey houses was soon smashed to smithereens. The fighting developed into the slow, grim pattern of the battle for Grozny, as Chechen fighters sat out the deadly barrage, running night raids under the tough but inspired leadership of Allauddin Khamzatov, the commander of Argun, a burly bandit who wore a solid gold chain and watch on his enormous wrists.

The battle dragged on for weeks, the casualties mounting on both sides, when suddenly on 22 March the Russians broke south, crossed the River Argun and moved round to encircle the Chechens, forcing the fighters to abandon the town. The Chechen defence seemed to unravel as Russian forces pressed their advantage and took two more major towns, Shali and Gudermes, by 29

March, just a week later. Both were huge prizes, giving Russia control of the eastern part of the republic. Gudermes, Chechnya's second biggest town and the main railway junction, 30 miles east of Grozny, came off largely unscathed, thanks to a deal between local elders and the Russian administration in Grozny. The fighters regarded it as a betrayal. Vladimir Zorin, the deputy Russian administrator in Grozny, saw it as a huge success that saved lives. In reality, with Russian forces virtually surrounding them, the rebels would have been pushed to defend it. Capturing Shali was a political coup for the Russians since it had been the temporary capital of the Dudayev government after Grozny fell. Surrounded on three sides by Russian tanks, and under heavy bombardment, Basayev ordered the fighters out, deciding not to waste their energy. They pulled back to the villages of Serzhen-Yurt and Agishti, nestled above in the foothills.

Serzhen-Yurt, just a few miles beyond Shali, was of far more vital strategic importance to the Chechens since it guarded the entrance to the gorge into the mountains and Vedeno. Vedeno was the prize, site of historical battles of the Caucasian wars, where Imam Shamil once had his headquarters. The ruins of the 20-foot-high walls of his white fortress still enclose the centre of the village and this was where Maskhadov now based himself. Vedeno was also the home of Shamil Basayev and a bastion of pro-independence fighters.

*

The generals were under pressure from the Kremlin to wind up the fighting before Victory in Europe Day on 9 May. Yeltsin had invited many of the world's leaders to Moscow to celebrate the fiftieth anniversary of the Allies' victory against Nazi Germany and wanted the war in Chechnya over and done with. By the end of April, Russian forces controlled much of the central plain of Chechnya. Kulikov announced that 80 per cent of Chechnya was won and ordered the most devastating bombing campaign of mountain villages and woodlands to break the final resistance. In a field along the western road, forty artillery pieces and multiple rocket-launching systems stood facing south to a string of three villages, Bamut, Stary Achkoi and Orekhovo, tucked on the edge of the plain where the wooded foothills began their rise to the great snowy ridge of mountains behind. Chechen fighters were firmly dug in in the otherwise deserted villages, and for months used the higher ground to repel any attack. Across the plains, now tinted pale green with the first spring grass, thick puffs of white smoke burst from the hillside as the Russian shells found impact.

Up in the woods Chechen fighters, guns over their shoulders, moved quietly up the hill. In low voices they greeted a group of men crouched around a campfire, propping their automatic rifles and shotguns against a tree and throwing their arms around each other in the traditional welcome. They paused barely ten minutes, just long enough to swap news of the previous night's shelling and Russian troops' movements. Then they disappeared, climbing into the thickly wooded hills to move out of range of the Russian guns. They were some of several hundred fighters defending the last villages in the western foothills, moving further up into the mountains in shifts to rest up. The forest, lush and green now spring had arrived, provided good cover for rebel camps. 'You will never go hungry in these woods,' said Hussein, a fighter who had spent his life hunting and riding in the area. He could name every tree – magnificent beech, huge wild pear, smaller trees bearing plums and berries, and every variety of Chechnya's ubiquitous hazelnut. He spotted a deer through the trees, and pointed to prints in the mud by a stream where a wolf had drunk.

At the bottom of a steep ravine sat several fighters, hunched around a fire in the cold morning air. More men emerged from a barely visible bunker, identified only by a layer of hefty logs forming its roof. It was one of the many hiding-places where rebels were resting, listening to the shelling rumbling in the distance. Even here though, in the boundless woods, Russia still had complete supremacy in the air. Helicopters came over morning and afternoon, hunting a prey they could not see but only guess was there. Further along, smashed trees, twisted metal and holes gouged in the earth showed where helicopters had attacked at random. Russian jets roared high above, heading deeper into the mountains on bombing runs. For the first time the fighters were living in the mountains like real guerrillas, exploiting the mountainous, wooded terrain to continue their fight indefinitely.

They held their positions, beating off repeated attempts by the Russians to storm the last villages. Bamut became a legend of resistance. The Russians claimed the fighters were holding out in deep rocket silos on the edge of the village but in fact the fighters lost control of them in April 1995 and for a year defended the village from the houses and steep wooded hillsides lining the narrow valley. The people from Bamut were among the fiercest, most independent of all Chechens and remained a thorn in Russia's side throughout the war.

On 9 May Western leaders attended a march past in Red Square, although in a muted sign of disapproval for the war in Chechnya they declined to watch a larger display of Russian military might later in the day. Yeltsin declared a ceasefire in Chechnya for the week of the celebrations but it was completely ignored by his generals on the ground, who continued a steady bombardment of villages in the hills. 'What moratorium?' muttered a fighter as he crouched low against a wall in Orekhovo, ducking his head as the shrapnel flew in close with a high-pitched whine. Meanwhile, veterans from the allied countries flew in to join Russian veterans gathered from all over the country. They marched together in the parade, a re-run of the victory parade by returning troops in 1945. The Chechens, needless to say, were not present.

Gaslan Umarov, proud wearer of the Soviet Order of the Red Star and the Order of the Great Patriotic War, donned his jacket laden with medals and stood by the bullet-ridden gate of his daughter's house in Gudermes for a family snapshot. Chechens had never been invited to march in Red Square, he said. There were 132 Chechens who were awarded the top medal, Hero of the Soviet Union, in the Second World War, but even then they never took part in the 1945 victory parade, and were sent straight to join the rest of their people in exile in Kazakhstan. Now he was close to despair. 'After fifty years of victory, look what happened to me. They burned my apartment, there is nothing left, not even so much as a spoon,' he said. He moved to his daughter's house which Russian troops sprayed with bullets during a firefight with Chechen fighters. 'We all lay on the floor, then went down to the bunker. I was in a bunker in 1942 and now again I am living in a bunker,' he said. 'Clinton is coming to celebrate Victory Day holiday and all this is happening.'

As the Western leaders departed after the festivities, Russian aeroplanes stepped up their raids. Tens of thousands of refugees who had fled into the safety of the mountains from Grozny were now caught with their backs to the wall. Running short of food and mad with terror from the constant bombardment, they fled back down the mountains, risking attacks on the roads and a hostile reception from advancing Russian forces. Queues miles long formed for days as refugees tried to pass through the Russian checkpoints back into the relative safety of Grozny.

The fighters were struggling now. Seriously outgunned, their ammunition and medical supplies running dangerously low, they were also losing men in the bombardments. They were close to the end of their military strength when the Russians took Chiri-Yurt, the last village on the plains in central Chechnya, on 20 May and cut the road above Serzhen-Yurt by the end of May.

There were some 250 fighters left defending Vedeno, and another fifty wounded, but when the Russian assault came on 6 June, it caught the rebels by surprise. Russian tanks crawled up the river-bed of a small tributary that brought them out on the plateau due west of Vedeno. At the same time paratroopers were dropped in above the village. The fighters, waiting for an attack straight up the valley, suddenly found themselves surrounded on three sides. Low on ammunition, they immediately pulled out, heading east through the woods towards Dargo. The loss of Vedeno forced Basayev to abandon Serzhen-Yurt too, and he and his fighters made the long trek on foot through mountain hamlets to join the others. 'We fought there to our last strength,' Basayev said a year later. For him and his fighters it was the lowest point of the war.

Maskhadov set off to report to Dudayev, who was in central Chechnya, in Shatoi. Dudayev had almost disappeared from sight since his last press conferences in Grozny, constantly on the move from one safe house to another. Now the Russians had split the Chechen front, cutting the President off from his Chief of Staff and top commander. Within two weeks Shatoi was to fall also. It was a dangerous journey for Maskhadov, with Russian paratroopers ranged in the mountains around. He drove up the rough mountain road from Vedeno through Kharachoi, which was already under rocket fire, past Lake Kezenoiam, and travelled round behind one of Chechnya's highest peaks, Mount Kashkerlam, that towers above the lake at 2806 metres above sea-level. At Makhazhoi he cut across to the main Argun valley and down to Shatoi where he met Dudayev. 'It was very important for us then how we would carry on, what to do next,' Maskhadov said. What he did not say was that they were close to defeat. They talked for hours and decided that Dudayev would take command of the western front and Maskhadov would move to Nozhai-Yurt and run the eastern front. They planned a guerrilla war where they would not try to hold fixed positions as such but look for ways to move around Russian positions and percolate back down to the plains.

Maskhadov set off on the return journey immediately, but paratroopers were already above Makhazhoi right on the Dagestan border and there was no question of driving this time. He took a horse and a Dagestani guide and, crossing high over the mountains, wound his way along the most remote territory before dropping down to Benoi to rejoin his staff. It took him two days. 'It was a very dangerous trip,' Iskhanov recalled. 'I did it myself twice – they are the highest mountains, if a plane or a helicopter comes there is nowhere to hide, the only thing you can do is quickly jump down a precipice to avoid it. There is absolutely nowhere to hide, the only salvation is if there are clouds or mist. Otherwise there is nothing.' The only light-hearted note was Maskhadov's stiffness after riding a horse for the first time since childhood. 'He could not sit down for two days after that,' Iskhanov laughed.

Fighters were preparing defences and building camps in the woods above Benoi, readying themselves to defend the last mountain villages but already contemplating a protracted and difficult guerrilla war in the mountains. 'I was sleeping badly, it was raining, sleeping in the woods was not fun,' Basayev jokingly recalled a year later. Iskhanov remembers it as the lowest time of all. 'It was after Vedeno, in Benoi, I felt that the people there and everywhere were not happy, in places there were atrocities, shelling, people were worried. There was a dilemma,' he said. 'It was there we started talking about how we could carry on.'

12

Terrorism and Talks

It was lunch-time on 14 June 1995, a hot midsummer's day in the slow-paced southern Russian town of Budyonnovsk. People were shopping in the sleepy market, policemen were walking home to lunch, the air was still in the tree-lined streets and the vine-covered courtyards.

Rima Kniga and her son Sasha looked out of the window of her house opposite the police station when a police car marked with a blue stripe drew up, followed by two army trucks. Two men in police uniforms climbed out and about twenty-five armed men in civilian clothes, all bearded, lined up purposefully against the wall of her house facing the station. 'They stood so calmly, they were not afraid of anything,' she said. Suddenly they opened fire, shooting furiously at the police station, smashing all the windows. Rima threw herself on the floor, dragging her son from the window. Then, as quickly as they had arrived, the men left, heading off round the corner towards the main square.

The head of the police criminal investigation department, a young officer called Nikolai, was sitting in his room on the third floor on the far side of the building when he heard shots and someone running along the corridor. He grabbed his pistol and ran out but saw no one. He raced downstairs, snatching the keys for the arms room, and gave out automatic weapons to the few people still around. Glass crunched underfoot from the smashed windows and a bullet-hole made a star-burst in the glass of the reception area. Someone said the gunmen had dragged off some female workers from the canteen. Nikolai and the others gave chase, running along the side streets towards the square.

The place was milling with gunmen. They had shot their way into the town hall and the telephone exchange next door and raised a green flag with a band of red and white stripes on its lower half. It was the Chechen flag of independence. Just a week after the fall of Vedeno, Shamil Basayev and a whole battalion of fighters had brought the war to Russia.

There began a week of terror and death that touched every family in the town and gripped the entire nation. Budyonnovsk, named after the famous Cossack General Semyon Budyonny, is a quiet provincial town of 60,000 inhabitants. It lies 100 miles from the Chechen border amid the rolling golden wheatfields and rich green pastures of southern Russia. Basayev and his group of 148 fighters raked the town with gunfire and seized thousands of people from the streets and their homes in the largest hostage raid in modern times. A furious gun battle broke out in the streets as Russian police pursued the fighters. Reinforcements, called in by the Mayor, arrived from the helicopter regiment based outside of town, driving into town in buses and immediately coming under fire. Dozens of civilians in the street were gunned down or caught in the crossfire. A young man was shot as he drove his motorcycle home to lunch. A civilian car lay abandoned on the corner of the square, its windscreen shot out and blood soaking the seats.

The battle raged in the centre of town for several hours. As more Russian assistance poured in, Basayev realized he could not hold the town hall: a tall, exposed building with large glass windows, it was hard to defend. The Pioneers' House at the end of the square, an old wood and plaster building, was on fire. He already had wounded fighters and sent two groups of them to the town hospital. He then ordered the fighters to round up more hostages and prepare a column of people to walk the mile to the hospital.

They worked along the nearby streets, bursting into courtyards and homes, grabbing anyone they found, many of them old men and women and housewives sitting at home. Olga Morzoyeva, aged eighteen, was snatched from her family house. She and her family were pottering around the yard at four in the afternoon, when suddenly the gunmen burst in and ordered them to get out quickly, her father Akhmed Morzoyev said. 'Her mother and another woman ran away, but they took her. On foot, at gunpoint,' he said.

The Chechens formed a huge column of hundreds of people along the street, urging them along at gunpoint, shooting over their heads to force back the Russian police. In a moment of black comedy, Basayev remembers an old woman stepping out of her gate staring around at the commotion. 'There's one old granny in a house on the way to the hospital. People are aware of what's going on, they all are crouching down, fighting is going on, the Russians are shooting and we are shooting, and the old woman comes out on to the street, and stands there, and I say, "Grandma, stop, come over here." She says, "Little son, what's going on, are you making a movie?" I say, "Yes, yes we are filming, Grandma, it's a war," and she comes quickly over.'

Russian troops had already blocked off the hospital, but as the swarm of civilians shuffled down the road they backed off and let the Chechens through with their human shield. The hospital corridors were already crammed with people, the Chechen fighters who had gone on ahead well in control. A former monastery set in walled grounds, the main hospital building housed general wards, including maternity and children's wards, for 400 patients. A surgical ward stood in a separate building behind. Scores of civilians, wounded in the firefight in town, were already there, as were a dozen wounded Russian servicemen from the helicopter regiment taken prisoner by the fighters as soon as they were ferried to the hospital. Together with the hospital patients, medical staff and now the whole column of hostages, there were at least 1200 people inside the hospital.

As night fell, the Chechens made their demands over the hospital telephone: Russia must stop the war in Chechnya, withdraw its troops and hold direct negotiations with Dudayev. Moscow immediately announced a state of alert in the region and Yerin ordered large forces of police troops to the town. Together with Stepashin, he left for Budyonnovsk. Already thirty-five people were dead and some fifty-seven wounded. Moscow was facing an appalling crisis, the single largest hostage-taking in the twentieth century. The Chechens had hit back just as Moscow was convincing itself and the world that it was winding up the war, and just hours before Yeltsin was to leave Moscow to join the heads of the Group of Seven leading industrial nations for a summit in Halifax, Canada.

*

Basayev was undoubtedly acting on his own in organizing and executing the raid on Budyonnovsk. Dudayev condemned the attack the following day. 'Such actions can only discredit the national liberation struggle of the Chechen people,' he said, forgetting that he had repeatedly threatened to take the war to Russia. Maskhadov said he only learned of it from Basayev's younger brother, Shirvani, the day after the group set off.[1]

A gifted commander, Basayev has described his main motivation for the raid as anger against Russia for the months of cruel war in Chechnya. He wanted Russia to experience what Chechnya had. At the end of May planes had bombed Vedeno, hitting a house full of women and children. Eleven of Basayev's relatives were killed, mostly aunts and young cousins. That bombing and the fall of his home village to Russian forces a week later tipped the balance. 'Before, I was not a supporter of that sort of action, to go and fight in Russia, because I knew what measures and cost it would entail, so I had always refused such things. But when last year we were thrown out of Vedeno, and they had driven us into a corner with the very savage and cruel annihilation of villages, women, children, old people, of a whole people, then we went. Then we felt better: "Let's go to Russia,

we will fight well there, we will stop the war or we will all die," '
he recalled the following summer.'² What he planned was very
like the centuries-old *nabeg*, where Chechen horsemen would
sweep down from the mountains in a lightning attack on a
Russian settlement to plunder and seize hostages.

Basayev is by no means a simple bandit. An extraordinarily
brave fighter even by Chechen standards, he also has a quick and
clever political mind. In launching a raid on a Russian town he
was dealing a calculated blow at Russia's political leadership and
its Power Ministries. He was also aiming for maximum publicity
for the Chechens' cause, determined to force Russian society to
wake up and act against the injustice of the war in Chechnya.
That his action would turn international opinion against the
Chechens did not concern him, since the world had offered little
help to Chechnya so far. Although he claims that he never planned
to take the hospital and civilian hostages, the Chechen traditions
of vengeance and hostage-taking run strong in his blood. To
make Russian society pay for the brutal war it was waging in
Chechnya was an inevitable step for a hot-headed Chechen
fighter.

Certain he would not get out alive, Basayev ordered his fighters
to round up hostages, thinking to take as many Russians with
him as possible. 'I thought, what difference is there, whatever
means I use, if they are Russian, they are jackals. My people are
more important to me than these Russian children or women,' he
said.

Born in January 1965, Basayev was, in his own words, an all-
Soviet kid. 'But by the age of fifteen, I knew that 360 Chechens
had defended the fortress of Brest, that forty-eight Chechens were
named heroes posthumously and then after the deportations were
not given the status of hero. The elders told us,' he said, sitting
out in a courtyard under the stars, talking long into the night.

The elder of two brothers, he was raised in the village of
Dyshne-Vedeno, just above the main village of Vedeno, a small

cluster of pretty houses among orchards, perched on the edge of cliffs above the River Khulkhulau. His father, Salman, a simple labourer, returned from exile and built his house in the same spot that his ancestors had inhabited since the eleventh century. A gentle, quiet-spoken man with a soft white beard and lively eyes, Salman Basayev brought up his sons on the tales of their ancestors. Almost every generation of the family have been fighters, protecting their homeland against invaders. One ancestor fought the Mongol hordes led by the fourteenth-century warload Tamerlane. Salman's great-grandfather, one of Imam Shamil's deputies, died in battle against General Yermolov. His father fought the Bolsheviks, only to die of hunger and cold in the first winter of exile in Kazakhstan. He lay in the snow unburied until the spring.

Salman himself grew sick in Kazakhstan and only later understood that it was because of the nuclear testing being carried out in the later 1950s. 'You know, they exploded atomic bombs above the ground at Semipalatinsk. We were in a four-ton tractor, three of us were sitting in it, it was thrown around and bounced high in the air, several times, up and down. It happened practically every three months or so. We were 500 kilometres away from it. There was a big wood and it was totally flattened. Everything glass was shattered. It was terrifying. A man could suddenly go blind. I was sick for a long time from it. They said it was some sort of plague, from ticks, in the limbs, which they had to treat. The men knew it was an atomic illness but they would not say. In the end I said it to them, "It is radiation sickness, isn't it?" '[3]

His father described the young Shamil as an attentive, thoughtful boy, who was obsessed with fairness. Basayev himself says he always wanted to be a detective. After military service he went to Moscow but, refused a place at Moscow State University, he dropped plans to study law and settled for land management, living in a hostel with African and Cuban students. He had a poster of Che Guevara on the wall of his room, a gift from one of the Cubans. Another hero was Garibaldi, he said. In a little green pocket-book he carries a quote from Abraham Lincoln about freedom thriving on the blood of its heroes.

He lived by trading foreign computers when they were still something of a forbidden fruit. Then, during the attempted coup in August 1991, Basayev joined over 100 other Chechens to support Yeltsin on the barricades at the White House. He abandoned that struggle to fly home as soon as he heard events were unravelling in Chechnya. He swiftly became involved in Dudayev's independence drive and was put in charge of the arms arsenal at the former Soviet army base of Khankala. In November 1991 he joined two friends and hijacked a Russian plane shortly after take-off from the airport of Mineralniye Vody. They flew to Ankara and demanded a press conference to protest at Russia's information blockade. After hours of talks with Turkish authorities on the tarmac they returned to Grozny without incident. It was the beginning of a career that Basayev sees as a struggle for freedom but that has labelled him forever as a terrorist.

He spent 1991 to 1994 readying for war with Russia. He claims that he learned his battle-skills fighting in Nagorno-Karabakh and the breakaway region of Abkhazia. He also travelled to Turkey, Iraq and Afghanistan to arrange military training for his men, although he says their experience was of limited use. Abkhazia, where he led a battalion of several hundred men for a year from 1992 to 1993, was the crucial experience, forging a solid comradeship amongst a number of fighters who were to become key commanders in the war against Russia. Despite his fearsome reputation and his low-key, unsmiling demeanour in front of the cameras, Basayev is both witty and personable. He inspires great loyalty and is at his happiest when telling battle-stories, making his men around him laugh.

He had little trouble finding the men and three women nurses to follow him on his raid into Russia. His cousin, Khalid Basayev, helped select them from 200 volunteers. 'We chose men who were most ready to go to their death,' Khalid said completely deadpan. 'We were looking among the brave and the desperate. There were some who had barely held an automatic rifle in their hands before. We were not looking for experience, but for someone who had strong nerves, who had not known fear, and also who had faith in God, who did not fear death.[4]

'We told the boys we were planning to go to Grozny, to blockade it completely and possibly never come back. We stressed that there was a full possibility of not returning. We refused those who had colds or fever. We told them we will not help you, if you fall, no one will bring you back,' he said.

Even Khalid, a grey-haired man in his forties, dressed in combat fatigues, did not know the ultimate destination. According to Shamil Basayev only five of them knew. Three of his closest deputies from Shali – Aslanbek Ismailov, a construction engineer who had fought in the Soviet army in Afghanistan, Aslanbek Abdulkhajiev, a roguish character with gold teeth, and Abu Movsayev, a former policeman – planned the transport and checked the route, travelling several times into Russia. Shamil himself organized the weapons. No one told Dudayev or Maskhadov, because to tell Dudayev would have meant his entire entourage knowing, endangering security, and the plan would immediately have been vetoed. 'The tactics were suicide. What president or commander would let them go?' Khalid said.

Today the real destination remains a closely guarded secret. Basayev has said he was heading for Moscow and the Kremlin but admits that is just a yarn he spins. Russian counter-intelligence chief Stepashin says they thought Basayev was heading to his old haunt of Mineralniye Vody to seize the airport. It is more likely that he was aiming for a military or industrial target or big city in southern Russia such as Stavropol, or even the military chemical weapons plant at Prokhladny in Kabardino-Balkaria. Some fighters say they were heading for the helicopter base outside Budyonnovsk. Whatever the case, they only ended up in the centre of Budyonnovsk because Russian police stopped them on the far side of the town and made them turn back to the police station.

Basayev says he spent $25,000 on the raid, buying two army trucks, two cars and enough ammunition to last a major siege, and using the rest to bribe the Russian police on the way. 'Boys in police uniform sat in the front in Zhigulis as an escort. We went looking like Russian mercenaries, we had trophies, black scarves (across our faces), and uniforms,' Basayev recounted, describing the look cultivated by Russia's contract soldiers in Chechnya. Those with the fairest looks were picked to be the drivers, the rest hiding inside the covered trucks. 'The police stop us, what have you got there? We say: "You dogs, we've been in Chechnya, spilling blood, and you dare stop us, swine, again you are going to check us, swine." When asked what they were carrying, the Chechens answered "Cargo 200", the military code word for dead bodies.' Even then the police wanted a bribe. 'They knew what was in the coffins, they think it's stolen goods. They want part of it, you have to pay for that. We used that idea because when a military column goes by there're always stolen goods. Officers, soldiers, they are all in it, for that reason we used that.' By the time they got to Budyonnovsk the bulk of the money was gone. On the edge of the town they found five police cars and eight policemen blocking the road. Two military planes buzzed them. Basayev knew the game was up and agreed to follow the police into town. 'What could we do in an open field? It is easier to fight in the town,' he reasoned.

The freedom with which such a large group of armed Chechens drove 100 miles into Russia enraged and embarrassed the leaders in Moscow. Yeltsin bawled at his ministers in a televised session of his Security Council and three ministers eventually resigned over the fiasco. Locals in Budyonnovsk angrily accused the police of corruption and negligence.

Budyonnovsk slumbered behind closed shutters the day after

the Chechens' rampage. 'Where's the war then?' a taxi driver shouted to a local man squatting by his gate. The man stared vacantly. Soldiers guarding the police station snoozed in the grass under the trees beside their armoured vehicles. The hospital, nestled in its walled grove of trees, was deathly quiet, troops in armoured vehicles surrounding it. The sun shone on the golden cornfields, burnishing the glossy coats of herds of horses grazing peacefully on the edge of town. But under the calm Budyonnovsk was gripped by anxiety. Relatives, desperate for news, gathered outside the police station where Stepashin, Yerin and Yegorov had set up their crisis centre. Two jets suddenly roared low over the town. Yerin emerged, dressed in a light suit and pale shoes of plaited leather, his thin hair carefully combed, promising that all would end peacefully. Few in the crowd believed him. 'Moscow is a long way away, they do not care, they do what they want,' said Nikolai Gusen, whose policeman son had been killed the first day. 'Human life does not mean anything to them,' another man chipped in, watching Yerin drive away.

Tense negotiations were going on by telephone. Basayev was demanding journalists be allowed in for a press conference. The Russians stalled, trying to bargain for a release of hostages in return. As the hot afternoon dragged on, Basayev ordered the first hostages to be shot. He says the Russian side had told him they had arrested 2000 local Chechens and said they would shoot them if he did not surrender. Basayev was unmoved. 'I said, "You bastards, go on, shoot them. If you are going to kill Chechens it is the same here as there, even more if they are Russian citizens, go on, shoot them. And I will kill ten here now, if you are going to blackmail me, you goats."'

Horrified hostages watched as fighters marched out five of the captured Russian pilots and executed them in the rose garden, just below the hospital windows. Basayev claims he executed twelve altogether, all members of the Russian forces. He eventually got his press conference that evening, although it was nearly aborted when Russian troops opened fire on the gathering in the hospital corridor, seriously wounding a woman surgeon. Basayev added to his demands a warning that he would blow up the whole hospital if there were attempts to storm it. He did, however, let out a handful of sick patients overnight, women and children, including two babies.

Yeltsin none the less left for the Halifax summit the following morning, two days into the crisis, leaving Prime Minister Viktor Chernomyrdin in charge. Halifax was an important summit for Yeltsin. Previously a supplicant begging to be admitted to the top table, he was this time hoping to come as a partner with more clout. Chechnya had seriously damaged his international standing and democratic credentials, yet he seemed to relish the fact that the Chechens had handed him a gift on a plate. Calling the Chechen attack 'barbaric', he told Russian television before flying out, 'there is one advantage. The world community has finally understood whom the federal forces are fighting.'

Another scorching day dragged by, interrupted only by the clatter of helicopters above the hospital and relatives clamouring outside the makeshift morgue set up in the town bathhouse. Women scrambled up into the refrigeration truck to look for missing relatives. Shaking and wiping sweat from their eyes, they emerged unable to speak, handkerchiefs pressed against their mouths. Another truck arrived from the hospital where the Chechens had handed over more bodies. 'Is there someone in yellow in there?' called a woman. 'I can see a policeman and someone in black,' a man perched on the roof of the bathhouse shouted down.

Doctors inside the hospital, alarmed at the massive overcrowding and worsening conditions when the water was turned off, asked Basayev to allow them to plead with the authorities to give the Chechens free passage. 'I said OK. We had been there one day. They went out, came back and said, "Nothing doing. Stepashin is there and Yerin. It's terrible, nothing doing, we talked but no one listened." They personally tried and they threw them out,' Basayev recalled.

Instead the Russians tried to use Basayev's own brother, Shirvani, to persuade him to release the hostages. At a meeting with Kulikov in eastern Chechnya Maskhadov agreed to send Shirvani to Budyonnovsk. Together with another commander, Magomed Khambiyev, Shirvani laid down his weapons and walked with Kulikov to his helicopter. 'That moment was real madness, my brother is in Budyonnovsk, I am under orders to go there, [trusting] just the word of a Russian, they could at any moment take me as a hostage,' he recalled. His instructions from Maskhadov were to find out and report back on the fighters' position in Budyonnovsk, for if it was desperate they would create a diversion. With Kulikov he agreed he would try to intervene for the sake of the hostages.

Without a weapon for the first time in six months of war, sitting among Russian generals, Shirvani says he cheered up when he saw the havoc in Budyonnovsk. 'I was satisfied with the way it had turned out. A destroyed town, burning, everywhere burnt-out cars, people in panic. Simply the picture ran past my eyes, that what had been happening for nearly a year in Chechnya, these boys had shown them here in Russia. They had opened people's eyes.'

Shamil threatened to shoot his own brother when he heard the Russians had brought him to mediate. With all the ministers listening in, Shirvani telephoned the hospital, 'Aslanbek [Abdulk-hajiev] picks up the phone. He asks me, "Did you come yourself or did they take you." I said I have an order from Maskhadov. He says, "Really?" I say, "Really." "If not we will shoot you," he says. That was an order from Shamil.' The word from Maskhadov was enough, however, and Shirvani walked into the hospital without incident. He spent over an hour there. He found the fighters well in control but he described the mood among the hostages as terrible. 'In the cellar I do not know how many people there were, many people, it was terrible, you could not walk along the corridors, they were everywhere, standing, on the floor,' he recalled. Shirvani emerged from the hospital saying he could not persuade his brother to give up but warning the Russians not to try to storm the building since there were so many hostages. On the surface Shirvani's visit achieved little to end the crisis, yet he almost certainly brought advice or orders from Maskhadov for Basayev to focus his demands on peace talks. It was only after Shirvani's visit that this became the main demand. Kulikov remembers Shirvani bringing out the message that Basayev would surrender if all bombing and military activities in Chechnya were halted.[5] The offer seems to have been ignored.

*

Russian forces stormed the hospital at 5 a.m. on the fourth day, in predictably heavy-handed fashion. Huge explosions rent the still dawn air and rocketed everyone in the town out of their beds. Heavy guns from armoured vehicles battered the walls of the building, throwing the hospital into screaming panic. Special forces troops, among them the elite commando group Alpha, burst over the walls and across the grounds towards the hospital buildings. The Chechen fighters were waiting, although Basayev had found twenty-one of twenty-four sentries asleep at their posts just an hour earlier.[6] Gunning furiously from machine-gun positions in the basement and on the roof, they now cut down the Russians as they approached. Snipers standing well back in the central corridor trained their sights on the approaches. Half a dozen armoured vehicles that moved towards the hospital were hit with grenade-launchers, exploding in flames.

Nikolai Karmazov, head of a surgical unit in a separate building, was already up and about when the assault began. 'I was on the first floor when it started. They were firing grenades, sniper and machine-guns. It was a nightmare,' he recounted later.

Basayev and his fighters were in the main building which took the brunt of the attack. 'There was fierce shooting, it was terrible, they took us from five sides, there was burning, we were shooting at each other, there were people killed and lots of wounded. I go down the corridor, and a woman says, "Ah, it's all right for you, it's *ghazavat*, but what are we to do?" The boys had already explained to them what *ghazavat* was. I said, "Pray to God,"' he recalled.

Three helicopters were circling overhead as members of Alpha reached the outbuildings. 'They came from the direction of the river,' Karmazov said. 'They shouted up to us at the window, asking if there were Chechens inside. We said no.' The crack troops burst into the building. 'Ten or fifteen of them came in – they were very strong, very tough-looking,' said Karmazov, a soft-spoken surgeon wearing a white coat and glasses. 'They were in camouflage, wearing big helmets, fully armed.' They escorted Karmazov and all but the most badly wounded of the 105 hostages out of the building at about 7 a.m. They ran 150 yards into buses, escaping unscathed. About twenty Russian soldiers, including two Alpha men with heavy wounds, were brought with them to the clinic across town, Karmazov said. 'I saw smoke rising from the building where the gunmen were, from the recovery ward and the blood transfusion section.'

Inside the main section of the hospital it was mayhem. Hostages were hiding under mattresses, scrambling into the central corridors to escape the incoming fire. Grenades were exploding on the walls of every room along one section. The Chechens were under intense pressure. Alpha broke into the main building, taking the ground floor, and the Chechens moved up into the upper floors, dragging heavy hospital machinery across the stairs and spraying the stairs with bullets. Then suddenly some of the hostages braved the bullets, flinging white sheets out of the smashed windows and screamed at the Russian troops: 'Don't shoot, don't shoot.' The fighters most likely forced them at gunpoint to make their desperate plea, although the fighters and some hostages deny it. Several of the hostages were killed, hit by incoming sniper bullets according to Pavel Chubov, a young surgeon in the hospital. Somehow their shouting was heard and the shooting died down. A doctor in a white coat emerged with a message, signed by hostages, begging the Russian forces to hold their fire. The town fell into a stunned stillness.

Contact with Basayev resumed. He had not wavered in his demands although he released about seventy patients, including women from the maternity ward. He still had well over 1000 hostages. There was another more stealthy attack two hours later. This time Alpha tried to take out the Chechen snipers and to make the Chechens expend all their ammunition. Their leader told the official army newspaper *Krasnaya Zvezda* that the Chechens were shooting from behind hostages standing at the windows. Two Alpha members aimed for the hostages' legs to make them fall, so a third sniper could take out the terrorist, he said. The Russians made a third attempt in the early afternoon. Deep booms resounded across the town dozing in the 40-degree heat as machine-gun fire rattled on and on. Two columns of black smoke rose from the central building when fire took hold in the north wing. The two sides called a halt while a fire engine came in to douse the flames. It was then that Prime Minister Chernomyrdin changed tack. The dramatic television pictures of women hostages screaming and waving sheets at the hospital windows had already been transmitted round the world and shaken the whole country. It was an absolute public relations disaster for the government. Suddenly Russian forces were seen as the brutal ones. The day's work cost the Russian forces five dead, three of them Alpha troops, and thirty wounded, although the Chechens claim the true figure was higher. Civilian casualties had risen to 121.

That evening Chernomyrdin called Sergei Kovalyov, who was already in Budyonnovsk, to ask him to negotiate with the terrorists. Kovalyov immediately talked to the Chechens by

telephone and early the following morning, with several colleagues, walked past the Russian guns into the hospital. He spent
nine hours on 18 June in the hospital working out an agreement,
quickly signing a draft handwritten paper with Basayev in the
morning, and then together with Basayev faxing and talking to
Chernomyrdin in Moscow throughout the long day. In an unprecedented step, Chernomyrdin actually negotiated direct with
Basayev over the phone. The atmosphere crackling with tension,
the Russian Prime Minister allowed television cameras into his
White House office to film his negotiations with Basayev. Basayev
was demanding an immediate ceasefire in Chechnya, the opening
of peace talks and safe passage for him and his fighters back to
Chechnya. Chernomyrdin demanded the immediate release of all
women, children, the old, the sick and wounded.

In Halifax Yeltsin, unaware of the mood-swing in Moscow,
said during a joint press conference with US President Bill Clinton
that he had given the order to storm the hospital before his
departure from Moscow. Red-faced, Yeltsin beat the air with his
fists above his head, saying the 'criminals in black headbands'
had to be 'annihilated'. His anger with the Chechens was palpable
and seemed to discomfort a subdued-looking Clinton. 'Yeltsin
could have only hindered the process,' said Yury Orlov, a human
rights activist who accompanied Kovalyov and two other deputies
into the hospital to negotiate. 'He certainly could not have helped.
Thank God he was not here.' Chernomyrdin, on the other hand,
had always been much milder on Chechnya.

Chernomyrdin spoke at least four times directly with Basayev.
The Chechens released 200 hostages during the day and Chernomyrdin eventually agreed to all their demands. He sent a peace
delegation down to Grozny to begin talks with Dudayev's representatives that same day. He ordered a ceasefire in Chechnya
from 8 p.m. that evening, and guaranteed safe passage for the
Chechens and 150 of their hostages on buses back to Chechnya.
The hostages were asked to volunteer to go on the buses, but

when Basayev did not have enough, he simply picked them himself. Chernomyrdin even announced his agreement to the conditions on national television. He called Arkady Volsky, an influential industrialist and close ally, to ask him to join the talks. 'Within a few hours we were in Grozny and sitting at one table,' Volsky remembered. Facing him was Usman Imayev, the Chechen Justice Minister and Dudayev's representative for the negotiations. He had heard his name mentioned on the radio while sitting in a bunker under bombardment in Bamut.

They set up a satellite telephone for Imayev to confirm to Basayev they were at the peace table. 'It was very interesting to see how they checked each other out,' Volsky recalled. ' "Is it your voice or is it a fake?" It was amazing. "Tell me who your aunt is, what is she called? And what did you do when we were on holiday there? And how were you dressed?" And then [Imayev] asks him, "And what wound did you get in Abkhazia when you fought there?" Only after an hour could they agree that they were one another.'[7]

In Budyonnovsk tensions suddenly rose in the middle of the day when Russian armoured troop-carriers advanced close to the hospital. Grabbing the phone to the Russian headquarters, Basayev threatened to open fire on them if they came any closer. 'It was a very unpleasant twenty minutes,' Orlov said the following day. 'It was either a provocation or we have this expression in Russian, a *bardak* [literally brothel or cock-up].' Eventually the vehicles backed off and Chernomyrdin came on the phone. It was not the only example of the danger of ill-disciplined troops and poor command. A Russian journalist, Natalya Alyakina, was shot and killed after being waved through a Russian checkpoint on the edge of town and a number of soldiers were seriously wounded when one of their own armoured vehicles fired into a wall behind them, spraying them with shrapnel. Yerin later admitted it had been a mistake to use young, inexperienced soldiers in the operation.

Chernomyrdin faxed a final agreement through at 10 p.m. but stayed at his office, talking twice more to Basayev during the night. The deadline for him to release the hostages at 5 a.m. on 19 June passed. The buses only arrived at the hospital at 6 a.m., fire engines roaring down the road after them. The sound of them brought crowds of people rushing out to wait for the hostages. It was a cruel false alarm. Negotiations dragged on for most of another long hot day, and it was only at 4 p.m. that a fleet of seven red buses finally drove out, bearing the hated gunmen away. The crowd whistled and booed as they went by. Russian soldiers manned the streets, training their guns on the buses. The gunmen inside stood immobile, staring straight ahead; tense, frightening dark silhouettes in the buses. The 100-odd hostages accompanying them looked out of the windows, pale, sweating and dazed. With them were a handful of deputies, including Kovalyov and Orlov, and sixteen Russian journalists. A lone gunman stood guarding the third bus full of wounded. A refrigerator truck carrying fourteen Chechen fighters killed over the last few days followed behind.

Only then did the bulk of the hostages emerge from their five-day ordeal, stumbling up the dusty road like war refugees. A team of doctors and nurses walked purposefully in a group to the main square to denounce Yeltsin and the Russian attempt to storm the hospital which they said cost dozens of lives. Hysterical scenes followed as many of the hostages defended the Chechen fighters, to the indignation of the townspeople. 'They shot at us, our own troops shot at us,' said Tatyana Rybakova, a teacher. 'The Chechens were good to us. They only want Russia to withdraw from Chechnya,' said Sveta Zhuravlyova, a young nurse. Suddenly bystanders started yelling at her. 'They are murderers, they killed over a hundred people here,' one woman screamed, making her burst into tears. As she tried to argue, her family dragged her away.

For the hostages on the buses the ordeal was to continue for another forty-eight hours. Basayev had negotiated a route cutting right across Chechnya and through Grozny, but Kulikov, who was at the Russian base at Khankala, learned about it at the last moment and, fearing a huge propaganda victory for Basayev, refused to allow it. 'He felt that he had won. He understood that they were letting him get away, and he decided to use it as an excuse to restore the Dudayev regime in Grozny,' Kulikov said. He sent up helicopters to track the convoy. 'We were told that twenty light cars were already accompanying them, and people in cars were already preparing to meet Basayev all the length of the road, and in Grozny they were already preparing green flags to meet Basayev.'

Kulikov sent one of his generals with a handwritten letter to Basayev threatening to fire on the column if he did not turn around. The general made it just in time, landing the helicopter right in front of the convoy. Basayev eventually turned round and drove all through the night around the top of Chechnya, arriving in the morning at the town of Khasavyurt on the eastern border.

Another stand-off developed, the Russians demanding that Basayev release the hostages at the border, while he insisted on taking them with him deep into the mountains to Chechen-held territory. Russian armoured vehicles drew up around the convoy, aiming their guns on the buses, but were quickly swamped by throngs of local Chechens who flocked around to greet the fighters and bring them food and drink. The hours ticked by as the wounded sweltered inside the buses in a 45-degree heat. Finally, after an eight-hour delay, they moved on, winding up through the mountains in the late afternoon to the village of Zandak, where the fighters met a hero's welcome from 500 villagers and fighters. The hostages sat in the buses watching, until finally Basayev sent them off. They headed home, free at last. They too were greeted like heroes, wriggling out of the bus windows, punching the air with their fists as hundreds cheered the buses into Budyonnovsk.

A storm broke and rain poured down, breaking the searing heat that had crushed the town for the last seven days.

Budyonnovsk was a pivotal episode of the war. Facing defeat, the Chechens had launched a ruthless raid that appeared suicidal both for themselves and their cause. Yet they emerged not only relatively unscathed but in a stronger position than before. They had won a much-needed ceasefire and forced Russia to be serious about peace talks. Basayev had become a hero at home and boosted the separatist cause as many were abandoning it. The Russians, handed the proof that the Chechens were terrorists, should have been able to take the moral high ground for once. Yet through their own incompetence and heavy-handedness they ended up the losers. In the final analysis, as many people died in the Russian attempts to storm the hospital as in the Chechens' original attack on the town. Many in the country, while loathing the Chechens, blamed the government for allowing it to happen. The raid was seen as a direct consequence of the war, and the law enforcement agencies were shown as incapable of protecting the population from terrorism. Chernomyrdin, criticized by hard-liners for giving in to the terrorists, won some popularity with the nation for solving the problem so decisively. Yeltsin's national standing had been dealt another blow, but ever the skilful politician, he moved quickly to mend matters. He sacked Stepashin, Yerin and Yegorov and appointed the head of the Kremlin Guard, Mikhail Barsukov, as the new head of the counter-intelligence service, now renamed the FSB. Kulikov was named Interior Minister and Vyacheslav Mikhailov Nationalities Minister. Yeltsin then set about assuming Chernomyrdin's popular role as the peacemaker for himself.

*

The peace talks in Grozny got off the ground at a great pace. The two sides met under the auspices of the Organization for Security and Cooperation in Europe (OSCE), sitting somewhat cramped round a table in a rented house in central Grozny. The good-looking young Justice Minister, Usman Imayev, his thick beard set off by a shaved head, led the Chechen delegation. Maskhadov joined the talks the following day as deputy leader of the delegation. The Russian delegation was led by Vyacheslav Mikhailov, with the veteran Russian centrist politician Volsky as his deputy. The convivial and dynamic Volsky was to prove skilful at defusing tension when the two sides were at loggerheads.

Both sides describe the negotiations as very tense, but within a few weeks they had reached common ground on several key issues and were even close to a political agreement. The shifting political currents on both sides made it much harder for both negotiating teams. On the Russian side the combination of Volsky and Mikhailov signified the ascendancy of a more pragmatic team in the government, patronized by Chernomyrdin. They had kept up contact with the Chechen side throughout the war and they seized on the chance of negotiations as an opportunity to outflank the hawks. But the Chechens soon noticed that there was a tussle going on on the Russian side – the negotiators in Grozny sometimes retreated from a position overnight after talking to Moscow.

The Russian team was also dominated by Kulikov, the top general in Chechnya, who was shortly to be named Interior Minister. A short, squat man who wears tinted glasses, he has been described as something of a Napoleon – small, aggressive and ambitious. He is also a skilled political operator. Highly educated, he can exude reason and charm when he wants to, but was tough about yielding an inch on key issues. 'He was a good general and an officer of his word,' Imayev recalled. 'If he said he would do something, he would do it 100 per cent, even if Moscow or his leadership didn't like it. But of course during the negotiations he said fifteen or twenty times, "That's it. We're ending the negotiations, we're starting the war." '[8]

The Chechens' negotiating position was complicated by Dudayev. At the time the Chechen leader was so invisible that there was speculation that he was out of touch with what was going on. In fact he was very much trying to keep control. He called five or six times a day to the OSCE satellite telephone and summoned the Chechen delegation back to his base in the village of Roshni-Chu every night for debriefing and discussions on what further moves to take.

On the Chechen side both Imayev and Maskhadov seemed keen to make a deal. Imayev was a sharp-witted legal expert who did most of the work of formulating documents himself. 'What was very difficult for the Chechen side was that we didn't have any advisers except the Almighty,' he said later, complaining that the Russians had whole research institutes to consult. However, his negotiating talents and his developing relationship with the Russians started to arouse suspicions in some of the Chechen leadership. Maskhadov, on the other hand, tried to keep a low profile during political discussions and sat silently doodling on a piece of paper. All the same, in his first major exposure to public scrutiny he impressed everyone with his intelligence and restraint and it was obvious that his negotiating position was closer to Imayev than to Dudayev. 'When you are fighting you need to fight and when you are making peace you need to talk quietly,' he said later.

Within a week of his arrival in Grozny Volsky went out to talk to Dudayev in person, meeting him at midnight in the mountains. It was the only meeting between a government official and Dudayev during the war. Volsky said he found an intelligent man whom Moscow could have dealt with if it had only been subtle enough. Volsky brought Dudayev the offer of a Jordanian passport, money and a plane, everything to persuade him to leave Chechnya, at which Dudayev took great offence. 'He said, "No, I am a patriot of my country, I will die here,"' Volsky recalled. They talked until five in the morning, discovering that they had many acquaintances in common from the Soviet military. Dudayev made digs at Grachev's use of tanks in the city and the performance of Russian aviation.

Volsky already had extraordinary proof that Dudayev had sources in Moscow which had effectively infiltrated the highest levels of government. He says that in February 1995 he wrote a confidential memorandum to Chernomyrdin on 'peace zones', only to find Dudayev saw it before the Prime Minister. Two days went by and the Duma Deputy Konstantin Borovoi came to see him and said, grinning, 'Arkady Ivanovich, I was in Chechnya yesterday and I met Dudayev. Dudayev was laughing and asked me to give you this memo back, and asked me to say that Volsky is a very good man but nothing good will come of his peace zones.' Volsky was appalled. When he sought out Chernomyrdin he found the Prime Minister had not even seen the memo. It was a devastating insight into how Moscow was failing to protect its own interests.

The incident suggested the Chechens either had a very well-placed agent in the Russian government or – more likely – they were bribing a very senior clerk. It was a graphic sign of how the Russian government was paralysed by corruption. It happened again several times during the peace talks. Imayev presented Volsky with a memo written by Shakhrai to Yeltsin on how he saw a way out of the Chechen crisis. 'He said: "Look, you are saying one thing and your people saying another."' Volsky is convinced it was bribery that caused the leaks, rather than internal sabotage, but, he said, the leaks came from an 'extremely high' level. It was yet more proof of how different parts of Moscow were simply working against each other.

*

The talks were the first chance for the international community to try to regulate the conflict. The Hungarian diplomat Sandor Meszaros, head of the OSCE Assistance Group in Grozny,

presided over the meetings, along with his deputy, French diplomat Olivier Pelen. A young Polish diplomat, Zenon Kuchciak,
perhaps played a more crucial role. Virtually left to his own
devices by the two senior diplomats, he literally lived with the
Chechen separatists for months, forging good personal contacts
that were to prove invaluable the following year.

The OSCE had established a presence in Grozny in April 1995
after sending a team on a brief visit in January. An incident at the
start of that visit set the tone for the OSCE's dealing with Russia
under Hungarian chairmanship in 1995. Hungarian diplomat Istvan
Gyarmati, who led the team in January, promised to take Sergei
Kovalyov with him to Grozny, but at the gates of the military
airport at Chkalovksoye Gyarmati's car was waved through and
Kovalyov was stopped. Kovalyov said he expected Gyarmati to
come back and insist that the man who was still after all the presidential human rights commissioner be allowed on to the plane,
but Gyarmati did not come back and flew on to Grozny without
Kovalyov. Gyarmati's report after the trip criticized Russia's use
of 'disproportionate and indiscriminate military force' in Chechnya
but in the same breath, in an almost ludicrous comparison, accused
both sides equally of atrocities. The Grozny team were clearly
getting instructions to tread softly in Chechnya and received very
little backup considering the importance of the task: there were
only six members of the team there, working day and night,
compared to a team of seventeen across the border in Georgia
monitoring the dormant conflict in South Ossetia. The following
year, under the Swiss professor Tim Guldimann, the new team
with the same mandate took a much more forthright approach.

The fifty-four-member OSCE was formed in 1975 to monitor
human rights and arms control. As a grouping of Western and
former Soviet states it automatically regarded Chechnya as part
of Russia, something that naturally annoyed the separatist negotiators. But its mandate in Chechnya was broad; the first task was
to 'promote respect for human rights and fundamental freedoms,

and the establishment of facts concerning their violations'. The Chechens repeatedly accused them of not bothering to investigate human rights abuses.

The main sticking-points in the negotiations were first of all Chechnya's status and then what should be done with Shamil Basayev, whom Russia regarded as a terrorist. The Russian side was unanimous on the main issue: no compromise on Chechnya's demand for independence. However, Volsky and Imayev spent hours on the steps of the OSCE house discussing the issue and talking round various possibilities for 'constructive ambiguity'.

In fact the two sides came close to a political deal, but reached an impasse. According to Volsky, the Chechens were considering declaring a moratorium on their claim for independence. They were suggesting a two-year moratorium, the Russians a five-year one, and the time out would allow a space for recovery and rebuilding of the war-damaged republic, paid for by 'contributions' from Russia. However, there were differences over who should be in power – Moscow was reluctant to let go of its puppet government led by Khajiev and Dudayev was not going to share power. The Chechens suggested they work out the military agreement and come back to a political agreement later. The Russians, who wanted all the issues contained in a single document, reluctantly agreed. It was undoubtedly a mistake on their part as many of the Chechen field commanders, who were sceptical about the peace talks, were intent on winning two to three months' breathing space in the fighting without giving any political concessions.

*

By the end of July the two sides were ready to sign the military deal for a permanent ceasefire and simultaneous disarmament by the Chechens and withdrawal of Russian troops. One army and one Interior Ministry brigade numbering approximately 6000 men would remain permanently in Chechnya. At the same time the Chechens could maintain self-defence units of fifteen to twenty-five armed men in every village until the republic organized official law enforcement bodies. There was also to be an exchange of prisoners. The big concession on the Chechen side was to promise to help in the 'search and arrest of Shamil Basayev and his group, accused of carrying out the terrorist act in the town of Budyonnovsk'. Maskhadov said that Basayev was resigned to them signing such a clause, although he, Maskhadov, was vehemently against it. In the end, they did include a clause, the phrasing of which was suggested by Basayev's brother Shirvani, and simply never acted on it.

On 30 July they were close to an agreement. The Chechens already had Dudayev's signature on a draft document. Both teams decided not to quit the premises of the OSCE until they had signed the deal. Shirvani, the younger Basayev brother, was sent off to Roshni-Chu with the final document for Dudayev to inspect. Imayev decided just to wait. As they dragged the discussions out long into the night waiting for his call, the Russians grew impatient. 'I was tired, I saw deceit, I saw craftiness, I saw unwillingess,' Kulikov said. 'I was ready to refuse. I said if we do not sign then that's it, we will end the talks.'

Shirvani reached Dudayev with the papers at 10.30 that night. Dudayev never called, and Imayev chose to interpret his silence as approval. At 4.15 a.m. on 31 July the two delegations finally signed the agreement.

When the Chechen delegation headed out to meet Dudayev that evening they met a frosty reception. Imayev was singled out for Dudayev's ire and roundly condemned by other members of the government sitting with the President. The two men had once been very close and Imayev had been one of Dudayev's two or three most trusted advisers, but they were now engaged in an open clash of wills. Imayev was dismissed and Dudayev rejected the accord, although the following day he appeared to reverse that opinion.

Ten months later Imayev summed up his opinion of his former President and accused him of jeopardizing the peace deal because of his personal ambition. 'It was typical dictator's behaviour. He felt that the negotiations were ending without his participation, that neither Yeltsin nor Chernomyrdin was intending to meet him, that everyone had forgotten about General Dudayev, and all the Chechens were talking only about the members of the delegation.'

Other Chechens said Imayev had been disloyal. Maskhadov said he had been too willing to sign a political agreement without approval from above. In any case, it was clear who came off worse from the row. From now on Imayev was an outcast on the Chechen side.[9]

The military deal formally still stood. Maskhadov was pleased with it, since the clause on the self-defence units meant he could maintain his fighting force. 'I saw that this document could stop the war and, most important, that I was left with real forces. If Russia broke the agreement, I could fight further,' he said.

There began a few extraordinary months of military cooperation. All over the republic Chechen and Russian commanders began to talk on the radio rather than shoot at each other, and organized disarmament ceremonies where the Russians paid out money as individuals handed in weapons. Shirvani Basayev returned home to Vedeno and invited the local Russian colonel to a traditional Chechen feast, gathering all the villagers in their finery and boiling up great vats of mutton. Maskhadov toured the republic with his Russian counterparts to persuade people to disarm. The Chechens drove in jeeps flying the Chechen flag amidst the Russian armour, as fighters up in the woods sent up a flare in salute, the white smoke bright against the dark green canopy of trees. The Chechens would hurtle along the roads in convoy, horns blaring, the green flags of independence flying from every car, bystanders, even small children, greeting them with shouts of 'Allahu akbar', raising their fists in the air. The Russian soldiers perceptibly relaxed, eating *shashlik* at tables under the trees in Grozny, chatting freely at checkpoints, happy that the night raids on their posts had eased.

Maskhadov established a remarkable rapport with Russian Lieutenant-General Anatoly Romanov, who was appointed commander of Russian troops in Chechnya after Kulikov left to take up the post of Interior Minister. Together they headed a special commission in charge of implementing the military agreement. 'I sensed a general who had had enough fighting like myself, who was fed up with war,' Maskhadov said later. 'He openly said to me, "Aslan, I am not going to shoot any more." That's what he said: "I'm not going to shoot any more, even if they order me to." '

'The language between Romanov and Maskhadov was a different one if you compare it to politicians',' Kuchciak recalled. 'They wanted to find something. They even kicked us out and said, "Please wait. We can tell nasty words to each other, we are soldiers, but later on we will tell you what we agreed in this nasty question." It was great,' he said.[10]

The pendulum soon swung back, however. Russian forces had resumed bombardment of villages in the mountains from the end of August and the incidents increased in intensity. The hawkish view again prevailed in the Kremlin. Moscow, fearful of letting Dudayev regain his authority, strengthened its support for the pro-Moscow government in Grozny. Mikhailov, now Minister of Nationalities, would leave for Moscow and return each time espousing a tougher line and repudiating positions he had informally agreed to. Dudayev was also provocative. His fighters were quietly gun-running into Grozny, flying through checkpoints under the cover of the peace-talks convoy. In Argun the fighter Allauddin Khamzatov brazenly took control of the police station at gunpoint and was blasted out by Russian helicopter gunships. The Chechens began to fall out with the two leading European diplomats. The Hungarian Meszaros was always measured and equivocal, whilst the short-tempered Frenchman Pelen seemed to sympathize openly with the Russians. Things became farcical when Pelen's dog Shatu pawed and licked the Chechen negotiators: Imayev complained that as a devout Muslim he was supposed to wash his clothes nine times every time the dog touched him.

The issue of the self-defence units became a major obstacle since it gave Dudayev a chance to reassert a presence in every village. Too late, the Russians said they would not allow the units in the area under their control, meaning 60–80 per cent of the republic. The Chechens turned to the OSCE for an interpretation of the agreement which clearly allowed for Chechen self-defence forces in 'all population centres'. The OSCE fudged the issue. Roman Wasilewski, the American member of the OSCE team at the time, wrote despairing memos as he watched the agreement unravel; he believed it was here that the OSCE could have played a crucial role as an assertive mediator and knocked heads together, but instead they did nothing. He thought the OSCE was in danger of falling into the trap of the UN Human Rights Commission in Bosnia – allowing the outside world to believe they were a useful presence while they actually had no positive influence on developments.

'The most important question, that of power, had not been decided,' Kulikov said, summing up the breakdown of the peace agreement. As summer turned to autumn the goodwill dissipated. A spate of kidnappings and banditry broke out. A Russian colonel and his driver, assigned to Maskhadov to take him through Russian checkpoints, were arrested and detained by the Chechen side. They were only released six months later, painfully thin and pale. The Russian Orthodox priest, Father Anatoly, and another priest from Moscow were seized by Chechen fighters after meeting the commander Akmed Zakayev to discuss prisoner exchanges. The Chechen side said they were all suspected spies. Father Anatoly never emerged alive and was probably killed in the bombing of Bamut, where at least a dozen prisoners died. While some kidnappings were acts of straightforward banditry performed by criminals, many were committed by fighters.

There was a paranoia about spies among some of them, as well as a very active Special Department, the military wing of the Chechen security service. It was almost certainly the Special Department which arrested and executed the American aid worker Fred Cuny and his three Russian colleagues when they travelled into Bamut in March 1995. Cuny had visited Grozny in February with Basayev. Appalled by the civilian suffering, he had lobbied hard back home for the United States to notice what was happening in Chechnya. In killing Cuny the Chechens killed a genuine ally and did lasting damage to their reputation abroad. In October 1995 the Chechen leadership seemed to be falling into a trap of paranoia that only played into the hands of their enemies.

*

In Grozny several car-bomb attacks, aimed at Moscow officials, rocked Grozny, one narrowly missing Yeltsin's new envoy in Chechnya and old comrade Oleg Lobov. The next, on 6 October, nearly killed General Romanov and left him in a permanent coma.[11] Moscow immediately blamed the Chechen rebels. They in turn blamed the Russian security forces or a 'third party', meaning the pro-Moscow Chechens in Grozny. It has never been established who did it, although a year later Moscow officials, including Volsky and Mikhailov, said that Dudayev's supporters could not be blamed for it. Romanov was heading for a meeting with Ruslan Khasbulatov and only four people knew about it, according to Volsky. Investigations showed that the devices used in the attacks on Lobov and Romanov were exactly the same and the detonation cord was not only the same kind but from the same reel. The evidence pointed to hardline elements in the Russian security forces or the pro-Moscow Chechen government, neither of whom liked the growing cooperation between the federal side and Dudayev's forces.

The attack on Romanov essentially ended the peace process. His replacement was Lieutenant-General Anatoly Shkirko, a much harder-line general, and the Romanov–Maskhadov commission stopped working. The Russians retaliated two days later with a devastating bombing raid on the village of Roshni-Chu, where Dudayev had been living, demolishing a whole street of houses, leaving six-foot-deep craters. It ended all chance of a political agreement. 'If there had not been the attacks on Lobov and Romanov which gave the excuse for the commission to stop working, I think we would have signed an agreement. I am 100 per cent sure of that,' Volsky said.

In October Moscow decided it was time for a change of leadership. Salambek Khajiev said he was fed up with being 'Prime Minister' of a puppet government. Khajiev had made an honest attempt to pull Chechens out of filtration camps and close down checkpoints and had set up the commission on missing persons with Hussein Khamidov at its head. But he was tarred with the charge of being a Russian collaborator and his writ increasingly ran no further than his government headquarters.

Doku Zavgayev, the old Communist Party boss, had been biding his time in Moscow since being ousted by Dudayev in September 1991. He had a modest job in the Kremlin administration as head of the 'department of social and economic problems of the republics'. In an interview in January 1995, as a telephone engineer fixed one of his government phone lines, the wily Zavgayev had insisted he was only a 'little bureaucrat'. But he took several long telephone calls from different Chechens and seemed to be fully in touch with what was going on.

He professed to condemn the war but he was also deeply contemptuous about the 'impostors' of the current Moscow-backed government. Khajiev, he said, did not have a 'milligram of legitimacy', while Umar Avturkhanov was a 'criminal' and

'Lefortovo [the Moscow prison] has long been crying out for him.' Zavgayev's answer to whether he wanted to return to power was carefully formulaic: 'The leader ought to be appointed by the people themselves,' he said.

In the autumn of 1995, Zavgayev believed that his hour had come and even that his last prediction might come true, that he could be 'appointed by the people'. He came back to Grozny as head of government and with the guarantee that there would be elections for head of the republic before the end of the year.

How it would be possible to organize elections in a region where a large-scale war was just resuming was never made clear. But they went ahead on 17 December 1995. At first Zavgayev's old enemy Khasbulatov thought he could steal a march on Zavgayev and decided to stand in the elections. Khasbulatov had been whiling away his time in his old job as Professor of Economics at the Plekhanov Institute in Moscow. He later withdrew his candidacy, saying the elections were turning into a farce. Zavgayev was duly elected with a large majority in which Russian soldiers, local government officials and even some Western reporters voted, but few ordinary Chechens.

Moscow supported the elections although in the peace talks it had always been stressed that they could only be held after the withdrawal of troops. The OSCE, with Pelen temporarily in charge, simply quit town, refusing to condemn the plan to hold elections. The Chechen separatists went on the offensive, disrupting the elections in two major towns, Gudermes and Urus Martan, by seizing control of the official buildings for the three days of polling.

The battle for Gudermes, led by a young relative of Dudayev, Salman Raduyev, and commanded at a distance by Maskhadov, turned into a full-scale, ten-day battle. The Chechens surrounded the Russian headquarters in the centre of the town, cutting their communications and trapping the soldiers. They repulsed repeated Russian attempts to break through with reinforcements.

Russia retaliated with helicopters, gunships and artillery, bombarding the town for six days after the fighters had slipped away. Nearly 300 civilians and sixty-eight Russian soldiers died. Dozens of buildings were burnt or damaged as Russian forces fought to regain control of the town they had taken peacefully just six months before. It was a bitter end to the year for the people of Gudermes, who huddled terrified and hungry in their cellars or tried to escape through the woods, dragging the wounded in sheets across the snow, under fire from Russian troops who refused to open a corridor for fleeing civilians.

Sergei Kovalyov had no doubt who to blame for the resumption of the war. 'I place Gudermes and all those elections in December 1995 on the conscience of that OSCE mission,' he said. If the OSCE had insisted elections were against the interests of peace, Moscow would not have been able to go ahead with them, Kovalyov said. 'It was not the attack on Romanov that started the war again, it was the December elections that started the war again. What was the start again of heavy, full-scale fighting? It was Gudermes. And Gudermes was right at the time of the elections.'

13

'A Semi-Guerrilla War'

Salman Raduyev was on a roll. Three weeks after his bloody attack on Gudermes he struck again, this time in Russia. He led a band of fighters across the Chechen border to attack Kizlyar, the old Russian fortress town on the Terek, now a substantial provincial centre in the republic of Dagestan. It was an almost exact repeat of the raid on Budyonnovsk. Chechen fighters burst into town at dawn on 9 January, shooting in the streets, attacking the police station, and seizing as many as 3000 hostages in the town hospital. It was Russia's worst nightmare, a copy-cat version of Basayev's deadly raid on Budyonnovsk, but which this time apparently had the full backing of Dudayev. It sent the message to the Kremlin that Russia could never be safe from Chechen terrorism.

Yeltsin called an emergency meeting of his top ministers, bellowing in fury at them for allowing Chechen rebels to launch a second raid outside Chechnya just six months after the last. 'We had received another blow,' he said in a televized meeting, staring down the line of military and security officials, who, heads bowed, stared sullenly at their notepads. 'How should we understand you, generals? Playing with toys, are you? It seems to us that the power structures, ministries, government, Security Council and Border Guards have learned little from one emergency situation, and have drawn few of the lessons they should have.'

The Power Ministers, namely Grachev, Kulikov, FSB chief Mikhail Barsukov and, in particular, Andrei Nikolayev, head of the Border Guards, took the brunt of the blasting. Ultimately, responsibility lay with them, Yeltsin said. 'The border guards overslept,' he growled, jabbing his index finger on the long Kremlin conference table. 'Several thousand of our servicemen are posted on the roads, and [the gunmen] went straight by. To let them cover such a distance having advance information about the group! . . . Reports came from every post, but they fell on deaf ears and no action was taken.' Nikolayev afterwards offered to resign, but it turned out that his men were not responsible and Yeltsin rejected his resignation.

Yeltsin went on to demand the 'most organized and decisive actions' to 'neutralize the bandits, painstakingly and thoroughly'. Barsukov was despatched to take charge of the operation in Kizlyar. It was a test for him and the FSB which he took over from Stepashin after Budyonnovsk. The FSB still had the best special forces unit in the country, Alpha, and now had a chance to show it was superior to both the Defence Ministry and the Interior Ministry, who between them had botched virtually every operation against the Chechens so far.

This time the Russian authorities faced a larger band of fighters, some 250 men, who were holding double the number of hostages. In Raduyev, they faced an excitable, not very intelligent fighter, who was full of wild threats and slogans and set on making himself a national hero in Chechnya. He called his band the 'Lone Wolf' and promised to fight to the end. 'We will reduce Kizlyar to ashes,' he told journalists that evening. 'After Kizlyar there will be another Kizlyar.'

Raduyev's original target was the helicopter base at Kizlyar. Helicopter gunships had become perhaps the most hated instruments of Russian aggression in Chechnya, attacking vehicles on the roads and often firing missiles into built-up areas. To wipe out a fleet of helicopters at their base and disappear back into Chechnya would undoubtedly have made Raduyev a popular hero at home. But the Russians were waiting for him and he arrived to find only two helicopters on the tarmac. His fighters quickly destroyed those but met strong resistance in the air-base and pulled back into town. They stormed through the streets, spreading out in groups, but as local police fought back, Raduyev found himself out of his depth. He turned to a commander one year his senior, Khunkar Israpilov, and asked him to take command.

In fact Raduyev had little military experience. Aged twenty-eight, he had completed his military service in the Russian army and then became a local leader of the Komsomol communist youth organization in Gudermes. Married to a niece of Dudayev, he claimed to have fought throughout the war, but only came to notice when he led the attack on Gudermes. A slight man with a long reddish beard and hooded eyes, his heavy lids slanting downwards at the sides, he has an almost Asiatic look. He laughs readily, showing a glint of gold teeth, and talks in stock phrases of Chechen bravado, professing fanatical loyalty to both God and his President. 'We made our oath to our President that we will be *smertniki* [suicide fighters] to the end and carry out his orders,' he said a few days later. 'The main slogan of our action is death or freedom.'

Israpilov, known to all as Khunkar Pasha, was by contrast a commander of proven ability and intelligence. He was a veteran of Abkhazia, like so many of the young commanders who rose to prominence during the war. With light, curly hair and hazel eyes, Israpilov has a crooked but winning smile that belies a ruthless edge and a love of battle. He only went on Raduyev's escapade, he said, because he suddenly found all his fighters had joined up. 'I was sure we would not come back from there. I knew we could not return from that attack without taking hostages and I knew the Russians would not let us get away like they did after Budyonnovsk.'[1]

Nevertheless, when Raduyev asked him to take command, he immediately gave orders to take the town hospital and seize hostages. Raduyev later said that taking hostages had always been his back-up plan anyway. What was clear was that these men, after more than a year of brutal war, had even less compunction about taking hostages than Basayev had, and despite their slogans of fighting to the death, their priority was now to get back home alive. The fighters raided two large apartment blocks near the hospital, barging into homes and ordering the residents out at gunpoint, shooting up the doors and corridors when the people protested. Grabbing more bystanders as they went, they pushed the hostages along to the hospital.

There were nearly 1000 patients and medical personnel already in the grey, four-storey hospital. Together with the hostages from outside, the gunmen now had between 2000 and 3000 people under their control. They forced the hostages up to the top two floors, setting up defences in the basement and the ground floor against an attempt to storm the building. It was only just in time. In the early afternoon Russian forces attacked, smashing all the windows and adding to the casualties as grenades hit the hospital walls.

Israpilov seized a walkie-talkie from a policeman who was among the captives and shouted over the noise that he would shoot hostages if the storm was not halted. 'I kept telling him I would shoot him. He was not paying attention, he was smiling, I could see he did not believe me. I shot him in the forehead,' he recalled matter-of-factly. 'I was demanding that they hold their fire. After that they did.'

By mid-afternoon negotiations were under way with Dagestani officials and Raduyev was back in charge. Knowing he would be in for trouble at home, he wanted to end the botched operation as quickly as possible. His patron, Dudayev, had already announced he had ordered the raid. 'Everything is proceeding under my strict supervision,' he said. 'I declare with a full sense of responsibility that one command from me is enough to begin or stop any operation.'[2]

Two days later he expanded further in classic Dudayev fashion.

'Gudermes was our last city – it was destroyed by Russian troops. We need housing, we need to accommodate our fighters somewhere, and, besides, our command. We need a new hospital – we have 200 wounded men. For this reason, we decided to create such conditions for us in a new Russian town. Kizlyar was picked precisely for this purpose. Three hundred years ago, this area saw the first clash between the Russian and Chechen armies. This is how the Russian–Chechen war began. An end to this war should also begin in this area.'[3]

Raduyev reached a deal with Dagestani officials and they pulled out of the hospital in a convoy of eleven buses and two trucks at 6 a.m. the following morning, taking with them 160 hostages from the hospital and a number of Dagestani parliamentarians. They bore away the bodies of seven dead Chechen fighters. Behind them they left a trail of nineteen dead and forty-nine wounded. Although the Chechen border lay only 10 miles away, they were taken on a roundabout journey of eight hours, trailed constantly by helicopters. They finally drove along a back road through the last village, Pervomaiskoye, past a Russian police post and headed over the Chechen border. Suddenly, as the first bus approached the bridge into Chechnya, a helicopter gunship opened fire, pitting the road ahead with a burst of its machine-gun.

Israpilov stopped the convoy. They were standing in an open field in the most vulnerable position possible, several hundred yards from the little border village of Pervomaiskoye. Israpilov immediately ordered the fighters to rush the Russian police post they had just cleared. Within seconds they disarmed the thirty-seven policemen from the Siberian city of Novosibirsk who were manning it. The police, so surprised and frightened by the aggressive Chechens, and with no orders to take them on, were overpowered without a shot being fired. The Chechens then rapidly fanned out through the village, splitting the hostages up into groups and taking cover in the small farm cottages. 'We found the village was completely empty. It was clear what they intended,' Israpilov said.

They expected an attack immediately but it took the Russians five days to gather themselves to the task. The fighters settled into the empty houses and put the hostages to work digging narrow trenches snaking across streets, under fences, through courtyards, right into the houses. Pervomaiskoye became famous afterwards for the ingenious trenches the fighters dug.

Russian forces began massing around the tiny village, with columns of armour drawing up on the roads and tanks fanning out in the snowy fields on three sides. Commando troops arrived in buses, parking along the side of the road, a couple of miles east of the village. They were unmistakable with their big helmets, wired with earphones and mouthpiece, masks and sniper rifles, as members of the special anti-terrorist unit, Alpha. An icy wind blasted across the open steppe, making standing still almost unbearable, and they hunched down in their seats in the buses. Across the fields behind a low line of trees lay their target, Pervomaiskoye, with its 500 residents and several dozen homesteads, school and mosque. Helicopters battered overhead, dropping flares that lit up the darkening sky. As night fell, yet more columns of tanks and trucks drew up on side roads. The Russians were preparing a major military operation.

The following day Raduyev was still full of bravado and threats while Israpilov appeared tense and wary. 'If Russia does not want a peaceful outcome, we are ready,' Raduyev said. 'We are soldiers. We do not care how we die.' His fighters milled around the village, among them five Arab *mujahideen* and six Chechen women fighters. The women were some of a small number who took up arms during the war. They wore green headbands like the men and camouflage trousers, something which still shocked in conservative Chechnya where women always wore long skirts and headscarves. Some were nurses and doubled up as cooks but others were real fighters, carrying Kalashnikovs over their shoulders. Khazman Umarova, a Chechen camerawoman, was among them, one of only two women who survived the siege.

Exhausted, the hostages – men, women and even some young children – huddled under blankets in one house. They were mostly Dagestanis, doctors and nurses from the hospital, workers and students grabbed from their apartments. Among them was twenty-five-year-old Raisa Magomayeva, who worked in Kizlyar's sewing factory. Her father, Salavdin Magomayev, a farmer from near Kizlyar, kept a lone vigil on the road outside the village. 'She is not brave, she will be sick with fear,' he said, staring up the empty road towards Pervomaiskoye. 'I will wait here until the very end.' He said he hoped the government would opt for a peaceful solution, 'but all this armour makes it much more difficult,' he gestured despairingly.

Villagers gathered uncertainly on the road outside the village. Some had sympathy for the Chechens, but most were angry that it had to happen in their village. 'They should wage their war over there, not here in Dagestan,' said Najmuddin Magomedov, director of a small printing press in Pervomaiskoye. Several villagers slipped back into the village to feed their livestock, and the fighters let them come and go freely. 'They are breaking down doors, helping themselves to food, and cooking,' said Akhmed Isayev, who found twelve fighters in his house. 'They said, "If we are not allowed to go, we will shoot the hostages and everyone."'

'We can understand that there is a war being waged against them in Chechnya and we understand why they did this, but why did they do it to Dagestan and why against civilians?' asked Magomedov. 'We always considered ourselves brothers of the Chechens. Our forefathers fought together for twenty-five years under Imam Shamil,' he said.

'I took in Chechen refugees, we all did. Five people lived in my house,' Magomed Magomedov, another villager, said.

*

The message from the Russian leadership was tough: the Chechens should release all their hostages at the border and proceed alone into Chechnya. The Chechens insisted they take the hostages with them as far as Novogroznensky, a village well inside Chechnya, some 30 miles east of Grozny. 'They are taking a very intransigent position,' said Alexander Mikhailov, the chief spokesman of the FSB. Mikhailov, who favoured loud checked sports jackets in Moscow, was wearing a black wool hat, with the grey fur collar of his field uniform turned up against the cold. 'Talks are of little importance now,' he said, adding that a storm of the village was inevitable. Army, Interior Ministry and FSB forces, including numerous special forces units, had the village surrounded. 'My personal opinion is that they should not be allowed to go free. They are bandits and they should be annihilated,' he said.

In Moscow Chernomyrdin, once more in charge of the hostage crisis as Yeltsin left for Paris to attend President Mitterrand's funeral, vowed to punish the 'bandits' but promised not to risk the lives of the hostages. He did not explain how they intended to do that. Yeltsin supplied one clue. Raising his arms to take aim like a boy playing war games, he said, 'We have thirty-eight snipers posted around the village to catch the terrorists.' The feeling in the government, the press and amongst the general public was that this time the gunmen should not be allowed to get away.

A period of waiting set in, apparently for talks, but it later transpired, for the Russians to organize their attack. The Dagestani officials walked out of the village to hold talks with the Russians and never returned, abandoning the rest of the hostages whom they had promised to accompany through to the end.

Raduyev released eight women and children, although one woman went back into the village to be with her husband.

On the fourth day hundreds of soldiers and officers, accompanied by special commando units, marched through the foggy dawn towards the village. A loud-hailer echoed back from the field: 'Release the hostages and we will guarantee your lives,' the voice said. Barsukov arrived to direct the operation in person, along with Kulikov. They gave the gunmen another twenty-four hours to release the hostages and surrender.

*

A barrage of tank-fire burst over the frozen white fields on the morning of 15 January, signalling the wait was over. This was no stealthy anti-terrorist operation, but an all-out air and artillery assault. Red flashes marked where tanks, dug in around the village, were firing. The shells landed with a muffled crump that resounded across the fields. The long, low white building of the school was the first to be hit. Bare rafters showed where a shell broke through the roof. Thick plumes of white smoke rose as more shells landed, then the building burst into flames. Black smoke mingled with the white, drifting across the village. A row of three houses was blazing, half hidden by a line of trees. Onlookers, many of them from Pervomaiskoye, stood and watched their homes being destroyed.

'The school is hit, that is the end,' said Imam Salakhov, wiping his eyes with his fingers. 'Where the buildings are burning, there in the centre, my cattle are there,' said one man, wrapped in a shaggy sheepskin coat. 'Listen to the heavy fire. There is a whole division drawn up around our little village,' said one white-bearded pensioner, his hand shaking on his stick. The barrage eased after half an hour, while machine-gun fire rattled on the west of the village, where the road led into Chechnya.

The fighters were spread out in groups through the whole village, leaning on mattresses in their trenches to guard the approaches. As the shelling eased they watched the Russian infantry try to run forward and opened up with machine-guns. Other fighters guarded the hostages in the houses. They ran from house to house as the artillery strikes resumed and hit first one part of the village, then another.

As the Russian infantry encountered heavy gunfire they called in assistance. Two of their tanks were already burning on the edge of the village. Red tracers carved through the sky in gentle arcs, followed by rapid explosions. A dozen helicopters toured the sky, flying low over the neighbouring village of Sovetskoye, the red Soviet stars visible on their grey bellies. Onlookers ducked as the gunships spat out their rockets with a deafening roar and tongues of flames right above them, launching volley after volley into Pervomaiskoye. Houses were now burning in the village centre, the red flames bright against the winter landscape.

Sergei, a senior lieutenant of a special forces unit, came back from Pervomaiskoye mid-morning, saying he had advanced as far as the school but the difficult phase still lay ahead. 'It could take some time, there are still a lot of fighters alive,' he said. 'We have to clean up by night-time, otherwise we'll be in big trouble.' The pressure was on to end the crisis quickly but as casualties were stretchered into a Russian field hospital near the battleground, it was clear the infantry were making heavy progress.

In Moscow, Yeltsin appeared on television hours after the assault began. He looked pale and hesitant, an increasingly distant and ill man. He told reporters he had been forced by the intransigence of the rebels to opt for a military solution to the hostage crisis. 'The operation was thoroughly planned. I cannot say there will be no casualties, but there will be fewer casualties,' he said. 'We must punish them and terrorism in general must be uprooted from the Chechen land.'

The day ended without success for the Russians, however. A handful of hostages made their way out of the maelstrom to Russian positions, but Raduyev, who still had time to make phone calls on his satellite telephone, said his fighters had repelled the attack. That night Israpilov sent out a reconnaissance team to check out an escape route and decided they could break through. He finally contacted the command in Chechnya for the first time. Basayev ordered them to stay in the village. 'I was furious they left Kizlyar too quickly. They had to try to win something out of this. I tried to reach Raduyev but he only answered after the first day of the assault. When he did I shouted at him, "If you are going to take hostages you stay there." Thank God for Pervo-maiskoye. If they had got back immediately they would really have been seen as terrorists, and Dudayev and Maskhadov too.'[4]

Fighting carried on into a second and third day, with helicop-ters returning to the attack, working at close range in the thick fog and snow. Big field-guns pounded without break, the men ducking away, fingers in their ears, as each gun jumped back-wards with the terrific force of the launch. At dusk the sound of Grad missiles roared across the fields hitting the village in bursts of three at a time, only a split second apart, shaking the houses in Sovetskoye a mile away. Nine-foot-long rockets, fired from multiple launchers, the Grads come in with the velocity of a high-speed train emerging from a tunnel. They make up with terrifying noise and explosive power what they lack in accuracy. Red fires lit up the black sky over Pervomaiskoye as the village burned for a second night, but the Russians were no nearer to taking it.

As the Grads blasted away at the little village of Pervomais-koye, news came that nine Chechen sympathizers had hijacked a passenger ferry in the Turkish port of Trabzon. Most of the 240 people on board were Russian shuttle-traders, about to return home to Sochi on Russia's Black Sea coast. The gunmen were Turkish but of Abkhaz and Chechen origin. Their leader, Muhammad Tokçan, a bearded thirty-year-old of Abkhaz origin, had fought in Basayev's battalion in Abkhazia. He threated to sail the ship into the Bosphorus strait and blow it up if their 'Chechen brethren' in Pervomaiskoye were not allowed to go free. The ship set sail, the gunmen visible on the deck, wearing masks and holding automatic rifles aloft. Yeltsin's Chechen problem had not only spilled into Russia but was spreading beyond its borders.[5]

Bogged down in the fighting in Pervomaiskoye and now faced with international crisis as terrorists threatened Russians abroad, Moscow was also losing the propaganda war. Yeltsin offered Turkey an anti-terrorist team to deal with the ferry hijackers, a strange offer when his best troops were pinned down by Chechen fighters at the time. FSB spokesman Mikhailov was no more subtle. He began claiming the Chechens had executed the remaining hostages. 'We believe the hostages are dead. Now we will destroy the bandits,' he said. The following day he admitted that he had lied about the hostages. By the end of the week, Mikhailov was fired.

*

Heads down, with a look of defeat, scores of weary Russian troops trudged down the road away from Pervomaiskoye the following morning. One Alpha commander, his face smeared with grime under his big helmet, said they had taken heavy losses. 'Twice SOBR [Rapid Reaction Unit] got into the village and twice they had to withdraw,' said another commando, dressed in the grey-blue camouflage of Interior Ministry troops, his face rubbed red from firing his rifle. 'They have heavy machine-guns and they moved them the whole time, they were hitting us from every side,' he said. 'We are pulling the troops out and we are going to screw them with Grads.' A couple of officers from SOBR hung back to make a call on a journalist's satellite telephone. Tough and athletic men in their early thirties, they said they had done two tours of duty in Chechnya. 'This was not an anti-terrorist operation, it was a battle to gain ground. And they were very good,' one said, 'they fought like lions.' His unit of fifteen men had got within 20 yards of the mosque in the village centre when they realized the Chechens were cutting off their retreat. 'The Chechens lured us into a trap, drew us into the centre and started surrounding us. Five minutes longer and it would have been too late,' he said. 'There are a lot of them, they are in good positions and they are well armed, better than us,' he added.

The Russian operation was looking like another fiasco. Some of the 100 wounded men flown to the airport hospital in Grozny told how they had been left freezing for days in the open fields, with little or no food or water, waiting for orders while the Chechens had time to organize their defences. Then they were sent in to fight with inadequate maps, communications, back-up and ammunition.[6] Alpha's trained experts were excluded from the planning and negotiations, which could have provided them with crucial information about their opponents, one Alpha officer said afterwards. The fighters had better communications and successfully listened in on the Russians, he said. 'They knew what units were moving in to fight, and when and where there would be artillery strikes.'[7] The Russians told of being hit by friendly fire from artillery and helicopter fire, and blamed poor planning that sent 500 men against over 200 when normal ratios for attacking defences demanded a ratio of five to one. Elite troops were wasted in an assault on a heavily defended village, a job regular infantry should have done, they said.

It was 17 January, the eighth day of the crisis, when the Chechens listened in on the Russians on their walkie-talkies and heard them pulling out their men in preparation for heavy bombing. They decided it was time to leave. Maskhadov and Basayev launched a rescue mission from Chechnya, gathering 400 men to break into Dagestan to create diversions. Some of them burst into Sovetskoye at 2 a.m. that night, shooting up the police post on the edge of the village, as the fighters and their hostages headed out of Pervomaiskoye. They left in groups of fifty, breaking through three rings of Russian encirclement, crossing a minefield under canon and mortar fire. Several of the frontrunners blew themselves up on mines, more were cut down by shell fire. The main body of fighters, among them Raduyev and Israpilov, followed. 'We were fighting for four kilometres,' Shamil, Radu-yev's deputy, said afterwards. Israpilov was wounded in the head and had to be helped through the last part. His younger brother was killed. One group lost their way on the unknown territory and inadvertently looped back, clashing with Russian troops a second time.

For the hostages who had been living at gunpoint for nine days now and under bombardment for the last three, it was the most terrifying ordeal of all. They left at about 3 a.m., in a bunch, with more fighters, leaving a last small group to guard their rear. Mortars, shells, machine-gun fire and rockets rained down on them from three sides as they ran blindly across the snowy plain, carrying the wounded, wading through a freezing river or balancing across the top of a gas pipe high above the water.

Ali Aliyev, a worker from a power station in Kizlyar, was one of a group of hostages made to carry four wounded Chechens. 'We saw flashes of firing on all sides,' he said. 'We were running. There was this horrendous noise, and I felt a blow on my leg.' The Chechen fighters kept going. 'They took their wounded with them. I pretended to be dead.' Wounded by shrapnel in the thigh, Aliyev lay in the snow on the battlefield until daylight, when Russian soldiers picked him up and sent him to a local hospital. Most of the others they found were dead, the trail over the border still strewn with half a dozen bodies of fighters and hostages two days later.

Yeltsin announced eighty hostages were rescued but at least eighty more made it into Chechnya with the fighters. Two days later over thirty of them lay side by side on wooden boards the length of a long underground bunker in Novogroznensky. They slept like the dead, motionless with an exhaustion that only comes from living through a battle. Many of them wore bloodstained bandages over shrapnel wounds. Arkady, a maths teacher and father of four, said they had feared to stay behind, convinced they would eventually be killed in the bombardment. 'In the mornings, we would look at our watches for the start of the helicopters. We understood we would be annihilated with the fighters. We did not know how we would survive and understood we had to get to the border.'

'It was hell on three sides,' he said of the escape. 'We thought when morning came the helicopters would come, so we hurried, but we were not quick enough. At about 6 a.m. they came. Three of them, constantly in the air and firing machine-guns at us. We had our faces in the ground and we went two kilometres in three hours,' he said.

'Do you know how a herd of sheep feels when the wolf is near? That is how we felt and the wolf [was] Russia,' said another hostage, Magomed. 'I feel they betrayed me, my own armed forces betrayed me,' Arkady said.

Raduyev, weary and concussed, claimed a great success. They had shown that the elite of the Russian army were powerless to defeat the Chechens. 'Seven times they stormed us and each time they were destroyed in flames. We beat the strongest men of the biggest army in the world,' he said, his brown eyes suddenly fierce and staring.[8] Raduyev was alone among the Chechen leaders to call it a success. Maskhadov, tight-lipped, deplored the taking of hostages and said Raduyev would be called to account for his actions. Basayev let fly at Raduyev for taking so many men on an operation that twenty could have performed and blamed him for the ninety-six fighters who died, the biggest loss for any rebel operation in Chechnya. Dudayev, who could not deflect all the flak, later said he had punished Raduyev.

The rebels sought to turn things in their favour with a series of press conferences in Novogroznensky, displaying the hostages before handing them over to Dagestani authorities, who returned some fifty bodies of fighters. It was a final embarrassment for the Russian leadership whose brutal pounding of the village had allowed the hostage-takers to retrieve some of the moral high ground. Militarily it was another humiliating defeat for Russia's armed forces. Their special forces and elite anti-terrorist units, supposedly the toughest, most professional men in service in Russia, had made little headway to free the hostages. Even backed by a powerful array of military hardware, they had failed miserably to make any impact on a band of Chechen fighters. The FSB, and Barsukov in particular, were shown to be no more capable than the rest of Russia's Power Ministries at crisis control, let alone at running a coordinated military operation. Barsukov revealed his mindset when in all seriousness he told a press conference that all Chechens were either 'thieves' or 'murderers'.

At the time Pervomaiskoye seemed to mark the low point of Yeltsin's presidency as dozens of Russians of all political persuasions condemned the brutality of the assault on the village, the constant lying about the operation and the President's blundering manner. It coincided with a purge of liberals from Yeltsin's administration. His moderate Chief of Staff Sergei Filatov was sacked and the hawk Yegorov returned to the Kremlin to fill his place. Yeltsin's comments about the thirty-eight snipers were lampooned in the press and on television and he seemed out of touch with what people were saying about him. Many former allies decided he had no hope of being re-elected President in June. Yegor Gaidar said his split from the President was 'final and irreversible' – a statement he had to retract a few months later with some embarrassment when Yeltsin unexpectedly gained a new lease of life.

The official death toll was sixty-nine, of which twenty-eight were civilians. The real figure was probably higher.[9] Relatives retrieved at least a dozen bodies from the smouldering ruins of Pervomaiskoye and the outlying woods after the storm. The majority of the hostages were Dagestanis and this was another terrible mistake Raduyev made, turning Chechnya's neighbour against it.

*

It was an easy two-hour walk at night across the border from Dagestan into Chechnya, not far from the point where Chechen fighters and their hostages crossed from Pervomaiskoye. Tramping in silence across the empty expanse of snow-covered fields, away from the last Dagestani village, we gave the single Russian post, looming dark among the trees, a wide berth. Less than forty-eight hours after the Chechen rebels escaped, there was no sign of the special OMON police who are supposed to patrol the border. Only Grad missiles firing somewhere in the distance into Chechnya sounded above the ice cracking underfoot. Flares fired over the ruined village of Pervomaiskoye lit the sky to the north. Raduyev and his fighters crossed this unmarked border in buses and trucks and two weeks later could have done the same again. We crossed a bridge and walked down a track rutted from tank-treads until we heard dogs barking in the first Chechen village ahead. Headlights were bumping along towards us. It was a group of rebels searching for missing fighters and hostages. They gave us a lift into Novogroznensky, a large village on the main highway where Maskhadov had set up his headquarters for the rescue operation.

His fighters had set off from here in open trucks, dressed in snow-camouflage, armed with grenades, Kalashnikovs and even swords, continuing on foot across the border. They even video-taped the occasion for the record. Days later they were still driving around in broad daylight, showing little concern for the Russian post on the edge of the village and the latest threats from Moscow to destroy all rebel bases.

'We control all the territory of Chechnya,' Maskhadov said. 'Russian forces control only the bridge they are standing on, only the ground of their bases.' It was not an idle boast. Six months after they were driven into the mountains facing defeat, the Chechen fighters were back in the plains, with a command network operating across the republic. They were moving around the country more freely than ever, with a confidence that came

from good organization. They had developed a stronger command system and better discipline. Almost every village had its
appointed commander, with fifteen to twenty-five armed fighters
under him, and up to 100 more in reserve whom he could call up
at short notice. Maskhadov made sure that another Pervomaiskoye could not happen. Fighters now waited for a written and
stamped command before leaving on an operation. The Chechen
fighting force was turning into a proper army.

They had used the few months during the peace talks to
percolate down from the hills, returning home, resting and
rearming. 'We are stronger than ever. In a year of fighting we
have learnt how to modify our methods,' said Umar-Ali Saidu-
layev, the commander in Novogroznensky, who was entertaining
a bunch of fighters in his living-room with videos and songs of
the war. The long summer rest had given them a vital breathing
space to win back their health and morale. They had also used
the time to stockpile weapons. Arms and ammunition were a
constant problem for the rebels in landlocked Chechnya. Unlike
the Afghan guerrillas during their long war against the Soviet
army, they had no friendly neighbour offering a safe haven and
an easy arms route. Nor did the Chechens have an open and
wealthy backer to provide them with Stinger ground-to-air
missiles.

They mostly bought weapons from the Russian troops in
Chechnya but there was no shortage of sources outside the
republic. The region was awash with weapons since the break-up
of the Soviet Union. Russian army bases were so short of cash
that soldiers were going hungry, and officers were without pay
and ready to do deals. Azerbaijan, where there was some sympathy for the Chechens and plenty of corruption, was another
source. The Chechens smuggled the arms in through Dagestan,
bribing the police and border guards or simply driving over
mountain tracks to avoid them. Many groups, if they wanted to
fight, had to organize their own weapons and ammunition.

One tough young fighter from Benoi, Sulunbek, described how with a group of ten fighters, one of whom was Georgian, he trekked across the mountains into Georgia to buy weapons in the winter of 1995–6. They bought twenty-five donkeys from Avars up near the border, leaving their guns as credit, and, on horseback, drove the donkeys over the high snowy passes for three days. They slept in the open, moving along small mountain paths to avoid any border guards. At the first Georgian village their donkeys were snapped up. 'We were rich men, we killed two sheep in Georgia,' Sulunbek laughed. Relatives of the Georgian fighter fixed them up with weapons in the capital, Tbilisi. 'We bought guns and ammunition, and artillery shells. It was cheap and they found what we wanted immediately,' he said. The weapons all came from Russian bases in Georgia, he added. They headed back to the village, loaded up the horses and walked back over the mountains.

It was a self-funded war. Dudayev did not hand out much money and many people were vying for it. There was some rancour that he gave Raduyev a lot of money but kept other commanders, including Maskhadov, short. Basayev for one organized his own funds through business contacts in Moscow and elsewhere. The large Chechen diaspora in Moscow, Jordan, Turkey and the United Arab Emirates was a key source and also provided help for wounded fighters who needed complicated surgery or prolonged treatment. Fighters came and went abroad at will and Basayev even boasted he had travelled to Russia after Budyonnovsk. Dudayev's son, wounded early in the war, was treated in Turkey. Raduyev, who was shot in the head in an ambush in March 1996, was operated on in Chechnya and then spirited away from the hospital at night. He returned months later, after receiving plastic surgery and a false eye abroad. He was one of dozens of fighters who slipped out of the country, driven by loyal supporters down into Georgia or Azerbaijan from where they could make their way to Turkey or further afield.

No foreign government overtly supplied military aid to the Chechens during the war although some helped train fighters. Iran actually sent a representative to offer Dudayev assistance before the war, according to Basayev. But the conditions, that it should be covert aid, made Dudayev, who desperately wanted international recognition, refuse, he said. The Saudi Arabian-based Islamic Relief Organization did set up in the region and was probably a source of substantial funds to the fighters. A semi-official organization, it channels relief aid to fellow-Muslims in many war-torn countries, funded largely by mosques and rich individuals at home for whom supporting the *jihad*, or holy war, is a religious duty. There are claims that the organization is involved in terrorism and that the Saudi government moved to take a closer hand over it. *Jihad* funding has become a small industry in itself and there is no doubt that the Chechens tapped into it. In February 1995 a Saudi Arabian, fighting under the alias Khatab, arrived in Chechnya. A veteran of the war in Afghanistan, he brought with him a group of *mujahideen*, mostly Saudi and North African Arabs. They are self-professed Wahhabis, belonging to the conservative Saudi religious sect, and join up to fight a *jihad* wherever needed. Khatab, a stocky man in his thirties, with thick curly black hair to his shoulders and a *keffiyeh* round his neck, is himself a Saudi, marked by his accent as north Bedu.

Like the Wahhabis in Afghanistan, Khatab has probably been more useful to the Chechens for his money than his military prowess. He did, however, lead a devastating ambush on a Russian convoy high in the mountains at Yaryshmardy in April 1996 that wiped out a large column, killing close on 100 soldiers. Copies of the videotape of the ambush in all its hideous detail are on sale in Grozny market, probably shot in order to raise more funds back home. Khatab's ambush caused a big stir in Moscow. Grachev almost resigned over it and was called to the State Duma to give an account of the ambush. It may also have brought the ire of Russian airpower down on Dudayev a few days later. Basayev led an even more devastating ambush on a Russian column twice the size a short while earlier in the narrow gorge up to Vedeno.

Sometimes it seemed as though nothing had ever changed in Chechnya. The tactic of luring a Russian column into the mountains and then attacking it from all sides, cutting off its retreat, harked back to Imam Shamil's famous victory at Dargo in 1845. Count Mikhail Vorontsov had set off confidently with a long column for Dargo which was then Shamil's mountain capital, but he advanced too far into the mountains, was cut off from his supply line and found his route back blocked. The 'biscuit expedition' as it became known was an ignominious defeat. Attacked on all sides in the Chechen forests, Vorontsov lost 984 killed (including three generals), 2753 wounded, 179 missing, three guns, a large sum of money and all his baggage. The British consul in Odessa, James Yeames, writing a report on the fiasco dated 26 September 1845, concluded that: 'On the present occasion the Sovereign's perfect satisfaction has been ostentatiously expressed; promotions have been made and other rewards lavishly bestowed, and nevertheless, it is certain that no previous expedition into the same country was ever more disastrous, by loss of life and other sacrifices than the last; nor more entirely fruitless in its results; for not a single native was won over to the Russian cause; no prisoners have been taken; not a gun has been recaptured; not a foot of the invaded territory has been retained; and Shamil's power in the mountains has been left unbroken, if not materially increased.'[10] If you substituted 'Shamil Basayev' for 'Shamil', the same passage could have been written about Chechnya 150 years later.

*

On the ground in Chechnya the fighters could rely on strong support from the local population. One spring night, a group of

armed fighters was taking us up to Basayev's mountain camp,
when our jeep came adrift fording the swift-flowing River Argun
just half a mile from a Russian post. We all bailed out into the
icy-cold water and one young fighter ran off for help. Within
minutes, although it was two o'clock in the morning, a Chechen
truck driver was dragging us out. In the next village a whole
family woke up to help, the boys working until dawn to fix the
water-logged engine, the mother, the local schoolteacher, supplying hot food and drying out our clothes. The fighters clearly had
friends they could rely on in every village, and the help was
instantly and unquestioningly given.

The fighters survived in the long Chechen tradition of outlaw
resistance that had its own codes of honour. They were not unlike
the Chechen *abrek* or 'bandit of honour', a Robin Hood figure
famous for his panache and impudent bandit raids on figures of
authority. As late as the 1970s a modern-day *abrek* called Khasaki
Magomedov was captured after being at large for thirty years,
protected by mountain villagers. The most famous Chechen
abrek, Zelimkhan,[11] lived at the beginning of the century and
came from the village of Kharachoi. The incapacity of the
Russians to capture him became a topic of national debate in the
newspapers and the State Duma. He repeatedly evaded capture
and was given refuge in mountain villages and shepherds' huts
despite vicious punitive penalties meted out by the Russians. He
was only finally killed in 1913 in a last shoot-out.

In the same steadfast tradition, ordinary villagers protected
Dudayev, Basayev, Raduyev and any fighter from Russian forces
with unstinting loyalty. There were many Chechen informers who
worked for the Russians or the pro-Moscow government, but the
code of honour, especially strong among the mountain *teips*,
proved an important life-source to the fighters.

The spring of 1996 following Pervomaiskoye was, however,
such a grim time for the Chechen people that support for the
fighters did start to wear thin. The peace process was buried and

there seemed no end to the war in sight. Russian forces vented their fury over Pervomaiskoye on village after village, penalizing the civilians since the fighters were forever elusive. They pushed hard to isolate Dudayev's supporters from the population and began to speak of them as a dwindling force of extremists. The campaign was led by the new chief of Russian forces in Chechnya, the brutish army Lieutenant-General Vyacheslav Tikhomirov. A tall man with a thuggish face, Tikhomirov showed his true colours early on. Asked in January to comment on remarks by Maskhadov that his men would cease attacking federal troops, he said, 'I do not respond to a gangster's statements.'

Hand in hand with the wily Zavgayev, Tikhomirov now pursued an invidious policy of threats and punishment, demanding villages expel all fighters and sign a 'peace protocol'. In return he promised not to attack the village. It was a one-sided agreement. The villagers had to allow the Russians in to check passports and search for fighters. If any fighters came back or a single shot was fired, the agreement was invalid and Russian military entitled to use force. 'It is not exactly a mutual agreement, it is like saying: if you sign, we will not kill you,' said one member of the OSCE team.

Novogrozny, where all the fighters had gathered with their hostages after Pervomaiskoye, became the Russian forces' first target. They signed a peace protocol with village leaders, gave a twenty-four-hour ultimatum and stormed the village. They moved quickly on, wrenching agreements out of a string of villages further south, shelling those that showed any hesitation in signing or seemed still to harbour fighters. Then they closed in on Shali, which had once more become the headquarters of the separatists.

Tens of thousands of civilians from the villages suddenly converged on Grozny in February to protest against the attacks. Camping out on the main square for a week in freezing temperatures, hanging banners from the bombed-out shell of the Presidential Palace, they demanded a withdrawal of Russian troops. It was a remarkable, spontaneous demonstration which thoroughly alarmed Zavgayev. Russian riot police in black masks finally dispersed them but not before some ten people had been killed. On 16 February the authorities razed the Presidential Palace to the ground – even ruined the Palace had remained a potent symbol of the Chechen fight for independence.

The pattern of violence spread to western Chechnya. The village of Sernovodsk, right on the border with Ingushetia and packed full of refugees, was now blockaded and bombarded. All male civilians who tried to flee the village were arrested and detained. No one, including the OSCE and international aid agencies, was allowed into the village for days while Russian troops stormed the centre, killing, pillaging and burning. Boris Kiev, the Mayor of Sernovodsk, escaped across the River Sunzha one night shortly after the storm began. He insisted the village had an agreement with Zavgayev's government and had even handed over weapons in a ceremony with Russian generals. 'We did everything possible,' he said a few days later. 'There were not any fighters. There were maybe local boys who had taken part in the fighting and had come home but we took the decision that no one could go around in camouflage. We made a rule that there should not be any fighters in the village and there were not.'

The fighters hit back with purpose, launching a three-day raid on Grozny itself. Dudayev had long urged his commanders to take back Grozny and now they wanted to prove they could strike where they wanted. They burst into the city at dawn on 6 March, attacking from three directions, surrounding outlying Russian posts and local Chechen police stations who were loyal to Moscow. Fierce fighting spread through the south, west and north of the city as fighters pinned Russian troops down in their posts and fought off reinforcements who tried to break through to them. The fighters pulled out on the third day, bearing off weapons and vehicles seized from the Chechen police, leaving the

Russians battered and jumpy in their posts. Russian officers on the main post on Staropromyslovskoye Chaussee said they took so many casualties that out of fifty-four, only thirteen were left. On the southern edge of the city, another post kept shooting wildly for days after the fighters left. They were eventually evacuated, their replacements saying they had turned 'evil' from the experience. Dudayev called the attack a 'little harassing operation' and warned it was only a rehearsal for something much bigger.

The fighters were waging what Maskhadov called a 'semi-guerrilla' war, defending strongholds in villages and at the same time running more and more ambushes and lightning raids. It meant some villages took a very heavy toll but Maskhadov said it was necessary. 'We wanted to prove one thing, that we will fight in every village. That in every village they will have that coming to them. They thought that when they reached [the mountains] that that was it, that everything was in their hands. And we said they will have to take every village. And we were in every village,' he said. 'They could even take the whole territory but they were never the ones in charge.[12]

Samashki was the next village for treatment, the fighters, still smarting from the previous year's massacre, determined to stay and fight this time. A savage ten-day battle ensued that cost both villagers and fighters heavy casualties. Russian forces took few chances, using heavy aerial bombardment, including fuel air bombs, known in Russia as 'vacuum bombs', which explode above ground with massive pressure, killing everything within a wide range. Andrei Mironov, an independent human rights activist from Moscow, documented the effects of the bombs in Samashki, carrying huge missile cylinders back to the capital for identification. The bombing left curious undulating destruction over a wide area and killed animals and people hiding inside, even in bunkers. Animals and humans alike showed bleeding from the nose and had died from collapsed lungs, doctors discovered.

*

A shaken Zavgayev redoubled his efforts to show Moscow he was in control after the March raid on Grozny. Hand in hand with the Russian generals, he bullied village after village to sign the peace protocols. For many of those on the federal side the conflict had become part of their careers. Certain groups of people – defence contractors, generals, corrupt politicians – were making money out of it. The state budget had committed millions of dollars for the restoration of Chechnya but it was very difficult to check where and how the money was being spent.

In the Communist period Zavgayev's time in power had been characterized by corruption across the board. The same story was to repeat itself when he returned to office in October 1995. He took as his deputy the Russian Nikolai Koshman, an official from the notoriously corrupt Russian Railway Forces. In an unholy alliance of commerce and politics, huge amounts of money were earned on the non-restoration of Grozny. The money was allocated by the chairman of the commission for the restoration of Chechnya, Oleg Soskovets. Under the first pro-Moscow government it started fairly modestly. Some 5.5 trillion rubles (more than 1 billion dollars) had been allocated to Chechnya during the nine months of Khajiev's government. It was hard to see what it was spent on because only a handful of buildings were ever rebuilt in shattered Grozny. Khajiev said most of it never left Moscow's commercial banks. One of Zavgayev's first acts was to dissolve the commission handing out compensation payments (that almost no one had received) and appoint a new one. Still no one received any compensation. Rumours circulated that places on the new commission had merely been sold to the highest bidder. In his first two months in office Zavgayev was allocated a huge 12.3 trillion rubles. The government Audit Committee that tried to investigate the expenditures discovered mass irregularities. It said it could find 'no legal basis' for the allocation of 11.2 trillion rubles of that amount.[13]

On the ground there were even more ugly practices. The French aid agency Médecins Sans Frontières took the highly unusual step of issuing a human rights report in April saying there was mass abuse of human rights in Chechnya. They said villagers under siege were being forced to pay the military for a so-called humanitarian corridor. Prices ranged between 50 and 60 million rubles (about $10,000) for the right of two to three hours' passage to safety. A bridge outside Shali became known as the 'Golden Bridge' where villagers made regular payments to the Russian generals to stave off attacks. When they ran out of cash they collected gold jewellery, giving the bridge its nickname.

*

In Moscow the Russian media, so outspoken in the first months of the war, virtually ignored the heavy fighting in 1996. President Yeltsin was facing re-election in June and as his campaign got under way, the Russian media grew more muted about the war, one of his biggest handicaps. Yeltsin was trailing badly in the polls against his main opponent, the Communist Party leader Gennady Zyuganov, and his supporters urged him to make peace in Chechnya to save his electoral chances. Among them was the young governor of Nizhny Novgorod, Boris Nemtsov, who collected a million signatures in his region pleading for an end to the war. Yeltsin announced a peace plan for Chechnya at the end of March, but it changed little and he persisted in supporting Zavgayev as the legitimate leader in Chechnya.

Moscow was in fact still pushing hard for a military solution. Russian forces fought one of their fiercest battles of the war trying for a month to dislodge rebels from the village of Goiskoye. The Chechen commander Ruslan Gelayev, second in the hierarchy of commanders after Basayev, drew Russian tanks into the village and then destroyed every unit. He was filmed at one point standing amid the smoking ruins of Russian tanks and dead soldiers, calling on the Russian command to come and pick up the bodies. The Russians only succeeded in taking the village after bombing it completely flat.

Yeltsin nevertheless started pretending the war had stopped, so anxious was he to remove it from the agenda. In April, when US President Bill Clinton flew to Moscow for a summit meeting, Yeltsin declared bluntly that 'Military actions in the Chechnya region are not going on'. Clinton was asked whether the United States should have been more critical of the war in Chechnya. 'I think it depends. Do you believe that Chechnya is a part of Russia or not?' Clinton replied. Then he sought to legitimize the Chechen war as a struggle to keep Russia together. 'I would remind you that we once had a civil war in our country in which we lost on a per capita basis far more people than we lost in any of the wars of the twentieth century over the proposition that Abraham Lincoln gave his life for, that no state had a right to withdrawal from our Union.'[14] The remark, which had not been cleared with the State Department, angered American officials who had been dealing with Chechnya and trying to find ways of making Moscow scale down the fighting.

Clinton's comments highlighted that the clear priority of the West was to help Yeltsin get re-elected. They were prepared to overlook what was going on in Chechnya. This exasperated opponents of the war. Sergei Kovalyov had an argument over this with Ernst Muehlemann, the Swiss general who was Chairman of the Council of Europe's Committee on Chechnya.

'[Muehlemann] thinks that if he is a general in Switzerland he understands everything in the North Caucasus because there are mountains there and mountains here,' Kovalyov said bitterly. 'I spoke to him and said, "What is your commission doing? What have you done? There are distinct demands to Russia written down, it is a condition of its membership. Why are you not demanding that the war comes to an end at once? This is what your commission ought to be doing – note the violations of rights, note the continuation of the fighting and present demands, that is what you ought to put forward at the Assembly." You know what he said in objection? He looked at me very intently and said, "What do you want? That Zyuganov and not Yeltsin is chosen at the elections."'

14

Death in the Gully

On 21 April 1996 Jokhar Dudayev drove up into a narrow gully in a copse above the village of Gekhi-Chu to make several calls on his satellite telephone. It was about seven o'clock in the evening, and still light. Alla, his wife, and his nephew Viskhan Dudayev accompanied him, along with several bodyguards and three close aides, Khamad Kurbanov, Magomed Janiyev and Ayub Ibragimov.

The Chechen President was living a life on the run. A wanted man since the Russian authorities issued an arrest warrant in January 1995, he was fiercely protected by his security people, and constantly on the move from one village to another to elude the Russian secret services. At the most dangerous time he had spent some months living in the woods with just a few body-guards. Yet he had managed to remain a voluble leader during the war. He broadcast regular speeches to his people on local television, bursting on to people's screens with his own Presidential Channel, beamed from a mobile transmitter in the mountains. His comments and reaction to every development cropped up constantly in the Russian media. He frequently gave interviews to journalists and he used his satellite telephone to call news agencies, friends and mediators in Russia and abroad.

Extraordinarily, after all the killing and destruction, and after his fighters had committed two terrifying hostage raids against Russian civilians, Dudayev was closer than ever to meeting Yeltsin in person. It seems that Yeltsin, with his eye on presidential elections, finally decided to see Dudayev to put an end to the hugely unpopular war that was damaging his chances of winning a second term.

Nationalities Minister Vyacheslav Mikhailov was working on a meeting with Dudayev through mediators, either the President of the Russian republic of Tatarstan, Mintimer Shaimiyev, or the King of Morocco, Hassan II, both of whom had offered their services. 'We proposed that the first meeting should be on the level of Shaimiyev and the second meeting should be with Chernomyrdin or with Yeltsin. A letter was sent to Chernomyrdin with regard to these proposals and Yeltsin made the decision that he himself would hold that meeting,' Mikhailov recalled.[1] On 20 April Chernomyrdin told a cabinet meeting that either he or Yeltsin would meet Dudayev.

The following day Dudayev was in the gully above Gekhi-Chu. He drove out of the village specifically to spare the village air strikes which frequently followed his progress. He knew the dangers. His aides set up the telephone to run off the car battery, placing the small portable dish on the ground ahead of the green four-wheel-drive Niva. Dudayev crouched down over the receiver just in front of the car with Kurbanov, his former Moscow representative, standing over him. Janiyev, a commander with a thick black moustache and whiskers, was standing at the open door of the car. Alla and Viskhan were some 12 yards below, where the second jeep was parked. The bodyguards spaced themselves around on look-out in the woods. Several times over the next half-hour the chief bodyguard Musa Idigov told Dudayev to cut off the phone when he heard planes. Dudayev told Alla to move away but he did not change location. Dudayev then called the Russian MP Konstantin Borovoi and Ibragimov slipped off to crouch behind the Niva and smoke a cigarette out of view of his boss. That is the scene Viskhan Dudayev remembers when he saw a flash in the fields to the north-east, where the Russian troops were positioned less than a mile from the village. Seconds later there was a huge explosion that threw everyone off their feet and hurled the Niva down the gully.

Dudayev, Kurbanov and Janiyev were killed instantly. Ibragimov, protected from the blast by the car itself, survived. The body-guards flung Alla behind a bank as a second explosion sounded not far off. Ramzan Basnukayev, the head of the Presidential Guard, rushed to the scene when he heard the explosions and found the guards had already borne off Dudayev. He gathered up the others, extricating Janiyev's body himself from the wreckage of the car. Ibragimov was wounded in the chest and was rushed to the nearby hospital in Urus Martan. 'Kurbanov had lost the top of his head, his sheepskin coat was torn to shreds,' Basnukayev recalled later.[2] They took Dudayev down to the village and Alla held him in the car and sat over him in the house, as it slowly dawned on her that he was dead.[3] She kept a vigil all night, praying over his body until all the senior field commanders within reach arrived for a funeral service the following morning. Basnukayev was among them, it was only then that he saw Dudayev's body. 'His forehead and face were burnt and his arm was in bandages,' he recalled. They prayed over the body, and then just three or four men of his personal guard took Dudayev's body away and buried him up in the woods. They are the only ones who know where he is buried, according to Basnukayev, and even Alla did not accompany them.

A deep crater marks the spot where the explosion occurred. Five days later trophy-hunters had cleared the crater of almost all the debris. The flattened wreckage of the Niva bore witness to the power of the blast. The most likely version is that it was a rocket, guided from a plane to home in on the satellite signal. The crater gave away little, it could even have been from a car bomb, planted by disaffected elements on Dudayev's own side. Basnukayev said he heard no plane at the time, although other villages said they did. Military analysts concluded that the Russians were capable of tracking the signal from a satellite telephone but had been lucky to have had enough time to programme in the coordinates and hit the target first time. A second rocket had landed a split second later, a good 100 yards away.

The timing of the attack just after Yeltsin had apparently agreed to meet Dudayev is another great enigma of the war in Chechnya. Borovoi believes that the Russian secret services were defying Yeltsin; they wanted to prevent any meeting between the two that might end the war and acted fast to get rid of Dudayev. They had been trying to kill him for years and they may just finally have struck lucky. Others have suggested the strike was straightforward retaliation for the ambush at Yaryshmardy. Perhaps the most likely explanation is that Yeltsin was preparing to negotiate with Dudayev, if he really had to, while continuing efforts to remove him altogether, which would suit him much better. If this version is true, the rocket found the Chechen President just before the negotiating team did.

*

In the last months of his life it took time and endurance to find Dudayev. He invariably gave interviews late at night, and journalists were escorted by armed fighters to a safe-house in rebel-held territory, usually in one of the villages in the foothills in central Chechnya, Alkhazurovo and Gekhi-Chu among others. On 16 March 1996 it took twelve hours to get to him, and eight changes of location. The last leg was a lurching three-and-a-half-hour ride in the back of a military truck, fording rivers and negotiating mud slides in the foothills of the Caucasus mountains to keep out of sight of the Russian guns below. At one point the truck sank deep into the thick mud, tipping at a 45-degree angle, until the Chechen fighters ordered everyone to climb out and walk. Snow still clung to the hillsides and a heavy damp mist chilled us to the bone.

Dudayev always looked immaculate, neat and clean in his field uniform and forage cap with the Chechen wolf emblem on the front. Even when tired and drawn, he showed a smiling self-conviction. He never expressed remorse for the victims of the war he had helped start. His favourite themes were the evil of Russian chauvinism and imperialism, which he dubbed 'Russianism', and the hypocrisy and short-sightedness of the West. His eyes glittered as he spoke, and he would clench his fists till they were white and the knuckles cracked. In that March interview, one of the last he gave, he talked for five hours, long past midnight, until the journalists facing him were practically falling off their chairs from exhaustion. He harangued us personally as hypocritical Western-ers, pretending to care about human rights, then supporting Russia with huge credits and in effect financing the war.

'You will bring tragedy to your homes and to Europe by aiding and abetting that regime,' he said. 'We have already raised our voices, the voices of drowning men. When we appealed to the West, when tanks were rolling over bodies, the West said it was an internal problem of Russia.' He went on: 'This is a very big mistake. Take my word for it, you have been mistaken. Even a few strong men can make the world bend to its knees or turn it to ashes.'

He showed a twisted concern about the effect of the war on his people, convinced that in the end it would be more damaging to Russia than to his tiny beleaguered nation. 'We are the main factor in continuing the war, and not Russia. We are much more interested in continuing the war than Russia, because, what is left to us? There is no production, buildings have been smashed, the economic process stopped, medical services destroyed, people are left with no jobs, no houses, no shelter, no bread. The men aged between fifteen and fifty know only how to fight. What am I going to do with them after the war ends? Put yourself in my place, what can I do?' he said. 'It is better to carry on the war, so that we are not the only ones to spill blood. Let the people who started it feel what war is, only then will they understand.'

Dudayev still had a strange obsession with Yeltsin, insisting the Russian President was not his enemy but then calling him an evil man and a murderer. 'We do not need any special status with a murderer . . . What they have offered us is to sit in a cage with a wild captive bear and shake him by the paw and look for reconciliation with a hungry bear.'

He dwelt repeatedly on his own death that night. Yeltsin had ordered his assassination at a Security Council meeting the day before, and commanded Grachev to accomplish a specific military task. 'The main plan is to kill Dudayev,' he said, adding that he had obtained the printed minutes of the meeting. 'The second is to start clashes and launch cruel and punitive operations to intimidate the population and to channel hatred against Dudayev as the main source who does not want peace.' Russia's security services would carry out the first task and Grachev the second, he said. Accompanied only by his chief of security and another senior commander, and armed with a pistol and a dagger, Dudayev seemed to have dispensed with his large retinue of fighter bodyguards. He said he had lost count of the number of assassination attempts made on him since 1991. Russian secret services had done everything to catch him, he said, including planting bugs in his car and giving one of his bodyguards at the peace talks a present of a commando knife with a transmitter concealed in the handle so that bomber planes could hunt him down.

*

The secrecy of Dudayev's burial gave rise to intense speculation that he was not dead at all, but had been spirited out of the country to return again one day. There were many mysterious details, not least that Dudayev's brothers in Grozny were not invited to the funeral. Chechens all over the republic held the three-day-long *tesir*, a mourning ceremony, slaughtering sheep and cooking them in great cauldrons, the villagers gathering to sit on long benches round a square, holding prayers and performing the *zikr*. Those in Dudayev's immediate circle were visibly devastated and yet the commanders, many of whom had been very close to their President, all swore allegiance to Zelimkhan Yandarbiyev, the Vice-President, who now took over as leader.

Ruslan Gelayev, the burly, red-bearded commander of the south-west front, who was fighting to defend Goiskoye even while holding a *tesir* for Dudayev, showed few outward signs of grief just days later. 'With Dudayev or without him, we fill fight for his ideas of freedom and independence,' he told reporters, standing relaxed and smiling in the courtyard of his house.[4]

Yandarbiyev and Maskhadov gave a joint press conference a few days later. It was part of a concerted effort the rebels made over the weeks after Dudayev's death to present a solid front to the outside world. They were calm and confident. Nothing would change, except Maskhadov would probably take on even more responsibility for the military campaign, Yandarbiyev said, since he, unlike Dudayev, had no military background. Their calm approach gave rise to speculation that there was a certain relief that Dudayev was now out of the way.

In another twist of fate Dudayev, the former Soviet general, became instantly mythologized on his death and traditional enemies of Russia honoured him as a great hero. Some deputies in the Polish Parliament rose to their feet to pay tribute to him. A street in the Latvian capital Riga was named after the Chechen leader. The greatest homage to Dudayev was in the Estonian city of Tartu, where he used to serve. His former military headquarters has been converted into a hotel and Dudayev's former office is now a hotel room with the Chechen President's portrait on the wall. 'He is a national hero,' said the blonde-haired, blue-eyed receptionist.

Yandarbiyev, who took over from Dudayev, was never an authoritative figure. He had spent most of the war penning pamphlets and writing poems, sitting out the bombing in the tiny mountain hamlet of Dzumsoi. The fighters and commanders, however, accepted him. They were determined to be seen to abide by their constitution and united in their desire not to let Russia exploit any internal differences. Yandarbiyev's very weakness also meant that no one was likely to take exception to him.

Dudayev's removal from the scene gave Yeltsin the opportunity to sue for peace. Presidential elections were less than two months away and Yeltsin knew he had to get Chechnya off the agenda. With Dudayev out of the way, things were suddenly easy for both the Russian and Chechen leadership. The Russians could wipe the slate clean with Yandarbiyev. This was something picked up immediately by Tim Guldimann, the energetic Swiss professor who now headed the OSCE mission in Grozny. Guldimann had rebuilt bridges with the rebel side after the disastrous end to his predecessor's mission the year before. Even though he never gained a meeting with Dudayev, the frequency of his contacts with the rebel leaders drew the wrath of the pro-Moscow leader Doku Zavgayev, who demanded that he be expelled from Chechnya – something which only enhanced Guldimann's reputation in the hills. On 9 May Guldimann met Yandarbiyev and discussed how and when a meeting with Yeltsin could be arranged. He twice flew to Moscow to confer with the Russian side. The Russians were particularly interested in whether there was unity in the Chechen leadership, and Guldimann conveyed the message that, broadly speaking, there was. Then he went to a two-day meeting outside Vedeno at which the entire rebel leadership discussed and approved the idea of a meeting between the two Presidents.

Aslan Maskhadov was in a good mood as he met four Western journalists the following day. He sat on a tree stump in the middle of a beech wood, his green camouflage fatigues blending into the trees. Heavily armed guards were concealed in the woods. 'Of course we are afraid,' Maskhadov said, looking ahead to the meeting. He said they had made the calculated risk of approving the meeting, knowing that they were thereby giving Yeltsin an election boost. But on balance they laid greater hopes with Yeltsin to deliver a peace settlement. Although they did not trust the Yeltsin regime, Maskhadov said, their memories of the Communist regime were too fresh for them to contemplate supporting

Zyuganov. 'The Communists deceived us more than anyone,' Maskhadov said. 'Our grandfathers believed in them.'

*

In May, Yeltsin's generals also finally provided him with some military successes. Russian bombers eventually flattened the village of Goiskoye, as well as the three villages that had withstood every previous assault, Orekhovo, Stary Achkoi and Bamut. They also occupied Vedeno and Dargo in the south-east. On paper, Russian forces controlled more ground than at any time during the war when Yeltsin finally extended the invitation to Yandarbiyev to come to the Kremlin and sign a peace agreement.

It was 27 May, just over a month after Dudayev's death, when Yandarbiyev flew to Moscow. He went in combat fatigues, accompanied by field commanders Akhmed Zakayev, wearing a black headdress with Islamic inscription, and Shirvani Basayev, in full combat gear and khaki beret, among others. Tim Guldimann was with them. It was a stormy meeting and nearly broke down in the first moments when Yandarbiyev rejected the seating plan. Yeltsin walked into the room, taking his customary seat at the end of the conference table, and bid the Chechens to sit down opposite the Russian team of ministers. Yandarbiyev refused, insisting he had come to a meeting between heads of state, not to a commission chaired by Yeltsin. 'We are not equal,' Yeltsin replied, staring down at the table, in television footage shown later that week. 'If we are not equal then we cannot decide anything,' Yandarbiyev said, standing above him, as Yeltsin's security chief Alexander Korzhakov moved in protectively. 'Sit down,' commanded Yeltsin. 'Sit down, did you hear? Sit down.' Yandarbiyev refused again, walking away and asking Guldimann to provide security for their departure.

'Close the doors. No one is leaving here,' Shirvani Basayev remembers Yeltsin thundering. 'It was very tense, they wanted to create psychological pressure,' he recalled.[5] Guldimann then stepped forward, clutching his briefcase in front of him, and addressed Yeltsin. 'Guldimann says, "Mr Yeltsin, this is not right. If you sit here, Mr Yandarbiyev should sit there." Like that, straight. I was amazed at his bravery,' Basayev recalled. In the end Yeltsin gave in. Pushing back his chair, he moved round to sit halfway down one side of the table in the middle of his ministers, whereupon Yandarbiyev sat down opposite. Yeltsin immediately complained that the Chechens had been hours late for the meeting. 'No one makes the President of Russia wait for even five minutes,' he said. Nevertheless, with elections less than three weeks away, he needed a peace agreement, and after two hours of discussions he watched while Chernomyrdin and Yandarbiyev signed the deal. They agreed to a ceasefire and an exchange of prisoners within the next two weeks.

Yeltsin had his peace deal and the Chechens had the direct meeting with Yeltsin they had always wanted. Yeltsin could no longer call them bandits after receiving them in the Kremlin, but they found that direct talks with him changed little. They had sometimes thought that if they could meet with Yeltsin and tell him how things were, he would relent in the war. But Shirvani Basayev says they came to the conclusion that Yeltsin was in fact 'very well-informed' and that he knew 80 per cent of what was happening in Chechnya.

The very next day, Yeltsin pulled the rug from under their feet, staging the most brilliant propaganda coup of his election campaign. As Yandarbiyev and his delegation were occupied for a second day of talks with Russian ministers in a government *dacha* outside Moscow, Yeltsin paid a flying visit to Chechnya to announce the war won and the 'bandit groups annihilated'. The Chechens were meanwhile virtual prisoners in the *dacha*, totally cut off from the media. They had had no idea of Yeltsin's plans, but had agreed to stay in Moscow when Yeltsin suggested they continue talks with Chernomyrdin the following day. The Prime Minister did not show up and they had to make do with

Mikhailov. They arrived back that evening in Chechnya, tight-lipped but in a way resigned, since it had so obviously been a pre-election stunt.

All the same, a peace of sorts held in Chechnya. The Kremlin kept insisting it wanted peace and the Chechens took full advantage of this. They very rapidly signed a second peace deal on 10 June in Nazran, the capital of Ingushetia, that agreed to a withdrawal of Russian troops by the end of August. General Tikhomirov signed it and said he would abide by it, although he was known to oppose it. So did two members of the pro-Moscow Chechen government. The signs of opposition were always there. Several bombs exploded by the road as Maskhadov's convoy swept home from the talks. Then Zavgayev's pro-Moscow government provocatively declared it would hold local elections for a Chechen parliament, flying in the face of the agreement just signed.

The rebels nevertheless held themselves in check, with Mask-hadov and Yandarbiyev repeatedly insisting they wanted to show their commitment to peace. In a move that signalled the level of cooperation now, they telephoned Chernomyrdin in Moscow. He assured them that he was also opposed to the local elections. 'When we heard that, we decided to hold ourselves back,' Maskhadov said. In turn Moscow made some gestures to peace. It closed down PAP-1, the notorious filtration camp in Grozny, and pulled out one regiment, sending it homewards amidst great fanfare for the benefit of the television cameras.

The local elections were widely boycotted in Chechnya but occurred without violence. Yeltsin won a second term as President of Russia after a major shake-up in his entourage. He brought on board Alexander Lebed, the charismatic former army general who had won 14 per cent of the vote in the first round. Lebed was appointed head of the Security Council. Yeltsin then sacked Grachev, Korzhakov, Barsukov and Soskovets in a dramatic clearout of the old guard who had dragged him into the war. Then he came through and won the election with a comfortable majority.

*

Less than a week after Yeltsin was re-elected, on 9 July, Russian planes bombed the village of Makhkety, high in the Chechen mountains. It was a calculated blow without provocation. Yandarbiyev had been using the village as a base in recent weeks and virtually the entire Chechen rebel leadership had gathered for a meeting there. Maskhadov was to have left the village the day before, but delayed his journey to wait for Sergei Drobush, Lebed's envoy, who was travelling down to arrange for the Security Council chief to visit Chechnya and meet the rebel leadership. The planes dropped huge bombs, completely demolishing the village hall and several private houses, and killing a dozen people, including children sheltering in a cellar. Tanks then started moving in to block off all the roads and tracks out of the village. Maskhadov immediately ordered his aide-de-camp, Iskhanov, to take Drobush out. They hurtled down the river-bed, Iskhanov knowing that if they met a tank they were both dead men. They got away only just in time. Fighters who attempted the same route half an hour later found it already blocked.

Yandarbiyev immediately drove to the edge of the woods, heading away on foot, then on horseback, travelling all through the night. By lunch-time the Russians began the assault, dropping paratroopers in positions all around the village. Maskhadov and Basayev split up and headed out south and west with the 150 fighters who had been in the village. 'We seemed to be practically surrounded,' Maskhadov recalled. 'For three days I went on foot, pushing through the encirclement. There were soldiers everywhere, everywhere was closed off, and they were bombing. We lived in the woods, with nothing to eat, nothing to drink. Three times we came up against Russian forces, and retreated.'

'We ate Yupi drink powder, it crackled in your throat, and we stripped leaves from the trees to eat,' said Jumbulat Samkhatov, one of Basayev's commanders. 'We wound our way through gullies and ravines, up and down.' The two groups met up again in the woods and finally broke through together. 'Two guides took us through Russian lines; we went through the Sharo-Argun, which is a terrifying river, it very nearly carried us away,' Maskhadov recounted. He turned down towards Duba-Yurt while Basayev headed up to Itum-Kale. The operation was a complete failure for the Russians. Every single fighter got out of the village safely and the bombing killed only civilians. Yet the scale and seriousness of the operation, coupled with a massive assault launched on the village of Gekhi on the same day, made it clear that Moscow was resuming all-out war. A vicious bombing campaign began again across the mountains above Shatoi.

For the rebels, the peace was over. 'It was a dangerous moment. You see, again, despite our bitter experience, we trusted in the measures the Russian side signed with us in the Nazran agreement,' Yandarbiyev said afterwards. Together they resolved to go on the offensive. It was time to take back Grozny.

15

Grozny Recaptured

Grozny in August was hot, dusty and slothful. The city, still in ruins, was slumbering through another sultry night when word came: 'The packet's gone.' It was the password for Chechen rebels all over the republic to launch their offensive on Grozny. They attacked at dawn on 6 August, infiltrating the city from three directions, in their most daring and ambitious operation of the twenty-month war. Over 1500 fighters poured in by truck and car in a carefully orchestrated assault. Moving fast, they headed for specific targets, attacking police stations and Russian army posts and bases on the outskirts. Some took up positions on the approach roads, guarding against Russian counter-attacks, while more fighters worked their way on foot towards the centre of town. Within hours they had overrun the key districts, laying siege to every Russian post and base on the way, and were advancing on the government compound in the centre.

Russian troops retaliated with a barrage of missiles and sniper fire on their immediate surroundings to keep the rebels at bay. Troops on the hills outside the city opened fire with tanks and mortar fire in support. Russian helicopter gunships and jets joined the battle, answering distress calls from Russian soldiers under heavy grenade attack inside their concrete block posts. Flying in and out of a thick pall of smoke from burning oil installations, they swooped down to fire rockets at buildings where Chechen fighters were taking cover. The rebels retaliated with fierce machine-gun fire from the roofs of apartment buildings, and swiftly brought down four helicopters. By the end of the day Chechen fighters were firing from within 100 yards of the central government compound.

Grozny was garrisoned with some 12,000 Russian troops. They guarded every bridge and main road, and had bases in every district, in factories and bus depots, behind barbed wire and messy sandbagged defences. Every single post was now coming under fire from Chechen fighters, who attacked with everything they had: mortars, machine-guns and sniper fire. At least one unit of Russian soldiers which ventured out from its checkpoint was ambushed and killed. Every detachment in the city was pinned down, unable to move. The roads from the main bases were cut. Troops in the nearby towns of Argun and Gudermes to the east of Grozny were also surrounded in their garrisons. Chechen fighters, better-armed and more numerous than ever, were dodging in and out of the ruins, moving freely through the streets. The city was all but captured in a single day. The Russian armed forces were facing their nadir.

'The actions in Grozny have a single aim – to show that the war in Chechnya is not over yet,' Maskhadov announced to a Moscow radio station.[1] He wanted to show the lie of Moscow's claims that virtually all the rebels were destroyed and the war won, he said later. He was fed up with Russian claims that his men were a rabble of bandit groups and the Zavgayev government installed by Moscow the real power in Chechnya. 'We proved that the Chechen armed forces are not "bandit groups", they are a real, powerful directed force, united under a single command, and the puppet power that the Russian leadership set up, this power does not exist, except in the bunker at the northern airport, nothing more, and when we want we can throw them out of there.'[2]

The Chechen action also seemed a calculated blow at Yeltsin, who was preparing to celebrate his inauguration for a second term as President in three days' time. Ending the war in Chechnya had been one of the corner-stones of his campaign for re-election, and it had blown up in his face. Now Yeltsin both promised to crush the rebel assault and tried to retain something of his new peacemaking image. 'Terrorist raids will be decisively put down,' he said. 'At the same time, even in this difficult situation, I continue to insist that there is no other way to settle the conflict in Chechnya other than the peace negotiations I began on 27 May,' referring to his Kremlin meeting with rebel leader Yandarbiyev. 'I will not allow anyone to talk to the federal authorities in the language of blackmail,' he added.

*

The fiercest fighting that first day centred around Grozny's Hospital No. 4. At seven in the morning the area exploded with gunfire as scores of Chechen fighters moved through the streets outside. Within minutes patients in the hospital heard the clatter of helicopters approaching and instinctively ducked as they fired their rockets with a roar and loud crack. Everyone who could move scrambled down to the ground floor, sitting on the floor of the wards, wherever they could. Wounded arrived almost immediately and the surgeons moved into the operating theatre with an injured Chechen policeman.

Ruman Ibrisova, one of the nurses, was climbing up to the operating theatre when disaster struck. As she opened the door, a rocket slammed into the theatre, demolishing the room and killing everyone inside. Thrown across the corridor by the blast, Ibrisova survived with a small wound, but three surgeons and four nurses, almost the entire medical staff on duty, were killed, as well as the policeman on the operating table. Ibrisova was left with a hospital full of more than 100 sick and wounded, many newly arrived with shrapnel and bullet wounds. Only two other nurses were with her as a terrifying air assault broke around them. Chechen fighters battling their way through to the town centre had been headed off by snipers and made a detour through the hospital compound. The Russian helicopters pursuing them turned their guns on the hospital itself.

'I was looking for people to donate blood, carrying the

wounded down, I was not thinking, I was just running, running,'
Ibrisova said after she escaped from the city two days later. 'We
took all the patients down through the afternoon, grabbing as many
medicines as we could, and all the time, bombs were exploding
on every side.' As evening came they evacuated the patients into
neighbouring cellars and buried some of the dead in the courtyard, although they could not reach all of those in the operating
theatre. The Chechen fighters urged her to evacuate the patients
from the city, telling her the battle would intensify. As fighting
still raged close by, Ibrisova pressed civilians in nearby bunkers to
help find transport. They loaded up the patients, tearing sheets
to fly white flags on the roofs of the buses, driving slowly out in
convoy. They came to a Russian post on the road west, where an
armoured column was massed ready to advance on the city. 'We
women walked out ahead, holding white flags up. I pleaded with
them, saying I was bringing out my patients. They let us through,
thank God,' she said, bursting into tears.

Hundreds of refugees were pouring out of the city by now as
the thick, black smoke from the burning oil station filled half the
sky. The sounds of heavy airstrikes and artillery resounded behind
them as they moved through the western suburbs, crossing paths
with fresh volunteer fighters heading in to join the battle. They
fled on foot, or crammed into small Zhiguli cars and open trucks,
along a muddy track through the woods. Chechen fighters
guarding the wooded trail suddenly yelled for people to take
cover. The beating blades of a helicopter filled the air and people
ran along the path, veering off into the woods, dropping belongings, calling to each other in fright. Two explosions burst ahead
of them in the woods, rockets fired by the helicopter that had
already wheeled away. The refugees pressed on in panic. Panting
and sweating, many had been walking for four or five hours from
their homes in the city centre. 'The fighters are everywhere, in
every house, in every street, they completely control the city,' said

Rosa Khazbeka, who with her neighbours was bringing out thirteen children.

They passed a group of volunteer fighters walking silently and purposefully in a line through the trees. They had hiked in from their village, easily skirting the Russian post on the edge of the town by cutting through the woods. Dressed in jeans and tracksuits, cheap gym-shoes on their feet, they dropped over a wall into the courtyard of a private farmhouse that was serving as a temporary headquarters. They carried Kalashnikovs, bought with their own money at the beginning of the war. A few had rocket-propelled grenades and launchers. Almost all had a dagger at their waist. They were not full-time fighters, one explained, but reserves, known to the commanders and ready for call-up when needed. They were part of a second wave of fighters who flooded into the city over the next few days, increasing their force to some 3000 men. Now they sat under the vines in the courtyard awaiting orders, listening to the shuddering explosions as ground-attack jets bombed the nearest suburb.

Another helicopter gunship came over, blasting Chechen positions just 500 yards away. The next second it swung round, firing two rockets which landed with a great bang near the compound. 'Swine,' muttered one fighter as he crouched down against the wall of the house. The helicopters circled away and just then their commander arrived, racing up the road and into the courtyard in a new white Volga car, followed by fighters in a Russian jeep. It was Akhmed Zakayev, a former actor at Grozny's theatre and one of the field commanders who had accompanied Yandarbiyev to the Kremlin to meet Yeltsin just two months before. He wore combat fatigues and his trademark black head-dress. Chechen forces were in full control of the city and had enough men and weapons to stay indefinitely, he said, smiling and embracing several of the new volunteers.

For the residents of Grozny, some 300,000 people, this was

the 'third war' in twenty months to force them down into their bunkers. Everywhere in the city was dangerous, there was no clear front line and no safe haven except underground. Gun and shell fire suddenly exploded in courtyards with no warning. Khadizhat Shakhtamirova was sheltering with her newborn baby in the cellar of a maternity home, just off the market in central Grozny. Out of food and water, with the babies screaming, she and six others decided to try to escape from the city. 'All the buildings were burning, it was terrible. Destroyed tanks, and APCs. It was a really foggy morning, it was like a terrifying movie playing in front of us, completely quiet. Somewhere further away there was bombing and shooting,' she recalled. 'We all ran, it was so frightening. Then suddenly a helicopter appeared and started shooting its machine-gun at us. It was a terrifying moment.'

*

It was only at dawn on the second morning that the Russian command organized a column of tanks and troop-carriers to go to the rescue of their trapped comrades. Troops from the 205th Army Brigade set out from the base to break through to the besieged men in the city. Among them was Sergei, a thirty-four-year-old sergeant, driving a big army truck with supplies. Wearing a black bandana and black T-shirt, he flung his flak jacket over the cab door to guard against snipers' bullets. They advanced deep into the centre and were within sight of the target, the government compound, when suddenly the column was ambushed. A tank in front hit a mine and suddenly Sergei felt his own truck shudder. He threw himself out of the cab, diving for the shelter of the nearest building, as the truck burst into flames behind him. Explosions shook the air and automatic gunfire broke out in every direction. Sergei and a few others battled their way, crawling and ducking bullets, through the shells of buildings destroyed over a year before. 'It took eight hours to fight our way up the street, just two hundred yards,' he said later. They finally broke through to the government building under cover of darkness. 'We needed more help than they did,' he said.

Russian troops and local Chechen police were inside guarding the three-storey, L-shaped building. There were no government officials. Zavgayev was safely in his rooms at the heavily fortified Russian base at the airport outside of town but his guards and police were trapped. They and the Government House were a main target for the rebels, who blamed the recent breakdown of the ceasefire and peace negotiations on Zavgayev's machinations. They nicknamed him Doku Aeroportovich because, they said, he rarely dared leave the safety of the airport. Across the street from the government house was a large contingent of Russian troops in the city stadium and adjoining buildings, among them special forces and a parachute unit. A group of Russian journalists were also in a hostel within the compound and were now sheltering in the bunker. They filed urgent despatches as they listened with growing alarm to the rebel advance, often contradicting the statements put out by the Russian command. Just north of the compound, residents took shelter in the cellar of their apartment block and listened in disgust to Zavgayev on the radio. 'The situation in Grozny is under our full control now,' they heard him saying against the din of incoming shells.

The Chechen fighters were by now in the telephone exchange, just 30 yards south of the compound, and opened up with grenade fire on the Government House. Snipers closed in on three sides, moving into apartment buildings and the old maternity home, as FSB troops abandoned it. Fire took hold in the apartments, gutting the buildings the whole length of one street. Then a grenade hit the arms store in the Government House and the whole building went up in flames. The men inside made a dash across the street. Sergei was among them, ducking under the Chechen gunfire. He was down to his last two magazines of bullets, he said: 'After that we just sat here without ammunition with all these wounded infantry.' The news of their failure had reached soldiers posted on the road outside Grozny. 'We heard a column was destroyed and bearded men are now driving around in our tanks,' said one Russian soldier. It was true. Chechen fighters had painted 'Bamut' on one tank and drove it jerkily back and forth on the street. They manoeuvred another tank into position under an arch and began to blast the government compound with heavy shells, provoking the Itar-Tass correspondent inside the bunker to report: 'We are perishing.'

*

The Russian command sent in several more columns over the next few days to try to relieve the besieged troops, but each time they ran into an ambush as the Chechens blew up the tanks and troop-carriers. Wrecks littered the southern road from Khankala: a huge self-propelled gun had broken off its base, the massive treads trailing like ribbons across the street. The bodies of Russian soldiers lay sprawled among the debris in a ghastly reminder of the New Year's Eve fiasco just a year and a half before. Another column, attacking from the northern airport, also came under a devastating assault. Units all over the city found themselves cut off without assistance. 'You telephone Moscow. They are saying on the television is it an insignificant conflict. What that really means is that we are surrounded and our checkpoint is being destroyed,' shouted one officer over his radio. Russian Interior Ministry officers from the Siberian town of Irkutsk gave a Russian news programme a recording of the radio intercepts from a group of six checkpoints talking with their headquarters.[3] 'A helicopter is coming to your assistance, over,' the command says. 'I have already been surrounded for eight hours, what other option can you offer?' the post replies. 'Expect help any minute. By our estimate help should be with you any minute. I am only a radio operator, over.' 'You are my countryman. I already have nine 200s [dead] and uncounted 300s [wounded]. I am still waiting!' the voice shouts back.

One watched helicopters float by, apparently oblivious to his calls. 'Helicopters! Helicopters! What kind of bloody aviation are you if you cannot even save your own men! What are you doing? Are you scared to come down lower?' Another: 'Our APC has been hit! About five hundred metres from the railway crossing. They are shooting our boys point-blank. Help us if you can, do you read me, do you read me?' another yelled. 'Understood, understood, but for now there is no help,' the command replied. 'We are out of ammunition! When is that column coming?' another called. All the checkpoints were taking casualties and, growing desperate, they started accusing the men in the bases outside the town of refusing to come to the rescue. 'I cannot even lift my head. We have to get out of here. Send a column, send a column so we can get everyone out of here. They are hitting us from all four sides. From four sides!' one officer shouts. 'They hit the column, do not try to leave,' the command replies. 'They hit the column. [Pause.] You are not even fighting!' the officer shouts back.

A force of some 900 men of the 276th Regiment did advance on the city from the east on 11 August, five days after the Chechens launched their attack. Zhenya, a twenty-two-year-old contract soldier, was with them. It was the third attempt by the Russians to break through to the centre. Ordered to take control of two central districts, they lost 50 per cent of their force, 150 dead and 300 wounded, in just two days. 'There's nothing strange in the fact that we took such heavy losses,' Zhenya said, adding that the Chechens had the advantage when fighting in the city. 'They are fighting on home ground. This is where they grew up. They know the back streets. Fighting in the open, it would be the other way round,' he said.

He was standing at the end of Mira Street where the buildings on either side were completely destroyed, a single battered wall sticking up out of the rubble. Just beyond, Prospekt Pobedy was like a forest, the ground strewn with broken branches and leaves downed by the gunfire. The place had been the scene of the deadly battle on New Year's Eve 1994 when a whole column of tanks and armoured vehicles was wiped out. A year and a half later the Russian command was still sending its troops in again in the same way, as if they had learned nothing from that disastrous mistake. Were they not inviting an ambush? 'Yes,' replied Zhenya, 'the tactics were bad ... It took us two hours to advance thirty metres.'

Some did break through, however, and soldiers at least managed to rescue the Russian journalists. The Chechen blockades were not totally solid. FSB troops in a hostel several blocks away from the government compound were surrounded and even talked to their Chechen attackers from an upstairs window. They refused to surrender, however, even after days under siege, and later broke out and escaped to the main compound. When the Chechens did storm the building they found plenty of weapons but only one dead man inside. Russian troops also burst out from one base in the north part of the city, in one of the nastiest episodes of the siege.

*

Movsar Tembulatov is the deputy head of Grozny's largest hospital, the Ninth City Hospital. In his white coat and tall white cotton hat, he projects an air of weary calm. He never left his post at the hospital throughout the entire war, but nothing had prepared him for the August siege. On the third day of the fighting, Tembulatov had over 600 patients and medical staff in the suffocating cellars of the hospital, with dozens of wounded arriving daily, when a group of thirty Russian soldiers burst in.

'One of the commanders, he was called Alek, he immediately said, "We are going to do another Budyonnovsk,"' Tembulatov recalled.[4] They told me they wanted to look through the hospital to see if there were fighters among the wounded. They said, "Someone is shooting at us from the roof." We said, "Take a look, there is no one here, no one is shooting from the roof," ' he said. They were tense, they were looking to hide, they thought there would be fighters here. Then when we explained there were no fighters they calmed down a little.'

The soldiers barricaded themselves into the hospital. 'They were all with their guns in different positions, on every floor there were machine-guns. We were all in the basement and they were up here, they took over everything,' Tembulatov said. The Chechen fighters quickly understood what had happened and took up positions in the buildings around but they failed to stop another two groups of Russian soldiers breaking through to the hospital from their base just 500 yards down the street. There were now nearly 100 soldiers in the hospital. 'We asked them why did you come here, why do you not go to your barracks, and they said they were given an order by their commander to hold the hospital,' Tembulatov said.

The soldiers seemed to have little stomach for their task. The nurses and doctors in the hospital described a frightened group of men who were reluctant to fight and even too scared to try to break out and run back to their barracks. They forced the nurses to go out and fetch their commander who lay wounded in the courtyard and made the doctors fetch in the bodies of their dead comrades from an APC that had been ambushed in front.

'Ten per cent of them were maybe courageous people, the rest of them were just out to save themselves, that was their mood. Whether they understood what they were doing was wrong, I don't know. But they had no fighting spirit. There were some who said, "Let's run to the barracks, it is not very far," but the rest did not support them,' Tembulatov recounted. 'There were ten or twelve conscript soldiers among them. They could not even lift their heads to look at you. Their unit had taken big losses,' Zarema Dadagova, a twenty-five-year-old nurse, recalled. 'The soldiers were hiding in the cellar with us. One said to me, "I have a wife and a son, I don't want to die." '

Conditions were growing desperate as the hospital ran out of food and water, and the Russian siege dragged into its fourth day. Finally the doctors and nurses negotiated with the Chechen fighters to allow the soldiers safe passage back to their barracks. They gathered some twenty nurses and doctors in white coats, mostly women, for they thought the Russian troops were less likely to harm them, and formed a human shield around the group of soldiers as they emerged slowly from the hospital. They walked up the street and round the corner to the Russian base where the soldiers told them 'Scram, fast'. Dadagova was among them. They fled down the street but as they turned the corner a barrage of mortars crashed around them, scattering the group. A doctor and a young girl were killed, and under heavy fire they decided to evacuate the hospital. It was a sickening episode, the Russian army had sunk to its very lowest, acting like terrorists in a spirit of fear and revenge.

*

The master of the attack on Grozny was the rebel commander Shamil Basayev. He sat in a tiny room in the cellar of an apartment building nursing a wounded foot. He wore a blue and white striped Russian army T-shirt and camouflage trousers and his head was shaved bald in the Chechen tradition, setting off his thick black beard. Relaxed, if in some pain, he had handed command over to his deputy, but had not left the battlefield. His cellar was right in the central market, just 200 yards from the front line, amid still-smoking houses and smashed apartment buildings. As he spoke, mortars landed regularly with a heavy crunch just a block away. The man who commanded the defence of Grozny during the early months of the war was back in town and presenting Moscow with a colossal challenge.

'The Russians could take the city back. It would take them half a year and they would have to destroy the town all over again. They could even take it in a month, but it would cost them ten to fifteen thousand men,' he said. By seizing the town he was forcing the Russians to fight at close quarters, something they did not like and did not do well, he explained. He had enough men and ammunition to hold on and also people organizing food and water and medical care for the fighters. 'So we will hang on and kill very many of their men, and then if our ammunition runs out and we have to leave, I can pull my men out in a day.' In the meantime he was making plans to attack the two Russian bases outside the city, at the airport and at Khankala, he said. Flies settled on the bloody bandage round his foot. A machine-gun bullet had broken a bone and hit a vein two days before, he said. 'For me, it is minor, a trifle,' he shrugged. He had been wounded several times during the war and still carried a bullet inside him. He could run if it were essential, he added, meanwhile he was on crutches. A pair stood in the corner.

He did not intend to attack and destroy every single Russian post around the town, just surround and persuade the men to surrender. 'If we run out of food we will eat Russian soldiers,' he said, with a laugh. 'That's a joke. They are all frightened that we will cut their throats,' he added. Asked if it was not reckless to humiliate Russia since it would probably bring terrible retribution down on the heads of his people, he snapped, 'Do you not think Russia has humiliated us for three hundred years? It cannot even feed its own people, that is humiliation. It should pay its hungry miners rather than spend the money on this war. Soldiers were eating dogs from the streets here in January, they were so hungry.'

His patience had run out, he said, after Moscow had gone back on its word to end the war peacefully and resumed blistering bombing raids in the mountains a month ago, just days after Yeltsin was safely re-elected. Despite obvious tiredness and a slight hand tremor, Basayev travelled across Grozny to see his deputy, Aslanbek Ismailov, who had taken over since he was wounded. He rode in a captured bank security van, the sort, with its cream body and bright green stripe, more often seen on the streets of Moscow than in a war zone. Inside Ismailov's office hung a huge wall map of the city, every Russian post and base outlined in dark ink, including the FSB hostel which was crossed out. But for those little circles, the vast expanse of the city was in Chechen hands.

*

Two Russian soldiers sat hunched on piles of sandbags by the door of their post on the bridge near the city canning factory. They were enjoying the warm sunlight, breathing in the fresh air after days and nights down below in their bunker. Things had eased up for them, they had agreed a ceasefire with the Chechens to stop shooting at each other. Their post was an ugly jumble of grey cement blocks and sandbags. The nose of an automatic rifle poked out of a tiny lookout hole in the cement tower, trained on approaching cars. A deep trench, protected by a bank of earth, ran round their little fortress. Only half of their group of fifteen, an Interior Ministry police unit from Orenburg in the Urals, was left. Andrei, a senior sergeant, came out to talk. Dressed in light green camouflage overalls, he jumped the trench, unarmed, his feet thrust into his boots, the laces loose. He stood chatting in the sun, apparently relaxed.

The soldiers were trapped, unable to reach their headquarters only half a mile away. 'There are fighters on both sides of us,' Andrei said, gesturing up the river and across the bridge. 'The fighters are not scared to move around and we are, that's the difference. They are the bosses here.'

In the first days of the siege they had half a dozen wounded and one killed. On his second tour of duty in Chechnya, he said, the rebel action had amazed them all. 'You always expect something when you come here, but we never expected this,' he said. 'We are astonished that they made it down from the mountains in half an hour. We sent out the wounded on our APC but they knocked it out on the way. The boys never made it, we do not know what happened to them.' The remaining men had survived repeated attacks by Chechen fighters over the last seventeen days. 'They sent a representative to suggest we surrender, but we refused. It would be stupid. We can continue. We have enough weapons and food. We have enough to live with.' In fact they had been slithering down the river-bank to fetch filthy water from the River Sunzha and were critically low on food until an old Russian woman risked angering the Chechens and brought the Russian boys food and water.

Just then two carloads of Chechen fighters screeched to a halt by the post to investigate the small gathering. The Russian soldiers quickly ducked back in behind their sandbags while the Chechens, Kalashnikovs aloft, shouted for the Russsian commander to explain what they were doing. 'Do not make them angry. These are our boys,' the Chechen leader told us, grinning as he jerked his head towards the Russian soldiers. Then, their authority asserted, they piled back into the cars and drove way. 'We feel it is like the theatre. They are directing and the end is unknown,' said Vadim, a twenty-two-year-old Russian conscript.

*

In Moscow, Yeltsin turned out for his inauguration, an ashen, lifeless figure who seemed to be going through the motions like a robot. It was later revealed he had suffered a minor heart attack in between the first and second rounds of the elections. Now he slurred his words, standing woodenly as he read the oath of office. The ceremony was short, Yeltsin's part kept to a minimum. He then turned and walked stiffly off the stage. Afterwards he was shown on television raising his glass to the 1000 guests at a banquet in the Grand Kremlin Palace as Chernomyrdin proposed a toast. Perhaps mindful of celebrating while tragedy was unfolding once more in Grozny, he later announced an official day of mourning. Already hundreds of Russian soldiers were dead.

Yeltsin did at least make some crucial decisions on Chechnya in the next few days. Two days after his inauguration he made his new Security Council chief, Alexander Lebed, presidential envoy to Chechnya. Lebed had been an outspoken critic of the war from the very start, and on the campaign trail argued that Chechnya should be allowed to leave the Russian Federation if its people voted to do so in a national referendum. But once he joined the presidential staff he began to parrot the official line. He said he needed time to find out the true state of affairs and assess the situation. Probably Lebed, who made no effort to hide his ambitions, was waiting for the right moment to act.

Yeltsin called in Chernomyrdin and Lebed for a two-and-a-half-hour discussion on the crisis in Chechnya on 11 August. It was the sixth day of furious fighting in Grozny and Russian forces were no closer to repelling their attackers. That day the 276th Regiment made its push into the town, only to be decimated in a Chechen counter-attack. Straight after the meeting, Lebed flew down to Dagestan. From there he took a car and drove into Chechnya, travelling without bodyguards through the night up into the rebel-controlled hills. It was a dangerous drive, especially at night when jumpy Russian soldiers at checkpoints fired at anything and everything and Chechen rebels were on the move. Lebed came under fire twice, once definitely from a Russian post, he said later. Undeterred, he drove on to the home of Rizvan Lorzanov, a wealthy industrialist who had offered his house in the village of Noviye Atagi for peace talks. There, at midnight, Lebed met Maskhadov, chief spokesman Movladi Udugov and Shirvani Basayev. They talked until four in the morning and agreed to call a truce. Lebed then got back in his car and drove back down the mountain. 'I liked Lebed,' the host, Lorzanov, said afterwards. 'He said he wanted to end the war and I think he means it.'

Lebed had left it that Maskhadov would meet his Russian counterpart, the acting Russian commander of troops in Chechnya, General Konstantin Pulikovsky, the following day to agree terms for a ceasefire. 'We came to the conclusion that Russia will of course be able to crush Chechnya if it wants to. But the question is, is it necessary? Should hundreds and thousands of lives be sacrificed to achieve this Pyrrhic victory?' Lebed said. Back in Moscow the following day, he gave a tumultuous press conference, blasting virtually everyone in the entire government and presidential administration for their poor handling of the Chechen war and the latest crisis. He slammed the press services of the Power Ministries who 'have lost their tongues' and said they should be sacked. 'Let them go fishing and grow raspberries at their *dachas*,' he said, while he praised the chief Chechen spokesman Udugov for beating them at their job. 'There is no more important question in Russia than that of Chechnya. It is an open bleeding wound,' he declared. But after a year and a half of war, there was no organized method to crisis-solving in the Russian government, no clarity on who should take decisions, and no one responsible for their implementation, he said.

He claimed they had handed him responsibility for Chechnya in the hope that he would fail. 'Someone very much wants me to break my neck over this assignment,' he said. 'We will see. I like tasks of the highest order of difficulty, they excite me.' He joked about coming under fire in Chechnya. 'They opened fire twice, but they did that tenderly – as you see, they missed.'

Lebed was in fact at his most confident in the thick of war. He saw active service leading a parachute regiment in Afghanistan and then spent several years scotching outbreaks of violence around the Soviet Union. He latterly commanded the 14th Army in the breakaway region of Transdnestr, where he ruthlessly but efficiently stamped out an incipient civil war. His base in Tiraspol stood out for being ship-shape and well run. Lebed said he was appalled by what he saw on the ground in Chechnya and angry to see the state of the soldiers. 'I expected that things there were not great, I even knew that. But I did not expect them to be so bad,' he went on. 'Those weaklings manning those checkpoints –

hungry, lice-ridden and underclothed – or rather, clothed in blouses, coats, vests and sweaters and shawls, some boots of unknown shape or purpose – they can by no means represent the Interior Ministry or the Defence Ministry. I also suspect that partisans during the Second World War were better clothed,' he said. He had found 'indifferent and war-weary people, a lack of command, of any coordination and unfortunately, pretty low morale'. In sharp contrast, 'The Chechens have always been good fighters, so they have to be treated with respect. They are fine soldiers and no one should refer to them by derogatory names.' That one quote was conspicuously absent from Russian media reports of the press conference.

Lebed's first trip to Chechnya proved a turning-point in both his and the Russian government's approach to the war. A plain-talking military man, Lebed was now the first government official to speak about the situation in Chechnya as it really was. He compared it to the Soviet army's experience in Afghanistan. 'When we were entering that country, 90 per cent of the population were welcoming us, lining the roads, flowers in their hands. When we were withdrawing from it, we were hated by everyone,' he said. The main opposition came from people who lost relatives in the war. 'They became wolves,' Lebed said. 'No army in the world has a chance against such people.' The Soviet army had not only destroyed Afghanistan but damaged itself in the process, he said. 'We did not simply leave, we left with war wrapped around the tracks of our tanks and the wheels of our vehicles, taking it home, and it flared up on our soil.' At a later press conference he talked movingly of meeting soldiers' mothers in Chechnya searching for their sons. 'You see the crowd of wretched soldiers' mothers with hope in their eyes. You feel bitter because you know that the glimmer of hope in many of these eyes is destined to dim.'

He abandoned the official line of supporting Zavgayev as representative of the government in charge. 'I am going to talk to anyone who wields real influence over the situation,' he said. 'But he does not control the situation, does he?' he said of Zavgayev, adding that the Chechen leader had lied about the real state of affairs in the republic. Zavgayev's star was indeed waning fast. When he arrived in Moscow for Yeltsin's inauguration, the President's new Chief of Staff Anatoly Chubais barely let him put his feet on the tarmac before ordering him straight back to Grozny. Zavgayev kept drifting back to Moscow, however. Lebed took him back down to Grozny on another occasion in his own plane. 'How else are we going to force the little coward to be in the place he is supposed to govern?' he said with a sly smile spreading across his battered face.[5]

Lebed announced after his first trip to Chechnya that he had been granted full control of the armed forces and all government bodies connected with the republic. On 14 August Yeltsin signed a decree confirming this. It was the green light Lebed needed.

*

In Chechnya, Maskhadov had met his Russian counterpart, Lieutenant-General Konstantin Pulikovsky, on the road outside Noviye Atagi to organize the ceasefire. Pulikovsky had refused to come to the house for talks, as Lebed had, and after arriving by helicopter, waited by the Russian post, surrounded by tanks and APCs. Pulikovsky had lost a son in the Chechen war and now, when they met, refused to shake Maskhadov's proffered hand. His attitude did not bode well for the ceasefire. After their meeting the Chechen side announced a ceasefire would begin at midday the following day, but the Russian command denied anything final had been agreed at all. A tense peace did begin, but Russian forces resumed shelling barely twelve hours later. On 15 August Lebed arrived in Chechnya on another flying visit, this time to talk to the Chechen rebel President Yandarbiyev as well as Maskhadov. He flew into the military base at Khankala and went on to Noviye Atagi in a military helicopter.

Lebed was becoming embroiled in a political battle in Moscow. When he returned from his second trip he launched into a verbal attack on Kulikov, who had until then overall command of Chechnya. Lebed blamed him for allowing the rebel attack to happen. Everyone in Grozny had advance notice of the raid, civilians had even packed up and left town, but the command did nothing to stop it, he said. Later, in a closed session of the State Duma, he said the FSB already had information of a planned assault in late July but the information went unnoticed. Of the 139 roads leading into Grozny, Russians troops controlled fewer than fifty, Lebed said. 'In my book they should have controlled either all 139 or none at all. It comes to the same.'[6] The Chechen police under Zavgayev were heavily infiltrated by the rebels to the point that the Chechen Interior Minister could not trust them and had to use Russian bodyguards. Lebed accused Kulikov of being directly responsible for the nearly 500 Russian servicemen killed, the 1407 wounded and the 182 missing in action in the August siege, as well as the unknown number of civilian casualties.[7]

'The Interior Minister of Russia has failed in discharging his duty to his country. It is my profound conviction that he can no longer stay in the ministerial post,' he said. He also accused Kulikov of getting in the way of his efforts to bring peace. 'General Kulikov has said he will not obey me. He thinks he is Napoleon,' he said. He then made an open challenge, calling on the President to choose between himself and Kulikov: 'Only one should remain in this system, either Lebed or Kulikov.' Kulikov said the accusations reflected Lebed's 'maniacal' quest for power, but nevertheless submitted his resignation. Yeltsin refused to accept it, though, and Lebed seemed to back off from further confrontation.

*

The power struggle between Lebed and Kulikov, who later admitted he was against making peace in Chechnya, had already precipitated more fighting. Planes and helicopters returned to the skies blasting the city of Grozny, just two days after the ceasefire was called. Then the generals went completely overboard. Pulikovsky issued an ultimatum to the rebels to withdraw from the city. He gave the citizens of Grozny forty-eight hours to leave the city before he launched 'massive military operations' to dislodge the fighters. Tikhomirov, the permanent commander in Chechnya, returned from holiday and voiced support for his deputy's ultimatum. The order, it seemed, had been signed by Yeltsin.

Lebed immediately rebuked the commanders for an ultimatum 'they had absolutely no right to give', but Yeltsin's press office confirmed that the President had personally formulated the command. Lebed said the signature was forged. A huge furore erupted as the question of who was running things in the Kremlin arose. Yeltsin had not appeared in public since his inauguration ten days before and was said to be away looking for a holiday home, although in reality he was still convalescing after his heart attack. In fact it may have been Lebed himself who gave the order. Kulikov describes a government meeting where Lebed laid out his plan. 'That ultimatum was agreed with Lebed. We had a meeting of government ministers and Lebed said, "I have discussed this. [The plan is] I leave [Chechnya], Pulikovsky gives his ultimatum and shakes them up a bit, and then I go down and cancel the ultimatum."' Kulikov recounted.[8]

Whoever gave the order, it caused an exodus from the city of Grozny like never before. Hundreds of cars, lorries and buses jostled on the dusty road leading east out of Grozny, the only exit guaranteed as safe by Russian troops. Children screamed as parents shouted at passing traffic for a lift, amid blaring horns and roaring engines. Trucks deposited refugees at an intersection and others scrambled into their places on top of piles of baggage.

'We heard on the television that we had forty-eight hours,' Idris Musayev, a doctor, said. 'The talks were just a game. We thought Lebed would manage it but for now it is all over.' Looking back at the city through the scrum of refugees, he said, 'They will storm it and then loot everything and it will be the civilians who will suffer.' Nearly 1000 vehicles were backed up for miles, three abreast in a traffic jam that snaked all the way into the city centre. Refugees trudged by on foot through the choking dust, carrying their possessions stuffed in yellow plastic bags. Tractors and trucks towed broken-down cars, many with smashed windows and pockmarked paintwork from the ten-day bombardment. One family perched on the back of a truck that had no trailer, clinging to the metal base as it crashed over potholes. Two teenage boys lounged in armchairs on top of another lorry loaded with household belongings. 'There will be a storm. One hundred per cent,' said Aina Itayeva, a mother looking for a lift with her two young children. 'Why should we not believe it when they already destroyed it once?'

The International Committee of the Red Cross appealed to the Russian command to extend the deadline, saying more than 130,000 people had fled the city, but at least as many remained behind. Now that the elections were over, Western governments joined the chorus of alarm, condemning the Russian threat and urging Moscow to refrain from further military action. US President Bill Clinton sent a letter to Yeltsin. 'The President has been deeply concerned about the escalation of fighting in and around Grozny,' said Michael McCurry, the White House spokesman. 'This cycle of violence must come to an end.'

Lebed, the troubleshooter, flew down to Chechnya amidst the uproar, saying he would resolve it by the morning and stop Russian troops from launching the threatened assault. 'We will no longer talk in the language of ultimatums,' he said as he set off for a meeting with Maskhadov. Pulikovsky had made a 'bad joke' and would be removed to another job. He sat face to face

with Maskhadov, upstairs in the large house of a Chechen
businessman, over a large colour map of Chechnya spread on a
table, at ease like a man playing poker, in his shirtsleeves, smoking
cigarettes from a black cigarette-holder. Asked if the bombardment of Grozny would stop, he said, 'I am going to Grozny to see
to it that things are quiet.' Late that night he went back down the
mountain to the Russian base at Khankala. General Tikhomirov,
who had served as Lebed's deputy a few years before in Transdnestr, greeted him with a broad smile, according to Russian
journalists accompanying him. The two men talked through the
night, only retiring at 5 a.m. Later that morning, 21 August,
Lebed was back in Noviye Atagi where in eight hours of talks he
finally clinched a deal with Maskhadov to end the fighting.
Russian troops were to pull out of Grozny to their bases outside
the town. The Chechens were also to pull back to their villages
and the two sides would set up joint headquarters around the city
to make joint patrols and keep the peace. 'We remembered we
both served in one army,' Lebed said, smiling at Maskhadov. 'We
many times believed in peace talks,' Maskhadov replied. 'Now I
want to take the word of an officer, that yes is yes, and no is no,'
he said.

Lebed flew back to Moscow looking like the man who had
saved the day, but Yeltsin refused to see him. The Russian
President had finally resurfaced in the Kremlin and had delivered
a swift rebuke to his Security Council chief. 'I am not completely
satisfied with Lebed's work. During the election campaign, he
said if he had power, he could solve Chechnya. Well, now he has
power and unfortunately I still cannot see any results,' he said,
adding, 'But we're not desperate yet.'

*

On the ground in Grozny, Lebed's success was immediately
apparent. Complete silence reigned in the city, for the first time
since rebels attacked over two weeks before. The road leading

east out of the city, a maelstrom of desperate refugees two days before, was empty. Dust blew along the deserted streets, stirred by the occasional car. A few residents were out fetching water in buckets, walking slowly, hugging the buildings. Stray dogs, barking frenziedly, chased the lone car that passed by. It was the only time during the whole war in Chechnya that the Russian side fully observed a ceasefire. Not a shot was fired nor did a single shell explode. On the ground Lebed was in control.

Across town, a sorry convoy pulled out of the centre behind a Russian military jeep flying a white flag. Four Russian army trucks each towed a broken-down APC, the battered armoured vehicles bumping along on flat tyres. Chechen fighters, armed with Kalashnikov rifles, grenades strapped to their chests, sat in the cabs alongside Russian soldiers driving. The Chechen commander Israpilov watched them go. His men had surrounded them, units from Russia's 101st Brigade, one of the most notorious serving in Chechnya, in their barracks inside three tall apartment buildings. Now he had an order to let them go. Beside him stood Russian Lieutenant-Colonel Igor Rudnyov, a red and silver medal for excellent service on his chest. This was Maskhadov and Lebed's peace deal in action. Men who had been fighting each other for the last twenty months were now supervising the peace together. The two men were organizing the Russian pullout from the city. Each column, each vehicle had a Chechen fighter sitting up with the Russian driver. Another joint convoy was touring all the besieged Russian posts with food and water, and evacuating the wounded. The Russian soldiers, unarmed, sat at the wheels, stony-faced. The Chechens, in euphoric mood, chatting and shouting to friends, climbed up beside them. Russian troops would withdraw within ten days, the Russian commander, Rudnyov said. A Chechen commander accompanying him added that the Chechen fighters would also be pulling out. 'Just those who are needed to guard the city will stay. The rest will go back to their bases,' he said. 'That's good,' the Russian said with a nod. 'No one won, there were losses on both sides, you cannot talk of winning or losing. We came to an agreement.'

It was a carefully orchestrated withdrawal to prevent any clashes, but there was no avoiding the fact that the Russian troops were in defeat. Down at heel, some angry, some depressed, they knew they were giving up the city to the Chechens. For a couple of months they were to man joint district headquarters to patrol the city and keep the peace, but from the start the Chechens were in charge. 'We just go along for the ride,' one Russian police officer said with an unhappy shrug.

*

For some men who had fought in the latest battle, Lebed's peace deal was too hard to swallow. It was nine o'clock in the morning and two soldiers were cooking up kasha – buckwheat – and tinned meat in a frying pan by the street. 'Do you have any vodka?' one asked. On hearing no, the older one looked away down the street, as if trying hard to contain his anger. They had lived through the heaviest fighting of all, ambushed as they came into the city, and then apparently forgotten as they hid in bombed-out buildings for days, with no food, no communications and running perilously low on ammunition. They met the news of Lebed's peace deal with leaden silence.

Dark, greasy stains marked where the bodies of dead Russian soldiers had baked in the hot August sun for days on the street. That morning soldiers with cotton masks over their faces had shovelled up the putrefying bodies into silver body bags, almost collapsing from the overpowering stench. Now a second group of Russian soldiers, led by a Chechen commander, was scouring the ruins for more bodies. A military truck, flying a white flag, followed behind them with their grim cargo.

A miserable group of Russian soldiers watched. They had been holding out in the ruins of a house for over two weeks, just 100 yards from the government compound, on what was the only clear front line in the city. They were still tense, demoralized and dog-tired. 'We did not even know that our guys were in the house across the way,' said Andrei, a skinny warrant officer with a thick moustache. He wore an old-fashioned uniform that looked too small for him. All he had known was that there were Chechen fighters who kept them pinned down in the rubble. None of the Russian soldiers had been issued with flak jackets. 'We're just cannon fodder,' Andrei said. They had even come under friendly fire when their column first advanced into the city centre in the pouring rain. 'They were firing on their own men. They fired on us and we fired on them. It was raining so hard I had to empty out my boots.'

A burnt-out tank lay amidst spent shell cases in the middle of the street, its gun turret upturned, blown clean off its body. Two tracked vehicles dragged it away down the street, its rusting iron hulk protesting as it grated against the tram-lines. The soldiers were waiting to be pulled out too. Andrei and his men, who were sleeping rough, were impatient to get out. But Sergei, standing at the gate of the government compound, was angry that Lebed was ordering them out and leaving the Chechens in charge. His black bandana, tight across his forehead, gave him a piratical look. 'Why did he start this ceasefire? We should have fought to the end. They should only pull out in order to give themselves a freer hand to attack the city,' he said. 'Raze the city to the ground and wipe out the whole nation, that would have been the answer. So many good guys have been killed. They died and I do not know why. When I came here I did not think there was much point in fighting. But then my friends died and have left behind families and children. How am I going to look them in the eye?' He refused to accept that the war was unwinnable despite the heavy losses his own battalion had taken. Fifty men were left out of 160, he said, and only two officers.

The soldiers in Grozny all felt the same on one thing. Their leaders had betrayed them, throwing them into Chechnya and then abandoning them. Now they were forcing them to accept defeat. Sergei was scathing about the senior commanders in Khankala who sent his unit into Grozny with no backup. 'All the generals were sitting in the coordination centre and there is this big bang. They are all concussed and Moscow is saying they are all heroes. They are like rats, they were all sitting there just waiting to be rescued.' In the end he felt no loyalty to them. After eleven years in service he was still a junior sergeant. 'I want to go up to warrant officer. If I do not get it I will leave. I have two young kids, Alex, five, and Zhenya, twelve. I need to bring them up.'

*

As the troops were pulling out, a strange ceremony was taking place in Noviye Atagi. Maskhadov was preparing his men to work together with Russian troops manning district headquarters. They gathered for their final orders, the Chechen fighters and Russian soldiers lining up opposite each other. The Russian general made a short announcement of the task in hand. Then it was Maskhadov's turn. He stood in silence, his hand on his chin, looking down at the ground. No one spoke, everyone waited, straining their ears. When he began his voice was full of emotion. 'Everyone had his own understanding of this war. This side,' he said, gesturing at the Russian soldiers, 'say they were protecting constitutional order, maintaining territorial integrity, that one can also understand. Our side were protecting our homeland against the destruction of a people. We want no one to be given the right to annihilate the Chechen people on Chechen land.' He looked sternly down the line of Russian soldiers. 'The most important thing today is to understand that we must not use war, force and barbarity as a means to an end, as so many politicians want us to, as a step to power. Please, for God's sake,' he said, his voice cracking, 'today it is very important that each of you understands that we are entrusting the way to peace to you and it depends on each one of you. You must go with any Chechen, stand next to him, serve next to him, live beside him, eat with him, drink with him,' he said to the Russians. Then to the Chechens: 'You all saw how they were bombing, killing, how your comrades were dying, but you must keep it to yourself, deep down.'

Joint relations were possible, he said, they had served together before. There were probably Russian officers he had trained now serving in Chechnya. He then blamed Russia's generals for dragging their army and their country to a dangerous all-time low. 'At the beginning of the war I said to Generals Babichev, Rokhlin, Kvashnin, "Stop this war, sit down with us and I, as a former officer of the Soviet army and the Russian army, I give you my word, let's think out how we can end this so the Russian army does not lose face." They did not want to. They thought killing us all would end it. So very unfortunately in the eyes of the world, and of all of us who used to think the Soviet army was great and unbeaten, at the hands of these generals, the army and the state are losing face.'

It was the ultimate irony that the rebel commander Maskhadov, who had led the final rout of the Russian army in Chechnya, was still underneath so deeply attached to the army that he was angry to see it brought so low. He quickly developed a rapport with Lebed as a general he could take at his word. He also recognized Lebed as someone who cared deeply about the state of the Russian army. Lebed had flown down to Chechnya after Yeltsin had refused to see him, determined to prove he could win peace despite the obstacles. The mood of the two men, Maskhadov and Lebed, was to make it work once and for all. They were after an agreement that would not only consolidate the ceasefire but seal the peace permanently. As the troops continued pulling out of Grozny into the big Russian bases on the edges of the city, Lebed spent long hours negotiating with the Chechen leadership on a political deal, occasionally taking time out to play chess with his host, Lorzanov.

By 31 August all Russian troops had left Grozny and Lebed and Maskhadov had a deal. They signed it with some ceremony in Khasavyurt in Dagestan. It was an amalgamation of many previous proposals but with one key difference. Any decision on Chechnya's status was deferred for five years and Lebed did not insist on phrasing that declared Chechnya as part of Russia. The document was titled instead: 'Joint Relations between the Russian Federation and the Chechen Republic.' It was full of lofty ideals about protecting human rights, the right to self-determination and the rights of ethnic minorities. The two sides would have five years to work out their 'joint relations', that is Chechnya's status, and an agreement on the issue must be reached by 31 December 2001, which will be after Yeltsin's second term as President has expired. The withdrawal of Russian troops would continue and a joint Russian–Chechen commission was set up to run the economy. The commission was a face-saver for Russia, since it did virtually nothing during its short existence and the Chechens soon took over.

The Khasavyurt agreement nevertheless caused an angry storm of protest in Moscow. Most of the press greeted Lebed's achievement coldly and many criticized him for 'losing' Chechnya. The Duma returned from its recess and deputies immediately denounced it as beginning the 'disintegration of Russia'. Kulikov criticized it as an admission of Russia's defeat in Chechnya, and called it 'high treason'. Later he said it was because Lebed agreed different terms than those already sanctioned in Moscow. Lebed hotly defended his plan. 'All talk that Russia is leaving Chechnya in shame is sacrilege. Russia is not leaving, it has only put an end to its shame,' he told Parliament. The war had killed up to 6000 Russian soldiers and wounded close on 20,000, he said. 'We paid a very high price for what could have been accomplished through

negotiations.' The following day Yeltsin finally met Lebed and
endorsed the plan, saying, 'The main thing is that the bloodshed
has been stopped.' The war he had set in motion had killed some
50,000 civilians, at least 6000 Russian troops and 2000 to 3000
Chechen fighters.[9]

The storm was aimed largely at Lebed personally, since his
overt ambition and harsh criticisms of virtually everyone had
made him many enemies. But the outburst in the Duma was also
an expression of Russian's pain and humiliation over the entire
débâcle in Chechnya. For the first time in nearly 300 years of
Russian expansion in the North Caucasus, the empire was
receding and its army in retreat. In a closed session of Parliament
Lebed had laid out the necessity of his deal. The decision to pull
out of Grozny had been a military one, the Russian army had
been at a complete loss as to what to do. 'When I arrived there
the Russian group of forces was on the verge of defeat – 1181
men were trapped without food, water or medicine. Ammunition
was running out. Units were starting to surrender. Not just
eighteen-year-old soldiers, but the whole army, the Krasnodar
OMON, a police battalion from Tolyatti,' Lebed said. 'Was it
really worth carrying on in such a situation? . . . There could be
no talk of victory.[10]

Lebed blamed the Russian defeat on the poor state of the army
– underfunding, lack of ideology and lack of good leadership.
The Russian soldiers in Chechnya were 'tired, exhausted and
indifferent to everything. Men who do not know why they are
there, who do not understand what constitutional duty means.
Nobody explained this to them either before they were sent there,
or after they got there.' The Chechens, on the other hand, were
'absolutely confident that they are fighting for their freedom,
people who have lost relatives, in short people who have a very
good reason to fight seriously'. The Chechens were even better
armed than the Russians, he said. The lack of a general headquarters to unite the Russian command he likened to 'delivering

your blows with the fingers of your hand spread wide. The one who does that simply breaks his fingers.'

But above all it was the futility of war that he stressed. 'In general I am fed up with making war. And then I know for sure that any war is first a deadlock and then a meaningless catastrophe. I know for sure that all wars, even if they are hundred-year wars, end in negotiations and peace. So, should one fight a hundred years and kill lots of people to come to a negotiated settlement? Perhaps we should start with it.' There was no doubting Lebed's determination to end the war, but his record was not wholly clean. There was a possibility that he had known and even agreed to the attack on Makhkety in July that triggered the whole August débâcle. Although Kulikov was still in command of Chechnya, Tikhomirov had visited Moscow just before and met his old colleague Lebed as well as Kulikov. After a year and a half of fighting his former Russian comrades, Maskhadov had few illusions. He said he did not bring it up with Lebed. 'I did not want to go over the war, let it be on his conscience. I wanted him to be a man who had not spilt blood. But in reality I do not know,' he said. He paused, then added, 'I do know one thing. That if the Russians had had the possibility to fight further then no one could have stopped this war. It simply was such that a politician who wanted to be the man to stop the war came along and those who were against him were just not able to carry on the war at that time.'

Lebed, upsetting everyone in government and embroiled in more and more controversy, was fired in October. But his deal in Chechnya held. Yandarbiyev came to Moscow to sign a further deal with Chernomyrdin on 3 October, and Maskhadov, donning a suit as Chechnya's Prime Minister, signed another one on 23 November. The same day, in a final big concession, Yeltsin ordered the last two brigades of Russian troops to pull out from Chechnya. The troops were all gone by the end of the year and a date was set for new Chechen elections. The war in Chechnya was over.

Epilogue:
Chechen Independence

On 27 January 1997 Chechens voted in presidential and parliamentary elections for a republic whose status no one had agreed on.

They put on their best show, determined to show pride amidst the destruction. No one could remember an election like it. The old men turned out in their *papakhas*, while their wives came behind, wrapped up in headscarves. At some polling stations there was a two-hour queue to vote and voting had to be extended for two hours until 10 p.m. 'I've never felt so good, my heart is rejoicing,' said eighty-one-year-old Rashid Bazayev, resting on a chair with his *papakha* and staff and waiting for the queue to subside a little.

The polling stations were makeshift clubs and schools. On the edge of Grozny, one technical college had no windows and was still shot up from the latest fighting. At one polling station the only light was provided by the lit flame from a rent gas pipe. The elections were conducted in an orderly fashion. There were signs in polling stations saying 'No entry with weapons' and these were observed. Chechnya has not disarmed – nor has it for the past 200 years – but no one was being intimidated to vote one way or another.

Everyone chipped in. Vakha Gaisumov had come from Moscow specially to set up a little polling station in Grozny for 496 refugees from the destroyed villages of Bamut, Stary Achkoi and Orekhovo. He was the chairman of the polling commission and his wife and daughter were his deputies. A man from Orekhovo had laid on a bus so that nineteen refugees from there could vote. One of those on board was Vakha Musayev, sixty-nine, who had twice made the *haj* to Mecca and was dressed proudly in his long green coat and hat with red and white bands.

It was a very ambitious election to hold so soon after the war had ended and the main point of controversy was that tens of thousands of refugees from the war now living in Russia, Kazakhstan and elsewhere were not allowed to vote, something that naturally benefited the rebel victors. Only those who could afford to fly into Chechnya or were close enough to be bussed in from border areas were able to cast their votes. In the end more than 400,000 Chechens voted.

Seventy-two foreign observers from the OSCE arrived to give the election a verdict on legitimacy. They stayed overnight in unheated rooms in the civilian airport before scattering out to five regional centres. Security was exceptionally tight and each pair of observers had three armed guards with them. The OSCE was strictly observing the election as though it were one in a region of Russia, although there was not a Russian election official in sight and all the candidates were supporters of Chechen independence. When pressed on this, the head of the OSCE mission in Grozny, Tim Guldimann, affected surprise and said, 'Of course Chechnya is a part of the Russian Federation.'

Election day seemed to confirm the impression that the war was over. The impact of the war was still dawning on Chechens and the evidence of it will surround them for years. However many times you see it, the appalling destruction of Grozny takes the breath away. In the centre of the city, where there used to be neo-classical civic buildings and tall apartment blocks, there are now blackened shells, heaps of rubble or simply large areas of sky. Long grass grows in what used to be the main square in front of a pile of rubble that used to be the Presidential Palace.

Away from the areas of the worst destruction some kind of life had returned. Buses were running. There were grey-uniformed traffic policemen on the streets attempting to fine you for going through the red light on one of Grozny's two traffic lights. The irrepressible Grozny market was swinging with life again, selling Iranian wardrobes, Italian clothes and kiwi fruit.

Valentina Malsagova, widow of the Chechen dissident Dziya-yudin Malsagov, had survived the war, but only just. Her flat in the red-brick building built by English oil workers in the 1920s had twice been in the thick of the fighting, first in January 1995, then in August 1996. Both times it had been looted, first by Russian soldiers, then by either fighters or freelancers. The other half of the building across the courtyard had gone up in flames in August. Her list of tragedies was not untypical for a resident of Grozny who had lived through the war. Her mother had died sick and untended in the first days of the bombing in her flat in the north part of the town. When they reached her it was too late. Her late husband's house and apple orchard in the village of Stary Achkoi had been levelled in the spring of 1996. Then, when the war seemed to be over, in October her younger son Oleg went missing. His body turned up a few weeks later with four bullets in it in a wood near the main road to Ingushetia. No one knows who did it but Valentina suspects it was departing Russian soldiers.

The pain of thousands of Chechens who are still searching for their missing relatives is an open wound that will never be healed. The task of Hussein Khamidov's Missing Persons Commission to trace prisoners or find and identify the many dead is a daunting one that will take years of determined application. The Russian mothers are no better off. Some are still touring Chechnya looking for their sons or searching through the hundreds of burnt and decomposed bodies in the military morgue in Rostov. As of April 1997 1,231 Russian soldiers were listed as missing in action and over 100 were thought to be still in captivity. 1300 Chechens are still lost without trace.

When Malsagova and her husband moved into her flat forty years before in January 1957, as some of the first returnees from

Kazakhstan, her husband was one of only two Chechens living in forty-nine flats. 'Now I am the only Russian left,' she says. Most of the Russians of Grozny have left or are leaving, driven out by fear of the future and crime, to which they are more vulnerable than others. Malsagova's main thoughts are on getting her pension, which has not been paid for eight months. Her daughter-in-law is about to resume 'shuttle-trading' to Dubai to try to earn some cash.

The Chechen authorities organized the elections in haste partly to consolidate their victory quickly and partly to fill the power vacuum left by the end of the war. As much as a President the country needed a Parliament to give some kind of representation to the different regions. It was the fifth since 1990. None of the others had lasted their full term. A field commander, Ruslan Alikhajiev, was named Speaker of the Parliament.

All sixteen candidates for President (of whom there were thirteen by election day) pledged they were committed to Chechen independence. The candidates included Dudayev's old ally, then opponent, Yusup Soslambekov, who achieved something of a record by getting a little over 500 votes or 0.1 per cent of the vote. Ruslan Khasbulatov did not stand. His brother was kidnapped just before the election and was released soon afterwards, evidently as a way of preventing him from standing. It was a vicious act that tarnished the elections, but Khasbulatov's hour had passed anyway.

It was an election fought among the victors of the war. The acting President, Zelimkhan Yandarbiyev, struggled right from the start. He had little personal clout in Chechnya and his only card was that he was the successor to Jokhar Dudayev, even, in the eyes of the naïve, the 'acting President' until Dudayev returned from the dead. Four days before polling day Yandarbiyev issued a decree renaming Grozny Jokhar-Ghala (Jokhar City). The population did not rise to the gesture. Field commander and former actor Akhmed Zakayev had plastered posters appropriately over the ruins of the Lermontov Theatre declaring that 'The rebirth of national culture is the basis of the rebirth of the nation'. Information Minister Movladi Udugov had the reputation of a fast-talking cynic and spin doctor, but had unconvincingly reinvented himself as the sober, black-suited proponent of 'Islamic Order'. As befitted his profession, Udugov had the slickest campaign adverts. He said his campaign money had come from 'friends'. The speculation was that it had come from Saudi sources.

It was soon obvious there were only two real candidates, the two main military leaders on the rebel side, Aslan Maskhadov and Shamil Basayev. They had very contrasting styles that represented the two traditional Chechen poles – the plains and the mountains. The thirty-two-year-old Basayev was true to his Vedeno roots, a flamboyant, unyielding highlander. The hostage seizure at Budyonnovsk made him, in Russia's eyes, an international terrorist, so a vote for Basayev was a slap in the face for Russia. He waged a combative campaign with big rallies in the centre of Grozny. He cracked jokes and took on hecklers. His campaign took an ugly turn in which he called his opponents 'crooks' and suggested Maskhadov would be soft on the Russians.

Maskhadov by contrast was a plainsman from the Nadterechny Region and very quiet and reserved. He was worried about his security and there were no big rallies. Groups of elders came to him for long discussions. Access to the press was very limited. His dignified and modest style went down well in a conservative society like Chechnya.

Maskhadov won handsomely in the first round, collecting 59 per cent of the vote. Had more refugees been allowed to vote, his victory would have been ever bigger. His victory was a vote for peace and pragmatism. For all their warlike traditions, Chechens are no different from anyone else in wanting a peaceful future for their children, jobs and stability. They saw Maskhadov as the man who could deliver that, as the man who could work with the Russians.

Maskhadov and Basayev were comrades-in-arms and there seemed to be little possibility of an 'Afghan option', as some Russian observers fondly predicted, in which the commanders on the victorious side started fighting each other. The solidarity principle between the victors was very high and the social mechanisms against internecine warfare was still very strong. This was confirmed two months after the election when Maskhadov appointed Basayev and the other top field commander, Ruslan Gelayev, to his inner cabinet. When Maskhadov travelled to Mecca in April, Basayev stood in for him as Prime Minister.

With Maskhadov elected, there was a strong feeling of *déjà vu*. Chechnya had returned to square one. Even perhaps to square minus one. Just as five years before, Moscow had a rebellious region on its southern rim which had declared independence. But there was a key difference. Moscow had burnt itself severely in trying to use force on Chechnya and for now was cowed. In his state-of-the-nation speech to both Houses of Parliament in March 1997, Yeltsin admitted as much. 'The Chechen crisis taught us much,' he said and went on to speak of rebuilding trust step by step through negotiations. It is unlikely that Russia really has taken on board all the lessons of the conflict in Chechnya and there is some evidence that it is back to its old tricks of covert destabilization, but for the moment it appears to have been persuaded to use diplomacy and economic levers rather than military might.

Another stark difference is the Chechen President himself. In Maskhadov, in contrast to Dudayev, Moscow had a leader it could work with. Even before the final tally was announced, Yeltsin had sent Maskhadov a telegram of congratulations carefully phrased to be ambiguous about Chechnya's status. It hoped there would be constructive partnership between the 'organs of power of the Russian Federation and the Chechen Republic'. Moscow then sent Ivan Rybkin, the Secretary of the Kremlin Security Council, to the inauguration. His predecessor Alexander Lebed also attended.

Yeltsin has softened his position on Chechnya and very obliquely admitted he was wrong about the war. When Yury Kalmykov, the only minister to stand up to him over the invasion, died in January 1997, Yeltsin was the first person to put a name to his public obituary. Not long afterwards, he presented a press award to Otto Latsis, the most prominent newspaper critic of the war. Yeltsin did this without once mentioning the word 'Chechnya' or expressing remorse, but it was a very indirect sign that he recognized his brutal stance in 1994 was a mistake.

But the cause of the war, Chechnya's bid for independence, remains unresolved. Independence is a tricky concept. Chechnya is now *de facto* independent of Russia. It has its own army, own government and is prepared to defend its borders. On the other hand, no foreign state has recognized Chechen independence or is likely to until Russia does so. This means, as one Chechen minister said, 'The United Nations does not even have the right to read our letters.' Maskhadov speaks of obtaining international guarantees to prevent Russia invading again but for the meantime he will have to rely on his own military strength.

And in many ways Chechnya is less independent than before. The short-term outlook for the country is very bleak. The economy has been devastated by the war. There is no oil flowing into the Grozny refineries, and only small earnings from the meagre 1.4 million tonnes that Chechnya extracts itself. Rich oil reserves in the Caspian Sea could provide a life-belt if transported through Chechnya's pipelines on the way from Baku to Novorossiisk, but any deal will be dependent on cooperation with Russia. Transportation costs will scarcely swell Chechnya's coffers, though, and Grozny desperately needs to rebuild its refining business, which will demand serious investment.

Economic pressure is a game Moscow is very good at playing. One of its last acts before pulling out was to restrict air traffic to Grozny airport. Hussein Khamidov, now named Minister for Civil Aviation, has opened the civilian airport but cannot receive large planes or flights from abroad. He faces months of negotiating with Russia to get the restriction overturned. The borders with Russia are open but the Russian Interior Ministry is boosting its presence around Chechnya and could later enforce a blockade if it wanted to. Russia is unlikely to stump up much financial aid for Chechnya since it is mired in financial crisis itself and the State Duma, dominated by nationalists and Communists, controls the budget. Moscow has promised to pay 'contributions' but is unlikely to sign a deal without winning political concessions from the Chechens, which in turn the Chechens will never give so soon after the war. Maskhadov hopes to look abroad for assistance and investment but there will be few takers. Chechnya will be stuck inside the ruble economy for a long time, which means it cannot raise its own credits.

Chechnya is now dangerous in a new way. Since the end of the war, law and order has virtually collapsed and the new leadership has not been able to impose discipline. Six foreign members of the International Committee of the Red Cross were murdered in December 1996 in what was almost certainly a politically motivated killing. All the foreign aid agencies pulled out of the republic and most will probably remain away until the case is solved. The republic is teaming with armed men with no obvious allegiance. Kidnapping for ransom has also spiralled out of control – in the first three months of 1997 six Russian journalists and one Italian were taken hostage in an atmosphere of worsening lawlessness.

Maskhadov tried to make his inauguration an international ceremony, but foreign delegations from the Baltics and Ukraine were denied Russian visas, a simple lever that Russia can still use until Grozny airport is allowed to open to foreign traffic. The Chechen diaspora, in Moscow and further afield, represents the best chance for reviving the war-torn republic. Satellite communications, television companies and travel agencies have already been set up in Chechnya.

In the meantime there will be poverty and a thriving black economy once more. There is every danger that it will again turn into a spivs' and mafiosi's haven as under Dudayev. The sense of *déjà vu* heightened in Grozny market. At the north end, in exactly the same place where they were three years before, knots of men in long dark leather coats were playing billiards and offering guns for sale.

The tragedy of Chechnya is that the war could have been avoided and pride satisfied on both sides if the Chechens could have struck a deal with Moscow on 'special status' or a moratorium on independence in 1992 and 1993. The Chechens could have agreed to it even if they didn't intend to observe it. Dudayev said several times that if he had had a face-to-face meeting with Yeltsin everything could have been sorted out. Possibly such a meeting would not have achieved anything. But more than 60,000 deaths later it would have been worth an attempt. While Moscow repeated the slogan of 'territorial integrity', Chechnya repeated the slogan of 'independence'. The issue was really one of freedom and human rights of a long-oppressed people. Using the formulae 'sovereignty' or 'self-determination', there were plenty of possibilities for constructive compromise.

If the Chechens had got a deal, similar to or better than the one Moscow struck with Tatarstan, giving them economic and cultural autonomy and control over the oil industry, the Chechens could have started out properly on the difficult road to state-building. Dudayev rejected the evolutionary approach in favour of a Bolshevik-style seizure of power. Moscow, with its historic ignorance of the region and imperialist arrogance, was too blundering to reach a compromise. But the war was about independence and it is now an issue drawn in blood. People who never thought about what it really meant to be independent have lost their homes to Russian bombing, seen relatives die, seen their menfolk disappear into filtration camps. Now, they say, how can we have the guarantee that it won't happen again one day and be regarded as an 'internal matter of Russia'? It is a hard question to answer.

Imperceptibly, however, the idea of letting Chechnya secede, one day at least, has come on to the political agenda in Moscow. Attitudes in Russia have changed. Opinion polls consistently show that the majority of Russians would be happy to 'let Chechnya go'. They are fed up with Chechnya, which is a source of consistent woe and pain from their television screens. By the year 2001, the deadline for deciding Chechnya's status, the public mood in Russia may have shifted even further. Russia will also have a new President in 2000.

For the West, Chechnya is way down on the list of priorities with Russia and not a reason to destabilize a relationship already made delicate by NATO expansion and the complex internal political situation. Questions have never been raised about the inviolability of an existing international frontier and are unlikely to start with small and troublesome Chechnya. The cue will be taken from Russia. The next five years will probably decide everything. The first question is whether Chechnya can survive at all, whatever its status. It has disappeared off the world news and has dropped well down the agenda of the Russian government. It will be very much up to the Chechens themselves to survive on their own.

Grozny–Moscow, April 1997

Appendix 1:
Cast of Characters 1990–1997

Aushev, Ruslan – Afghan war veteran and President of Ingushetia from March 1993.

Avturkhanov, Umar – Head of the Chechen opposition Provisional Council, 1994. Member of pro-Moscow opposition government, 1995.

Babichev, Ivan, Major-General – Commander of the western group of forces in Chechnya during invasion and storming of Grozny, 1994–5.

Barsukov, Mikhail – Leading Kremlin hawk. Head of the counter-intelligence service, the FSB, 1995–6.

Basayev, Shamil – Most famous Chechen field commander, who commanded Central Front and led raid on Budyonnovsk, 14–19 June 1995. Runner-up in Chechen presidential elections, January 1997. Deputy Prime Minister in new Chechen government.

Basayev, Shirvani – Younger brother of Shamil, field commander, Prefect of Vedeno from 1995–7.

Beno, Shamil – Chechen Foreign minister in 1992.

Borovoi, Konstantin – Liberal Russian politician and Member of Parliament.

Chernomyrdin, Viktor – Russian Prime Minister since December 1992.

Deinekin, Pyotr – Head of the Russian air force since October 1992.

Dudayev, Jokhar – President of Chechnya from November 1991 until his death in April 1996.

Filatov, Sergei – Kremlin Chief of Staff, 1993–6, patron of the Chechen opposition.

Gaidar, Yegor – Acting Russian Prime Minister, 1992. Thereafter head of the liberal Democratic Choice of Russia party and leading critic of the Chechen war.

Gantemirov, Beslan – Organizer of the paramilitary National Guard that helped Dudayev to power in 1991. Mayor of Grozny, 1991–3 after which he went into opposition to Dudayev. Again Mayor of Grozny, 1995. Arrested and imprisoned in Moscow, May 1996.

Gamsakhurdia, Zviad – Nationalist dissident, elected President of Georgia in 1991. Overthrown in the New Year of 1991–2, took refuge in Chechnya. Died in 1993, trying to retake power in Georgia.

Gelayev, Ruslan – Second most senior Chechen field commander, commander of Western Front.

Grachev, Pavel – Russian Defence Minister from 1992 until June 1996, commander of invasion force.

Guldimann, Tim – Swiss head of the Assistance Group of the Organization for Security and Cooperation in Europe in Chechnya from January 1996.

Gyarmati, Istvan – Hungarian diplomat, headed OSCE delegation to Chechnya, January 1995.

Imayev, Usman – Head of Chechen Central Bank, then Justice

Minister. Head of Chechen delegation at talks in summer of 1995 until dismissed by Dudayev.

Iskhanov, Hussein – Aide-de-camp to Aslan Maskhadov, 1994–6.

Israpilov, Khunkar 'Pasha' – Chechen field commander of Eastern Front, co-leader of hostage raid in Kizlyar and Pervomaiskoye, 9–17 January 1996.

Kalmykov, Yury – Russian Justice Minister. Resigned in protest over invasion of Chechnya in December 1994. Died in January 1997.

Khajiev, Salambek – Leading opposition figure to Dudayev. Prime Minister of pro-Moscow Chechen government in 1995.

Khamidov, Hussein – Pilot. Headed commission on missing persons in Chechnya. Minister of Civil Aviation in new Chechen government from autumn 1996.

Khasbulatov, Ruslan – Leading opponent of both Dudayev and Yeltsin. Speaker of the Russian Parliament, 1991–3. Jailed for his part in resistance to Yeltsin in October 1993. Released in February 1994. Ran anti-Dudayev 'peace mission' in 1994.

Korzhakov, Alexander – Yeltsin's leading aide, chief bodyguard and head of presidential Security Service. Sacked in June 1996. Elected to Russian Parliament in February 1997.

Kostikov, Vyacheslav – Yeltsin's press secretary, 1992–4.

Kotenkov, Alexander – Deputy Nationalities Minister, who coordinated aid to the Chechen opposition in 1994. Now Yeltsin's representative in Parliament.

Kovalyov, Sergei – Dissident turned human rights activist. Deputy of the State Duma, presidential Human Rights Commissioner and most prominent critic of the Chechen war.

Kozyrev, Andrei – Russian Foreign Minister, 1991–6.

Kuchciak, Zenon – Polish diplomat. Member of the OSCE mission in Grozny from April 1995. Deputy head of mission from January 1996.

Kulikov, Anatoly, Colonel-General – Commander of Russian forces in Chechnya from February 1995. Russian Interior Minister from July 1995.

Kvashnin, Anatoly, Lieutenant-General – Deputy Commander of the North Caucasus Military District and Deputy Commander of Chechen operation, December 1994.

Labazanov, Ruslan – Convicted murderer. Joined Dudayev's guard in 1992. Went into opposition to Dudayev in 1994. Murdered in 1996.

Lebed, Alexander – General turned politician. Came third in June 1996 Russian presidential elections. Appointed Secretary of Kremlin Security Council and Special Envoy to Chechnya. Signed peace agreement with Chechens in August 1996. Sacked from Kremlin in October 1996.

Lobov, Oleg – Old Party comrade of Yeltsin's. Secretary of the Kremlin Security Council, then Special Envoy to Chechnya in 1995.

Mamodayev, Yaragi – Chechen businessman who bankrolled Dudayev's political campaign. Served in his government until he went into opposition in 1993.

Maskhadov, Aslan – Deputy Chief of Staff of Chechen Forces, 1992–4, Chief of Staff 1994–6. Signed peace agreement with Alexander Lebed in August 1996. Chechen Prime Minister, October–December 1996. Elected President of Chechnya, 27 January 1997.

Meszaros, Sandor – Hungarian diplomat, who was head of first OSCE mission in Grozny in 1995.

Mikhailov, Vyacheslav – Russian negotiator. Nationalities Minister and head of Russian negotiating team in Chechnya from summer of 1995.

Ochirov, Valery – Air force general, former comrade of Dudayev's. Worked in the Kremlin until 1996.

Pain, Emil – Kremlin analyst, adviser on nationalities policy.

Pulikovsky, Konstantin, Lieutenant-General – Russian commander in Chechnya in 1996.

Raduyev, Salman – Chechen field commander, married to Dudayev's niece, leader of hostage raid on Kizlyar and Pervomaiskoye, 9–17 January 1996.

Rokhlin, Lev, General – Commander of Northern Group of Forces in Chechnya, 1994–5. Conqueror of Grozny. State Duma Deputy and Chairman of Duma Defence Committee from 1995.

Romanov, Anatoly, Lieutenant-General – Commander of Russian forces in Chechnya in 1995. Badly wounded in bomb blast in October 1995, since which he has been in a coma.

Rutskoi, Alexander – Russian Vice-President, 1991–3. Organized attempt to overthrow Dudayev in November 1991. Now Governor of Kursk region.

Shabad, Anatoly – Liberal Russian Member of Parliament, 1990–5.

Shakhrai, Sergei – Chief Russian policy-maker on Chechnya, 1992–4. Nationalities Minister, October 1992–May 1994. Kremlin Deputy Chief of Staff since December 1996.

Soskovets, Oleg – Leading hardliner in Russian government,

1992–6. Special Representative to Chechnya in 1995. Sacked from government in June 1996.

Soslambekov, Yusup – Chechen politician. Close ally of Dudayev until 1993, when he went into opposition.

Starovoitova, Galina – Adviser on nationalities policy to Yeltsin, 1990–2. Now Member of Parliament.

Stepashin, Sergei – Head of the counter-intelligence service, the FSK, until June 1995. Currently head of government administration department.

Tikhomirov, Vyacheslav, Lieutenant-General – Commander of Russian forces in Chechnya, 1996.

Udugov, Movladi – Chechen Information Minister, 1991–6, then First Deputy Prime Minister in Chechen government.

Umkhayev, Lechi – Organizer of Chechen National Congress in 1990. Now head of Daimokkh Party in Chechnya.

Urnov, Mark – Head of Kremlin Analytical Centre, 1994–6.

Volsky, Arkady – Influential industrialist and politician. Deputy head of Russian delegation at talks with the Chechens in the summer of 1995.

Vorobyov, Eduard, Colonel-General – First Deputy Commander of Russian Ground Forces. Resigned 22 December 1994 rather than take command of the Chechen operation. State Duma Deputy from December 1995.

Yandarbiyev, Zelimkhan – Chechen Vice-President, April 1993–April 1996. Then Chechen President until losing presidential elections in January 1997.

Yegorov, Nikolai – Leading supporter of the Chechen war.

Nationalities Minister, May 1994–June 1995. Head of presidential administration, January–July 1996. Died April 1997.

Yeltsin, Boris – Russian President since June 1991.

Yerin, Viktor – Russian Interior Minister, January 1992–June 1995.

Yushenkov, Sergei – Liberal politician. Chairman of Russian Parliament's Defence Committee, 1993–5.

Zakayev, Akhmed – Former actor at Grozny State Theatre. Field commander of Western Front, then Presidential National Security Adviser and Chechen negotiator and Minister of Culture.

Zavgayev, Doku – Communist Party boss in Chechen–Ingushetia from June 1989 until ousted in September 1991. Head of pro-Moscow Chechen government, October 1995–August 1996.

Zhirinovsky, Vladimir – Extreme nationalist Russian politician, whose party won the majority of seats in parliamentary elections of December 1993.

Appendix 2: Maps

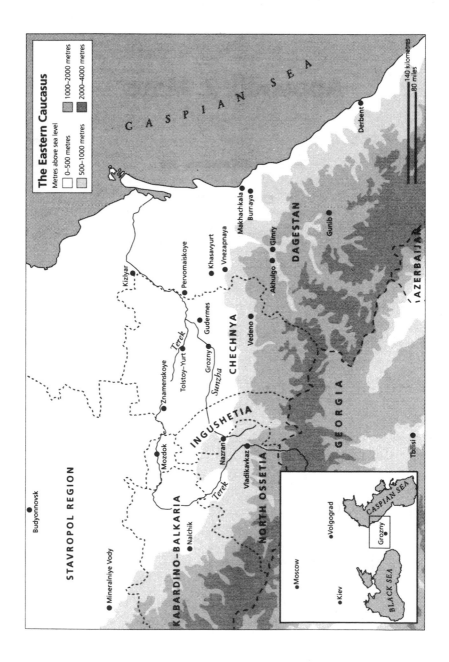

The Eastern Caucasus

Metres above sea level

- 0–500 metres
- 500–1000 metres
- 1000–2000 metres
- 2000–4000 metres

CASPIAN SEA

140 kilometres
80 miles

Derbent

Makhachkala
Burnaya
Gunib
Glinry
DAGESTAN
Akhulgo
Khasavyurt
Vnezapnaya
Pervomaiskoye
Kizlyar
Gudermes
Vedeno
CHECHNYA
Tolstoy-Yurt
Grozny
Znamenskoye
Terek
Sunzha
AZERBAIJAN
INGUSHETIA
GEORGIA
Mozdok
Nazran
Vladikavkaz
Terek
NORTH OSSETIA
Tbilisi
KABARDINO–BALKARIA
Nalchik
STAVROPOL REGION
Budyonnovsk
Mineralniye Vody

Moscow
Kiev
Volgograd
CASPIAN SEA
Grozny
BLACK SEA

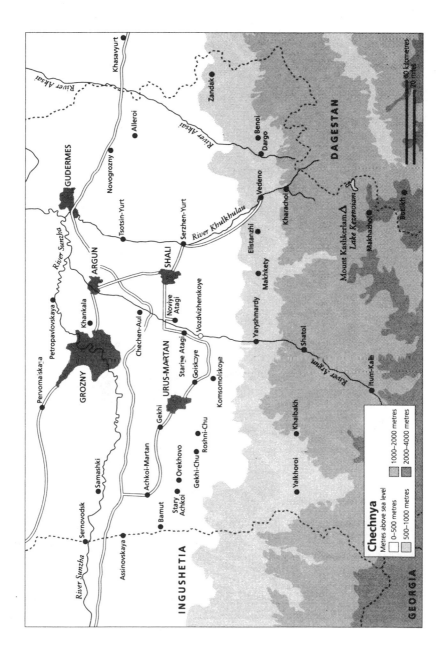

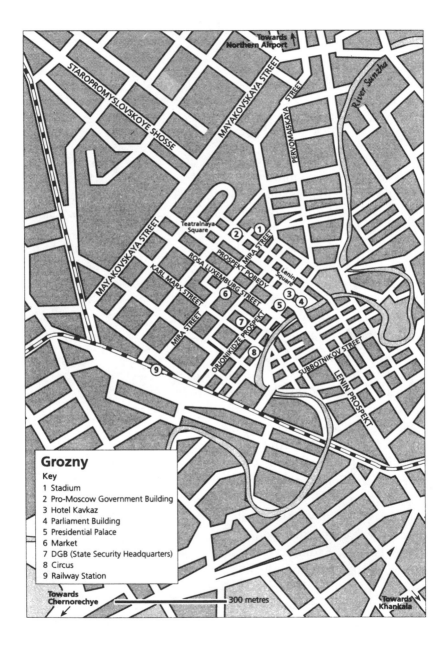

Grozny

Key

1 Stadium
2 Pro-Moscow Government Building
3 Hotel Kavkaz
4 Parliament Building
5 Presidential Palace
6 Market
7 DGB (State Security Headquarters)
8 Circus
9 Railway Station

Towards
Chernorechye

300 metres

Towards
Khankala

Towards
Northern Airport

Acknowledgements

Special thanks to Marc Champion, editor of *The Moscow Times*, for his impressive commitment to covering the war in Chechnya and his valuable judgements. And to Tanya Stobbs of Macmillan who commissioned the book, and our agent Clare Roberts for her interest and support.

Also to: Alvi Abayev; Aiza Abazova; Vakhid Akayev; Andrei; Dmitry Balburov and Sanobar Shermatova of *Moscow News*; Richard Beeston and Irina Malyavkina of *The Times*; Chris Bird, Isabelle Lasserre, Jean-Baptiste Naudet, Lawrence Sheets and Sebastian Smith for their company and their sat-phones; Matt Bivens; Charles Blandy; Heidi Bradner, Michael Yassukovich and Thomas Dworzak for their photographs; Musa Damayev; Aslan Dukayev; Natasha Fairweather and Chrystia Freeland for their comments on the manuscript; Didier François; Irina Gaidarova and Natasha Yevseyeva of *The Moscow Times*; Bill Gasperini; the *Independent* foreign desk for putting up the war insurance; David Isby; Andrew Jennings for his material from 1993; Peter Jouvenal; Robert Kee; Pyotr Kosov; Viktor Listov; Robin Lodge; John Lough; Azamat Nalgiyev; Valentina Malsagova; Sonia Mikich for the use of her documentary material; Vyacheslav Nikonov; Alan Philps, Nanette van der Laan and Marcus Warren of the *Daily Telegraph*; Andrei Piontkovsky; Arkady Popov; Vladimir Povetkin; Nigel Ryan; Anders Saether; George Shabad; Viktor Sheinis; Charles Tchokotoua; Valery Tishkov; Khazman Umarova; Mairbek Vachargayev; Arkady Volsky; Olivia Ward; Paul Wokke for his help with the maps; all our fellow journalists who were such good company during tough times; Georgina Wilson and the Gall family for their love and insights.

Most of all our thanks to the many Chechens, some of whose names we don't even know, who showed limitless hospitality and unstinting kindness, often risking their lives to help us in extremely dangerous times.

Notes and References

1. New Year's Eve

1. Interviews with Viktor Kim, Nikolai Ryabtsev, Mamed Kerim-Zade and Nikolai Zarovny from the Maikop Brigade, by CG in the southern Russian towns of Volgodonsk, Romanovskaya, Maikop and Adler 7–10 January 1997. The 131st Brigade takes its name from Maikop where it is based. The soldiers serving in it came from all over Russia, although the majority were from southern Russia.
2. The Russian side claimed there were huge numbers of foreign volunteers or mercenaries fighting on the Chechen side but there were in fact very few. The three Ukrainians were the only ones seen by journalists during the battle for Grozny. Russian claims that there were teams of 'Baltic women snipers' lay in the realms of fantasy. Some Arab fighters arrived in February 1995 but never numbered more than several dozen.
3. Interview with Zupkukhajiev by CG, 2 July 1996.
4. Interview with Chauvel by CG, 8 October 1996.
5. Interview with Yushenkov by the authors, 29 October 1996
6. Interview with Shabad by the authors, 19 November 1996.
7. Interview with Gyarmati by Jörg Haskemeyer, Westdeutscher Rund-funk (ARD-TV), 4 July 1996.
8. The size of the 131st Brigade in Chechnya is a closely guarded secret, as is the total number of dead. Even the men themselves had no clear idea. Conscripts put the size of the force in Chechnya between 1000 and 1500. One officer said 1200 men went into Grozny and 200 came out alive. Zarovny, quoting another officer, said 1500 went in and 153 came out. A documentary film made by a local Rostov television company in 1995 said 700 men went in, 200 came out, and 100 armoured vehicles were destroyed.
9. Interview with Kovalyov by the authors, 10 December 1996.
10. The Chechens were more interested in counting knocked-out vehicles than bodies. Basayev claims his fighters took 150 prisoners and

knocked out 221 pieces of armour on New Year's Eve. It was only in mid-January that the first official casualty figures emerged. In Moscow a deputy of the Federation Council, quoting official sources, said that 394 Russian servicemen had been killed and more than 1000 wounded to date. A day later military sources in Mozdok quoted by Russia's Interfax news agency put the figure of dead at 1160. The reality by then was probably over double.

11. Interview with Fedulov by CG, 26 September 1996.
12. Interview with Alexander Zavyolov by CG, 10 October 1996.
13. N. N. Novichkov, *Vooruzhenniye Sily v Chechenskom Konflikte* (*The Russian Armed Forces in the Chechen Conflict*), Moscow, 1995.

2. The French of the Caucasus

1. John Baddeley, *The Russian Conquest of the Caucasus*, London, 1908, p. xxxv.
2. Adolf Berzhe, *Chechnya i Chechentsy* (*Chechnya and the Chechens*), Tiflis, 1859, p. 86.
3. A. P. Ippolitov, *Etnograficheskiye Ocherki Argunskago Okruga* (*Ethnographic Sketches of the Argun District*), Tiflis, 1868 pp. 17–18.
4. Ernest Chantre, *Recherches Anthropologiques dans le Caucase*, Lyon, 1885–7.
5. Yan Chesnov, 'Trudno byt' Chechentsem' ('It's hard to be a Chechen'), *Nezavisimaya Gazeta* 22 September 1994.
6. Leonardo Sciascia, *The Day of the Owl*, trans. Archibald Colquhoun and Arthur Oliver, London, 1987, p. 95.
7. John Baddeley, *The Rugged Flanks of the Caucasus*, London, 1940, vol. 1, p. 11.
8. Ibid., p. 9.
9. S. Belyayev, *Desyat' Mesyatsev v plenu u Chechentsev* (*Ten months in Captivity with the Chechens*), reprinted Grozny, 1991, p. 6.
10. Adolf Berzhe, *Kratky obzor gorskikh plemyon na kavkaze* (*A short Survey of the Mountain Tribes in the Caucasus*), Tiflis, 1858, p. 35.
11. Alexandre Benningsen and S. Enders Wimbush, *Mystics and Commissars, Sufism in the Soviet Union*, London, 1985, p. 8.
12. Vakhid Akayev *Sheikh Kunta-Khaji: Zhizn' i Uchenie* (*Sheikh Kunta Haji: Life and Teaching*), Grozny, 1994, p. 100.

3. Conquest and Resistance

1. One of the survivors of the battle, Pieri's adjutant, Pyotr Bagration, survived to become one of the most famous soldiers of the Napoleonic War and died at Borodino in 1812.
2. John Baddeley, *The Russian Conquest of the Caucasus*, London, 1908, pp. 147–8. Baddeley's *Russian Conquest of the Caucasus* has only recently acquired a rival of the same standard – Moshe Gammer's *Muslim Resistance to the Tsar*, London, 1994.
3. Ibid., pp. 137–8.
4. Ibid., p. 153.
5. Ibid., p. 136.
6. Quoted in ibid., p. 340.
7. Quoted in ibid., p. 268.
8. Yavus Akhmadov, *Imamat Shamilya – Godudarstvo Gortsev Chechni i Dagestana (Shamil's Imamate – the State of the Mountain Peoples of Chechnya and Dagestan)* in *Chechentsy Istoriya, Sovremmenost' (Chechen History and Contemporaneity)* ed. Yu Aidayev, Moscow, 1996, p. 183.
9. To this day, however, there is a widespread folkloric legend that they will some day be under the rule of the English (the 'Ingiliz'). Some Chechens even mention a specific period of time – seven years!
10. The best account of Shamil's life is Lesley Blanch's *Sabres of Paradise*, London, 1960, a breathlessly told but extremely well-researched account of the Caucasian Wars.
11. Quoted in Zaindi Shakhbiyev, *Sud'ba Checheno-Ingushskogo Narodo (The Fate of the Chechen–Ingush People)*, Moscow, 1996, p. 196.
12. *Bolshevitskoye Rukovodstvo. Perepislka. 1912–1927 (The Bolshevik Leadership. Correspondence. 1912–1927)*, Moscow, 1996, p. 120.
13. Abdurakhman Avtorkhanov, *The Chechens and Ingush during the Soviet Period and its Antecedents* in *The North Caucasian Barrier*, London, 1992, p. 165.

4. The Deportations

1. Interview with Akhmatov by T de W, 23 August 1996.
2. *Chechentsy Istoriya, Sovremmenost'* (*Chechen History and Contemporaneity*) ed. Yu Aidayev, Moscow, 1996, p. 263.
3. The figures are from *Komsomolskaya Pravda*, 23 July 1996.
4. This and subsequent reminiscences of the deportations from interviews by T de W in Chechnya, January 1994.
5. Beria and three of his deputies, Bogdan Kobulov, Ivan Serov and Sergei Kruglov, were awarded the Order of Suvorov First Class for their work in the deportations of the Chechens and the Ingush. It was a medal usually awarded for extreme bravery at the front. Gvishiani and twelve other officers were given the Order of Suvorov Second Class. 259 junior officers were given the medal 'For Courage'.
6. S. Gayev. M. Khadisov and T. Chagayeva, *Khaibakh: Sledstviye Prodolzhayetsya* (*Khaibakh: the Investigation continues*), Grozny, 1994, p. 264.
7. Ibid., p. 73.
8. Abdurakhanan Avtorkhmov, *The Chechens and Ingush during the Soviet Period and its Antecedents* in *The North Caucasian Barrier*, London, 1992, p. 147.
9. Dziyauyudin Malsagov, who was one of a party sent into the mountains to reconnoitre Sheripov's band, said that it consisted of only about a dozen people.
10. Moshe Gammer, *Muslim Resistance to the Tsar*, London, 1994, p. 278.
11. Gayev, Khadisov and Chagayeva, op. cit., p. 251.
12. Khrushchev also used the commission to move against Kruglov, who had just served ten years as Interior Minister, who was expelled from the Communist Party and died in 1977, and Serov, who lost his job as head of the KGB, but later managed to resume his career and became a Hero of the Soviet Union. He died only in 1990. Gvishiani was not touched. He had been pardoned after Beria's death and was made a Lieutenant-General. He died in Tbilisi in 1966. The other leading organizer of the deportations, Bogdan Kobulov, was shot with Beria in 1953.
13. Interview with the authors, 22 October 1996, and Gayev, Khadisov and Chagayeva, op. cit., pp. 101–2.

14. See Robert Conquest, *The Nation Killers*, London, 1970, pp. 105–6. Conquest's book and Alexander Nekrich's *The Punished Peoples*, New York, 1978, although twenty years old, are still the authoritative works on the deportations.

15. A. I. Kokurin, *Spetspereselentsy v SSSR v 1994 godu ili god bol'shogo pereseleniya (Special Deportees in the USSR or the year of the big deportation)*, Otechestvenniye Arkhivi, 1993, No. 5, p. 104.

16. Interview with Khajiev by T de W, 2 October 1996. Khajiev's father is Avar. He was deported with his Chechen mother.

17. The Germans were only allowed to leave in 1972, the Tatars in 1991 and the Meskhetian Turks of Georgia have never been allowed back.

18. Alexander Solzhenitsyn has repeatedly said Chechnya should be allowed to secede from Russia after 'returning' these three northern regions. General Alexander Lebed also used to support this stance.

5. Dudayev's Revolution

1. Interview with Yandarbiyev by the authors, 21 October 1996.

2. Quoted in Jokhar Dudayev, *Ternisty Put'k Svobode (The Thorny Road to Freedom)*, Vilnius, 1993, p. 197.

3. Interview with Muzayev by T de W, 20 November 1996.

4. Interview with Gakayev by T de W, 10 January 1997.

5. For a detailed description of the unrest see Aleksandr Nekrich, *The Punished Peoples*, New York, 1978, pp. 151–4.

6. Interview with Iskhanov by CG, 8 July 1996.

7. Interview with Magomadov by the authors, 22 October 1996.

8. Interview with Zavgayev by T de W, 26 January 1995.

9. Dudayev, op. cit., p. 121.

10. Ibid., p. 85.

11. Interview with Fyodor Kulikov by the authors, 17 March 1997.

12. Interview with Baskhan and Bekmurza Dudayev by T de W, 19 May 1996.

13. Dudayev, op. cit., p. 50.

14. Interview with Mall by T de W, 9 December 1996.

15. Interview with Laaneots by T de W, 9 December 1996.

16. The story that someone unfurled an Estonian flag at the base appears

to be a legend. Such an overtly nationalist gesture would have landed Dudayev in big trouble at the time.

17. Interview with Starovoitova by T de W, 1 November 1996.
18. Quoted in Yury Shchekhochikin, 'Malen'kaya Pobedonosnya Voina' ('A Small Victorious War'), *Literaturnaya Gazeta*, 2 August 1995.
19. Interview with Khajiev by T de W, 2 October 1996.
20. Interview with Khasbulatov by the authors, 1 October 1996.
21. Interview with Gantemirov by Matt Bivens of the *Los Angeles Times*, 11 March 1995.
22. Interview with Ivanenko, *Rossiya*, No. 5, 1995.
23. Interview with Volkonsky by T de W, 9 December 1996.
24. Interview with Gorbachev by T de W, 25 September 1996.

6. Independent Chechnya

1. Interview with Khajiev by T de W, 2 October 1996.
2. Interview with Beno by the authors, 19 October 1996.
3. Kirill Svetitsky, 'Kriminal'ny sled mera Groznogo' ('The Criminal Traces of the Mayor of Grozny'), *Izvestia*, 11 October 1995.
4. Interview with Vachargayev by the authors, 12 May 1996.
5. Interview with Imayev by T de W, 20 May 1996.
6. Interview with Kozyrev by Sonia Mikich, Westedeutscher Rundfunk (ARD-TV), 26 July 1996.
7. Deinekin press conference in Moscow, 10 April 1996.
8. Ochirov agreed to a brief meeting in which he confirmed the above details but declined to give a formal interview.
9. *Argumenty i Fakty*, February 1996, No. 6.
10. Galina Starovoitova, 'Rossiya i Chechnya: smertel'noye ob'yatiye' ('Russia and Chechnya: a lethal embrace'), *Moskovsky Komsomolets*, 14 March 1995.
11. Interview with Gaidar by T de W, 9 October 1996.
12. Interview with Abasova by T de W, 4 January 1997.
13. Interview with Umkhayev by T de W, 26 October 1997.
14. Viktor Sheinis and Boris Zolotukhin, unpublished parliamentary commission report on Chechen–Russian relations 1991–1994, p. 47.
15. The telegram numbered VCh-PII-37791 was obtained privately by the authors.
16. Interview with Aushev by the authors, 18 July 1996.

7. A Free Economic Zone

1. Interview with Shakhrai by T de W, 3 December 1996.
2. See Emil Pain and Arkady Popov, 'Chechenskaya Politika Rossii 1991–4' ('Russia's Chechen policy 1991–4'), collection of articles in *Izvestia*, 7–10 February 1995, p. 12.
3. O tom kak Dudayev ne vpisalsya v rossiiskii rynok' ('How Dudayev did not fit into the Russian market'), *Kommersant*, 18 September 1996.
4. The findings of the parliamentary oil commission were published in the newspaper *Patriot*, No. 40, 1995. Other details are from Yelena Kolokoltseva, 'Chechnya: Finansovy Aisberg' ('Chechnya: a Financial Iceberg'), *Moscow News*, No. 78, 12–19 November 1995.
5. Quoted in Yury Shchekochikhin, 'Malen'kaya Pobedonosnaya Voina' ('A Small Victorious War'), *Literaturnaya Gazeta*, 2 August 1995.
6. Reported in *Segodnya*, 17 September 1996.
7. Jennifer Gould, 'Chechen Instability Puts Cap on Oil Pact', *The Moscow Times*, 11 March 1993. According to Usman Imayev, the state of Texas signed a document recognizing Chechen independence.
8. The best account of Dudayev's visit to London and the business dealings of the Utsievs is in Andrew Jennings, 'From Marx to the Mafia', *New Statesman and Society*, 14 May 1993, and 'Oil, Money and Murder in Chechnia', *The Nation*, 20 September 1993. The story of the aftermath and the murder of Karen Reed, the sister-in-law of the Armenian, is told in Jo Durden-Smith, 'Unfinished Business', *Sunday Telegraph* Magazine, 28 April 1996.
9. Christopher Elliott, 'Murdered Russians planned £170m deal with fraudster', *The Times*, 18 March 1993.
10. Interview with Imayev by T de W, 20 May 1996.

8. A Small Victorious War

1. Interview with Pain by T de W, 3 November 1996.
2. Interview with Shakhrai by T de W, 3 December 1996.
3. Yegorov met Dudayev privately in May 1994 at the trade fair in the Black Sea port of Sochi. According to one story Dudayev, who had not given up his Communist ideals, asked Yegorov to sell him a

statue of Lenin. See 'O tom kak Dudayev ne vpisalsya v rossiiskii rynok' ('How Dudayev did not fit into the Russian market'), *Kommersant*, 18 September 1996.

4. Interview with Gromov in *Obshchaya Gazeta*, No. 3, January 1995.
5. Kotenkov refused the authors an interview.
6. Interview with Khasbulatov by the authors, 1 October 1996.
7. Interview with Shakhrai by T de W, 3 December 1996.
8. When the Russians invaded Labazanov did not carry out his pledge to fight them. He stayed in Tolstoy-Yurt and was co-opted by the Russians, eventually becoming a colonel in the FSK! He was killed in a brawl by one of his own guards in May 1996.
9. Pavel Felgenhauer, 'Chechen Rebels Bypass Moscow', *The Moscow Times*, 20 October 1994.
10. Nikolai Topuriya, 'Est' li u oppozitsii kosmonavty?' ('Does the opposition have cosmonauts?'), *Nezavisimaya Gazeta*, 1 October 1994.
11. Yekaterina Domnysheva, 'Kak gotovilas' chechenskaya voina' ('How the Chechen war was prepared'), *Izvestia*, 10 December 1996.
12. Interview with Kozyrev by Sonia Mikich, Westedeutscher Rundfunk (ARD-TV) in English, 26 July 1996.
13. Interview with Kalmykov by T de W, 19 September 1996. Kalmykov died on 16 January 1997 of a heart attack at the age of sixty-four.
14. Interview with Yushenkov by the authors, 29 November 1996.
15. Answers by Stepashin to written questions from the authors, February 1997.
16. Interview with Borshchyov by T de W, 23 July 1996.
17. Interview with Grachev, Interfax, 7 December 1995. The other interview was in Ogonyok, 22 May 1996.
18. Interview with Urnov by T de W, 4 December 1996.
19. e.g. in *Argumenty i Fakty*, No. 34, August 1996, where Korzhakov puts the blame firmly on Grachev. This should be seen in the context of an old rivalry – in another interview, asked what Grachev's qualities were, Korzhakov said laconically, 'Pavel Grachev is a good organizer of parades'.
20. Interview with Kovalyov by the authors, 10 December 1996.
21. Interview with Alla Dudayev, *Izvestia*, 8 June 1996.

9. Russia Invades

1. Radio journalist for Columbia Broadcasting System.
2. Interview with Vorobyov by the authors, 19 July 1996.
3. Interview with Mikhailov by T de W, 28 February 1997.
4. Interview with Volsky by the authors, 15 January 1997.
5. Interview with Kovalyov by the authors, 10 December 1996.
6. Interview with Gaidar by T de W, 9 October 1996.
7. Interview with Maskhadov by Anders Saether, Norwegian TV 2, 24 August 1996.
8. Interview with Maskhadov by CG, 26 October 1996.
9. Interview with Iskhanov by CG, 8 July 1996.
10. Interview with Zupkukhajiev by CG, 2 July 1996.
11. Interview with Khansultanov by CG, 18 December 1994.
12. *Segodnya*, 27 December 1994.
13. *Izvestia*, 18 January 1995.

10. The Battle for Grozny

1. Rokhlin agreed to give an interview to the authors although in the end he never did.
2. Interview with Chauvel by CG, 8 October 1996.
3. Interview with Povetkin by CG, 7 January 1997.
4. Charles Blandy, Conflict Studies Research Centre, Sandhurst, England.
5. *The Moscow Times*, 10 January 1995.
6. Interview with Naumov by CG, 10 October 1996.
7. Interview with Fedulov by CG, 26 September 1996.
8. Interview with Kovalyov by the authors, 10 December 1996.
9. Interview with Iskhanov by CG, 8 July 1995.
10. Aslan Maskhadov, *Chest' Dorozhe Zhizni* (*Honour is Dearer than Life*), 1997, p. 18.
11. Interview with Maskhadov by CG, 26 October 1996.
12. Interview with Valentina Krayeva and her son Alexei Krayev, or Alyosha, by CG, 7 January 1997.
13. Akhmed was killed in August 1996 in Grozny when the Chechens attacked and recaptured the city.
14. Frederick Cuny, 'Killing Chechnya', *New York Review of Books*, 6

April 1995. To give an idea of the scale of bombardment in Grozny, Cuny compares it to the shelling in Sarajevo, which at its height amounted to 3500 detonations *a day*, while in Grozny it reached 4000 an *hour*.

15. Interview with Andrianova by T de W, 12 February 1995.
16. Interview with Kulikov by the authors, 17 January 1997.
17. Interview with Amadov by CG, 11 January 1995.
18. The human rights organization Memorial estimated the death toll in Grozny was between 27,000 and 30,000 people. There is no other estimate of the civilian losses and the Russian government later adopted the Memorial figure as official. It is however thought by some to be too high, calculated on a survey of 400 refugees who listed all the people they knew who had died in their area.

11. War Against the People

1. Interview with Khamidov by CG, 29 August 1995.
2. Interview with Lorzanov by CG, 17 August 1996.
3. Interview with Mosarov, by CG, 24 October 1996.
4. Mosarov was transferred to Mozdok and only released two weeks later. While there he was twice driven out of the camp when soldiers said the International Committee of the Red Cross were coming to visit, returning when they had gone.
5. Interviews by T de W, 10–11 February 1995.
6. A copy of the statement dated 26 December 1994 was shown to CG at the local administration in the neighbouring town of Sleptsovsk, 10 January 1995.
7. Interview with Kulikov by the authors, 17 January 1997.
8. Interview with Damayev by CG, 20 October 1996.
9. Interview with Fedin by CG, 20 October 1996.
10. Interview with Shabad by the authors, 19 November 1996.
11. Journalists who gained access to Samashki a few days after the massacre found dozens of used syringes and ampoules littering the streets and courtyards and listened to villagers' stories that soldiers were shooting up on the streets and acting crazy. The ampoules contained Promodol, an anti-shock tranquillizer, and Dimedrol, a powerful narcotic, both issued to soldiers in their first aid kits. Russian pharmacists later confirmed that mixed with alcohol the drugs could result in extremely aggressive behaviour. Although

Interior Ministry officers deny it, drug-taking is common in the Russian Armed Forces and the stories from Samashki's residents are wholly credible.

12. Interview with S. by CG, 14 January 1997.
13. Umakhanov's story comes from *By All Available Means: the Russian Interior Ministry Operation in the Village of Samashki, April 7–8, 1995*, a report by the Memorial Human Rights Centre, Moscow, whose team spent months investigating the massacre.
14. Interview by CG in Samashki, 30 April 1995.
15. From the Memorial report.
16. Elmurzayev began to make more and more contacts with the Dudayev side as the war progressed. He was murdered in unexplained circumstances in June 1996.

12. Terrorism and Talks

1. Interview with Maskhadov by CG, 26 October 1996.
2. Interview with Shamil Basayev by CG, 7 July 1996.
3. Interview with Salman Basayev, aged sixty-one in 1996, by CG, 19 March 1996.
4. Interview with Khalid Basayev by CG, 7 July 1996.
5. Interview with Kulikov by the authors, 17 January 1997.
6. Keston News Service, August 1996.
7. Interview with Volsky by the authors, 15 January 1997.
8. Interview with Imayev by T de W, 20 May 1996.
9. Imayev retired to his home village of Kulary where he set up a self-defence unit of fighters. In the autumn of 1996 he disappeared. He was rumoured to be in Turkey but close acquaintances said they feared for his life.
10. Interview with Kuchciak by T de W, 19 May 1996.
11. Romanov as of June 1997 is still lying comatose in Burdenko military hospital in Moscow. Doctors have said he is unlikely to improve further. His office in the Interior Ministry in Moscow remains waiting for him, manned by his deputy.

13. 'A Semi-Guerrilla War'

1. Interview with Israpilov by CG, 9 July 1996.

2. Nadezhda Chaikova, *Obshchaya Gazeta*, No. 1, 11–17 January 1996.
3. Yulia Kalinina, *Moskovsky Komsomolets*, 11 January 1996.
4. Interview with Basayev by CG, 7 July 1996.
5. After three days the ship reached the edge of the Bosphorus, but as the crisis in Pervomaiskoye ended, the hijackers threw their weapons into the sea and surrendered to Turkish authorities. Tokçan and his band were eventually given prison sentences of varying lengths in March 1997.
6. Alexander Kakotin, Yury Snegirev, *Izvestia*, 19 January 1996.
7. *Ogonyok*, No. 5, January 1996.
8. Interview with Raduyev by CG, 22 January 1996.
9. Dagestani authorities said forty-three Dagestanis died overall, fifteen of them police and troops and twenty-eight civilians, split almost equally between Kizlyar and Pervomaiskoye. Russian military casualties were also unrealistically low. The official count was twenty-six dead, but Russian media reported at least 100 wounded passed through Grozny's hospital and as many as 100 Russian dead. The figure of ninety-six Chechen fighters dead is widely accepted. Most of them died during the final break-out, seven were killed in Kizlyar, and eight in Pervomaiskoye itself, according to Raduyev. Among the dead were four Chechen women fighters and two Arabs, a Syrian and an Egyptian. The last two are buried among thirty-five of the fighters at the cemetery in Tsotsin-Yurt.
10. Moshe Gammer, 'Vorontsov's 1845 Expedition against Shamil: A British Report', *Central Asia*, Vol. 4, No. 4, 1985, pp. 14–15.
11. His full name was Zelimkhan Gashmazukayev. He was sent to prison in 1901, at the age of twenty-seven, on a murder charge, evidently a vendetta killing. He escaped, vowing to free his two brothers and father. He roamed Chechnya, defying capture and executing devastating attacks on Russian parties before dying in a final shoot-out.
12. Interview with Maskhadov by CG, 26 October 1996.
13. Yulia Kalinina, 'Zolotoi Telyonok Chechenskoi Respubliki' ('The Golden Calf of the Chechen Republic'), *Itogi*, 21 May 1996. The biggest beneficiaries were the Moscow commercial banks appointed to handle the financing. They often dithered in allocating the money, reaping the rewards of high interest rates.
14. David Hoffman, 'Yeltsin Turns to Clinton for Help in Chechen War', *International Herald Tribune*, 22 April 1996.

14. Death in the Gully

1. Interview with Mikhailov by T de W, 28 February 1997.
2. Interview with Basnukayev by the authors, 22 October 1996.
3. *Izvestia*, 8 June, 1996.
4. Until Dudayev is given a public burial there has to remain some doubt about his death. His nephew is reported to have filmed the funeral, and the Chechen Interior Minister, Kazbek Makhashev, says he has photos of Dudayev's body, but neither film nor photos had been made public as of June 1997.
5. Interview with Basayev by the authors, 20 October 1996.

15. Grozny Recaptured

1. Ekho Moskvy radio station, 6 August 1996.
2. Interview with Maskhadov by Anders Saether, Norwegian TV 2, 24 August 1996.
3. Nail Salikhovsky obtained the recordings for the Russian news programme *Vzglyad*.
4. Interview with Tembulatov by CG, 25 January 1997.
5. Michael Specter, *The New York Times* Magazine, 13 October 1996.
6. 'Yesterday in the Duma . . .' Olga Gerasimenko, *Komsomolskaya Pravda*, 16 October 1996.
7. There is no figure for civilian casualties in August although the ICRC treated 500 alone in their headquarters in central Grozny where they set up an emergency operating theatre. In a subsequent review they estimated 3000 people were in need of treatment from war injuries received in August and before.
8. Interview with Kulikov by the authors, 17 January 1997.
9. The human rights organization, Memorial, estimates 50,000 civilians died during the war. By the autumn of 1996, 4000 Russian soldiers were officially listed as having died in the war. Lebed said 3826 had died; 1906 were missing in action, 90 per cent of whom were probably dead. Independent estimates put the figures as high as 10,000. Maskhadov estimates 2000 Chechen fighters died. Shamil Basayev says he thinks it is between 3000 and 4000, many of whom were only volunteer or part-time fighters.
10. *Komsomolskaya Pravda*, 16 October 1996.

Index